MW00711528

Joe McDaniel (signature)

31206

The Boys of Willingham High
_1958-1970_

Joe S. McDaniel
(Foreword by Ed Grisamore)

Indigo Custom Publishing, LLC.

Publisher	Henry S. Beers
Graphic Designer	Daniel Emerson
Operations Manager	Gary Pulliam
Associate Publisher	Richard J. Hutto

© 2005 by Indigo Custom Publishing

All rights reserved. No part of this book may be reproduced in any
form or by any means without prior written permission from the publisher,
except for brief quotations used in reviews written specifically for inclusion
in a magazine, newspaper, or broadcast media.

Printed in the USA.
2nd printing.

Library of Congress Control Number: 2005925944

ISBN: 9780976287568

Indigo custom books are available at quantity discounts
with bulk purchase for educational, business, or sales promotional use.
For information, please write to:
Indigo Custom Publishing, LLC., 3920 Ridge Avenue, Macon, GA 31210, or
call 866-311-9578.

Dedication

This book is dedicated to my parents,
Billie and Dot McDaniel,
who had the good judgment and foresight to buy a house
and then build a home in South Macon.

It is also dedicated to the hard-working, God-fearing men and
women who chose to live, work, shop, educate, worship, and create great
lives for their families.

Finally, 31206 is dedicated to the 2,000-plus young men
who walked in the halls, ran on the fields, studied in the classrooms,
and represented their school, A. R. Willingham High School,
throughout its 12-year history.

To God be the glory.

Table of Contents

Acknowledgements

Harry Bowen and Ed Grisamore are two primary reasons *31206* was written. Understand - Harry graduated from Willingham in 1965, while Ed finished at Riverwood High School in Atlanta a half-generation later. Still, both are proud sons of Macon. Harry, however, is a proud son of South Macon.

The Bowen Brothers, George and Harry, have done well in business for over 20 years by selling high-quality men's clothing in an atmosphere which is friendly, professional, and inviting. My inclination has been to stop in frequently just to chat with the owners and whoever happens to be in the store. Both Bowens are from South Macon and grew up on San Juan Avenue near Houston Avenue. They attended Charles H. Bruce School, but while Harry went to Willingham High, George, his older brother, graduated from Lanier.

It is common knowledge that if someone grew up in South Macon, the Bowens will know who they are, what their parents did, and remember some identifying characteristic about them. Throughout the years, Harry and I agreed that South Macon had produced its share of characters, but we also agreed that Willingham had an inordinate number of highly-successful, prosperous graduates who have thrived in life. Harry stated several years ago, that someone should write a book about Willingham graduates who have done well in life. He admitted, "I already have a name for the book – *The Boys of '06*."

Fast-forward to November, 2003. I was riding to Columbus, GA, with Ed Grisamore, a highly-talented, creative columnist with *The Macon Telegraph*, and we were on our way to an Allen Levi concert. Ed suddenly stated, "Joe, you have a book in you." Taken aback, I asked what he was talking about, and he replied, "With all of the people you have known through your years of coaching, working at Mercer, 20 years on staff at Mabel White Baptist Church, and now at Mid Georgia Ambulance, you must have some interesting stories at your disposal."

I related to Ed that Harry Bowen had suggested that someone should chronicle the successful lives of South Macon boys who graduated from Willingham. After consulting with my wife and praying about that unenviable task, the die was cast. *31206* was officially underway.

This book includes only 25 of 1,900-plus men who grew up in South Macon and graduated from Willingham. The school had only 11 graduating classes in its 12-year existence. Every graduating class from 1960 to 1970 would be represented. Each man in the book has been successful in life, both personally and professionally, though they may not be the richest, most powerful, or influential.

31206 is simply about 25 guys that I was able to locate, and who have led quite interesting lives with stories that need to be told. The deeper I dug and the longer this project took, the more I realized that I would barely scratch the surface of successful Willingham graduates.

Please understand – there are way too many Willingham Rams to include in this one volume. Does that mean that *31206, The Sequel,* is forthcoming? Let me answer this way – "Ask any woman who has just gone through nine months of pregnancy if she wants to have any more children?" "Probably not" is the likely answer.

One thing that has greatly impressed me with the fellows in this book is that none of them felt worthy of having their story told. None of them. Flattered? Yes. Honored? Absolutely. Worthy? Not even close. "Flattered" and "honored" were the two recurring responses that I received when I told them I was writing a book and wanted to include their story.

The 25 interviews were a blast and were, quite frankly, one of the best parts of this entire process. We reminisced, laughed, told stories – many of which were actually true - about the old days, and we dredged up memories from our wonderful past that had been dormant far too long.

Though *31206* has taken about 18 months to interview, transcribe, write, re-write, proof, re-proof, and then print, the inspiration for this book has obviously been in the works for several years. What started out as a book with about 12 to 15 guys ended up being a research project of gargantuan proportions. For each man/chapter, I sought out between five and ten references who have known each at some level. Their stories about their South Macon friends truly made the book. I am extremely grateful to those who took the time to call back, e-mail, mail, fax, write, and reply to my questionnaire. You all have been vital to any success that *31206* will have.

The original plan for *31206* was to schedule a few brief interviews, write their stories, add a couple of pictures, and call it a book. Before I knew it, 25 men had been located and interviewed, and I soon realized that an untold number of deserving, highly-successful Willingham graduates would be left out. That one thought grieves me more than anything about writing *31206*. Simply put, everybody couldn't be in it. While these 25 men are all successful in life in different ways, practically every one would mention three or four of their classmates who would be far better candidates for the book than they were.

Transcribing the interviews, which were recorded on tapes, as well as taking shaky notes written in a self-taught, modified version of shorthand, was difficult, but bearable. Following-up with over 200 references was a 'bear,' and, it seemed to take on a life of its own, but the results were worth it. The best part of interviewing their references was that I received some amazing insights into the lives of 25 men, some of whom I did not know previously. These references were siblings and parents, children and business associates, high school buddies and college teammates, coaches, teachers, politicians, and community leaders, along with neighbors and friends. Communicating with the likes of former Attorney General Griffin Bell, coaches Vince Dooley and Jim Donnan, Senators Sam Nunn and Saxby Chambliss, lawyer/author Bob Steed, Dr. Ravi Zacharius, state representative Larry Walker, Coca-Cola President Steve Heyer, and countless others was more than a pleasure; it was an extreme highlight of the project.

* * * * * * * * * *

31206 contains two special sections that may be of interest to the reader. One is a chapter about Willingham's faculty and staff. I had the honor of interviewing five people who had deep roots and great influence at Willingham and possessed an untold number of stories, anecdotes, and memories about their days on Canterbury Road. I want to thank the faculty and staff of Willingham who helped mold and shape the lives of literally thousands of young men. Here is a brief summary and update on five familiar people:

• Fred Johnson became Willingham's principal in 1959. He was raised in North Georgia and was at Pearl Harbor when it was bombed on December 7, 1941. Mr. Johnson, nearly 90-years old, is married to the wife of his youth, and lives in Macon.

• Billy Henderson, Willingham's only head football coach in the school's brief, 12-year history, now lives in Athens with Fosky, his wife of 58 years. The coach works out daily at the Athens YMCA and still remembers names, numbers, and great plays from his teams at Willingham.

• Mary P. Smith, nicknamed 'Rock' by one of her students, was referenced, along with Leonard Pridgeon and Mike Garvin, as one of the finest teachers at Willingham. Her ability to remember facts and details about the students whom she taught was truly amazing. She still lives in the same house which she lived in while teaching at Willingham in the 1960's.

• Mike Garvin taught math and coached at Willingham from 1959 through 1967. Then he coached Mount de Sales Academy to three state football championships in four years. Garvin lives in Macon with his wife, Carolyn, and they have three married sons and two grandchildren.

• Mary B. Lamback, Willingham's tennis-playing secretary, issued more hall passes and late-slips to delinquent students than the law allowed. She was much, much more than a secretary. She was a counselor, mentor, mother figure, and friend to an immeasurable number of Willingham boys.

Another chapter in *31206* is a tribute to six Willingham graduates who, because of their deaths in the Vietnam War, were not able to continue on in life. Their lives were valuable, nonetheless, and they are heroes to the rest of us. Those six men from Willingham are:

• Willis Furney, class of 1964
• Carson Hardison, class of 1962
• Terry Jackson, class of 1965
• Bricey Lamb, class of 1964
• Frank Ruis, class of 1966
• Johnny Sharpless, class of 1969

As members of the Willingham High School family, we honor and thank these six men – our friends, former classmates, Willingham graduates, and sons of South Macon - for their willingness to serve when they were called. May they rest in everlasting peace.

* * * * * * * * *

I want to thank numbers of people who have helped this book become a reality. First, Cynthia, my wife and the love of my life for 36 years, has been extremely supportive and patient while I have spent countless numbers of hours of what was previously considered family time at the computer. Her advice, support, and insights were invaluable.

Our daughter, Krista Dillard, and son, Chad McDaniel, along with their spouses, Steve and Stephanie, were great sources of encouragement as well. Cynthia and I have the best children and in-laws that anyone could ask for. Likewise, they have given us four of the cutest, smartest, most wonderful grandchildren on earth – Jackson, Betsy, Stafford, and Lindley. I love you all, and I thank God daily for blessing me with you.

My parents, Billie and Dot McDaniel, probably wondered why I would spend so much time writing a book about things that happened 40 years ago, but after they began reading the chapters and remembering Willingham boys from a by-gone era, they both became excited about each succeeding chapter. My mother, who quizzed me in spelling during my elementary school days, was an excellent proof-reader. My only regret in this entire process of *31206* is that my dad passed away on June 20, 2004 (Father's Day), and he never got to hold the final edition of his son's book in his calloused, hard-working hands. Regardless of this book's success, Billie McDaniel would have been very proud.

Mrs. Margaret Phillips, my seventh-grade teacher at Charles H. Bruce School, displayed the patience of Job while serving as my chief proof-reader. When I handed Steve Smith's story (his was the first to be completed) to her, I said, "Mrs. Phillips, I write like I talk, which means you're gonna see some incomplete sentences, sentence fragments, and Southern vernacular."

When I would bring manuscripts for her to review, she must have wondered, "Didn't that boy learn anything about grammar, composition, and punctuation at Bruce School?" I told her, "Mrs. Phillips, I didn't know a dangling participle, misplaced modifier, or a split infinitive when I was in the seventh-grade, and I sure as heck don't know what they are now!" I thank her, nonetheless, for her diligence and attention to details. I also appreciate the encouragement that she gave to me, a 'rookie, wannabe-writer' who took on a writing project that was way over my head. Just as she did at Bruce School some 45 years ago, she rescued me once again in 2005. Thanks, Mrs. Phillips.

I want to thank Mrs. Pam Wacter, the daughter of Mary P. Smith, and former principal of Central High School for being such an excellent proof-reader. That is such a difficult and thankless task. Thanks, Pam, for a job well done.

I appreciate the consistent encouragement of one of my life-long friends, Claudie Brown. He called me frequently during the past 18 months to monitor the progress of the book. I don't know who was more excited about the completion of *31206*; Claudie or me.

Ed Grisamore has published four outstanding books and has a fifth one, *It Can Be Done: The Billy Henderson Story*, in the works. Ed's human-interest columns in *The Macon Telegraph* have entertained and informed the citizens of Macon and Middle Georgia for many years. Without his insistence that I could actually 'pull this off,' I never would have tried. Not only did Gris give me practical pointers about basic writing techniques (like beginning a story with a 'hook' so people would want to continue reading), he directed me to Henry Beers at Indigo Publishing who published the book. Henry, Gary Pulliam, and Daniel Emerson, my new friends at Indigo, were wonderful, patient, and extremely helpful.

I am grateful for the initial nudge that Ed Grisamore gave me. The fact that he would even consider writing the preface for *31206* was an honor within itself.

Hemmingway? Faulkner? Grisham? Nah. I'll take Ed Grisamore's writing every time.

* * * * * * * * * *

I especially want to thank the 25 Willingham graduates who are the objects of this book. They were helpful, cooperative, and always encouraging. What I like most about these men, however, was the humility they displayed by being included in *31206*. That impressed me even more than their amazing stories.

Please understand that these 25 guys from South Macon and Willingham aren't any more special than the other 1,900-plus Willingham graduates. They are, however, all outstanding men who grew up without pomp and privilege in the blue-collar, working-class side of town and have carved out successful lives the hard way. They sacrificed and worked for what they achieved, and all are better men for it.

I am hopeful that reading *31206* will be time well-spent. I trust that the stories of these 25 men will encourage you, and show you that anything in life can be accomplished with drive, determination, goals, and faith. It is my sincere hope and prayer that lives will be enriched and readers will be edified as they read these stories of men who defied conventional odds to become all that God created them to be.

Thanks for taking the time.
Joe S. McDaniel
Proverbs 22:1
2005

Foreword
By Ed Grisamore

I have, for some time, been feeling sorry for Joe McDaniel.

After all, people say we look alike. They claim we could have been twins separated at birth.

All over town, people call me "Joe." And folks reach for Joe's hand and call him "Ed." When someone asks me, "You know who you look like?" ... I can usually fill in the blank.

Actually, I'm flattered to be thought of in the same breath as Joe McDaniel. It's Joe who deserves the sympathy card.

I'm flattered, because I have never met a finer man. He is one of the true saints in my life.

He is a man of high morals and boundless enthusiasm. I have rarely seen him without a smile on his face. Joe is one of those folks you know is happy, because he never gives you a reason to believe otherwise.

His love for people is unconditional. He is a devoted Christian, son, husband, father, grandfather, and friend. Is there any greater calling in life?

That's why Joe was the perfect person to write this book. In it, he honors a band of brothers, not only from the same zip code in South Macon, but who embody his same spirit.

Page after page, story after story, is a tribute to men who are the products of their own greatest generation. They shared the same school, the same neighborhoods, the same sandlots. They did not grow up licking silver spoons. They used knives and forks on their meat and potatoes. And they said grace at every meal.

They grew up with backbone and a strong moral compass. They knew the difference between right and wrong. They were taught the value of hard work. They were not afraid to sweat and bleed.

They were committed. They built solid careers and wrote impressive resumes by keeping faith as their cornerstone.

Perhaps, most importantly, they never forgot their roots.

31206. You can go home again.

There could have been no more worthy ambassador to write these stories than Joe Mac – the preacher, the trooper, the poor guy who looks like me.

He lived among them. His feet are grounded on the same soil, embedded in the same cornerstone. He is proud to hold them up as guiding lights.

Their lives are quite extraordinary. You'll find Joe there, too.

Introduction

What kind of name for a book is *31206?* First, 31206 is the zip code for South Macon, GA. Some readers might recognize more famous zip codes like 90210, the zip code for Beverly Hills, CA, since it became a highly-popular, made-for-television series. However, 31206 is, without question, the antithesis of the Left Coast's zip code and their way of life. Whereas 90210's clientele flaunted glitz, hedonism, glamour, and superficiality, the zip code, 31206, - in the 1950's and 60's - was made up of down-to-earth, God-fearing, hard-working, honest citizens.

The book, *31206,* is the story of 25 men who grew up in South Macon, GA, the blue-collar, working-class section of town, graduated from A.R. Willingham High School for Boys, and achieved a level of success and accomplishment that is significant and worthy of print. For those who did not live in Macon, or who knew nothing about Willingham, a school for boys may conjure up thoughts of elitism, prep schools, and military academies, or possibly a correctional institution for wayward youth. Those would all be wrong, though Willingham would have its fair-share of 'characters.' For long-time residents of Macon, they knew Willingham High to be the epicenter of life in South Macon.

Super Omnia Integritas is a Latin phrase that was imprinted on each Willingham senior ring and was on the school's official shield. It was translated to mean Above All Integrity. The 25 men of *31206* who are listed below are all men of integrity, though none of them is perfect. Each of them has faults, though few of their faults are listed in this book. *31206* is not a 'tell all' or an expose. It simply chronicles each man's story about growing up in South Macon and attending Willingham, and it gives us insights into how and why success came their way. Likewise, each man had final editorial rights to his own chapter, thus approving what was written about them.

The boys, now the men of *31206,* are listed below, along with brief biographical sketches.

- Bobby Bryant (1963) is the Willingham graduate who has been most widely known. At the University of South Carolina, he was drafted by the New York Yankees and the Boston Red Sox but opted for a 14-year career in the NFL with the Minnesota Vikings.
- Dr. Skeet Heard (1966) was one of the top ENT surgeons in the state until he cut off his right index finger in a freak accident with a circular saw. Undaunted, he simply went to law school, graduated *cum laude,* and now practices law in Macon.
- Willie Goolsby (1970) was a four-sport letterman at Willingham and has coached in Macon for over 30 years. One of his athletes, Antonio Pettigrew, won an Olympic gold medal in the 4-by-400 meter relay in the 2000 Sydney Olympics.
- Dan Strickland (1966) went from Willingham High to Johns Hopkins.

Today, he is known as one of the top innovators in the world. His excellent work eventually brought him to the executive committee of The Coca-Cola Company in Atlanta. Dan is in charge of Innovation, Technology, and Stewardship at Coke.

• William Bradshaw (1968) progressed from very limited means to own and operate eight automobile dealerships in two states with plans for more in the near future. In addition, he is the 2006 chairman-elect of NADA (National Automobile Dealers Association), an organization comprised of more than 20,000 automobile dealers.

• Judge Bill Self (1967) succeeded his father, the renowned Judge Tilman E. Self, as judge of the Probate Court of Bibb County. He has made quite a name for himself locally as a lawyer, judge, actor, musician, and chef.

• Darrell Young (1966) was featured in *Georgia Trend Magazine* in the 1990's. He went from being a struggling salesman to become president and CEO of HBO, a leading medical software company based in Atlanta, and has written a book about leadership.

• Tommy Reid (1961) was one of the finest athletes in Willingham's history and had an All-SEC baseball career at UGA. He later won the Georgia Senior Amateur golf title. Reid's career has been in corporate accounting.

• Roy Mann (1961) was Reid's running-mate in baseball at Willingham and at Georgia. He went on to have a brief, but distinguished military career before becoming a successful banker in Augusta and Macon.

• Eddie Battle (1960) was captain and quarterback on the first football team at Willingham High. He also was the first Willingham athlete to win a college scholarship. He married his high school sweetheart and now owns Astro Pools in Macon.

• Connell Stafford (1966) was Sam Nunn's top assistant when Nunn served in the U.S. Senate. Stafford worked for Coca-Cola for 25 years in government relations and now works for Troutman Sanders Public Affairs Group in Atlanta.

• Ben Hinson (1970) bought two old worn-out ambulances and began an ambulance service in 1977. Now, he has over 165 employees, nearly 30 ambulances, and operates in four cities. He has been a guest of President and Mrs. George Bush on several occasions.

• Dr. Billy Browning (1969) went from being a Clinical Psychologist in Atlanta to becoming a corporate coach and an Organizational Psychologist. The Brownings now live on Lake Burton in Rabun County, GA.

• Dr. Wilfred Anderson (1965), Willingham's first African-American student, had a long, successful medical career as a doctor serving in public health in Cleveland, OH. He worked for IBM in the late 1960's and now owns Anderson Systems, a computer service.

• Jim Wooten (1963) has been selected as one of the "100 Most Influential Georgians" for seven of the past eight years by *Georgia Trend Magazine*. Wooten is considered to be the conservative voice of the *Atlanta Journal-Constitution's* editorial board.

- Jim Lambert (1964) lost his first wife to the dreaded disease, lupus, but found his mission in life, Angel Flight, by combining his love for flying with helping families in crisis. He owns Allen and Lambert insurance agency in Macon.
- Rick Bennett (1970) got his start in the business world with a large accounting firm in Atlanta. He and a fellow accountant founded their own company, Bennett Thrasher, which is now one of the leading CPA firms in Metro Atlanta.
- Oney Hudson (1970) grew up on a farm in South Bibb County. After having success as a farmer, he went into corporate and residential development in recent years. He is largely responsible for the growth and development in South Bibb County.
- Mike Cheek (1962) had a career, most recently as the COO of a major global leader, which allowed him extensive world-wide travel experiences. He will also serve as a vice chairman of the 2008 Ryder Cup at the Valhalla Golf Club in Louisville, KY.
- Mark Stevens (1970) achieved notoriety as the catcher on Willingham's only state championship team in baseball. Since then, he has been highly successful in the banking industry and was the founding president of New Southern Bank in Macon.
- Dr. Steve Smith (1969) went from being a high school teacher and coach to success as a principal in Bibb County. He later became the superintendent of the Lowndes County (Valdosta, GA) school system, one of the top school systems in Georgia.
- Dr. Pete Gaines (1963), one of Willingham's all-time great athletes, played football at the University of Georgia and was on Coach Vince Dooley's first squad. Gaines has been a successful dentist in Macon for over 30 years.
- Prentice Knight (1963) found professional success as a college professor at the University of Kansas and at Dartmouth College. Now, he works for CoreNet Global as one of the most prominent and well-respected 'thought-leaders' in the corporate real estate world.
- Dr. Mike Willoughby (1960) was the top academic student in the first graduating class (1960) at Willingham. After graduating from Mercer and then Tulane's Medical School, he settled in Virginia and has had a successful OB-GYN practice.
- Dr. Kim Johnston (1970/71) was the last official graduate of Willingham High. After graduating from the Medical College of Georgia, he returned to Macon in 1987 and now is a partner in the Georgia Neurosurgical Institute.

* * * * * * * * * *

After World War II and on into the 1950's and 60's, South Macon went from being a nondescript area of Macon to a section of town that would experience astounding growth. South Macon was a great place to live and grow up. It was made up of safe, stable neighborhoods which stretched from John W. Burke School on Second Street to the Peach Orchard beyond Broadway to John H. Heard School in South Bibb County to Agnes Barden School in Bloomfield. Just about every home within those boundaries was made up of solid citizens who cared about God, family, education, honesty, and providing a better life for their children than the lives they experienced growing up.

Crime was practically non-existent in South Macon for several reasons. First, who would you steal from, since most people had few material possessions? Families ate meals together, rode or walked to neighborhood churches, and parents insisted that their children respect adults. Classroom teachers were right, and they were seldom questioned for their discipline and teaching methods. If a child got a spanking in school, he could generally expect more of the same – and maybe worse – when he got home. Two-parent homes, which included stay-at-home-moms, were the overwhelming norm in those days. Drugs were something that you purchased legally at locally-owned pharmacies like Powell's, Hogg's, Dixon's, and Massey's, all located on Houston Avenue.

Families, who actually owned cars, would frequently leave their keys in the ignition so they would know where to find them. Houses may or may not be locked at night, and front doors were left open so a window (or attic) fan could draw the night air through sweltering bedrooms after dark. Air conditioners? Televisions? Those were rare commodities in many South Macon homes in the 1940's and 50's, but, as the 'Greatest Generation Ever' became more prosperous and the country rebounded quickly after the War, South Macon began to grow at an alarming rate. New neighborhoods sprang up quickly; strip-shopping centers were being built, and South Maconites were introduced to new grammar schools named Jessie Rice, W.T. Morgan, Minnie Burghard, James H. Porter, and Joseph N. Neel. Like Bruce, Weir, Heard, Burke, and Barden, they also became feeder schools for Willingham High.

Good people lived in South Macon. Proud people. Hard-working people who had big dreams for their children. They were in the early stages of experiencing the 'American Dream.' Owning a home with a yard and a car were about as good as it got for those families who endured the Great Depression. Having excellent grammar schools within walking or bicycle-riding distance was icing on the cake for these young families. Boys and girls had school grounds and backyards to play in and safe neighborhoods to roam during the day. Seldom were South Macon streets, in those days, occupied late at night, other than on weekends, when high school sporting events took place.

Prior to the construction of Willingham and McEvoy, South Macon students proudly attended Sidney Lanier High School for Boys and A.L. Miller High School for Girls after completing grammar school. In those days, Macon was one of the few cites in the country which segregated its students in two ways – by race and gender. Before integration, white students went to Lanier and Miller, while African-American students, both male and female, attended Ballard-Hudson High School. However, as Macon began to grow, and industry began to expand into the Middle Georgia area, it was imperative that the Bibb County Board of Education keep pace with that growth and build new public schools. Thus, Peter G. Appling, a new school for black students in East Macon, was built, while Willingham and McEvoy were built in South Macon to accommodate the growing number of students from the Baby Boom which began in 1946.

Much of South Macon's growth had to do with Robins Air Force Base, located approximately 18 miles south of Macon. Consequently, living in South Macon significantly cut the distance and travel time for those who worked at the base. Most residents of South Macon considered their communities to be desirable places to live and raise families. Their schools and neighborhoods were looked upon with a sense of pride and respect. The houses weren't large, and the lawns weren't rolling and expansive, but, for the most part, they were painted, clean and well-kept.

Conversely, it was widely known that Maconites from other areas of town didn't look at South Macon with the same respect and admiration that South Macon saw in itself. There were some who simply labeled it as a section of town that they considered 'less than.' For South Maconites, there was no better place in the world to live and raise a family. For people outside the South Macon community, many would not have considered living there if the rent were free. South Macon, for the most part, was seen as the working-class section of town. Sociologists would classify its populace on a socio-economic grid of Macon as somewhere between upper-lower-class and lower-middle class citizens.

Generally, people either loved living in South Macon and calling it home – or they moved.

* * * * * * * * * *

Historically, Macon, Georgia, in the 1940's, 50's, and early 60's was quite typical in many ways of Southern towns with populations between 50,000 to 100,000 citizens. There were two school systems in Macon/Bibb County, though both were under the umbrella of the Bibb County Board of Education. One school system was for white students, and the other was for black students. Both systems were governed by an all-white Board of Education. The operative term in local education circles back in those days was 'separate, but equal.' Regardless of a person's philosophy, the two cultures in Macon seldom had reasons to encounter each other, which was especially true with the two school systems until 1964-65 when integration began in Macon in extremely small increments.

Sidney Lanier High School for Boys and A.L. Miller High School for Girls, along with Dudley Hughes Vocational School, had been the only options for public secondary education in the white community for as long as Maconites could remember. At the same time, Ballard-Hudson was the high school which educated African-American students in Macon and Bibb County.

Lanier was the flagship school for Macon's white community and was known state-wide and nationally for its top-notch education, discipline, highly-educated faculty, military prowess (Lanier had an ROTC program which was recognized nationally), state championship teams in all sports, and was well-known for its grueling college preparatory curriculum. However, as Macon began to grow in the late-1940's, and South Macon's population began to experience rapid growth as well, the need for another high school in Macon became evident.

In September, 1958, the Bibb County Board of Education presented the grateful residents of South Macon with a brand new secondary school named A.R. Willingham Boys High School, named in memory of Mr. Alfred Ross Willingham, a long-time, successful entrepreneur, civic leader, and Board of Education member. The rambling, one-level school building was located on Canterbury Road off Pio Nono Avenue and was across a soccer field from McEvoy, its new sister-school which was already one year old. Margaret McEvoy High and Willingham High quickly became points of pride for a part of town that had no identity and very little to take pride in.

With a new, young, energetic faculty, a creative music and band director, and an athletic coaching staff that was second-to-none, Willingham High School was off and running in the 1958-59 school year. Rising seniors at Lanier were allowed to complete their last year of high school at Lanier High; thus, Willingham began operations without a senior class in its first year of existence. With Willingham becoming a reality, suddenly South Macon had its own new school to rally around. The new school produced a sense of pride and excitement which was never thought possible by South Macon residents.

No more driving 30 minutes from the south part of the county near Heard School to get to Lanier. No more traffic to negotiate for Agnes Barden parents carrying their students to be educated on Hendley Street and Montpelier Avenue where Lanier and Miller were located, respectively. South Macon had its own school now. No longer would Charles H. Bruce or Cynthia H. Weir school boys have to forego athletics, because getting a ride home after practice had been practically impossible. No longer would residents of the Peach Orchard community be subjected to long morning and afternoon school bus rides on a Yellow Hound. Now, residents from the south side of town had their own school to support, and it was in close proximity.

Transportation was a big deal in the 1950's. Most families with modest incomes and with one spouse working were doing quite well if they owned a family car. Carpooling to Warner Robins for work was a necessity. To have two cars made a family an anomaly in those days.

Thus, with Willingham High located in the middle of the South Macon community, it became possible to play football for Billy Henderson's Willingham Rams in the fall and spring or be in Jim Littlefield's Pride of Dixie Marching Band. In years past, staying after school at Lanier to play sports, march in the Lanier band, or participate in other activities was very difficult for families without a car or with only one vehicle. Willingham made it possible to stay and play. The high school experience suddenly became a lot more fun with many more opportunities for a large portion of Macon.

The sense of pride that Willingham and McEvoy brought to the South Macon community was unbelievable. With a highly-motivated coaching staff, headed up by a Lanier graduate named Billy Henderson, the school chose Rams for their new nickname. In the eyes of the Willingham community, Rams was a highly-favored moniker, compared to their cross-town rivals, the Lanier Poets. Who – for crying out loud – could rally around a Poet, of all things, when you could be a Ram? It was no contest.

In their eyes, the residents of South Macon had finally arrived. And they knew it, and they loved it. So what if Lanier and Miller combined for all of those years of history and tradition? Willingham and McEvoy students didn't seem to care. Plus, beating your wealthy, affluent, local rivals in athletics only validated the new school. South Macon boys would now have the ability to be elected president of the Student Council, the Beta Club, or the senior class. Thus, a brand-new rivalry was created in Macon between the old-line, tradition-heavy Lanier Poets and the upstart Willingham Rams. Comparisons between Lanier and Willingham over who was better were inevitable. For example,

• Lanier had pride and tradition; Willingham had pride and the jump-start of a new tradition,

• South Macon had the Westgate Shopping Mall; Lanier had everything else in town,

• Lanier had 19 straight wins over Willingham in basketball; Willingham had six straight wins over Lanier in football,

• Lanier had ROTC, military uniforms, and shiny black combat boots; Willingham had dress-right-dress, P.E. uniforms, and bare feet,

• Lanier had what seemed like 100-years of a rich heritage; Willingham had 12-years of blue-collar opportunities,

• Lanier colors were orange and green; Willingham colors were blue and white,

• They were the Poets; we were the Rams,

• They had the Pig N Whistle; we had Fincher's Barbeque. We won!

It is true that Lanier High School produced an enormous number of highly-successful graduates in its long and storied past. Doctors, lawyers, bankers and financiers; entrepreneurs, business owners, politicians, and industrialists; educators, professional athletes, and even an astronaut walked their hallowed halls as proud Lanier Poets. And rightly so.

But Willingham was new, equally-proud, and ready to challenge their much older cross-town brothers.

Sadly, with the stroke of a pen by the powers-that-be, circa 1969-70, the rivalries and traditions of those two fine schools would all be gone, and not just for Willingham/McEvoy and Lanier/Miller. Things would never be the same again for Ballard-Hudson, Peter G. Appling, Dudley Hughes Vocational, and five-year-old Mark Smith/Lasseter. Though the names of the schools would be forever changed, the traditions, friendships, and great memories would linger on in the minds and hearts of their proud graduates.

* * * * * * * * * *

As Willingham and McEvoy began their new missions as the educational hub of South Macon, new businesses began to locate there to take advantage of a burgeoning population. Shoney's, McDonald's, and other fast-food restaurants began to compete with the long-time establishments – Fincher's Barbeque and NuWay Wieners – for South Macon dollars. Small, strip-shopping centers began to spring up throughout the south part of Macon on Pio Nono, Rocky Creek, and in Bloomfield, but in September, 1961, Westgate Mall, the first indoor shopping mall in the entire South, opened its doors on Pio Nono Avenue in the virtual heart of South Macon.

First, Willingham. Then, Westgate. South Macon had arrived once again.

Now, Maconites from areas of town like Vine-Ingle, Shirley Hills, and Idle Hour who wanted to shop in Macon on a steaming-hot, humid day in August, or on a cold, rainy day in February, had a choice. They could either search for a parking space on Cherry Street downtown and pour their coins into a parking meter and walk for blocks to shop at Joseph N. Neel's, Davison's, or R.S. Thorpe's, or, they could drive to South Macon, park close to the building, and shop in total comfort in Georgia's only climate-controlled shopping mall.

Westgate and Willingham became important locations and landmarks for South Macon and helped authenticate a growing section of Macon. But as important as South Macon's growth and progress were, and with a deep sense of pride that the community soon developed, the real treasures of South Macon were found in the young men and women who were educated in her schools, worshipped in her churches, shopped in her stores, practiced and played on her fields, and lived in her neighborhoods.

Nearly 2,000 boys/young men/male students/Rams graduated from Willingham from 1960 through 1970. The 25 men who are featured in *31206* are only a few examples of hundreds of others just like them who graduated from Willingham and achieved measures of success in life. It is the author's hope that the reader will appreciate each man for who he is and for the things he has accomplished. Each has his own story, and all were influenced in different ways by teachers, parents, coaches, pastors, neighbors, siblings, and friends.

In the creation of *31206*, some common threads wove their way into the fabric of the book. Of 25 men in this book, only two of them – Dr. Wilfred Anderson and Judge Bill Self – had parents who graduated from college. Several men in *31206* were raised by parents who did not graduate from high school, but several only completed the third or fourth grades. It became apparent that college-educated parents were not determining factors in the success of their children. Time and involvement in their sons' lives, however, were extremely important. Some guys were raised by their mothers; most had two parents in their homes. Regardless, each man of *31206* was raised in a home where there was unconditional love and were encouraged to be their best.

Discipline in the home, along with high expectations from the parents, was important in the development of each man. These men were expected to do their best in whatever they undertook, be it academics, a part-time job, or athletics. Parents' roles in the home were to guide their children into adulthood so they would become productive, successful men. Even busy parents were involved in their children's education, and PTA and Booster Club meetings were well-attended because of the school's expectations of its parents. The school expected commitment from its students, and their parents seemed equally committed to doing their part to help the school in any way possible.

Participation was much more important than being a spectator when these men were young. Each guy in *31206* was not only a participant but a leader in athletics, band, clubs, or student leadership in high school. Though the choice of sports and organized activities was miniscule in the 1950's and 60's when compared with today's offerings, the young men at Willingham still found avenues of involvement in some form of extracurricular activity.

The church and faith in God were common threads in the homes of these men. Parents took their families to church and most of these men were actively involved in the life of their church. Pastors were frequently mentioned as mentors and role models. Likewise, various adults - teachers, coaches, neighbors, parents, and other authority figures - were vital in the growth and development of these men.

The boys, now the men, of *31206* have lived full, meaningful, extraordinary lives. Growing up in South Macon, these guys may not have had everything they wanted, but they had everything they needed. Now, their stories have been told, and they have made the rest of the South Macon community proud of them.

Go Rams!

Rams to Gamecocks to Vikings

Bobby Lee Bryant
Class of 1963

*Trust in the Lord with all your heart, and lean
not to your own understanding. In all your ways
acknowledge Him, and He will direct your paths.*
—Proverbs 3:5-6

Willingham had just beaten its arch-rival Lanier, 7-6, to clinch their third consecutive win against the Poets, so it was time to celebrate. But, with players and coaches already beginning to enjoy the hard-earned victory in the dressing room, halfback Bobby Bryant sat alone. Crying. Bobby recalled, "Coach Henderson walked over to me, and it was like he knew what I was thinking. He said, 'Bobby, you're going to go to college.'

"Even though we had just won our last game of the season against Lanier," Bobby said, "I was sitting there thinking that I hadn't heard from any colleges, and all of a sudden, it's over. This would be the last football game I would ever play. My parents, who had 11 children, didn't have money for me to go to college, and no schools had even approached me about a scholarship. Since my sister, Helen, and I would be the only ones in our family to actually finish high school, I had no one at home to advise me about going to college or my future."

He stated, "I was 6'0" tall, weighed 145 pounds, and only played in five games my senior year, because I broke the navicular bone in my right wrist in the first game of the year. I didn't play the previous season, because Coach Henderson and I had a disagreement, and I quit; so a football scholarship didn't look like a possibility. I still had basketball and baseball to look forward to, but I figured my football career was officially over."

In high school, Bobby was an 'A/B' student, but sports would be the avenue that would bring him self-respect and notoriety. "I enjoyed sports, and I regret not playing more varsity football than I did. Socially, I was a shy kid, was insecure with girls, and felt a bit inferior because our family was poor. I didn't have many close relationships during my high school years other than being part of the teams. Sports were my avenue to success, and I got a lot of joy from playing ball, which made me feel better about myself."

Coach Johnny Stallings, who was on the first coaching staff at Willingham when the school opened in 1958, was a Lanier graduate and, like Bobby Bryant, he was also a former South Carolina Gamecock. Stallings had been coached by Billy Henderson during his freshman year at USC, and, after injuring his knee, assisted Henderson as a freshman football coach. Thus, when Henderson got the Willingham football job, he invited Stallings to join him on staff. Stallings recalled, "Bobby was one of the two best athletes that I have ever coached. C.J. Williams, who played for me at Woodward Academy and later for Georgia Tech, was also a tremendous athlete and could do everything like Bobby.

"Bobby was great in every sport – football, baseball, basketball, and track. The state record for the 440-yard dash back in 1962 was about 48:8, and Bobby ran 49:2. In the Columbus Relays he ran the 440, the 440-relay and mile-relay, and high jumped and broad (later renamed 'long' jump) jumped. He was some track athlete. I remember in Columbus when Bobby was about to run the 440 while the high jump was about to start. I spoke with the coach who was handling the high jump and told him Bobby would high jump as soon as he finished the 440. After the race, Bobby ran over to me and said they scratched him from the high jump. I told the coach to let Bobby pass until the bar goes up to 6'1" - and Bobby still won the high jump. If my memory is correct, he jumped about 6'3" that day. Bobby stayed pretty busy by practicing baseball three days a week and doing track two days."

Stallings expressed mild surprise that Bobby had such a long and successful NFL career. "For someone who was Bobby's size to play on defense in the pros for that long and that well is a real accomplishment. On the other hand, a lot of players that were drafted in late rounds, or who weren't drafted at all, end up being good professional football players. Bobby had such a tremendous work ethic and great athletic ability."

As Bobby's high school career wound down, a couple of smaller schools, Presbyterian College and UT-Martin, showed some interest in him but offered no scholarships. However, the University of South Carolina pursued him as a defensive back and kick-returner. Coach Weems Baskin, a football recruiter and the track coach at USC, knew about Bobby primarily because of his success in track, so the South Carolina Gamecocks offered Willingham's Bobby Bryant a football scholarship for the 1963-1964 school year.

The coaching staff knew that they were getting an excellent athlete. Little did they know they were getting a high-quality, high-character young man in the same package, a true student/athlete who would make the university and the entire USC community proud.

South Carolina was a great fit for Bobby. According to Tom Price, the USC Gamecock historian, "Track coach Weems Baskin hoped that Bobby might help his track team as a sprinter or hurdler, in addition to playing football under head coach Marvin Bass."

Price wrote in his article, *Catching up with Bobby Bryant*, in October, 2003, on the USC Gamecock website, "Instead of running track, in the spring, Bryant turned to baseball as a left-handed pitcher, and became one of the best of that era on both the gridiron and the diamond. He never weighed more than 172 pounds and his nickname at Carolina was 'Bones.' After a year of freshman teams (in an era when freshmen weren't allowed to play varsity sports in college), Bryant was a regular for three seasons in both sports and was named first team All-

Atlantic Coast Conference in both football and baseball as a senior. He won
the Anthony J. McKelvin Award given annually to the outstanding athlete in the
Atlantic Coast Conference. *The New York Daily News* and the *Detroit Sports
Extra* named him to their All-America teams. Bobby played in the East-West
Shrine Game and the Hula Bowl."

Price continued, "Bryant said probably his biggest football thrill as
a Gamecock occurred in the only game that USC won his senior season.
Paul Dietzel replaced Marvin Bass as head football coach in 1966, and the
Gamecocks traveled to Raleigh to play North Carolina State in the dedication
game at Carter Stadium. Bryant returned a punt 98 yards for a touchdown
that sparked Carolina to a 31-21 win. Thirty-seven years later, Bryant said, 'It
was probably a mistake for me to field the punt at our own two-yard line, but I
received a couple of key blocks from teammates, and everything worked out.'
The 98-yard return is still a school record for the longest punt return, though
Bryant also had a 77-yard punt return against Louisiana State in the 1966 season
opener.

"In baseball, Bobby was the first University of South Carolina pitcher to
strike out 100 batters in a season and once pitched a 13-inning complete game,
1-0 win, over the University of Maryland. In another game, he walked the first
two batters in the first inning and picked both of them off base. Bobby was
drafted for baseball by the New York Yankees in 1966 and by the Boston Red
Sox after his senior season in 1967. In the NFL draft, the Vikings chose him in
the seventh round in 1967, the 167th player selected that year, but he was the
first Gamecock selected. Defensive back Stan Juk was drafted by the Miami
Dolphins, and tackle Paul Phillips was picked by the San Diego Chargers that
year."

Coach Marvin Bass, former head football coach at South Carolina, has
been around football for a long time. He was an assistant coach at several
schools, including Georgia Tech under the legendary Bobby Dodd, and coached
professionally for the Buffalo Bills of the NFL and in Canada. Bass recalled
fond memories of his three-year association with Bobby Bryant at South
Carolina. "Bobby was one of those self-made guys. I believe he's one of the
best defensive backs to ever play in the NFL and there are lots of other coaches
in the pros who felt the same way. Bobby was not only talented but was one
of those dependable players that you knew would give everything he had every
time he stepped onto the field, both at practice and in games. He paid attention
to details and was so easy to coach. Bobby was a total team player; he listened
when the coaches talked, and he was very intelligent. He was a man of high
character, he had great manners, and, whatever the situation was, in sports or in
life, he always responded with greatness."

Coach Bass (85) is now retired and lives in Blythewood, SC, near
Columbia. He continued, "Bobby may not have looked like a great football
player at 170 pounds, and he didn't have that physical package that everybody
used to look for, but he had everything else. Bobby had a feel for the game,

incredible toughness, he was athletic and fast, and just knew what to do and when to do it. About Bobby Bryant, there's just nothing bad that can be said."

Coach Dick Weldon, USC's offensive backfield coach, head recruiter, and baseball coach, gushed with praise when asked about his former pitcher. "Bobby Bryant is not only one of the finest athletes I have ever been around, but he's one of the finest individuals I have ever met. He's one of the truly great ones that I have known in my entire life."

After Bobby graduated from the University of South Carolina in 1967 with a BS in Business Management, many observers from his hometown wondered if Bobby was making the right career choice by choosing to spend his Sunday afternoons covering wide receivers like Lynn Swann, Fred Biletnikoff, Otis Taylor, and Bob Hayes (known at one time as the World's Fastest Human after winning the 100 meters in the Olympics) while tackling the likes of Walter Payton, Larry Czonka, O.J. Simpson, and the rest of those big, fast, physical tailbacks and fullbacks.

So, Coach Weldon, were you surprised when Bobby chose pro football over pro baseball?

"Just a little, but Bobby would have been successful in whichever sport he chose. He was just an amazing athlete. One of my favorite memories about Bobby is when he pitched a one-hitter against North Carolina, and we beat them, 1-0. It was the finest performance I have ever seen. I would have pitched him every game if I could have gotten away with it."

In Bobby's first year playing varsity football at Carolina, he played defensive back and ran back punts and kickoffs. Weldon said, "He had an amazing body—all bone, muscle, and sinew. Bobby may have been skinny, but he could fly, and he had plenty of heart and desire. That combination will take you a long way in life and in sports. I think part of the secret to his success was that he took care of himself, both physically and spiritually. Bobby had no bad habits like a lot of college students and was very committed in his Christian faith. On top of that, he was just tough as nails.

"Sure, Bobby was an incredible pitcher in baseball, and he was amazing as a defensive back and kick-returner in football, but I think Bobby's greatest achievement was being named the ACC's Most Outstanding Athlete in 1966, because our football team won only one game the entire season.

"It's easy for coaches to have high opinions of outstanding student/athletes like Bobby Bryant, but you could talk to any of his former teammates, and they would have the same high opinion of him. His teammates thought he was a great athlete, teammate, and a great person as well. You can probably tell that I can't say enough good things about Bobby Bryant, and, in my book, he has no flaws and no down-side. You won't hear many coaches say this, but he's just one of my heroes."

Bobby was drafted as a pitcher in a late round by the New York Yankees after his junior year at Carolina but didn't sign, because the Yankees didn't offer a very large contract. After his senior year, Bobby was drafted by the

Boston Red Sox, but he had already decided to play professional football. The Minnesota Vikings of the NFL drafted Bobby after his senior season in the seventh round as a 170-pound cornerback. Bobby laughed, "My nickname at South Carolina was 'Bones' and with the Vikings, it was 'Skinny.'" Regardless of his size, Bobby Bryant confounded any doubters by playing defensive back and returning punts and kick-offs for 14 years.

When questioned about his lack of size regarding his 14-year career in the NFL, Bobby said, "I attribute my long career to the toughness that I got from my mother. She weighed 95 pounds and had eleven children. My mother was tough and lived to be 99 years old. I believe the Lord made my body where I healed pretty fast from injuries. After coming back from broken bones or pulled muscles, I still ran as fast as I did before the injuries, and I never feared getting hit again either."

Bryant's list of teammates on the Vikings includes at least five who are in the pro football Hall of Fame in Canton, OH: Fran Tarkenton, Alan Page, Ron Yary, Carl Eller, and Paul Krause. "Alan Page, my roommate in Minnesota, became a lawyer and a Minnesota State Supreme Court Justice. We still gather for Vikings' reunions periodically, so I get to see those guys again. Doug Sutherland, Wally Hilgenberg, and Karl Kassulke were some of my best friends from those days with the Vikings."

The Minnesota Vikings roster from 1969 throughout Bryant's career reads like an NFL all-star team: Fran Tarkenton (qb), Alan Page (dl), Carl Eller (dl), Jeff Siemon (lb), Chuck Foreman (rb), Ed White (ol), Ahmad Rashad (wr), Sammy White (wr), Ron Yary (ol), Matt Blair (lb), Paul Krause (db), Jim Marshall (dl), and Mick Tinglelhoff (c). Those Vikings teams were led by Hall of Fame coach Bud Grant. The Vikings defense, with Bobby Bryant at cornerback, earned the nickname, "The Purple People Eaters," for their aggressive, attacking style and physical play, and became the standard by which defenses were measured in that era. The Vikings had an amazing run of highly-successful seasons when they went 12-2 in 1969, 1970, 1973, and 1975, and went 11-2-1 in 1976 with a defense that ranked second out of 28 teams in the NFL.

When asked if being on four Super Bowl teams and playing in two Super Bowls were the high points of his pro career, Bobby quickly answered, "No, primarily because we played so poorly. I had knee surgery in 1970, so I didn't get to play against the Chiefs, and, in 1975 against the Steelers, I didn't play because of a broken arm. I played in 1973 against Miami and against the Raiders in '76. Sure, the Super Bowls were really fun and exciting, and it was great just getting there, until the kickoff. Then it went downhill fast. We just didn't play well at all in any of the four Super Bowls."

The real highlights of Bobby's professional football career came in 1986 when the Minnesota Vikings named him to their Silver Anniversary team as a cornerback, and, again in 2001, when he was named to the Vikings 40th Anniversary team. Bobby said, "That is a pretty elite group for me to be part of and may be my biggest thrill."

Bobby made All-Pro in 1975 and played in the Pro Bowl in New Orleans. He recalled, "I think my best year in the pros may have been my rookie year in 1969, when I intercepted eight passes in the first nine games, before tearing up my knee." Bobby led the NFC in interceptions in 1973 with seven, while two AFC defensive backs led their conference with eight that year. He ranks second on the Vikings in career interceptions with 51. Hall of Famer Paul Krause, who is the NFL's all-time career interception leader with 81 intercepted 53 passes while playing with the Vikings. To give some context to the outstanding interception numbers that he amassed as a Viking cornerback, Bobby led high-profile defensive back and future Hall of Famer Deion Sanders in career interceptions going into the 2004 season.

"I was never looking forward to retiring from the Vikings, but I knew that the day would one day arrive," Bobby recalled. "I didn't want to be a 37-year-old backup defensive back, but I knew, because I had been injured recently, that they could get a younger, cheaper cornerback than me. I think I was ready when retirement came, and I was never under the pretense that I could play football forever. Plus, we had a new defensive coordinator, and the bump and run-type coverage was just coming into the league, where the cornerbacks play right up on the line of scrimmage and make contact with the receiver when the ball is snapped. You had to play man-to-man coverage all over the field, and I knew I couldn't play that style anymore. Also, I pulled a hamstring in the preseason, so my career came to an end."

Doug Sutherland played defensive line for the Vikings and was a teammate and roommate of Bobby Bryant. Sutherland, a 14th-round draft choice out of University of Wisconsin-Superior, a Division III school, was part of the heralded Purple People Eaters defensive unit of the Vikings. "I replaced Gary Larson, who was an original member of that front four. Bobby and I played and roomed together for four or five years. I've always had such great respect for Bobby, and I felt worse when he retired from pro football than when I retired."

Doug Sutherland was asked what he remembered about Bobby Bryant?

"You mean Skinny Minnie?" he laughed. "We used to say, 'He's not skinny; he's tall. That's all.' Bobby's just the greatest! In fact, the highlight of my entire career and the happiest moment in football for me was when we were playing Dallas in 1972, the year we played in the 1973 Super Bowl, and Bobby intercepted a pass near the end of the game and ran it back for a touchdown. That touchdown clinched the game and guaranteed that we were going to the Super Bowl, so it was a pretty happy moment. Bobby was such a big-play guy."

Sutherland continued, "Bobby was kind of like the Evil Kneivel of pro football in that he broke just about everything that could be broken. He obviously wasn't the largest individual to ever play corner and ended up with dislocated shoulders, broken wrists, legs, bad knees, anything that could be broken – he had it broken, but he was just tougher than nails.

"And what a tremendous athlete Bobby was. I played softball with him a few times, and he could throw a ball from the fence to home plate like it was on a rope. His arm was amazing, even after breaking his wrist and arm, and he was a great basketball player as well. Bobby was one of the fiercest competitors to ever play. I mean, he'd come back into the huddle in football with the Vikings, and he'd start yelling at our big old defensive linemen, 'Can't you guys put any heat on that quarterback? I can't cover these guys back here forever!' But that was just Bobby.

"Bobby could get pretty crabby at times, but we all knew that was because he wanted to win so badly. He'd be yelling and getting mad about something, and 'Stubby' Eason, our equipment manager, would give Bobby the wrong pair of pants or the wrong pair of socks on purpose just to watch him go off! It would make him crazy before the game, but that meant Bobby was ready to play."

The Vikings obviously had a number of characters in their organization in the 1970s and '80s. Stubby Eason was also one of them. Sutherland recalled, "Stubby (now deceased) was our equipment guy, and the reason we called him 'Stubby' was because he was short, and he only had one leg. I felt bad about people calling him 'Stubby,' but he insisted on us calling him that. Stubby was great, though, and he would sit up on a table in the equipment room and ask a rookie to help him take off his shoe because he was tired. Stubby would loosen up his artificial leg while the rookie wasn't watching; then, the rookie would reach down and pull Stubby's leg completely off. The rookie would just about die! We had a great time on that team, but you always had to keep your head on a swivel! It was like a big kindergarten party."

Sutherland said, "Bobby got more out of his body in professional football than, perhaps, he should have, and I was sorta like that. I was a very low draft choice from a D-III school, and I never should have made it in the pros. However, Bobby was a tremendous, all-around athlete, and he worked hard at it. It didn't just happen for him. He was committed and trained hard to be the best."

Bobby Bryant coached the Minnesota Vikings basketball exhibition team for several years, and Sutherland remembered that they must have played about 180 games one year. Sutherland said, "When Bobby played, we hardly ever lost a game. He was like a coach in the locker room, yelling at guys because they weren't playing hard or something. They thought it was supposed to be for fun, but Bobby hated to lose in anything. When he was coaching, he'd take some guys out of the game, and they almost came to blows a few times, because he was such a competitor. His intensity and wanting to win at any cost drove him to be better than other players. That was Bobby's shtick – he didn't care if he broke both arms making a tackle, because he was gonna stick his head in there no matter what.

"Bobby had the respect of everybody on the team. The crazy thing is that he never made a lot of money in football, because every time he was about to renegotiate his contract, he always got hurt. He was trying to negotiate a contract coming off knee surgery or shoulder surgery. You talk about 'buzzard luck,' he had it. It was so unfortunate, because he was such a great guy and had a great career.

"Skinny Minnie. He was the best!"

Fred Zamberletti (72), an Iowa native, has lived in Bloomington, MN, since 1961 when the franchise was founded and served as the only athletic trainer in Minnesota Vikings' history. He began working with the Vikings when he was only 28 and has seen literally hundreds of athletes don the purple, white, and gold. Zamberletti said, "I don't think anybody in this franchise, pound for pound, has ever made more big plays than Bobby Bryant. He might have signed a major league baseball contract as a pitcher had he not fractured both navicular (wrist) bones in college. Bobby was tough, and I guarantee that he could play in the league today. His type of game in the secondary would fit right into today's schemes.

"I remember when we were playing against the Packers in a big game one year, and it was late in the fourth quarter and the game was close. The Packers had a big running back, Jim Grabowski, who played at Illinois, and he was running a sweep on fourth-down. Bobby flew up to the line of scrimmage and stuffed Grabowski for a three-yard loss and helped us beat Green Bay. But, the biggest win the Vikings ever had in our franchise's history was against the Cowboys in Dallas in the last game of the season. Whoever won that game went to the Super Bowl, and we were heavy underdogs. Bobby intercepted a Roger Staubach pass and ran it back for a touchdown."

Zamberletti recalled that Dallas-Minnesota game in vivid detail. "They came into that game with all of those Pro Bowl athletes like Staubach, Bob Hayes, and all of that speed on offense and defense. Harvey Martin, Too Tall Jones, and Jethro Pugh were all riding together when I got on the elevator with them. They were relaxed, laughing and joking, and eating popcorn before the game. They acted like it was going to be another scrimmage or something. We went in there and whipped their butts that day."

Fred continued, "Bobby constantly made big plays, and on the day of a game, he was like a 'banty [bantam] rooster.' He was just ornery as can be and was all over the place. The equipment manager hated to see Bobby coming into the locker room, because every time Bobby came in there, he complained about his gear, his socks, anything. But that was Bobby's ritual on game day.

"I followed Bobby's career closely, because it was apparent that he wanted to be the best and do something with his life. One year, he led the league in interceptions and was having a great year until he dislocated his shoulder and had to have surgery again. He always responded well after he got hurt; he worked hard in rehab and got himself ready to play again. We didn't have the modern medicine then that we have now, or he may have played even longer. Bobby sure earned his pay while he was in Minnesota. At the time he was up here, our front four were getting all of the publicity as the Purple People Eaters, but if Bobby had been on any other team, he would have gotten a lot more recognition."

Zamberletti was convinced that Bobby had a long, productive career, because he was such a good athlete. "He had speed, athletic ability, he knew when to break on the ball and when to jump a receiver's route, plus he had amazing instincts. And those hands! If he ever touched it, he could put the ball away. He makes these guys today look like they're playing in junior college. Bobby was just so tough, especially for his size. I've seen him fly up to the line of scrimmage and just throw that skinny body at the knees of those big fullbacks. Those big plays were pretty important to me; I've filed them away in my memory-bank over the years, and Bobby made as many plays as anybody. Some guys were special for the way they played the game, and Bobby's at the top of my list.

"I'm happy that Bobby is successful today, and it's because he has found peace within himself. Bobby is happy today, and Stephanie is a big part of that. I think Bobby has found serenity in his Christian life, which is really important to him."

* * * * * * * * *

The fact that Bobby Bryant was an outstanding all-around athlete has been well-chronicled and was a point of South Macon-pride since the early-1960's, well before he became a four-sport letterman at Willingham. Bobby recalled his Bruce School days, "In grammar school, we played football in cut-off jeans, and many on our team played barefoot. Billy Smith was my first coach, when I was in the fourth grade. When I was in the seventh grade, Franklin Jacobs coached us to the Pony Bowl, the city's elementary school football championship game played on Thanksgiving Day. Billy Smith and Franklin Jacobs both taught me a lot about sports and competition."

Bobby Bryant family: daughter Jennifer Halligan with husband Steve and son Miles.

Margaret Phillips remembered the toughness and lack of fear that Bobby possessed, even at an early age. "Having taught both Bobby and his twin-brother Billy, my most vivid memory of Bobby during his days at Bruce School was in the Pony Bowl football game in 1954. That was the first year that Bobby was old enough to play, which meant he was a fourth grader. Truly, he was never big enough. Joseph Clisby School was Bruce's opponent that day, and their star was a big boy named Bobby Mangan, a huge seventh grader who was maybe a half-ounce below the 150-pound weight limit. Mangan broke loose on the opening kickoff and was heading for a touchdown, when Bobby chased him down and grabbed onto Mangan. Bobby was hanging onto Mangan like the tail of a kite, and he finally tackled Mangan before he crossed the goal line."

Bryant remembered that play. "That was the play where I bit my tongue. I had a bad habit of sticking my tongue out when I played ball. Another memory that I have from that game was at half time. We were losing to Clisby, and our coach said, 'A fourth-grader is the only one on this team with any guts.' You don't forget those moments."

Bobby later captained and quarterbacked his Bruce School team to a second Pony Bowl appearance. In basketball, he led his team to the city championship, scoring on a long, one-hander from about 30-feet out in a triple-overtime, sudden-death thriller over Cynthia Weir School at Memorial Gym in Macon. A true left-hander, he pitched Bruce to the city baseball championship, while his brother Billy was his catcher, and a younger brother Dennis a fifth grader, played infield.

Willingham High School's coaching staff knew that they were on the verge of getting a special athlete when Bobby arrived on campus in 1958. Bobby enjoyed considerable success in football as a wingback and defensive back, despite a broken hand in his senior year which limited him to only five games. In basketball, Bobby was moved up from the ninth grade team to the varsity and became an impact player for Coach Martin Allman's Rams. In baseball, he was a wicked, left-handed pitcher and an outfielder with incredible range. However, as talented as Bobby was in those three major sports, several of Bobby's high school coaches agreed that track and field may have been his best sport. Bobby high jumped 6'1" in the days before the Fosbury Flop became popular, ran the 440-yard dash in 49 seconds, and ran on the mile and 440-relay teams.

"We had some tremendous athletes at Willingham in those days. Marcus Bowen and Pete Gaines played three sports at Willingham and went to the University of Georgia on football scholarships. Jimmy Clay, Tack Mote, and Jimmy Hammond were good friends of mine and were great teammates. They helped Willingham develop a strong, competitive athletic program in Willingham's early days."

As one of, if not *the* finest athletes to ever grow up in Macon, Bobby Bryant may not have had numerous scholarship offers for football as a senior in high school, but, as already noted, he did have a choice of professional sports. Bobby's football and baseball coach, Billy Henderson, commented about Bobby, "Without a doubt, Bobby Bryant was one of the finest athletes I have ever coached. He had speed, savvy, intelligence, and desire. Bobby also had character. It is well-known that Bobby and I had a confrontation on the practice field when he played football for us as a junior. I learned that it wasn't smart to give an ultimatum to a player in the heat of the moment. Good things don't happen for anybody when you give ultimatums. I think Bobby and I both learned a lot from that incident."

Several teachers greatly influenced Bobby's education. "Eunice Odom was my English teacher when I was in the seventh grade at Bruce School. I really enjoyed the way she taught, and, therefore, I always did well in English. She gave me a strong foundation in grammar." Bobby mentioned other teachers in high school that he particularly liked - Mike Garvin in algebra and Daisy Beatty, his typing teacher. I liked their teaching styles and enjoyed their classes." Not one to hold a grudge, Bobby, likewise, lauded Billy Henderson as one of his most meaningful teachers.

"I have had a lot of people who have been highly influential in my life. First, my father, Lloyd Lewis Bryant, taught me the value of hard work. My mother, Ella Mae Bryant, raised eleven children and worked hard to give us the best life she possibly could. Most importantly, my high school coaches - Billy Henderson, Martin Allman, Johnny Stallings, Henry Middlebrooks, Billy Beale, Dave Hill, Mike Gavin, and others—coached me and taught me how important it was to work hard, have integrity, always doing your best, and they emphasized the importance of teamwork. Neil Bowen was my South Macon Little League baseball coach and was a father figure to me in many ways. My pastor at Mikado Baptist Church, E.C. Sheehan, and my Sunday School teachers all played a big part in my development as a Christian."

Pete Gaines and Bobby Bryant grew up two blocks from each other on Grenada Terrace. Pete recalled, "Bobby didn't have a car in high school, so he rode to school with me. I remember the day Bobby signed a bonus with the Minnesota Vikings and bought his first car. We all thought he was crazy, because he played cornerback at USC at about 170 pounds and chose pro football over major league baseball.

"Bobby was an amazing athlete. He could pick up a tennis racket and be good at it. We watched him play in several Super Bowls and I remember how Bobby would hit 'em low and cut a ball carrier's legs out from under him, rather than trying to tackle a runner up high. It must have really worked for him, because he had a long, successful pro football career."

Bobby reminisced, "While growing up on Grenada Terrace in South Macon, I remember there was always a game of some type being played in one of our backyards. We usually had enough kids to have two teams, plus, we only lived about a half-mile from Bruce School, which had a ball field and asphalt outdoor basketball courts.

"I remember at Willingham, Coach Henderson used to tell us how Lanier students and players thought they were better than us, because he was trying to get us fired up to play Lanier. I guess we probably thought they were better off financially than we were, but I never felt that Willingham was inferior in any way. Though we were a new school, our teams were pretty good. I guess I did feel that South Macon was poorer than the Lanier side of town."

Bobby, do you think your life is better or worse because of where you grew up?

His reply was, "I think the choices you make and the people you are exposed to, taught by, and play and work with are much more important than where you live. Learning discipline, the value of work, honesty, and teamwork were valuable lessons I learned early in life."

* * * * * * * * * *

Tom Price, the USC Gamecock historian, wrote about Bobby in 2003, "Contacts made during a 14-year National Football League career with the Minnesota Vikings resulted in a post-football career in sales for Bobby Bryant. The former all-star Gamecock defensive back, who played longer in the NFL than any other University of South Carolina alumnus, now lives in Columbia, SC, and is a sales representative for Harmon Autoglass Glass Doctor, a glass replacement firm that is based in Minnesota.

"Bryant remained in the Minneapolis area when he retired from professional football in 1981, but four years later, returned to Columbia to work for Boyd Management, a

Two Vikings: Nate Wright (43) and Bobby Bryant (20)

property development and management firm run by Ken Wheat, another former Gamecock football player. Bobby left Boyd Management in 1990 for his present job with Harmon. "I knew some people back in Minnesota who worked for Harmon," Bryant explained.

Bobby met his wife, the former Stephanie Vakos, in Minneapolis when he was playing for the Vikings. Stephanie said, "I am a second generation Greek-American from Wisconsin and was working for two ex-Green Bay Packers, Fuzzy Thurston and Max McGee, and a third partner, a fellow Greek, who recruited me to come work for their chain of restaurants, The Left Guard. They decided to open a restaurant in Minneapolis with a Viking theme and transferred me there to help open the restaurant and work as the assistant manager."

Stephanie explained, "Karl Kassulke, the strong safety for the Vikings, was hired as the restaurant's celebrity host. Karl was from my hometown, Milwaukee, and our parents lived only a few miles apart. We became friends and often traveled together to visit our families. One night Karl invited me to a Viking dinner where he introduced me to Bobby. After that, Bobby and I kept bumping into each other, and I would often see him at The Left Guard. We even doubled-dated to a University of Minnesota basketball game, and we spent all our time talking to each other and ignoring our dates. After the Super Bowl in Houston, we literally ran right into each other in baggage claim, and that's when he asked if he could call me. We began dating, and shortly after, I left the restaurant business to become a flight attendant with Northwest Airlines. I thought I would have more free time, but, unfortunately, I was always on 'reserve' and was flying most Sundays. About a year and a half after we started dating, we were married on July 12, 1975, and we actually had a 'big, fat Greek wedding,' just like the movie! Shortly after our marriage, I retired from Northwest to become a full-time Viking wife and fan.

"Coming from a staunch, Green Bay Packer-supporting family, I was almost disowned by marrying the 'enemy,' but, thankfully, the Vikings were much more successful than the Packers in those days, and it didn't take long to convert my family. Bobby acquired quite a Greek fan club from my large, extended family that crossed the country, and he almost always had someone at an away game cheering for him."

Stephanie was attracted to Bobby from their very first meeting. "He was, and still is, a gentleman. Bobby probably is one of the last true Southern gentlemen, and, after working with so many 'un-gentlemanlike' football players, it was refreshing to meet someone who knew how to treat a lady. But it wasn't just with me. Bobby was so sincere and personable with friends or strangers. He has never allowed his football fame to go to his head, and he has never flaunted it. Bobby has kept a unique humility about him, and you will never hear him brag about his football career. In fact, I'm usually the one who tells everybody. He was a little embarrassed when I wanted to display all of his memorabilia in our recreation room. Bobby has never thought of himself as any better or more important than anyone else just because of the success he's had in sports. His honor and humility, along with his strong sense of responsibility and commitment, are some of his greatest strengths and assets."

Recalling when they first moved to South Carolina, Stephanie said, "Our older son, Blaze, was almost six, and he had only seen Bobby play basketball in the off-season for various fundraisers and charities with other former and current Viking players. We signed Blaze up for a soccer camp, and one day after practice the coach asked Blaze if his dad was 'the Bobby Bryant who played pro football with the Minnesota Vikings?' Blaze told him, 'No, my dad only played basketball with the Vikings.'"

Stephanie credits Bobby with being a wonderful husband and father who always thinks of others before himself. "He has a heart of compassion, a generous spirit, and he's the one who stops to help someone who is stranded and generously gives of his time and money wherever there is a need. That is part of what has made him successful in life. Hard work, determination, self-discipline, integrity, and commitment are all part of who Bobby Bryant is, but his faith is the driving force behind his success, and the glory goes to God for what he has achieved in this lifetime.

"Besides being a great athlete," Stephanie continued, "he's done a great job being my husband for nearly 30 years, which is practically a record in this day and age! Bobby has raised a daughter and two very fine sons, and he models his Christian faith and character to them." Jennifer, Bobby's daughter by a previous marriage, is an architect who is married to Steve Halligan, and they live in Minnesota. Jennifer presented Bobby with his first grandchild, Miles, who is three years old.

Bobby spoke about his two sons, Blaze and Brady. "When they were growing up, I had mixed emotions about them playing football. Physically, they were late-bloomers like me, but both were excellent soccer players in high school. Brady continued to play soccer in college and now plays professionally in the U.S. Soccer League for the Wilmington (NC) Hammerheads. Blaze's interest is in computer graphics, and he hopes to make that his career."

"One of the best things that Bobby does," according to Stephanie, "is to share his faith with others. He has that opportunity when he speaks at various events, and his message is that fame, fortune, and material possessions are not what life is all about. Bobby tells them that they can have eternal life by trusting in Jesus Christ and what He did for us on the cross. That is really where true happiness and contentment lie. It's great how God has used Bobby's sports career and his testimony to touch so many lives with the gospel."

Stephanie concluded, "Athletically, I believe Bobby will be remembered as a poor, skinny, Southern boy with tremendous athletic ability, who made it in professional sports despite all the odds. Personally, Bobby will be remembered as a man of character and integrity, with a strong faith and big heart."

Stephanie and Bobby are active members of Cornerstone Presbyterian Church (PCA) in Columbia. Having been raised at Mikado Baptist in Macon, his Christian faith is extremely important to him. Lauding his mother's character and Christian faith, Bobby said, "My mother taught us that the most important thing that we would ever do in life would be to put our trust in Jesus Christ for eternal life. I have had the opportunity to lead several people to a saving knowledge of Jesus Christ. That is the best and most exciting thing that I have ever done."

Bobby has received numerous honors since the completion of his athletic career. He has been inducted into the South Carolina Sports Hall of Fame, the Georgia Sports Hall of Fame, and the University of South Carolina Sports Hall of Fame. Bobby stays active and fit by continuing to play softball, golf, and training with weights. He is also on the Board of the Midlands Fellowship of Christian Athletes organization.

"I hope I will be remembered as a good Christian, a good husband, father, and a good friend," Bobby concluded. His family and friends will make sure that he will be remembered as all of those things and much more. One thing is for certain, however. The Minnesota Vikings from the frozen North had a lot more fans in the deep South, particularly in Columbia, SC, and Macon, GA, when number 20, Bobby Bryant, was roaming their secondary from 1968 till 1981.

You can bet the name, "Bobby Bryant", will be remembered in those three locations for all of the right reasons.

The Vikings trainer, Fred Zamberletti, said it best when he concluded his remarks with deep conviction, "Tell Bobby that I'm still a big fan of his."

Bobby, so are the rest of us.

(*Some information for this chapter was taken from the University of South Carolina webpage, http://uscsports.collegesports.com/sports/m-footbl/spec-rel/ 101003aaa.html, and the Minnesota Vikings webpage, www.minnesotavikings.com.)

Bobby Bryant family: Bobby, Brady, Stephanie, and Blaze.

Nunn But Coke

Connell (Connie) Stafford
Class of 1966

The day is sufficient unto itself for my needs.
— *Author Unknown*

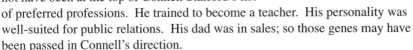

While he was growing up on Beddingfield Avenue in South Macon, a career in politics would not have been at the top of Connell Stafford's list of preferred professions. He trained to become a teacher. His personality was well-suited for public relations. His dad was in sales; so those genes may have been passed in Connell's direction.

However, Connell gave his first political-type speech as a junior in high school, not helping someone in their race for the Senate or Governor, but assisting a South Macon friend who was running for president of their high school fraternity. Not realizing at the time that he had a God-given ability to speak with conviction and passion, Stafford was almost single-handedly responsible for his friend's election, despite the fact that Willingham boys were virtually never chosen in those elections. Fraternity presidents, historically, were Lanier or Stratford boys, not Willingham Rams.

Darrell Young, the high school fraternity brother, said, "Connell gave the most eloquent, impassioned speech on my behalf that we had ever heard. It was so powerful that, somehow, I began to wonder if he was actually talking about me. It was just incredible what he said and how he said it. We knew at that moment that Connell had some special qualities that other high school guys at Willingham didn't possess."

Connell Stafford, known in his younger years as "Connie", was the second of three boys – Terry (61), Connell (56), and Mark (50). Their mom died in 1980, and their dad, who began his career with Coke in 1945, died in 1988. Connell grew up on Beddingfield Avenue and attended Charles H. Bruce Elementary School. He graduated from Willingham in 1966.

Stafford attended Georgia Southern University (then, Georgia Southern College) in Statesboro, GA, where he majored in Psychology. He later earned a Masters Degree in Government from American University in Washington, DC. Upon graduating from Georgia Southern, Connell taught geography and history at Florence Bernd Elementary School in Macon, GA, on a provisional teaching certificate. Without his realizing it at the time, politics would soon enter into his life in an unusual way and never leave.

As a young, concerned sixth- and seventh-grade teacher, Stafford realized, "Florence Bernd School had old, out-of-date text books. I went to our principal to find out why our students' books were so bad and why other Bibb County schools had new books. Somehow, I never got a clear answer. I was told to go to the superintendent's office and ask them. No one at the board office could give me a straight answer either. I had a terrible time getting any resolution about this matter, and the worst part was that my reasonable questions went unanswered."

To this day, Stafford remains unsure why he was so bothered about such a simple matter as text books. "If someone had said, 'Connell, your school doesn't have new textbooks, because your principal chose to buy gym equipment, new televisions, desks, or video projectors instead,' I would have been fine with it," Stafford said. "There may have been a simple, rational reason, but no one could answer my questions. And that was one thing that I couldn't get out of my head.

"My genesis in politics began that day when I asked what I thought was a simple question," Stafford remembered. "It just wasn't fair to those children, and in the process of trying to figure it all out, I somehow became interested in the field of politics. And I have been at it since I was 23 years old. That's 33 years, to be exact."

Thus, Connell Stafford began his life in politics by trying to bring about change where he thought change was needed and to make things better for those around him.

"My first real foray into politics occurred in Macon when I worked in Emory Greene's campaign for mayor. Emory Greene owned a service station at Seven Bridges in South Bibb County that was called Greasy Greene's Corner. He ran against Ronnie Thompson, but lost. Later, though, Em went on to become chairman of the Board of Commissioners in Bibb County," Stafford recalled. "I just remember wanting to help someone who was interested in helping kids in education, and Emory Greene was that man."

Connell went from losing a local election in Macon to helping Sam Nunn in his bid for the United States Senate in 1972. Nunn won his first Senate race, and Connell Stafford became the Executive Assistant to Senator Sam Nunn from Perry, GA. Nunn's seat in the Georgia House is now held by Rep. Larry Walker, also of Perry, and a good friend of Connell's.

"When I first met Sam Nunn, I was a school teacher in Macon," Stafford recalled. "He came to speak at a Middle Georgia legislative forum. There I learned that he was planning to run for the U.S. Senate, and shortly afterwards, I went to work for him. I was in charge of the 'youth campaign' in his 1972 campaign. Then I went on staff with Senator Nunn in Washington, DC, until 1977."

Stafford said, "I admired the Senator's tenacity and his intellectual abilities. He was such a smart guy, and he never gave up. My responsibilities in his office were related to the oversight of special constituent projects. And since 1972, I have spent 33 years in politics in some capacity, either in Macon, Washington, DC, with Coca-Cola, or with Troutman Sanders in government relations."

Sam Nunn said about his long-time friend, Connell Stafford, "When I first met Connell, he was a young liberal. Today, he is an old conservative, but he really hasn't changed much. Connell has remained dedicated to the principles of honor and integrity. I consider him to be a very savvy guy who knows Georgia business and politics. He has been a very effective spokesman for Coca-Cola, and a strong community leader."

Senator Nunn observed Stafford's strengths, "He has good judgment and a very good feel for people. He has the ability to get along well with all types of people, because he is an excellent communicator. Connell Stafford is well-liked by everyone who knows him. I consider him to be a real friend, and he is a man who has many friends.

"People like Connell, and they trust him," Senator Nunn continued. "I think he will be remembered as a real leader and a person who had a constructive influence on both his business and his community. Of the many things that Connell has done well, I think he has contributed positively to state and national policy. He has been a moderating and positive influence on Georgia's political life.

"To me personally, Connell Stafford is a trusted friend and advisor," Nunn concluded. "And he is also a devoted husband and father."

After seven years in politics with Senator Sam Nunn in Washington, Stafford had an opportunity to go to work for Coca-Cola in 1979. His dad had worked at Coca-Cola in Macon since 1945 and drove a route truck to nearby Warner Robins, where he also worked in vending repair.

"My dad worked at Coke, and I had always wanted to work for Coke as well," Stafford said. "I left Washington to go to work for Coca-Cola and became one of their 'government guys' for the next 25 years. When I was about to end my political career, Earl Leonard, who was working for Coke, asked me, 'When you leave Washington, would you be interested in working for Coke?' And of course, my answer was an instant, 'Yes!' My world had somehow come together again. I could now work for Coke and continue to work in government. Life really has been good, and over the past 25 years, I have had two fabulous bosses, Earl Leonard and Ovid Davis—both great men."

The Rev. Dr. Victor D. Pentz is the Senior Pastor of Peachtree Presbyterian Church in downtown Atlanta. He spoke of his friend from Macon, "Connell Stafford is a Christian leader as well as being a model husband and father of two successful daughters. His greatest achievement is seen in the sheer love the Stafford women have for him. He is held in high esteem and affection by all of us here at Peachtree Presbyterian Church."

Connell has many strengths which have allowed him to be a success in government, politics, and business. According to Stafford, "I think perseverance may be my best quality. I have a strong resolve and determination that I believe is a result of being grounded in my Christian faith. As a child, I grew up at Tabernacle Baptist Church in Macon, GA, and now I attend Peachtree Presbyterian Church in downtown Atlanta with my family. My faith is very important in my life.

"Likewise, inquisitiveness has always been a part of my makeup as well," Stafford continued. "I have never been afraid to ask questions of people. I also like to be around 'genuine' people. I don't put any value in what I consider 'artificial' people.

"I believe people who are truly successful in life really enjoy what they do. One of the things that I have enjoyed most about my many years with Coke was working in a company which cared about communities and gave millions of dollars to charities every year," Stafford said. "Coke, which operates in over 200 countries, has always had programs that helped people simply get through the day. We enjoy helping people when they need disaster relief or other assistance. It has been great fun working for Coke, and I feel like I have been involved in something that was lasting and worthwhile."

Connell Stafford is a lot of things in the corporate world today. He is politically connected like few others. He is a great friend to scores of people, and is on a first-name basis with some of the most recognizable corporate and political leaders in America.

Griffin Bell, the former Attorney General of the United States under President Jimmy Carter, is currently Senior Counsel with the prestigious international law firm of King & Spalding, LLP. Judge Bell said of Stafford, "As you know, Connell has a bright mind and a very pleasing personality. I first knew him when he was an assistant to Senator Sam Nunn. I have followed his career at the Coca-Cola Company and now, in the Troutman Sanders firm, with much interest. He is an outstanding Georgian and American. Connell reflects great credit on Macon."

Bob Steed, law partner with King and Spalding, knows Connell Stafford extremely well. Steed, an alumnus of Mercer University, author, and humorist (Steed wrote in his book, *Willard Lives*, that 'Mercer University's School of Law was founded in 1826 for students who were too poor to go to Emory, and too proud to go to Georgia.') remembered several stories about his Macon friend.

"We called Connell 'The Possum!'" Steed said, "He is remarkably like his two mentors at Coke, the late Ovid Davis and the formidable Earl ('Boss Hog') Leonard. They taught him that all a lobbyist needed to be successful was a good personality and an unlimited expense account. It was said of Ovid Davis that he could walk on the beach without leaving any tracks or walk in the sun without casting a shadow. 'Possum' has this same talent for secrecy and circumspection."

Steed continued, "Because of Connell's nature, folks just like to be with him. He would invite four or five federal judges to lunch at Coke and ask Judge Bell, Sen. Sam Nunn, and me to come along. All invitees would work their calendars in such a way as to be present. During these sessions, Connell would yield the floor to the others and always get the best out of them.

"I told him once that if he ever offered for public office, his campaign slogan ought to be 'Connell Stafford: He's smarter than he looks!' He is a marvelously persuasive operative. He could sell air conditioning to Eskimos. A.R. Willingham School for Boys should be very proud of Connell ('The Possum') Stafford," Steed laughed.

One of Connell's best friends is a Perry, GA, native, Larry Walker, the majority leader in the State House of Representatives for 16 years. Walker said, "Connell Stafford is one of the most genuine people you will ever meet. He is extremely bright, and he seems to know everyone, but he will always be 'good old Connell.' I've never met anyone quite like him.

"Being the head of Government Affairs for Coke has taken him all over the world," Walker stated. "In fact, he and I have fished in Costa Rica and have stood by each other at the base of Christ on the Mountain in Rio de Janeiro, Brazil, where we touched the statue of Christ. We have traveled to Greece, Italy, and Paris. Connell is simply a great American."

Larry Walker concluded, "Connell is such an entertaining guy. He does an amazing imitation of Judge Griffin Bell, so one day, Connell and I were sitting in the Capital City Club and decided to have some fun. We decided that Connell would disguise his voice as Judge Bell and call Sam Nunn, tell him to drop what he was doing and get over to the Capital City Club at once. When he arrived, he would see the two of us and know that we had set him up. Fortunately, we didn't have enough nerve and decided it was a bad idea."

* * * * * * * * * *

In Stafford's 56 years, he has accomplished a great deal and has met an amazing number of powerful and influential people, but for all he has achieved, without a doubt, he is most proud to be a husband and father.

Connell and Shay Stafford have been married for 29 years. They have two daughters – Ali (25), who is a teacher in Atlanta, and Jenna (24), a student at the University of Georgia in Athens. "I married well!" Connell gushed. "My marriage to Shay and having two wonderful daughters are at the top in my list in life. I did that right, and I feel that God has really blessed me in life."

Shay Stafford described her husband, "Connell is a character. God really made an original when He made him, and you will find no one else quite like him anywhere. I love the fact that he is his own person. He does what he thinks is right, despite what others might think. He is never one to worry about the superficial things of life. He has a strong faith and is very well-grounded.

"Connell has an amazing ability to analyze situations and is very intuitive about people and events," she said. "He also has exceptional skills to deal with people and genuinely cares about them. Connell has a great appreciation for this country, and he has excellent knowledge of how it works."

Shay continued, "Connell is highly respectful of people, regardless of their position in life. Friends mean everything to him, but if you cross him, he won't forget it. He is a 'team player' and always encourages his team or organization to work together. He accomplished his work through relationships. Connell is not a 'Power-Point presentation' kind-of-guy. His style is a prime example of 'servant leadership.' In fact, several people have used that term to refer to Connell's style of operation.

"Connell does not pretend to have all the answers. He likes working with others, and, though many people have reported to him through the years, I have never heard him say that an individual 'works for him.' Rather, it is always that he 'works with someone.' Never have I sensed that he feels superior to anyone, and he is always looking out for other people. My husband is much more interested in what is in your head and heart than 'what you are wearing, where you have been, or who you know.'"

* * * * * * * * * *

Medora S. (Medie) Wiley, Stafford's administrative assistant for seven years at Coca-Cola, concurs with Shay Stafford that he was easy to work with. Likewise, Wiley observed Stafford's strong love for his family and said, "Connell is so proud of his girls, Ali and Jenna, and is totally devoted to them and his wife Shay. A strong 'sense of family' is very important to him. Connell believes that family comes first

Staffords and friends: Connell, Paul Kinney. Shay, Rich Horne, Jenna and Ali Stafford

and always encouraged the people in his department to take whatever time they needed to deal with family issues and problems at home first."

To those who know and love Connell Stafford best, he is seen as a funny guy who is loving, thoughtful, generous, and kind. Ovid Davis, Earl Leonard, Roberto Gouizetta, and many others at the Coca-Cola Company liked to refer to Stafford (for somewhat different reasons than Bob Steed) as 'The Possum' because he would frequently 'play dead' in a meeting. Connell felt no compulsion about revealing what he knew or thought about a subject which was being discussed. Nonetheless, he was carefully listening and filing away important information.

Connell Stafford has an amazing sense of humor and is prone to pull practical jokes. One of his classics took place years ago when a young man who worked with Connell at Coca-Cola spilled some ink on his suit pants. He was quite upset, because he was scheduled to go to a reception and dinner later that evening and wouldn't have time to go home and change clothes.

In an effort to help, Connell suggested that the young man give him his pants and stay in his office with the door locked. Connell told the young man that there was a One-Hour Martininizing Cleaners nearby, and he would do the young man a favor and take his pants to be cleaned. So the young Coca-Cola employee agreed that, under the circumstances, that would probably be the best thing to do.

Connell did not have the guy's pants in his hands more that two seconds before he ran upstairs to a senior officer's office to show him the 'trophy' that he had in his possession. The two of them concocted a story about how the chairman of Coke, along with the senior officer, needed to see the young man in his office immediately. They phoned the young man and ordered him to come up to the 23rd floor right away.

The poor guy nearly had a heart attack!

With a remarkable sense of humor, Stafford loves to imitate people and is pretty good at it, according to friends and family. He once hosted a luncheon for a group of attorneys and Judge Griffin Bell was in attendance. Judge Bell was always one of Connell's favorite people, and according to Shay Stafford, "Connell can do an imitation of the Judge that is sometimes better than the Judge himself."

Connell had never done his 'Judge Bell impression' in front of the Judge until the day of the luncheon. Connell stood up and began telling one of the Judge's stories in his best 'Griffin Bell impersonation.' Not to be outdone, the Judge then stood up with Connell in mid-sentence to complete the story himself. The former U.S. Attorney General of the United States and Connell Stafford from Beddingfield Avenue in South Macon, in tandem. What a pair!

* * * * * * * * * *

Connell's older brother, Terry Stafford, who still lives and works in Macon, has faced many challenges in his lifetime. Terry was severely injured in an automobile accident as a child, but miraculously was able to graduate from high school, and gained employment at nearby Robins Air Force Base. Connell is extremely loving and supportive of his brother.

Terry later became a husband, but sadly, about two and a half years ago, Terry's home burned to the ground, and his wife died in the fire. Connell has helped Terry in every way possible since that catastrophe by making certain that he had what he needed to get back on his feet again. Connell takes care of his brother's business and financial matters and stays in close contact with his older brother. They both enjoy their close relationship.

"Connell loves to help and mentor young people in whom he sees great potential," said Shay Stafford. "He assists them in finding the right job and encourages them to get the education that they need. I particularly remember one young man from a South Georgia farm. Connell encouraged him and entered him in competition to become a Coca-Cola scholar. Because of this scholarship, the young man was able to graduate from Yale University and has a wonderful job today."

Matt Echols is the head of State Governmental Affairs at The Coca-Cola

Company. "Connell hired me as a summer government affairs intern for The Coca-Cola Company in 1995. He took a chance on a young kid from Hiram, GA, and gave me the opportunity of a lifetime. Terms like 'loyal friend,' 'uncanny instincts,' and 'intuition,' plus the ability to relate to people, make him successful. And he can read people and situations better than a CIA spy."

Echols continued, "Connell has a special talent for immediately making everyone around feel comfortable, and he can relate to anyone on almost any level. Like most great leaders, Connell believes in hiring people with the best skills and judgment for the job. Then, he gives them the flexibility to make their own decisions and do the job the way they think is best. He is not a micro-manager. He lets his employees make decisions and then backs up those decisions.

"Connell is one of the most talented government affairs professionals in the country. He always took his work very seriously but never took himself too seriously. I will always be indebted to him for his helpfulness in getting my career started," Echols concluded.

Shay Stafford continued about her husband, "Connell is so caring and thoughtful. When business travels frequently kept him away from his family in the early years, he would generally call us three times a day. The first call would be early morning to check on everyone's plans for the day. He called after school to see how Ali and Jenna's day went. He would call again at night to say, 'Daddy loves you.'"

"Frequently, Connell took both girls to work with him on Saturdays, where they loved to play office with their daddy nearby. When they were little, he bought a trailer for his Snapper tractor so he could give them a 'hayride' while he cut the grass. Now that our girls are in their 20's, he continues to be a big part of their lives, whether it is picking up some tickets to an event he knows they would love, or buying a dress for a special occasion to surprise them. Connell even presents them with a basket of make-up every year at Christmas. I, personally, would not begin to attempt such a thing, but they are always well-pleased."

Shay continued, "As a husband, he is so very thoughtful of me and is appreciative of almost everything that I do for him. On a special birthday, he took me on a surprise-destination trip to San Francisco and had a beautiful, seated dinner for about forty dear friends, complete with hand-painted invitations. He had a video produced for me on another birthday. What is important to me becomes important to him as well. Connell is very respectful of me, and he values my opinions. For that I am most grateful."

Stafford's extended family is very important as well. Not only does he love his family in Macon and organizes 'get-togethers' for them, but he adopted his wife's family in North Carolina as his own. Each year at Thanksgiving, Connell has a bushel of oysters shipped to Shay's Uncle B's house so they can shuck oysters together in the picnic shelter, regardless of how frigid the weather.

"Connell loves throwing a party so he can enjoy his friends," Shay said. "It may be 'carrying-on' over a game of croquet, cooking rooster-pepper sausage for the family's Christmas Eve brunch, or simply swapping good stories over a meal. Connell adores taking friends and family to places they have never been. He especially loves people who have a love for life. Those folks may be his barber, his doctor, the security guard, or the hostess at a restaurant he frequents. He will send cartoons, newspaper articles, a cake or cookies, a bottle of wine, or a book to them. Connell is forever thinking of how life might be made better, or more interesting, for other people. He truly lives his Christian faith, and he makes his family proud of him everyday."

* * * * * * * * * *

Though Connell Stafford has truly lived and worked in a highly competitive market, and has rubbed elbows with some bright, wealthy, influential, and important people, he still remains a very proud son of South Macon.

"I feel so lucky to have grown up on Beddingfield Avenue in South Macon. That was a wonderful street in a great neighborhood. Mike Bassett, Harry Bowen, Danny Strickland, my brothers, and all of the other people my age had so much fun growing up together. I have great memories of playing touch football or baseball until dark in the vacant lot on San Juan Avenue every single day and wearing the knees out of our jeans. Our street was a dead-end, and I remember walking through a field at the end of Beddingfield to get to Houston Avenue so we could catch the bus to town, or to go eat at Fincher's Barbeque. Those are some great memories."

Stafford recalled, "I attended Charles H. Bruce Elementary School, which was only about a half mile from my house. Mrs. Marian W. Smith was my sixth grade teacher and taught history, government, and social studies. She was my favorite teacher and was just wonderful.

"I also loved my high school experience at Willingham," Stafford said. "It was a '10.' We had the greatest rivalries in the state in all sports against Valdosta, LaGrange, Moultrie, Albany, and Lanier, our cross-town rival. Willingham had great athletes, coaches, and many outstanding teachers like Mike Garvin in math and Leonard Pridgeon, who taught chemistry.

"We used to go 'up the hill' to McEvoy, the girls school, each morning before school and visit. That was the only time we would see girls all day. On the other hand, attending an all-boys school may have made the time we spent at McEvoy even more important," Stafford said. "Athletically and academically, I thought Willingham was just the best.

"However, I began to realize that I lived in a 'different' section of town when I was in high school. In those days, Macon had high school fraternities, and I was in A.O.S. Fraternities were about the best way in high school to meet girls socially and to meet other guys from Lanier. I realized that many people in Macon lived differently from us, but I never felt second-rate in any way. I was proud to have grown up in South Macon, and even though we were different socio-economically, I never felt bad about where I was raised. It was just not an issue with me."

It is also readily apparent that Stafford has not forgotten where he was born, raised, and educated. In conversation with him, there is a genuineness about him that belies his success and status in the business, corporate and political worlds. Likewise, one quality that Stafford continues to demonstrate is that of humility. In a conversation with Connell, you quickly observe that he wants to know about you and your life. He seems to be constantly probing and asking questions of others. In a corporate world, where many upper-level leaders appear to be 'full of themselves,' Connell veers dramatically from that method of operating.

Perhaps he learned that lesson from his early mentor, Emory Greene, who was such an influential political figure in Macon and Bibb County. Greene served as chairman of the Board of Bibb County Commissioners until his death in February of 1990.

Stafford remembered about Greene, "Emory Greene never forgot where he came from. He had a serious interest in, and was always a part of, the working class. He had a great sense of humor. I learned a lot about life, politics, and hard work from Emory Greene. He was such a great influence on me as a young adult."

Connell Stafford's list of friends, acquaintances, and references are impressive, to say the least. The list includes politicians, lawyers and judges, public servants, secretaries, and high-ranking corporate officers. Interestingly, those who know Stafford best like his easy manner of dealing with everyone, regardless of their status in life.

Medie Wiley described her former boss, "He is a very caring, compassionate person who lives by the 'Golden Rule' at all times. He has such a way of making people feel that they are important and special. Everyone, regardless of age, loves Connell. He also has great rapport with people from all walks of life. He could make an ambassador or a person with little education or training feel entirely comfortable. He treated them all the same."

Wiley continued, "He was not a micro-manager. People who reported directly to Connell knew what they were supposed to do, and he had enough faith in them that he was not constantly following up or monitoring their work or time. This kind of relationship was built on trust and confidence. Connell Stafford is one of the finest men I have ever known," Wiley concluded. "Working as closely as we did for seven years, there was not one time that I was disappointed in his style of work, integrity, professionalism, or leadership."

Jimmy Williams, the retired Chairman and CEO of SunTrust Bank, is on the Board of Directors of Coca-Cola, a position which has brought him into close contact with Connell Stafford over the years. "I have known Connell since his early days with Senator Sam Nunn. He came to Coke on the heels of Ovid Davis and Earl Leonard. I got to spend time with Connell at Ichauway Plantation, owned by Mr. Woodruff of Coca-Cola," Williams said. "Connell entertained the likes of Secretary James Baker, Governor Lawton Chiles of Florida, senators, and politicians. People enjoyed being around Connell, because he was such a gracious gentleman and had such a wonderful personality. He was a guy who always did his homework and was very bright. He had good instincts and a humble nature, but he could be very firm as well.

"I got to know Shay and Connell more personally when she and I were on a pastor-search committee for Peachtree Presbyterian Church. My wife and I enjoyed our association with them immensely," Williams concluded.

Lonice Barrett is the former Commissioner of the Department of Natural Resources for the state of Georgia. He was recently appointed by Governor Sonny Perdue to be in charge of the New Georgia Commission. Barrett had this to say about Stafford, his long-time friend. "Connell has a great public servant ethic. He was, and continues to be, very astute and extremely knowledgeable about state government. He is as savvy as anyone I ever have known. Connell was great at making deals, he knew everybody, and he was always willing to intercede on projects of importance for Georgia. He never did anything for his own personal gain. Whatever has been good for Georgia has been his driving force. This state has been his love," said Barrett.

"Connell is a genuinely warm and sincere person with a great sense of humor," he continued. "He also has a very quick grasp of issues. Professionally, I considered him to be a person who sought to get to the bottom line quickly, but not so soon that he would fail to get or listen to – as Paul Harvey says – the rest of the story. To his credit, Connell was never prone to knee-jerk reactions. He would never do something until he had the full story and all of the facts. What a great, often-overlooked trait that is."

Barrett continued, "My generation of Georgia leadership will always remember Connell as an integral part of The Coca-Cola family. I will think of him as my cherished friend, confidant, pal, and inspiration. I have never heard a word from Connell that wasn't designed to uplift, encourage, and inspire someone else.

"Connell is the father of two daughters, and he has a great, personable, loving wife. To me, he is a 'Norman Rockwell-type figure.' I would love to have known his parents. They must have been great people, because 'this fruit didn't fall far from their tree.' Connell Stafford is my friend forever," Barrett concluded.

Connell retired from Coca-Cola in December, 2003. The Troutman Sanders Public Affairs Group (TSPAG) in Atlanta quickly hired him to deal with government relations. Former Georgia governor, Carl Sanders, is one of the founders of the company. Since he is not a lawyer, Stafford's responsibility is primarily being involved with political and government issues for the firm.

Norman Underwood, a senior partner with Troutman Sanders, observed the three major phases of Stafford's life. "One, right out of college, Connell was a teacher and then Sam Nunn's Congressional Assistant. The second phase of his life was his years at Coke, where he was involved in corporate America. He had opportunities that few Americans can experience. He was on the management team of the most successful corporation of American capitalism – Coke – which had unparalleled sustained growth and economic success, which is rare in U.S. history. And Connell Stafford was a major part of that great corporation.

"Third," said Underwood, "he has now gone to work with us at Troutman Sanders Public Affairs Group. We were happy to have him on board because of his previous successes. He serves as an intermediary between corporations and policy-making America. Connell can give wise counsel to smaller businesses who want to be successful and to large businesses who want to continue to be successful. He also talks with governors, legislators, and Congressional staffers about how policy is viewed by corporate America.

"It is impressive to see someone like Connell, who has been in politics and business, and has the real image of integrity and maturity. He lives his life in a way that reflects his personal values. He is solid and achievement-oriented. Connell has an appealing streak of humility as well," Underwood continued.

"Connell had the perfect temperament and background to be successful at Coke," Underwood concluded. "His temperament was shaped by solid values and hard work. He wasn't born with a silver spoon in his mouth, and he hasn't forgotten his roots. He relates to people so well, and he can cross lines with those who have little formal education or those who are the top people in corporate America. He is a man with great ability who is very bright, and those are rare gifts."

Though Stafford's life took on a new challenge at age 55, he has continued to be active in civic affairs, as well as in government and politics. He is a member of the Gridiron Society at UGA, serves on the Board of Trustees at Georgia Southern University, and serves on the Georgia Technology Authority in Atlanta. Likewise, he is on the Jekyll Island Foundation Board and is a member of the Little White House Foundation. Though no longer serving, Stafford enjoyed his associations as a board member for Camp Sunshine, a children's cancer treatment facility camp outside Atlanta, where children with cancer would be brought to camp for two weeks.

"My wife and two daughters are my major hobbies these days," Stafford said. "I love to play golf, and I enjoy the mountains at our place near Brevard, NC. I also enjoy reading biographies of political figures.

"I hope I will be remembered as someone who was not arrogant, but who was humble and honest," Stafford reflected. "Maybe it's due to my Baptist upbringing, but I have always cared more about the well-being of others than I did about myself. I have been very fortunate to have had such wonderful associations with Coke, a career in government, and now with Troutman Sanders. I have a terrific family. Life has really been good. I feel that God has truly been holding me in the palm of His hand."

"We were fighting for the American Girl...Democracy, Coca-Cola, Hamburgers, Clean places to sleep, for The American Way of Life."

Col. Robert L. Scott, Jr.
God Is My Co-Pilot
1943

Shay and Connell Stafford

Turn A Sow's Ear Into a Silk Purse

Dr. Robert Willard (Billy) Browning
Class of 1969

*"And Josiah did right in the sight of the Lord, and
walked in the ways of his father, David,
and did not turn aside to the right or the left."*
　　　　　—II Chronicles 34:1-2

Marie Browning sent her three sons—Butch, Billy, and James—
three blocks away to Bruce School for an education. She took
them to Macon Evangelistic Church on Lackey Drive off Houston
Avenue to learn about the Lord. However, she personally taught her boys life
lessons that were both social and Christian, so when they grew up, they would
become gentlemen, productive citizens, and godly men. Her middle son Billy
recalled, "My mother had a profound effect on my life and development. She
taught me that it's OK not to know something, so you just figure it out in life.
You just watch and learn. You look around and see the people that do know
what to do, and know how to act, and model what they do. Don't feel bad that
you don't know something; that's just an opportunity for you to learn, because
you're smart enough to learn it. She was so affirming to my brothers and me,
and what my mom has overcome in life is incredible. My mother is a saint.

"She taught me that adversity is never a reason not to do something.
Hardship and adversity have nothing to do with whether or not you ought to
do something. The question is 'Is it the right thing to do?' That was, and is,
her motto. My mom was the youngest of 11 children. The doctor told her dad
that there were complications when she was about to be born, and he could
save either the wife or the baby, but not both. Her dad said, 'I've got ten other
children. Save my wife. I need her more than I need another daughter.' But my
mom made it, nonetheless, along with her mother. My mom is now 80.

"Something that brings tears to my eyes is the story my mother told me that
happened to her when she was 11 years old. She always wanted a bicycle, but
her family didn't have any money to get her one. On Christmas, she got up early
to go into the room where the presents were. It was dark, so she walked with one
hand against the wall and her other hand reaching out into the room, because
she knew there was a bicycle in there, and she didn't want to bump into it, turn
it over, and wake up the family. Of course, there was no bike for her. Several
years ago, I found something that my mother had really wanted for a long time,
so I went out and bought it for her. I told her, "This is for the bicycle that you
always wanted but never got.' She may have had to wait 70 years for something
special, but now she had it. That was a great, great moment for both of us."

When asked who had the greatest influence on his life, Billy's answer was easy. "My mother. She taught me that self-image had nothing to do with where you lived or what you have or don't have. It had everything to do with the character of your soul and that nothing was impossible for people who applied themselves and used their God-given talents. Nothing was impossible, so I just grew up assuming that anything in life was possible. She modeled a life that was dedicated to God. Through her influence, I became a Christian and experienced God's power to forgive and transform my heart, mind, and actions."

Browning has vivid memories of his childhood, coupled with life lessons, from growing up on Flamingo Drive. "I recall going to school with holes in my shoes, and my socks getting wet. That's when I learned that if you wanted dry socks, you had better avoid the mud puddles. That became a metaphor for life, of sorts. The other thing I learned at an early age was that if I didn't button my sports coat, then it didn't look too small, and I could wear it an extra year or two.

"Nobody in our neighborhood had any significant financial means. We were all relatively poor, but when I was in elementary school, our poverty was compensated by love at home, and because of my mom, I didn't know we were poor. My dad wasn't home a lot because he was usually working. At Willingham, I knew that there was a real difference between those of us in South Macon and those who lived in other parts of town. It was then that I realized that I had actually come from an impoverished background, and that lots of people had it a lot easier than we did, but I took pride in the fact that my family played whatever hand we had been given. I was taught not to whine. There were no points for whiners. Whining got you nowhere."

Fred Browning, Billy's dad, taught him the value of hard work. Billy recalled, "His idea was that there was no degree of poverty that you couldn't overcome with hard work. He taught me to do things right the first time and the ultimate person you had to please was yourself, so you do things right, regardless if anyone was looking or not. That was his hallmark. He became a builder/construction contractor after having worked in several professions prior to settling on construction. Though he ended up doing fairly well in construction, he was one of the best salesmen I've ever seen. My dad didn't finish the 11th grade, but everybody loved my dad because he had such a big heart. He'd give people stuff when he really didn't have it to give, but he also taught me the value of giving and sharing. His life embodied 'It's better to give than to receive.'"

My pastor, Joe Andrews, was a big influence on me as well. He taught me kindness, gentleness, and focus. He also taught me how to deal with distractions and how to compartmentalize in life. The most successful people that I know have the ability to go from one task, client, or patient quickly and smoothly and compartmentalize. As a clinical psychologist, I was trained to do everything I could for a patient while I was present with them. I was working long hours five days a week, and I would go from one patient to the next to the next with only a 10-minute break, where I would chart their sessions, maybe go to the restroom, return phone calls, and go right into another session. While you are with someone, that's your opportunity to make a difference in their lives. Then, you have to shut the door on that one, and open the door on the next one. You may be celebrating with a client one minute and then weeping with the next client. You may be dealing with a serious trauma after that. Joe Andrews taught me a lot about compartmentalizing, focus and being able to set things aside to be more effective in what I do."

* * * * * * * * *

"Willingham High School was a great experience for me," Browning said. "I was involved in all kinds of activities there: Key Club, Beta Club, athletics. My friends in those days were Billy Beale, Jr., Charles Evans, Terry Sark, Mike Pyles, Richard Thomas, and Mike Odom, who played on the tennis team with me. The relationships I had with such high-character guys and the academic preparation that Willingham offered served me well as I built a foundation for my future."

Two teachers came to mind that were exceptional in Billy's academic development. Polly Banks was his third-grade teacher at Bruce School. She lived on Ormond Terrace around the corner from Billy's house and had a way of making her students feel special. Billy said, "She told me that I had talent, ability, and a good mind. She convinced me that I had value, so I began to believe it. She was a teacher, and if she said it, then it must have been true. Who was I to not believe her?"

Mr. James Hinson was Billy's science teacher in junior high and took Browning under his wing. Hinson affirmed Billy for his academic ability. Though Billy was always a strong student in the classroom, Hinson had the ability to challenge him and bring out the best in him.

As a proud son of South Macon, Browning became keenly aware in high school that many saw Willingham as second-rate. He stated, "I was aware that society saw us as sub-par; however, it taught me the same lesson that I learned from my dad – 'I just needed to work a little harder.' I never considered our lot in life as debilitating or irreversible. Being poor was just a temporary condition for us, and it wasn't irreversible. At Willingham, I learned that we couldn't afford to own a silk purse, and I saw Lanier people as having silk purses, figuratively speaking. My dad taught me to buy a sow's ear and turn it into a silk purse, and that's what he did.

"That lesson carried over into my adult life. The first lot that my wife and I bought in Dunwoody Club Estates in Atlanta was the 'dog lot.' It was the worst lot in the entire neighborhood. When I was counseling at the Atlanta Counseling Center, we didn't have enough money to buy a nice place, but I went and bought that problem-plagued lot, improved it, and then built a home on it. I was able to sell it and made a great profit. That's what it means to 'buy a sow's ear and turn it into a silk purse.'

"The fact was that I was from South Macon, and you don't complain about it. You just get some sow's ears and turn them into silk purses, and when you do that a few times, you begin to build some financial security; so that's what I did. I suppose I could have gone into real estate in Atlanta and done well, but psychology seemed to be my calling in life. Plus, I was able to help people in many different areas as a counselor and later as an organizational psychologist."

Billy believes that his life is much better because of where he grew up. "Where I came from has helped me to be sensitive to the importance of helping others because I have been helped by so many, and the truth of the matter is that people who haven't experienced pain and poverty and dealt with them properly can end up pretty phony and arrogant. When you find somebody who has faced their pain, then that is a sterling friendship possibility."

* * * * * * * * * *

After graduating from Willingham in 1969, Billy attended Asbury College in Wilmore, KY, and earned a Bachelor of Arts degree with a major in Psychology in 1973. He came back South, attended Georgia State University in Atlanta, and earned a PhD in Clinical Psychology in 1981. Billy began his professional practice at the Atlanta Counseling Center.

Billy recalled his post-doctorate days at the University of Alabama-Birmingham and another teacher who influenced him profoundly.

Dr. Billy Browning 'Catch and Release'

"Dr. Allen Shealey validated me in a way I had never experienced when he told me that of all the interns he had in the last ten years, I was tops, and that boosted my confidence like nothing that I had ever experienced. From that time forward, I learned a serious life lesson. It's one thing to know that you know something, but it's another thing to know that you know that you know it. I knew—because of my association with Dr. Shealey."

Having grown up at Macon Evangelistic Church, Billy Browning was fully aware that evangelical churches who had visitors on Sunday would visit those same guests on Monday or Tuesday nights. Little did he know that after his first visit to the Christian and Missionary Alliance Church in Atlanta, his life would be changed forever. A beautiful young Delta flight attendant, Sandy Wimpey from Orlando, joined two fellow parishioners from the CMA Church for visitation and dutifully visited Browning at his apartment. They were married two years later in 1976.

"The two best things that I have done in life," Browning said, "would be surrendering my life to Christ at age 12 and marrying Sandy. She is the most wonderful person I know, and we have had over 28 great married years together.

"The next best things in my life would be the privilege of getting an education and serving as a leader. Leadership is a privilege, and leadership is nothing but influence. Going back to my mom's lessons in life, she taught me how to learn, and she began to instill leadership principles in me at an early age. She told me to observe people with character, and when you don't know what to do, observe what they do.

"Because of my upbringing, I didn't know how to act in some social settings. I never thought I'd be a member of a country club (Waterfall Country Club in Rabun County) or fly in corporate jets. I didn't even know where to go to get on one. Some of the people that I coach in the corporate world sometimes want you to go and fly with them, and it doesn't matter where you are because you can have a conversation anywhere. On one occasion, we were supposed to meet with some clients and spend the day together. I pulled my car into the parking lot, and the CEO said, 'Come on, Billy. Follow me. And he drove right into the hangar. When we all returned at the end of the day, a red carpet was rolled out to his plane. All of our cars are pulled alongside each other with the driver's-side doors open, and the engines running. I'm just laughing to myself. It was unbelievable. It was like something people would do for a celebrity, and I wondered, 'Who's that for?'

"Some places that I'm privileged to speak will have a limo waiting at the airport. To this day, I still walk out and look around to see who the limo is for," he laughed, "because I'm just not a limo-kind-of-guy. An entire limo just for me? Incredible!"

* * * * * * * * * *

Dr. Billy Browning is convinced that great leaders are really influencers, and he was greatly influenced by Dr. Carl Bramblett, his mentor during post-doctoral days at Georgia State. "Dr. Bramblett took me under his wing and talked to me about my skill sets and abilities. He told me that I needed to get out of the clinical arena and move into the business and corporate world. He trained me for a year and a half; I traveled with him, and he personally helped launch my consulting career. Moving into the corporate world was a wonderful way to leverage my time and energy in terms of the value that I created. I learned that real leaders figure out how to find great value in what they do and get paid well for doing it. Thus, I entered the corporate world as an organizational psychologist and a corporate coach, partnering with Dr. Tim Irwin to form the consulting firm, Irwin and Browning.

"I have learned that the world is made up of two types of fundamental people—those who are influencers, and those who are influenced. The questions have to be asked, 'Do our circumstances influence us, or do we influence them?

Do we influence people, or do they influence us?' It all boils down to that level for success in life."

Billy had a unique opportunity regarding influence and leadership several years ago. He told the story, "I got to spend time with five guys; four of the five were in their 30's and 40's, while the other was in his 50's. We met at Gurney's Spa and Resort, north of the Hamptons in New York, which is an area that probably has the most concentrated wealth on the planet, and here they were consulting with me, a guy from South Macon, about significance, and what success in life really is. Three of them were billionaires, and two were multi-millionaires. For 24 hours, we reflected on what to do when you can't spend all the money you have and what do you do with your life to have an impact? I remember just pausing and thinking about how good God is to allow me to be able to help influence people's lives."

So, did they come out of the meeting feeling like they had a purpose?

"Yes. I talked with them about four categories, or four quadrants, of their lives. These four quadrants are competency, currency, quality of life, and significance. Those are the four accounts that every living human being makes trade-offs with in their life, and here's how it works:

1. *Competency* means the more I grow in knowledge and skill, the more value I bring to my company, organization, or community. I must continue to provide greater value to my organization, so the answer is to never stop learning. In other words, don't let your brain get soft. That's the South Macon version!

2. *Currency* comes in a variety of forms. I don't believe financial currency is the only kind of currency. It doesn't matter what form the currency comes in, because successful people figure it out. Currency can be four things, and everybody that works in life is working for one of these things :

a. Steady income. We seek this so we can pay our bills.

b. Wealth accumulation. Once we get a steady income, then we can begin to accumulate wealth.

c. Brand identity. There are people who love working for someone, or for a company so much that, even though they could make more money or have greater benefits elsewhere, they want to stay with that brand. Virgin Brand, Ted Turner at TBS, and Coke are examples. People love working in those places, because they strongly identify with that person or that brand.

d. Professional/industry affiliation. This is like working for a group of doctors where you build credibility. Later, perhaps, you go out and launch your own company or practice.

3. *Quality* of life has to do with the amount of stress, travel, leisure, family, and community involvement that you need. What kind of margin do you demand in your life, or are you just about tapped-out? Margin is the amount of discretionary time that you have in your life

and how you determine to use it.

4. Significance is made up of our passion, mission, impact, and influence. Successful people figure out which trade-offs they will make. For example, a golfer may sacrifice wealth and quality of life because he is interested in traveling to build his competency as a golfer and to ultimately pursue his passion. Early in my career, I traded off my quality of life, because I traveled all over the world for four or five days a week for fifteen years. My work would take me to Europe for a day, but there's not enough money out there today for me to leave my wife and travel like I did in the past. That's because quality of life is much more important than the money.

"The quality of life quadrant is so important," Browning emphasized. "I'm now focusing on significance and quality of life, because I've built the competency, and I've continued to grow in that area. I'm not sitting back in life now, but the point gets to be, 'How much do you need?' Am I going to chase another dollar? What is more money versus significance, impact, and eternity? I'm playing this game of life for the significance and the quality of life."

So, was that a pretty humbling experience, and was the information you shared with them original, or did it come from somebody's book?

"Well, that weekend caused me to think about what's important in my own life, as well as trying to give those men some direction," Browning said. "I prepared that information specifically for them and that weekend, and I feel like what we did brought together a lot of my thinking about life and 20 years in leadership. It helped me to assemble what I really believe about God, giftedness, opportunity, and values."

Billy continues to use the four quadrants in his corporate connections and in leadership opportunities. "I was at breakfast recently with an executive in Atlanta who worked for a large corporation and was personally struggling with life. I wrote those four things – competency, currency, quality of life, and significance – on the back of a napkin at the OK Café in West Paces Ferry on Northside Drive. I gave it to him and told him this is something he needs to think about. I ran into him two weeks later, and he said, 'Our meeting must have been providential, because I was offered the CEO job with a company for a fabulous salary with stock options. I pulled out the napkin and talked to my wife about our conversation, and we decided the quality-of-life quadrant was so important that I'm not willing to trade it. Thank you.' That's an example of providential influence and impact, and that entire story came off the back of a napkin.

"See, I believe that's what life is all about: having your life count. And when your day is surrendered to the sovereignty of God, then you're in a real position to have a meaningful life that can impact others in a positive way. The problem with most people is that their life is not surrendered to the sovereignty of God; so they are trying to figure it out on their own. The sovereignty of God means that God can do as He pleases in your life."

Billy Browning's Christian faith is the basis for all else that he does in life. One of his closest friends is Ravi Zacharius, founder and Chief Executive Officer of Ravi Zacharius International Ministries for the past 20 years. Ravi previously served in evangelism for the Christian and Missionary Alliance denomination, based in Colorado Springs, CO. Considered by many to be the finest apologist in the Christian world today, Ravi Zacharius debates and lectures on college campuses and in public forums all over the world. The two met at the First CMA Church in North Druid Hills, Decatur, GA, in 1985, when Billy was Ravi's Sunday School teacher.

"Truthfully, Billy's assets and strengths are that he is a man with many special talents," Zacharius said. "First, he is a systematic thinker. Whether it's fly fishing, carpentry work, psychology, corporate administration, or leadership, whatever he does is done systematically. Billy is a linear thinker and a package thinker. He can process mentally the steps that need to be taken to get from one point to a wonderful conclusion. He can, better than just about anyone, see the entire specter of a situation and find the correct conclusion."

Zacharius continued, "Second, when Billy is talking to you, he is extremely focused. He bores down on the conversation that you are having, but his primary strength is his deep faith in the Lord which orders all else in his life.

"Billy is comfortable in many arenas and with many subjects. He has such diverse friends, many of which are youth. My children—Sarah (29), Naomi (26), and Nathan (23)—called him 'Uncle Billy' when they were young. They continue to stay in touch with him and will occasionally stay at Billy and Sandy's home on Lake Burton.

"The best thing Billy has done in his life, second only to knowing the Lord, has been his marriage to Sandy," Zacharius continued. "They are such a precious, wonderful couple."

"Third, Billy has long been obedient in the same constant direction. He has not veered from his strengths. Billy has the ability to help guys in the corporate world 'unpack' things that are deep inside. His perceptions and judgments have been spot-on with executives that he has interviewed. He is much like Billy Graham in that he has stayed on target with his calling. Billy Browning has stayed with his love and his strengths."

Echoing what many of Browning's friends have observed, Zacharius explained, "Billy has always had a boyish attractiveness about him. He loves simple jokes and will laugh hilariously. He and a friend from Alaska went fishing 15 years ago and something funny happened. They still get together and will retell the same silly story, and there will be gales of laughter. He consistently laughs at and tells the silliest jokes. I believe his boyish innocence helps keep him humble."

Billy, likewise, has a light side that many individuals who are in counseling or corporate situations with him may miss. But not Ravi Zacharius. "Billy loves to play party games and has such fun, whether it's Charades or Name That Tune. He really gets into it. His intensity is always present, and you can easily see that he has a competitive spirit. He loves to win. There is such charm in his being a young man."

Many of their friends are unaware that Browning and Zacharius are fans of Elvis Presley. "We found out years ago," Ravi recalled, "that we both loved Elvis. On one of Billy's milestone birthdays, Sandy had a party for him, hired an Elvis impersonator, and we all loved it. Now, when one of us has a birthday, we will send the other some Elvis memorabilia. In fact, Billy has an Elvis clock that I gave him, and it's hanging on the wall in his shop. On the hour, Elvis's hips will swivel."

Ravi Zacharius continued about his friend, "I have observed three things about Billy's life.

1. No matter how busy Billy is, and he has a very demanding schedule, he is always an available friend. He is never too busy to return a phone call or to help someone in need.

2. No matter when you last saw Billy, you can pick up where you left off with him. We only see each other two or three times a year, but there is always this sense of excitement when we get together with Billy and Sandy.

3. He has such a love for his extended family. He really misses his father, who died years ago, and he has such a tender heart for his mother. He, likewise, loves his two brothers and their families. That speaks so well of Billy as a man, and he has never forgotten where he came from.

"Billy is just a gem of a guy," Zacharius concluded. "In this world, where we seek out heroes, Billy Browning stands head and shoulders above others. His life is to be emulated. He has had amazing success in life, though it has never gone to his head. In short, he is simply profound and is profoundly simple."

Dr. Comer Cherry is a cardiologist who lives and practices in Tallahassee, FL. Cherry, his wife, Marilyn, and their family split time between their Tallahassee home and Lake Burton in northeast Georgia, which is where he and Billy Browning met. Dr. Cherry, in responding to a telephone request to speak about his friend, said, "My wife told me that my reaction to your telephone call perhaps said more about Billy than anything else I had to say. The emotions I had were fear and dread. I really welcomed the opportunity to comment on my good friend, 'flyfishbb@aol.com,' but I had this burden of responsibility to compose something that was worthy of the man. I wanted to say something that captured his uniqueness, something that was not ordinary, mundane, contrived or trite, because Billy isn't. To the extent that this chapter on Billy Browning will be part of his legacy, I wanted to provide information which would help encapsulate his special character.

"I believe Billy Browning has been successful in life because, like no other person I know, he has adopted the right priorities, in the right order, with the right balance, and he consciously intends to keep it that way. It all begins, and maybe ends, right there. His first priority is his relationship with God. He follows Jesus's example and arises early in the morning, before others are awake, in order to have quiet time for prayer, meditation, and Bible study. His second priority is his relationship with his wife, Sandy. He schedules time for her and encourages her spiritual and social development. Billy talks over all major decisions with Sandy. When he's away on business, he calls her nightly, and they often pray together. They are a team. Billy's third priority is the rest of us - his Mom, his extended family, and friends. His next priority is his professional life, and finally, the 'everyday furniture' of our worldly existence."

Understanding Browning's intense professional travel schedule, Dr. Cherry continued, "Sometimes, these priorities get shuffled, especially with Billy's busy professional life, but he purposes to keep his time, focus, and energy marshaled to 'majoring on the majors' and 'to get the big rocks in first,' to use a Stephen Covey (author of *Seven Habits of Highly Successful People*) metaphor.

"Much of Billy's success is due to two women. He 'chose' a good mother and a good wife. Marie Browning, his mom, is a strong, Southern lady, and a steel magnolia. She read her spirit into Billy at an early age, and because of her, it has never occurred to Billy that he would be anything but successful. She encouraged and nurtured him, and she gave him her sense of purpose and values which are Christian values. Then, at the right time, she passed the torch of encouraging her son on to his bright, beautiful, devoted wife. From the beginning, Sandy realized Billy's potential and put aside her own professional ambitions to complete him, support him, and to be for him whatever he needed. I think her lifetime Bible verse for her husband, Proverbs 22:29 (NIV), speaks volumes about Sandy. That verse says,

'Do you see a man skilled in his work?
He will serve before kings;
He will not serve before obscure men.'

"Billy would be the first to admit that he would not be the man he is today without both of these women and their devotion to him."

Dr. Cherry continued, "Billy and Sandy Browning filter all of their major decisions through Scripture. Their paradigm for life is that the Bible is the inerrant, infallible Word of God, and that it speaks to every issue in our 21st Century existence. Their desire is to be obedient to the written Word of God. Billy and Sandy pray about every major decision and wait on God for His answer before proceeding. As arcane a concept as this may be to many people, they schedule a period of time for prayer and fasting in decisions which require a significant alteration of their lifestyle.

"Billy has a superior ability to make people that he's counseling or conversing with seem valued and heard. To use a breast-feeding metaphor, Billy always 'latches on.' Nobody would ever say he is clueless about any subject, but if there was such a word, they would probably say that he is 'clue-full.' In spite of his busy schedule, and it is extremely busy, Billy makes you feel like you are the most important person in the world and your problem or issue is the most important thing that he is going to deal with. Billy doesn't seem distracted or act like he's multitasking when you're talking with him, but to be perfectly honest, he sometimes is. Somehow, Billy has learned to compartmentalize so that he is not distracted with everything else he has going on. Billy has a demeanor of competence and excellence that just sort of leaks out his pores."

Dr. Comer Cherry said about his friend, "Billy has a unique ability to formulate practical solutions for complex problems and then articulate them clearly, understandably, and in a way that can be remembered and acted on. People always leave Billy's counsel with an action plan that is clear and do-able. He is the most creative person I've ever met professionally, architecturally, socially, and in every other way. Most of Billy's creativity is considered 'in the box,' but some of his creative solutions, when required, are clearly 'outside the box.'"

Aware of Billy's penchant for doing things the right way the first time, Cherry said, "He gives meticulous attention to detail and won't accept anything short of perfection. Some have found him difficult to work for because of this. I didn't know his dad, who was a building contractor, very well, but Billy may have gotten that trait from him. Billy has boundless energy - until 9 p.m. Then he's dead meat! After 9:00, you could just as easily carry on a conversation with a corpse. His life is 'up early and to bed early.'"

Comer Cherry and Billy Browning have been friends for many years. Cherry said, "The best word I could use to describe Billy as a friend is 'there.' If you need him, Billy shows up, and is there for you. He is loyal and puts a great deal of time and energy into maintaining friendships. I would say that Billy is one of, if not my best, male friend. He makes me feel like I'm special to him, though I have the sneaking suspicion that I share this feeling with 10-20 other guys. At a recent conference, the leader asked us how many people we knew really intimately. I answered 'four,' and Billy was one of them. He allows himself to be vulnerable and lets people get to know him. Billy deals with different people in different ways. The Cliff Notes version of this trait is that, if he perceives you to be honest, straightforward, and amiable, he deals with you straight up, generously, and personally. If he perceives that you are the least bit devious, adversarial, or dishonest, then he either avoids you, or, if he is required to work with you, 'manages' the relationship."

Browning's friends all seem to concur that he is a man of many strengths and assets. Cherry described his friend as 'energetic, bright, and a quick-read.' Cherry said, "He has a charismatic aura and demeanor which is unexplainable. At the same time, he is generous with his time and resources. Billy is unique in that he puts time into relationships and people. It never occurs to him that he won't be successful. One of the mantras of his personal and professional life is to 'end well.'"

For those who know Billy best, they are impressed, not only with his sharp mind, but his amazing sense of humor. Cherry recalled, "Sandy has appropriately nicknamed Billy, 'The Hummer.' When he's working around the house and yard, he gets several projects going at the same time and goes from one to another, working feverishly and frenetically for a few minutes at each project, and then moves to the next and the next and the next before returning back to the original project. He looks just like a furious hummingbird going from flower to flower, sucking it dry. Thus the title, 'The Hummer.'"

In conclusion, Dr. Cherry said, "Billy Browning probably thinks that his legacy will involve his creative accomplishments in his professional life or his architectural or developmental achievements. Most people, however, tend to remember personal qualities and attributes. If my friend Billy pegged-out tomorrow, I would remember him as an exceptionally talented, creative, warm, and energetic man who spent his life giving himself away. Of all the good things that I could say about Billy, the best things are that he is sold out to the Lord, is sold out to his wife and marriage, and to his extended family and friends. Billy married well and has spent time and energy honoring and nurturing his marriage covenant with Sandy. He has scheduled time daily to be alone with the Lord for prayer, meditation, and to study God's Word. Billy has been obedient to God's call on His life. He also makes people a priority and spends himself in service to them."

As an organizational psychologist and corporate coach, Billy has had the opportunity to travel across America and around the world. He has counseled with clients at AA&T, CNN, Georgia Power, and numerous other notable companies. Michael T. Felix, President and CEO of AT&T Alascom in Anchorage, AK, has worked extensively with Browning in recent years, and the two have become close friends. Felix said, "I've learned a lot from Billy and use it almost everyday in my personal and professional life. When I think of Billy Browning, I think of a verse in the Old Testament, Micah 6:8, that says, *'Do justly, love mercy; walk humbly with your God.'*

"When I first got to know Billy, he had just come out of his doctoral program and was working as a clinical psychologist at a Christian counseling center in Atlanta. I was a beginning-level manager at an upstart telecom company which eventually became Sprint. I was employee No. 70, and the year was 1982. We would meet together on a regular basis and would frequently have dinner together at Williams Seafood on Clairmont Road in Atlanta. Billy and I would talk about our careers, current jobs, aspirations, and the foundations that got us where we were. I remember being amazed at how well-developed his own personal mission statement was, as well as his unwavering sense of purpose. They would be his guiding lights through a career with twists and turns, but he always had a well-defined direction and a clear vision for what the end-result would look like. Billy's strong sense of purpose in life kept him from trying to be something that he wasn't, and he always played to his strengths. He never compromised, or said, 'I think I'll just settle for being *here,* rather than spending the time and energy to get *there.*'"

Felix said, "For Billy, nothing but the ultimate goal would ever suffice. He had an uncanny ability to visualize the goal and then stay focused on getting exactly where he intended to get, no matter the path. This was probably most evident in watching him build several houses over the years. In an almost perfectionistic way, he became affectionately known to his friends as 'Rip-it-out Billy,' because he would insist that his subcontractors do exactly what they had agreed to do and exactly as he had envisioned the end-product being. If the job wasn't done like it was supposed to be, then Billy would ask them to rip it out and do it all over again. He could see a piece of property and visualize the end-product of the house, as well as the view. In the meantime, everyone else was focused on the shape of the lot, the slope of the land, and the trees. None of that made any difference to Billy. And so it was with his lot in life.

"Even though Billy was years ahead of the rest of us, he was always very patient and compassionate with those who were still trying to figure things out. He has always been generous with his time, as long as he sensed that people were honest about their journey, and, though he was always polite, he wasted no time with the idiot who wanted to play games. While Billy is a very private person, I think his sense of who he is—and the very nature of his business as a counselor and corporate psychologist—helped him have the kind of boundaries that kept those who played games at a distance."

When Felix was asked, 'And who is this Billy Browning?' he replied, "He is a man of absolute integrity, much like Joseph of the Old Testament, but he is not so serious that he can't laugh at himself. He's an integrated man with no segmentation. The man you see in front of captains of industry is the same man, and is no less pretentious, as when he's tying flies before going fly-fishing. One of his strengths is that he is a life-long learner. I think he's drawn to people whom he believes he can learn from, and in every situation I've seen him, even as the teacher, he has taken away something of value.

"Billy Browning is a lover of life and a generous man who learned early on that when you truly love something, you give it away. He gives his life away every week. Billy is a lover of laughter. In fact, one time he and I almost got thrown out of the restaurant at Callaway Gardens for laughing at a silly little joke I had told. Somehow, it struck us both as funny, and we couldn't stop laughing. We ended up laughing at each other!

"He is a lover of his wife. In my business, I can tell a lot about a man by how he treats his family. In fact, I never hire a direct report without seeing that person in a setting with their spouse. I'd hire Billy in a heart-beat simply based on how he treats Sandy. On the other hand, me hiring Billy Browning would be roughly akin to Inspector Clouseau hiring Sherlock Holmes."

Mike Felix concluded, "It is always evident that Billy Browning loves his God. His humble walk and unshakable faith have carried him through some difficult times and very dark days in his life, but through it all, he has remained steady, focused, and resolute to get to the goal. Billy would be the first to admit that his success in life wasn't really his at all, but rather God's goodness and grace that 'placed him before kings - as a man skilled at what he does, which is a rough paraphrase of Proverbs 22:29."

Bill Johnson and Billy Browning have been friends for over 30 years. Johnson, of W.B. Johnson Properties, has been in business since 1967. He began with Waffle House 38 years ago and has been in real estate and hotel development worldwide in recent years. Johnson developed Ritz-Carlton Hotels world-wide and also developed the 191 Premier Building in downtown Atlanta Monarch. He has also been a partner in creating the extraodinary Waterfall Country Club overlooking Lake Burton in Rabun County near Clayton, GA. He is a past-chairman of Trustees of Berry College in Rome, GA.

"I first met Billy Browning in the early 1970's at the Christian and Missionary Alliance Church in Atlanta," Johnson said. "I have been so amazed at how smart Billy is and how quickly he picks up on things that most people don't get. He is unique in that he is both street-smart and is brilliant, educationally. I have observed Billy during our time as Trustees at Berry College when he was unaware he was being watched. Billy is a Christian man who cares deeply about people, and I know that he is a man of great honesty and integrity. He is articulate, highly educated, and has the ability to draw the best out of those around him. Billy is amazing with team-building and has added to the success of many major corporations."

Bill Johnson continued, "Billy is unique in many ways. For example, he has built several traditional homes and has included an outhouse-type restroom indoors in the last two of them. He is equally creative and exciting in business. One thing I like a lot about Billy is that he doesn't take himself too seriously.

"He is an excellent provider for his wife, Sandy. Billy is an extremely generous man and has helped me with funding for over 900 college scholarships from a foundation that I created. It was a thing of beauty to see him in strategic planning with the trustees of Berry College, because Billy has been doing that type of thing with major corporations for years. Today's kids need direction, and Billy gives them that direction. He is an outstanding counselor, and he affirms those he deals with. He has the unique ability, like no one I have known, to point them in the right direction."

Johnson continued, "For all that Billy Browning has accomplished, I attribute much of that to his upbringing as a kid. He has worked hard and received a quality education, but with all of the success that he has achieved, he has never lost sight of where his accomplishments have come from. Billy has always given God the credit for his success. He is such a unique and wonderful person, and he constantly thinks of others. Billy cares deeply about people and hurts for them. Some that I have known may be able to fake that, but Billy doesn't fake it. It is just so easy to brag on Billy Browning."

Bill Cox, the former head of Programming at the TBS Superstation in Atlanta, has known Billy for the past four years. Cox said, "He was my coach for Executive Leadership and worked with me and other senior staff members of the TBS Superstation. Billy understood television dynamics surprisingly well, and seemingly, adapted his standard principles of coaching to our industry. He was exceptionally helpful in dealing with corporate structure issues, personnel issues, leadership enhancement, and process development for all areas at TBS. The great thing is that he was open to discussing personal issues that could cloud our work effectiveness at times. At that, he was as good as any psychologist that you could find anywhere."

Cox noted, "His gentlemanly manner disarmed people, but it didn't prepare them for the depths of his insights. He focuses solely on the person that he is with and not on someone else in the room that might be more compelling. Billy would say something astonishing to you with such clarity, something that you already should have known because it was so vital to you, but it was something that you might have missed. And that something would lead you to peace because of its understanding.

"Billy cares deeply about your hidden strengths, pain, vulnerabilities, confusion, and especially about your soul. He sees straight into you, because he is not cluttered with judgment. One of Billy's real strengths is the fact that he believes deeply in people, even if they have proved they cannot be trusted. He still believes in their ability to change and wants to make a difference in how they achieve those changes.

"He is an extraordinary communicator, his eyes probe, and his words are laid out simply and beautifully in a way that lets you understand what you need to know." Drawing on a fly-fishing metaphor, Cox continued. "He is totally persistent and determined to straighten out all of the crossed-up lines that are inside you, much like a rod and reel that has gone haywire. Somehow, Billy does that in a way that let's you straighten out every tangled, tedious knot, and lay the line out clearly, rather than just cutting the line. Billy helps you see where you have been and where you might want to go.

"I think Billy will be remembered as a truly positive note to the frequently discordant music of the world. He is like the perfect chord that brings harmony to those around him. As a tall, soft spoken guy, Billy has such an easy manner. He also has a heart, a brain, and a fisherman's attitude which is to keep plugging away, and you will be just fine," Cox said.

Cox, along with others who have worked closely with Browning, knows of Billy's keen sense of humor and noted, "I think that Billy is a closet-performer. I think he would love to shine for a moment on the stage and then leave with a benevolent smile, happy that he's done well."

"Has Billy been successful in life?" Cox was asked. "Absolutely. And he really, really has made a difference in my own life. Love, curiosity, courage, and faith have made Billy successful in life. I love the guy, and he has kept me and many others from drowning so many times that they ought to name a Lifesaver flavor after him. I consider us to be good friends, as does Billy."

Executive Vice President and Managing Director of CNN International, Chris Cramer, is responsible for all the CNN channels and services outside the United States, including global newsgathering. Before arriving at CNN in 1996, Cramer was the head of newsgathering for BBC News and was based in Great Britain. Cramer said, "Billy came highly recommended to me when I sought out the best professional support in the South for a new senior management team here at CNN International. As well as a long association coaching the international management team for about three years, Billy has also been my personal coach of choice for a senior executive program for the last 12 months at Turner Broadcasting."

Cramer continued, "Billy is the most accomplished listener that I have ever worked with. His ability to cut through the crap and determine the kernel of a problem is uncanny. Billy quickly teaches senior managers that 'Leading is as much about coaching and nurturing as it is about decision-making.' As a mentor-par-excellence, he is, simply put, a brilliant resource for managers at every level.

"Many business leaders and corporate chiefs seek him out for counsel on day to day management issues, and his 'take' on a problem is frequently unique. Billy once suggested to a CNN management team that sarcasm was not necessarily something the team all benefited from. However, Billy was told, in no uncertain terms, that journalists couldn't live without it. Thus, Billy and the team begged to differ and moved on.

"Perhaps the best things that Billy has done in his professional life," Cramer concluded, "are to realize that you work to live, not live to work. He is arguably the most balanced, successful executive that I have ever met."

Ronnie Bates is the senior vice president of Planning Sales and Service for the Southern Company. He and Billy Browning met in 1993, when Bates had just moved to the Georgia Power Company from Mississippi Power. Bates, who has had a 29-year career with the Southern Company while holding several managerial and executive positions, said, "Professionally, Billy is prepared at all times, and he knows his chosen field like few others in the industry. His real strengths are his personal value-system, and his willingness to walk his talk. Billy combines these two strengths so well and really connects with people that he is doing business with. He contributes genuine advice and gives counsel with a sincere, personal touch. If Billy had a weakness, it would be that he is so busy and his schedule is so crowded that we don't have enough time to visit with each other. He is a man who truly understands the real meaning of success. In my opinion, Billy pursues activities that benefit others and has invested his life in people."

* * * * * * * * * *

Dr. Billy Browning has traded his frenzied schedule with maximum travel for a simpler life with purposeful focus and a more manageable pace. He and Sandy have an interest in antiques and travel throughout North Georgia, as well as making an occasional trip to England. Sandy named their home on Lake Burton 'Desired Haven,' from a scripture passage, Psalm 107:30, that says, '... *and He guided them to their desired haven.*' He has been an avid fly fisherman for years, fishing the streams of Alaska and Montana, (while using the very un-

South Macon-like 'catch and release' method). Billy is currently restoring 'pond yachts' and a turn-of-the-century walnut bureau, just for fun. He has created scores of original lamps in his high-quality wood shop. Sandy joked, "If you stand still long enough, Billy will make you into a lamp."

He commented, "I have narrowed my focus in life to three things—the first being my church, where I teach a Young Adult Sunday School class. Next, I mentor a young fellow in Clayton every Sunday morning over breakfast. My third focus is my profession as a corporate psychologist. I still carry a heavy work load, and client service is very important to me, but my travel has been curtailed a bit. I have the unique privilege of working with CEOs and board chairmen, which is both challenging and exhilarating, but the primary function of my work these days is to train leaders."

When asked how he would like to be remembered, Billy concluded, "It would be presumptuous of me to even think about being remembered, but I would consider my life to be a success if someone said, 'Billy used every God-given talent and ability that he had to honor the Lord and to help people improve their lives. And he did it passionately.' That would be a successful life for me."

Dr. Billy, Sandy, and "Oreo" Browning

100 Most Influential Georgians

James Roger (Jim) Wooten
Class of 1963

Life is mostly froth and bubble,
Two things stand like stone,
Kindness in another's trouble,
Courage in your own.
   –Adam Lindsay Gordon,
   Australian poet (1833-1870)

Georgia Trend Magazine's January, 2005, issue listed Jim Wooten of *The Atlanta Journal-Constitution* as one of the "100 Most Influential Georgians." Making Georgia Trend's list, however, was not necessarily news in the Wooten household, since Jim has made the magazine's list of the "100 Most Influential People in Georgia" for seven of the past eight years. *Georgia Trend's* 2005 issue said of Wooten, the associate editorial page editor of the *AJC*, "As the conservative voice of the newspaper's editorial page, he offers a right-wing perspective in his column three times a week. With a Republican governor, GOP control of the state Senate, and a vocal conservative population stirred by radio talk shows and higher taxes, Wooten commands a growing readership."

To glimpse into his past, circa 1955, the thought of Jim Wooten becoming a member of the editorial board of a major, Southern, metropolitan newspaper would have been an incredible stretch. To say that Jim has come a very long way in a journalism career that began during his high school days at Willingham is a bona-fide understatement. Growing up in government housing was one thing. Growing up as the fourth of six children in a single-parent home in South Macon was another.

"I grew up in the Pendleton Homes public housing project on Houston Avenue and was a fifth-grader when my father divorced my mother and vanished from my life," Jim said. "When he left us, there was my mom, with no marketable skills, and six children. Our family had to go on welfare, and we moved into a three-bedroom apartment in Pendleton Homes the summer before I entered the seventh grade at Charles H. Bruce School. My dad was not very diligent about paying child support; so my mom took a job working as an aide at Lockhart's (later renamed Goodwill) Nursing Home on Houston Avenue to supplement our limited income."

Wooten told of his love and deep admiration for his mother in an atypical Mother's Day column in 1995. It was a rare column, because in the words of his wife Ann, "Jim almost never writes about his family. He says he doesn't want to exploit us for column material. Once, he even referred to me as 'a relative by marriage.'"

Thus, when Jim wrote the following column about his mother in *The AJC* on Mother's Day, 1995, it took on an air of added importance.

One Woman's Strength

My father I could take or leave. Poor fellow married too soon, fathered too many, worked too hard to earn too little. Life was to depart a houseful of children on Monday and return to a drawerful of payment books on Friday. After a while, the urge to run – to see Milwaukee in the winter or San Antonio in the summer, to drive a Buick automobile or to taste saltwater taffy – took hold. He was gone. Just gone. Maybe to Milwaukee. Or Abilene. Maybe to taste the taffy. But gone.

The collection man with his payment book came. And my mother faced. him. He sent his take-back truck for the TV and the stove and the washing machine. And my mother faced them. They came for the car. And my mother faced them.

Lightly schooled, the result of childhood illness, not yet through her 30's and suddenly alone in a rented house with six children, she faced them. If you can fend for yourself, you must. If you can't, and we four who were younger could not, I will take care of you. How, I don't know. Or where. But the family will stay family, father or not.

From that promise sprang countless indignities a proud, defiant woman could not have imagined. Social workers asking personal questions. Welfare bed-checkers counting heads and dispensing morality. Public housing functionaries functioning to kill enterprise but never the roaches. Bill collectors and con artists, always on the stoop, hustling misery.

She faced them.

And amid the misery of broken lives and generational despair, in the center of public housing, she built for us a protective cocoon to shield her children from the indignities and hurt headed our way.

She faced us, too. This is not you, she said. Free yourself. Improve your life. Walk out with pride.

At 4 a.m. on winter Sundays, she would rouse my two baby sisters from their sleep and drive me over my route to deliver The Macon Telegraph and News. It didn't speed delivery all that much, really. And once, she ran over my foot. But she was my buddy, and it didn't matter. Sunday mornings, with the world asleep, was our time.

So it is among the retained images of my childhood, not the sounds of a mother's homilies, but of the strength with which she bore the Earth's burdens. She did not speak her love, often, nor did I. But its presence, at unexpected times, was visible as the puffs of winter's breath as we talked in the Sunday-morning chill. I felt loved. In the

brown checkered coat she could not afford, I felt it, and in the chocolate
cake she baked because I craved it, I saw it. It felt there.

She is 72 now, stubbornly independent, determinedly and defiantly
on her own. Before soliciting support, she would dine on saltines
in hell. It is that defiance, that fiery, determined, headstrong and
unyielding defiance that spared a family from a wretched fate.

To see it there now is to realize the price dependency extracted
then. How unnatural and painful it was for her to face strangers and
ask for help or grocers and clothiers to ask for credit. But nobody ever
lost a dime betting on my mama. Never.

Men do not say what they feel often enough. So it is that I have not
told her. For facing all those people and all those mornings for all of
us, Mama, I love you.

"A single mom with six children was fairly traumatic in those years,"
Wooten said. "It was especially tough on my mother, because the youngest girls
in our family weren't old enough to be out on their own. The older girls did get
part-time jobs to help bring in some income, and, after several years, my older
brother, Elbert, then 17, joined the Air Force and left home. But things began to
get better during my senior year at Willingham when my mom got remarried and
moved to Conyers, GA. I stayed in Macon to finish high school and lived with
one aunt on Virginia Avenue and with another aunt, Stella Mae Ward, who ran
a boarding house on New Street. I had no car when I was in high school, so I
either caught the bus or rode to school with a friend, David Tucker."

On a somewhat light-hearted note, while living with his Aunt Stella in her
boarding house, young Wooten had the dubious challenge of rooming with an
older man who was an alcoholic. The man drank all of Jim's British Sterling
cologne, a treasured gift from Jim's girlfriend.

"I am proud to say that despite our difficult upbringing, all of my siblings
have done well. It was very important to us that we got out of Pendleton Homes
and not continue to live in public housing, but there was no way that my mom
could support a family as large as ours without public assistance," he said.

Spending time with Wooten revealed that he had great memories from his
formative years in South Macon. "It was a safe place, and there were no class
issues to deal with in those days," he recalled. "I didn't feel or observe any
class distinctions, even though some in South Macon were poorer than others.
Basically, all of us were in the same narrow income range since there were
no rich people. Nobody felt that they didn't belong. I remember being self-
conscious about living in public housing, but I never felt 'looked-down upon.'
No one 'lorded their wealth,' as meager as it may have been, over anyone else."

To Wooten, South Macon was the embodiment of America with its solid
work ethic. "Even in those days, people were upwardly mobile though they
were working blue-collar jobs. People who lived in the Bloomfield area of
South Macon were pretty affluent folks in those days. Parents sought a better
life for their children than what they had experienced and wanted to help the

next generation become successful. To me, South Macon was a sense of what America was all about. We were not aware of anger and hostility or divisions and strife in the world. I remember that we felt comfortable there. It was a different day back then, because we didn't 'smart off' to our neighbors, and it was very common for parents to discipline other children who weren't their own."

* * * * * * * * * *

Though Jim, for the most part, grew up with no dad in the home, he sought out and found responsible male adults who could give him emotional support, direction, and encouragement. One of those men was Otho Pirkle, a guidance counselor at Willingham, who took a personal interest in Jim. "Otho Pirkle knew I was poor, and I worked in the lunchroom. He got me out of kitchen duty when I became a junior to allow me to have some dignity. He was amazingly insightful and was conscious of my young ego. He didn't want me to feel degraded or 'less than' the other boys. He saw to it that I was moved into the position of 'lunchroom counter,' a job with a bit of responsibility where I would count the number of people who were eating lunch each day. Mr. Pirkle was also a bi-vocational preacher in Cordele (I think) and would occasionally take up a love offering to help me. Sometimes, he would bring groceries to our family. He had great sensitivity regarding my teenage ego by putting me into a situation where I wouldn't feel degraded. He didn't want others to see me in such a subservient position at school. He truly was an inspiration to me."

Otho Pirkle, now 82 and retired in Macon, has fond memories of his young friend from their days at Willingham. "I remember Jim Wooten very well. We came from similar backgrounds, both of us growing up in families with limited financial means. Likewise, Jim, by the time he reached Willingham High School's eighth grade, which is when I came into the picture, had a mother at home with few marketable skills who was trying to provide for him and several siblings with no father in the picture."

Pirkle met Jim early in Wooten's career at Willingham. "He was easy to know, very pleasant, polite, always with a smile on his face, and most appreciative of any help or assistance that was provided for him," Pirkle recalled. "I was a guidance counselor, and he spent a lot time in my office, assisting me in making information available on colleges, trade schools, and industry. The staff at Willingham worked with me in arranging some financial assistance for Jim when it was available. He benefited from the student lunch program, and I was able to use him for odd jobs around our home after school, which helped him earn a little spending money. Jim worked a paper route for *The Macon Telegraph*. In fact, our house was on Jim's route, which naturally led to his spending a lot of time in the neighborhood and around our house. The rural churches where I served as pastor heard me mention his plight and what a worthy, honest student he was. From time to time, they would send food and money for his family."

E.J. Hancock, who taught Jim in the ninth grade, was another male teacher at Willingham who inspired him. "Mr. Hancock was extremely knowledgeable about science and biology. I learned a lot from him at a time when high school boys like me were trying to define who we were through conversations in class that always seemed to wander away from the appointed subject matter. He taught us how to treat women. I remember him as a man of virtue, wisdom, solid values, and a thoroughly decent guy who knew himself well."

Fred Tucker, now deceased, was the district circulation director for *The Telegraph and News* in the '60s, and had a strong, positive influence on Wooten when Jim was growing up. Wooten joined Tucker in delivering newspapers to customers the carriers had missed and would pal around when Fred went to collect from his paper boys on Saturdays. "We developed a father/son-type relationship and had great conversations about father/son things," Jim recalled." I learned a clear sense of how to behave and how to treat people. He took on the father's role in my life."

Additionally, Jim had numbers of excellent teachers in his elementary and high school careers. Margaret Phillips was one of his seventh grade teachers at Bruce School and got him interested in reading via a reading program. Wooten recalled about Mrs. Phillips, "She was very spirited and enthused about that reading program. Mrs. Phillips encouraged me to read; she had an enthusiasm about learning that was inspiring, and I related to her quite well."

In high school, Jim became editor of the *Ram-Scott*, the Willingham-McEvoy High School yearbook. Though he ultimately worked for several daily newspapers throughout his journalism career, Jim was not originally drawn to newspaper work at Willingham, opting instead to spend time directing the yearbook staff.

Jim Wooten held Betty Lou O'Keefe (who later married Denmark Groover, a prominent Macon lawyer) in high esteem, because she believed in him as a student and took an academic interest in him. "Ms. O'Keefe, my senior English teacher at Willingham, was perhaps the first teacher to see writing potential in me," Wooten said. "She took several Willingham boys to Wesleyan College to hear the symphony for the first time in our lives. In my senior year at Willingham, I had no plans to go to college because I had no money. My immediate future was to go to work and save some money and then give college a try. Ms. O'Keefe was the advisor of the yearbook and began to talk to me about furthering my education. I told her 'I'm not going because I can't afford it,' but she replied, 'No, no, we can't have that.' So she arranged a Saturday interview with Johnny Mitchell, the Director of Admissions at Mercer University. Based strictly on her word and strong recommendation, Mercer accepted me on the spot."

Knowing little about the college scholarship possibilities, O'Keefe helped Wooten with scholarship applications. "She helped me get the Winn-Dixie Scholarship even though I never worked for them. That scholarship was one of those situations where I had to receive a recommendation from the mayor of

Macon and a state senator. Ultimately, I enrolled at Mercer and was considering their ROTC program because they offered a monthly stipend. I soon learned that the ROTC program also required that you purchase a military uniform which cost $75, so I opted out of the program due to a lack of funds."

After he graduated from high school, Wooten's mom and step-father moved to Atlanta. "My step-father took a job with the J.P. Stevens Cotton Mill, and I also took a job at the mill and lived with them in the summer so I could save some money. In August, the Winn-Dixie scholarship – all $375 of it – was approved so there was enough money for me to start at Mercer. I showed up at Mercer in the fall but was still flat broke. It had taken all the money I had to just get enrolled, so I got a part–time job with Brown's Bookstore in Macon and looked for other work. Since I lived downtown with my aunt, I could walk to Mercer or to Brown's Bookstore. I dated a girl who was going away to the University of Georgia, and she told me about a job that involved working weekends at *The Macon Telegraph*, so I went to work there part-time."

Jim attended Mercer University for one year and then made plans to transfer to UGA. "I simply ran out of money," he said. "Mercer, as a private school, was expensive, so I took a job working at *Blue Bird Body Company* in nearby Fort Valley, but I also kept the job at the paper. *The Telegraph* offered a full-time job for the summer, which was better than the hard work at Blue Bird, as well as driving back and forth to Fort Valley daily."

Peyton Anderson, the publisher of *The Macon Telegraph*, had this great deal where he would take one kid from the Macon community each year and give them enough money to go to college. The only stipulation was for them to go into journalism. Macon guys like Lanier's Tom Johnson, president of CNN and former publisher of the *Los Angeles Times*, along with Bobby Lamb and Rick Parham of Willingham, had previously won the Peyton Anderson Scholarship."

He continued, "Peyton Anderson made the prospect of getting through college considerably easier for me, because his scholarship gave me $500 a year which paid for everything. I left Mercer and later enrolled in the Henry Grady School of Journalism at UGA. During my college days at Georgia, I went to work for the *Athens Daily News*, a start-up newspaper where I worked 40-hours a week. I chose to work at the *Daily News* rather than for the *Red and Black*, the UGA campus newspaper, because they actually paid me and the school's paper didn't. My schedule was going to school during the week and then driving back to Macon to work at *The Macon Telegraph* on Saturdays. I had no social life in college, so I didn't get to enjoy the college experience at all. I would really like to go back to college some day simply for the joy of learning, as well as getting another degree."

* * * * * * * * * *

After working for two newspapers for three years and completing his Bachelor of Arts Degree in Journalism in 1967, Jim faced even more daunting challenges in the next stage of his life. "When I got out of college, the Vietnam war was raging. I knew that sooner or later I would get drafted, so I volunteered one morning. That afternoon, there was a draft notice in my mailbox. I enlisted in the U.S. Army and then went to Officer's Candidate School at Fort Benning in Columbus and was commissioned a second lieutenant in the infantry. From there, I went to Ft. Campbell, KY, at the time Vietnam was really going full blast."

So, Jim, were you scared?

"Through the early process of Vietnam, I confronted my mortality and came to terms with death, pretty much like everybody else I knew," he recalled. "Yes, death was something I approached with great trepidation. I had just read *A Street Without Joy*, a fatalistic outlook about Vietnam. We all knew what was going on there."

Wooten stated, "I arrived in Vietnam just after the Tet Offensive and had gone through Jungle Survival School. I was assigned to the American Division, the division of Lt. William Calley and the My Lai massacre. We didn't think the American Division was very good for infantry officers, because its reputation among young lieutenants was that it was quite undisciplined, not taking needed precautions to protect the troops, so I was not very thrilled to go in with them. This seemed to heighten my sense of fatalism even more. The day I got 'in country' in 1969, there was heavy combat involving the First Brigade of the Fifth Infantry Division that was stationed on the DMZ. They took a batch of infantry lieutenants, of which I was one, and sent us north. Our contact with them broke off more quickly than was expected, so the Army was left with a temporary surplus of infantry lieutenants. Thus, because of the luck of the draw, they sent me up to Dong Ha to be a liaison with the first ARVN Division of the South Vietnamese army to help coordinate base defense."

Subsequently, when Vietnam fell to the North Vietnamese, the first ARVN Division folded. "I spent about six months working with them, going out on missions with them, and trying to coordinate sectors of defense. Then a new public affairs officer came in, saw my credentials in public affairs, and chose me to go and assist him. For the last two months of my duty there, I worked in public affairs."

Jim stayed in Vietnam approximately 10 months before returning to the States early. "My biological father had resurfaced in our lives; he had a heart attack and was in a hospital in Savannah. Without my knowledge, I came home to discover that my older brother Elbert was also in Vietnam at the same time I was there, and, since I only had a short time left, they allowed me come home. My father recovered from this particular heart ailment but died about three years later. My relationship with my father was quite distant. I could handle him leaving me, and even if I could have understood why he left my mother, I still couldn't reconcile the notion that he had abandoned my younger sisters."

Returning to the United States, Jim asked for an assignment close to Georgia and was assigned to Fort McPherson. "I was in casualty notification, which meant that I didn't have to notify the next of kin, but I arranged for someone else to do this for the families of those who died in Vietnam. When I got out of the Army in 1971, with my background and experience as a newspaper employee, I found that I was very employable, which was a very good thing."

Looking back, 1967-68 were important years in Jim's life for reasons other than graduating from the University of Georgia and enlisting in the United States Army. While he was in journalism school in Athens, Jim met Ann Jarrett, a journalism student from Cartersville. They were married in 1967; he graduated in June, 1968, and they are still married today. Ann earned her degree in journalism from UGA before returning to Athens to pursue a Masters degree in journalism. Interestingly, she changed career paths, went back to Middle Tennessee State University in Murfreesboro, TN, and got a master's degree in storytelling, which is actually a degree in English. Her business card reads, "Ann Wooten, Storyteller."

Their daughter, Jennifer Towns Wooten, was born in 1973 and got her degree in Communications. She worked for Georgia Public Television for a year before going back to school and is now working toward a degree at Kennesaw State (GA) University with hopes of becoming a veterinarian. Her plans are to attend UGA or Auburn's vet school. She has been married to Derrick Faur since December 2, 2000.

* * * * * * * * * *

In 1971, Jim's newspaper career took off with a two-year stint at *The Atlanta Journal,* covering metro-Atlanta counties, as well as the Sam Nunn Senate campaign.

His journalism career picked up speed in 1972 when he went to work for *U.S. News & World Reports*, covering Jimmy Carter's campaign for President. It was highly unusual for U.S. News to hire someone under 40, because their editors thought it took that long for writers to get the necessary experience. After Carter was elected, *U.S. News* wanted young Wooten, a native Georgian, to move to Washington and cover the White House. However, Ann Wooten, an only child whose parents lived in Georgia, wanted their daughter, Jennifer, to know the South.

"I knew the Labor Editor's job at *U.S. News* was already filled so I felt safe when asking for it. I knew if I was offered the Labor Editor's job, I would have to move to Washington, D.C. I thought applying for a job that was already taken would buy me about five or six more years in the South. However, the editor called me and said the Labor Editor job I had asked for was mine, and, 'When could I report?' I gave them a date and realized that I was going to have to get an apartment in Washington. I liked the magazine but didn't feel comfortable adapting to their writing style. I knew I'd either have to adapt to their writing-by-committee style or leave."

Durwood McAlister, who became a long-time friend, had hired Jim out of the Army to work for *The Atlanta Journal*. When he was faced with the prospect of moving to Washington away from his wife's elderly parents, Wooten asked McAlister, who was about to be named editor of *The Atlanta Journal*, to consider him for future openings as an editorial writer. Jim said, "Durwood McAlister finally had an opening in Atlanta, and I returned to the *AJC* in 1978. I have spent the last 27 years as a reporter, city editor, assistant managing editor, and editorialist."

Wooten has been highly-successful in his 27-year tenure with the *AJC*. He has won the Walker Stone Award for Editorial Writing, given by the Scripps-Howard Foundation for editorials on abuses of state pension funds. He, likewise, directed a local news staff of approximately 100 reporters and editors for three years, before returning to editorial writing in 1986. He was named Associate Editor of the combined *Atlanta Journal-Constitution* editorial pages in 2001.

It would be a serious understatement to say that Durwood McAlister has the greatest admiration for Wooten. McAlister wrote the following excerpt to detail his respect for Jim. "When Gov. James M. Cox bought *The Atlanta Journal* in 1939," McAlister said, "he made an announcement in the paper offering his conception of the function and duties of a newspaper." In Cox's statement regarding a newspaper, he said,

'It should tell the truth as only intellectual honesty and discern the truth. It should do what is in conscience needful and right. To try by vague and pointless preachment and evasion to please everyone is bad faith. Persisted in, it pleases none and exposes a lack of character which the people will soon appraise.

'In our civilization, the interests of the classes are organized and guarded by their own skilled agents. The masses are not so protected. The press should never be unmindful of this fact. It should hold itself above the partisanships of classes and groups, for its right function is to bridge these gulfs with the tolerance and reasonableness of the strong, while yet protecting, without coddling, the weak against abuses of power – that is the everlasting labor of self-government. In the field of this labor lies a peculiar opportunity and obligation of the press.'

McAlister said, "I quote this at length, because the phrases that Governor Cox used to describe a good newspaper seem to me to be talking about Jim Wooten, newspaperman. Intellectually honest, conscience-driven, and very sensitive to the needs of the poor and weak, Jim is unwilling to coddle those who claim victim-hood without cause. Jim Wooten is a strong voice of tolerance and reasonableness."

He continued, "Jim's character is his strength. In a world increasingly filled with cynics, phonies, and finger-to-the-wind chameleons, Jim stubbornly refuses to leave his beliefs and principles. It is that absolute integrity which drew me to him as a young reporter and has distinguished his career in the decades since.

But beyond integrity, Jim Wooten possesses a remarkable, innate wisdom, the kind that seems to come to those who come through hard times and difficult situations and are strengthened in mind and spirit."

In addition to their professional relationship, McAlister has known Jim to be a loving husband, doting father, and a loyal friend. "It pleases me to no end to be able to sing the praises of Jim Wooten," he offered. "I have long felt that the best day I ever had as editor of *The Atlanta Journal* was the day I persuaded Jim to turn down an opportunity to go to Washington, DC, to cover labor news for *U.S. News & World Report* so that he could join me on the editorial board of the *AJC*. I would happily have worked for him if our roles had been reversed."

Journalist-in-waiting: Jim Wooten 5th grade

Linda Lanier Fortson has known Jim Wooten, professionally, since the 1970's when she was an intern at the *Atlanta Journal-Constitution*, a reporter at the Macon Telegraph, and as both southeast regional correspondent and southeastern bureau chief for *U.S. News & World Report*. Today, Fortson is the owner of her own public relations firm, Lanier Communications, and works out of her office at home in Atlanta.

"I've known Jim in many incarnations, first meeting him in the summer of 1971, between my junior and senior years in college, while interning at *The Atlanta Journal*. Jim was a rising star reporter and was one of the best writers at the paper. I naively thought that, if I had the same early newspaper experience as Jim, then I could write as well. He wrote a letter of recommendation for me to *The Macon Telegraph and News*, where I became a beginning reporter. When Jim became the southeastern bureau chief of *U.S. News & World Report* magazine, he remembered me when there was an opening as a regional correspondent. I came back to Atlanta, became good friends with Jim and his wife, Ann, and subsequently was their daughter Jennifer's godmother. When I married and had a child, Jim and Ann became our daughter's godparents."

Fortson had an opportunity to know Jim Wooten as he matured from a young reporter, who had just returned from Vietnam, to being her boss at *U.S. News*. She recalled, "Jim has been an important part of my life as both a friend and co-worker. I have been impressed with his life and career from the time he was the editorial page editor at the *Atlanta Journal* to his continued service to his country as he served admirably in the National Guard until his retirement from the Guard. I have observed and admired Jim at his daughter's wedding in Atlanta, his mother's funeral in Macon, and in his present position as the conservative voice in his column at the *Atlanta Journal-Constitution*.

"Jim's greatest strength is his deep-bedrock will that is masked by what seems to be such a quiet nature. However, as one would define character, Jim has it in every area of his life. He has given much of the credit for what he is today to his mother, a woman that he has described in print as 'lightly educated.' It has been well-documented that Jim lived in the Pendleton Homes housing project in Macon after his father abandoned the family. The six children helped their mother financially in any way they could. As a nine-year old boy, Jim sold drinks at wrestling matches to earn money, as well as selling potholders and Bible verse cards door-to-door. I think much of the authoritative quality and strength of his current columns, many of which I disagree with, are based on his struggles as a child to simply survive. Anyone who can come out of what Jim faced growing up, and become a fair-minded leader in journalism, a wonderful husband, father, and friend, is going to be formidable in life."

Fortson has known Wooten to be ingenious, determined, compassionate, and always with a sense of humor. "Jim will be remembered, first and foremost, for his work in journalism in Macon, Vietnam, Atlanta, and the Southeast. He has successfully carved out a niche as a conservative columnist in a rapidly changing world of journalism, and has always been a great citizen while serving the March of Dimes, Red Cross, and in Georgia's Selective Service."

Her favorite Jim Wooten story, because it is so much the essence of the man, took place on an annual *U.S. News & World Report* meeting in Washington when all the regional bureaus gathered. "Jim sensed a certain regional paternalism from our nation's Capital bosses who felt that Southerners were perceived as 'quaint' and that our minds ran at the speed of our slower Southern accents. Jim donned a Panama hat and proceeded to wave away imaginary gnats with it as he waited for the elevators. He became the stereotype of all-things Southern from his speech ('Y'all come back now, ya heah?') to his very demeanor. Everything he did was so exaggerated and so transparent to me, though many of the Capital-types never got it. Jim had a great time with his little game which was capped off by the grand finale at a cocktail party. In the midst of a luscious spread of hors d'oeuvres, with the editors listening, Jim poked with his finger at a caviar canapé and asked them for their enlightenment: 'Is that fish eggs?' he wondered out loud? They assured him that it was caviar. Jim's innocent response was, 'So *that's* caviar!'"

Fortson concluded, "No one has ever loved his wife, child, family, or friends more than Jim. He is honest in his dealings with everyone. The opposite of truth is something that Jim simply doesn't comprehend. As a friend and career mentor, I know that he will 'tell it to you straight' when no one else will. He is that rare confidante."

As previously mentioned, *Georgia Trend,* which is one of the state's leading business magazines, referred to Jim as the conservative voice of the *AJC's* editorial page. "In years past," Jim stated, "the morning paper, *The Atlanta Constitution,* was considered liberal, while the afternoon paper where I worked, *The Atlanta Journal,* was a more conservative voice. As I previously worked with the *Atlanta Journal,* our country gradually evolved from men getting home early in the afternoon and reading the evening paper to men leaving early for work, reading a morning paper on the way to work, then working late, and arriving home late. Today, only Las Vegas and smaller communities have evening papers."

In 2001, *The Atlanta Journal and The Atlanta Constitution became the Atlanta Journal-Constitution.* Suddenly, the melding of two long and proud newspaper traditions became one morning voice. As evidenced by his contemporaries at the *AJC,* Wooten has been a balanced, even-keeled voice of reason throughout his newspaper career, both in Washington and Atlanta. Lyle Harris, a native of Brooklyn, NY, and a Howard University graduate, sent the following e-mail to Wooten after the editorial boards of the morning and afternoon newspapers consolidated. "While I disagree with you on many matters of substance, I just wanted to say how much I appreciate your measured demeanor, thoughtful insights, and the spirit of camaraderie that you bring to the morning meetings. Would love to hear and see more of that in the weeks ahead. It has truly been a rare pleasure."

* * * * * * * * * *

As Wooten has moved deep into his late-50's, his life has increasingly become one of great discipline and restraint. Jim, for many years, has been religious about diet and exercise and, unlike virtually all of his high school classmates, he has not deviated five pounds from his high school weight. To a large extent, Jim's health-consciousness has much to do with his family's health history. As the fourth of six children, Wooten realized that good heart-health was not in his favor. His brother Elbert retired from the Air Force at age 37 and has survived six bypasses, while two Wooten sisters have had bypass surgery. His dad, at 54 and granddad at 45 both died from heart disease. At age 59, Jim takes every precaution as he eats right, does cardiovascular exercise, works out with weights on a regular basis, and has periodic physicals.

Jim Wooten is a quality citizen whose resume reflects his desire to make a difference in the community where he lives. He has been the Southern Region chairman of the American Red Cross Blood Services, a member of the regional selection committee for White House Fellows, and president of the Georgia Press Association, becoming the first to be elected from the *AJC* in the GPA's 177-year history. He is also actively involved in the Friends of the Smyrna Library and is a founding member of the Smyrna Cemetery Association. Additionally, Jim has been involved in cleanup projects in the metro-Atlanta area with people who need to do community service after violating city ordinances. Wooten today is involved in the Inquiry Club, the oldest debating club in Atlanta, which meets at the Piedmont Driving Club once a month.

Wooten, a colonel in the Georgia Army National Guard, retired in June, 1999, and was promoted to Brigadier General on the state retired list. He also received the Legion of Merit Award, one of the nation's highest military awards for service. Jim was involved in public affairs with the National Guard and with the Selective Service System for over 25 years.

He still gets together in Atlanta and visits, periodically, with several Willingham High School friends: Rutledge Beacham, Wayne Brannan, Wallace Bates, Mark Bowen, and Pete Gaines. Rick Parham, the son of Joe Parham, former editor of *The Macon News*, and Jim's roommate in college, still stays in touch with Wooten.

"I spent 25 years around a lot of other guys in the military. I loved it, in part, because they were different from those that I worked with at the paper and because they had the same types of values that I had. I knew how military guys would perform under certain circumstances. I got to know them in Vietnam; we had instant rapport, and I knew how they would respond. Those were honorable men, and when I get together with these guys from Willingham, I know them and what their values are. I know how they will treat me and perform, and there's instant rapport with them, even though it's been over 40 years since we've been together in school. I know how they will act and who they truly are."

The love of friends and family has always been important to Jim Wooten, dating back to his days in South Macon. Though his mom died in 1995, he had remained close to her through the last years of her life. "I admired what she had been able to endure to hold the family together," Jim said. "In fact, the older I got, the more I appreciated her."

Jim, likewise, has a keen appreciation for those things that he deems to be important in life as well. He was the keynote speaker for the University of Georgia's College of Journalism and Mass Communications convocation. His remarks contained a Top Ten List of Admonishments.

Item One: Watch television intelligently. It performs a role in shaping our culture that can be more dominant than that of schools, churches, and even parents and friends.

Item Two: Become involved in something that matters more than you do. Life is never more exhilarating than when the success of the cause you are involved in is more important than you are. Maybe it's a social cause, environmental or humanitarian causes, political campaign, or a religious movement, but other than falling in love, there's no greater emotional and spiritual high than that which comes from devoting your energies to pursuits that matter more than you. Find a cause greater than the individual.

Item Three: Volunteer. Each of us has an obligation to public service, and I'm a real proponent of military service, especially for a group whose values and judgments define the society in which we live. We have an obligation to America, to our fellow man, that cannot be fulfilled by pinning on a ribbon and walking or marching. It requires active and meaningful involvement in public life.

Item Four: Appreciate the cannas and the crepe myrtles. After returning home from military life, I made a conscious decision to look for crepe myrtles and canna lilies that grow in profusion across the Southern landscape. When you resolve to look for something that brings you pleasure or makes you happy, as I did, it's amazing what you will see.

Item Five: Never trust information off the Internet. Sure it's there voluminously, easy to access, authoritative and the medium of this generation, but there's as much misinformation circulating there as there is information that's accurate.

Item Six: Don't make babies with people you're not married to. Though you may be financially successful, it is terribly harmful and generationally harmful, especially to the children of the poor. Don't be reckless with people's lives.

Item Seven: In a world where morality is often situational and values relative, there are absolutes. There are absolute rights and absolute wrongs that don't depend on the situation. There are some principles and obligations that are non-negotiable. You are personally responsible for all of the choices that you make or don't make.

Item Eight: If what you're doing is heading toward something where your parents will have to bail you out, don't do it. You are personally responsible for all the choices you make or don't make.

Item Nine: Open a Roth IRA. If you save $1.50 a day by avoiding junk food, alcohol or tobacco, by the time you're ready to retire, you would have accumulated $290,363. You get rich not by winning the lottery or developing an Internet start-up company. You get rich by living within your means and putting a little aside early.

Item Ten: ...is a message to be superimposed on all the other honorable advice you'll ever get in life. The essence of the message is URGENCY. You are on the verge of life's great adventure with all the time in the world, or so it seems. The truth is that you don't have time to be lazy, and you don't have time to waste. As William Faulkner said in *Big Woods*,
'You can't be alive forever, and you always wear out life long before you have exhausted the possibilities of living.'

Jim concluded his remarks to the young UGA journalists with a prophetic poem from Dr. Seuss:

You have brains in your head,
You have feet in your shoes,
You can steer yourself
Any direction you choose.
You're on your own.
And you know what you know.
And you are the guy who'll decide where to go.

So, Jim, what does life hold for you in the future? Where do you see yourself going?

"I want to look forward to going to work every day," he said. "I, also, would like to go back to college just to learn and study literature or history. I have been able to speak about journalism in college classes at Georgia State, UGA, Kennesaw State, Clayton State, and Georgia College and State University. My wife and I have traveled in spurts to places like Seattle, Las Vegas, San Francisco, Ireland, Europe, and Germany, and have enjoyed those trips a great deal."

He concluded, "I just want to be able to look in the mirror, and like who I see."

In all likelihood, with his history, Jim will like who he sees.

Ann and Jim Wooten

Willingham. A Beautiful Place!

Dr. Wilfred Louis Anderson
Class of 1965

To whom much is given, much is required.
–Luke 12:48

The strong, clear words of 88-year old Estizer Dyer Anderson, the mother of Dr. Wilfred Anderson, came across the long-distance phone line like the voice of a welcomed friend. "As far as Willingham is concerned, it's just a beautiful place. We have never complained about a single thing that happened at the school. Willingham helped make my son the gentleman that he is today. Wilfred was praised when he did well, corrected when he did wrong, and the correction was always done in the right way. We felt welcomed there, even though there were those who weren't particularly glad Wilfred was there.

"I have such great admiration for my son and for what he did in high school," Mrs. Anderson said, "and I am so proud of the fine man that he has become."

The school year, 1964-1965, was a memorable one in Macon for many reasons. A.R. Willingham High School, heretofore an all-white, all-boys' school, would become an integrated school for the first time in its brief history. Wilfred Anderson, a 16-year old rising-senior, and his friend, Javors Lucas, were prepared to become the first African-American students to enroll at Willingham in September, 1964. Wilfred recalled, "Javors was going to Willingham with me, but at 7:25 that morning, he called and said his mother chickened-out, and he wasn't going to Willingham after all."

So, Wilfred, what were you thinking when your friend had to back out on you?

"I remember feeling much worse than I thought I would feel when I learned that Javors wasn't going to Willingham with me. I had never figured on being the only black student at Willingham, and if I had signed up to go to Willingham several months beforehand and had known that I would be the only black person there, I would have thought about that decision a lot more. However, my mother was pleased that I chose to attend Willingham, but she was also scared for her oldest son."

Wilfred had a very good experience in his one and only year at Willingham. "From my perspective, I didn't experience a lot of problems related to my attending Willingham. My point of view was to try to bring people over to my side. Early in my senior year, there may have been some hostility toward me, but, by the time the band took our trip to New York City in the spring, there was no animosity at all. I had a great time at Willingham, and academically I did well, especially in my math and science courses. Mr. Leonard Pridgeon was my physics teacher, and I really liked his class. My other favorite teachers were Jim Littlefield and Charles Bird, who taught English."

Naturally, there were a couple of isolated incidents that happened during Wilfred's one year at his new school. He said, "My first day at Willingham, some guys threatened me, but the second day of school, the Willingham football team came and sat down with me for some reason. I ate with the football team at lunch. I don't know how it happened, but they sort of adopted me, and nobody was going to mess with those guys."

He recalled, "There were just some small problems here and there, and I remember when a guy physically threatened me once. I had pretty much walked away from those encounters most of the year, but I recall that I grabbed the guy, held him out over a railing, and he thought I was going to drop him. The football coaches broke that one up. Somehow, we ended up being friends later on. Of course, I was 6'4" and about 190 pounds; sort of tall and lanky, but I was at least big enough to be a threat, so people really didn't bother me much.

"I'm glad I went to Willingham," Anderson confessed. "Early in the year, people would only allow themselves to get so close to me, but, by the middle of the year, I really had become part of a new family, and I was having so much fun that I didn't want to leave. Going to Willingham was one of the best decisions that I have ever made in my life."

* * * * * * * * * *

Wilfred Louis Anderson was the oldest of Louis and Estizer Anderson's six children, five of whom graduated from college. The Andersons, both graduates of Tuskegee Institute in Alabama, placed a premium on education in their home. Louis earned a master's degree in accounting and sold insurance for Allstate, while Estizer taught home economics, music, and health-related subjects at the secondary level. Estizer Anderson recalled, "We raised our children in church in Macon, and we attended the Episcopal Church, as well as Turner's Tabernacle, Tremont Temple, and Stewart Chapel. Our children have graduated from Fisk, Tuskegee, Hampton, and the University of Georgia, and two of them, Wilfred and Louis Jr., became doctors."

Mr. Anderson died several years ago, while Mrs. Anderson, now 86, lives in an assisted-living complex in Atlanta and is a bright, delightful Southern woman. Wilfred recalled, "At the first PTA meeting that my mother attended after I transferred to Willingham, people were going around the room introducing themselves. My mother said, 'Hello. I'm Estizer Anderson, but I expect y'all already know me.'"

When asked if it was a difficult decision for her son Wilfred to leave Ballard-Hudson High School to attend Willingham for his senior year, Mrs. Anderson answered without hesitation, "No! Wilfred made the decision on his own, and, as a family, we were behind him completely. Personally, he was really quite reserved, but he was ready to be accepted at his new school. Wilfred wanted to make a good, positive impression at his new school, since he was the first Negro student at Willingham. Our race had many young men who had low opinions of themselves, but Wilfred wanted to change other people's perceptions of black people. He wanted others to see that we were ladies and gentlemen just like they were."

She continued, "When Wilfred first enrolled at Willingham, there was a police presence, but we were assured that he would be well-cared-for. Despite a few misgivings about his attending Willingham, Wilfred didn't hesitate. He felt that he had to do this on his own, and he did. We were somewhat frustrated as parents, wondering if anything might happen to him. We were the cowards. Wilfred had such a way of disarming people, and he represented our family so well."

Mrs. Anderson stated, "The fact that Wilfred was musically talented and could play almost every instrument in the band helped him a lot. Mr. Jim Littlefield, Willingham's band director, seemed to have some concerns about Wilfred playing in the band, but he soon learned what a great musician Wilfred was. Mr. Littlefield ended up being one of our best friends and biggest supporters. We had a lot of respect for him."

Bill Self, Judge of the Probate Court of Bibb County, was a band member with Wilfred, and recalled a specific incident involving Wilfred's arrival at Willingham. Self said, "Jim Littlefield, our band director, spoke pointedly to the band before Wilfred arrived as our first black student and band member. He told us in no uncertain terms, 'We're going to deal with this issue. Wilfred is a member of this band, and he'll be treated like every other member of this band.'"

Self continued, "Because of Wilfred's sense of humor, he made things easier for all of us. I remember a comment that he made in the band room one day, 'When the cheerleaders get here, they're going to notice me, because I'm the tall, dark, and handsome one in the band.' Jim Littlefield wisecracked, 'Well, at least you're tall and dark.'"

Wilfred Anderson laughed with fondness about his one year in the Willingham band. "Get this - I was in the Willingham Pride of Dixie Marching Band! I was the only black guy in the band, and we were the only band to play at the Barry Goldwater presidential rally that came to Macon in 1965. I remember that two blacks were in attendance at the rally that day—my dad and me."

He continued, "There was a time that we were going on a band trip. Jim Littlefield called me into his office and spoke directly, 'If you can't go with us, then we aren't going.' He didn't ask me if I wanted to go. It was, 'Look. We're going and you're going.' I always thought he should have at least asked me if I wanted to go, but he never wavered. As a band, we had the opportunity to go to the World's Fair in New York City at the conclusion of my senior year. Mr.

Littlefield told me that I could take a friend who would room with me. I invited Frank Brunson, who, at the time, played first trumpet at Ballard-Hudson, my former school. The guys in the band were going to stay four to a room, and since Mr. Littlefield couldn't put me in a room by myself, and since Frank and I were the only 'brothers,' we got to sleep two to a room. That was not a bad deal for us. Frank practiced with us before the trip and liked what we were doing so much that he came over to Willingham for his senior year, just as I did."

Part of Anderson's mentality about transferring from Ballard-Hudson to Willingham for his senior year was a practical matter.

"The background was that my parents sent me to kindergarten when I was only four years old, because they thought I was ready for school. I was supposed to be in kindergarten for two years, but the people at the kindergarten wouldn't keep me there for the second year; so my parents moved me into the first grade at Eugenia Hamilton School when I was barely five. Nobody in my class really knew that I was the youngest one there, and, of course, I was younger than all of the girls. I just never told anybody how old I really was.

"Back in those days, if your parents went with you to the driver's license bureau and filled out a form that said you were 15, you got your learner's permit to drive. I got my learner's permit at 14 because my dad lied about my age. Then, I got my driver's license at 15. That's another reason that I went to Willingham for my senior year. Otherwise, I would have been going on to college and would have been two years younger than the girls that I would be dating. I could have finished at Ballard-Hudson after my junior year because I had completed enough academic courses to graduate early, and I had already been accepted at Fisk University in Nashville, TN. So, my choice was to go on to college at 16 or go to Willingham for my senior year."

Wilfred confessed, "I was 26 years old before I began to tell people my real age."

* * * * * * * * * *

After graduating from Willingham, Wilfred Anderson attended Fisk University and graduated in 1969 with a BS degree in chemistry. Wilfred was computer-savvy when he was in high school and said, "I taught myself computer programming back in 1966. Then I taught computer programming when I was an undergraduate student at Fisk. There was only one computer on the Fisk campus, and it wasn't any more powerful than a calculator that you can buy now. Fisk set up a computer course, and I taught an 'FYI course' for high school science teachers who were studying at Fisk. I was 18 and was their laboratory proctor, and we spent six weeks studying programming in 1967. In 1969, when the people at IBM came to Nashville and saw what I was doing, they hired me to work in their research center in Yorktown Heights, NY. Thus, I was at IBM's research center in 1969 when I actually graduated from college. I worked there for a year before I went to medical school."

Unquestionably, Wilfred was on the front-end of the computer wave in the late 1960's. He laughed, "I learned computer programming before Bill Gates did, and, professionally, working with computers is probably where I should have stayed. I was working with IBM when the medical school at Washington University in St. Louis accepted me. While I was considering what I wanted to do with my life, they offered me a full scholarship, so I didn't think I had much of a choice. I hated to leave IBM, which I now believe was an error on my part. If I had to live my life over again, I probably would have done that part differently, because I certainly would have made a lot more money in the computer field."

After being accepted into Washington University's Medical School, Anderson did his residency at the University Hospital in Cleveland where he met his wife. Wilfred completed his medical training and became an MD in 1974 before going to Case-Western Reserve University in Cleveland for two years of a surgical residency. He worked in the emergency room for about a year and left there to go to establish a clinic for the City of Cleveland's Health Department.

Though he had amazing expertise in the computer-world, Anderson was asked if he had a good career in medicine.

"I have, but a medical career is still limited by something," he explained. "See, you're still a worker, and it's something akin to being a factory worker, except there's a much higher pay scale. In a sense, you're on an assembly line, and these parts come through your office, only they aren't parts – they're people. With computers, your imagination is the only thing that limits what you can do and how far you can go."

Wilfred had his own medical practice, rather than being a part of a larger medical practice. He commented, "After my second year of surgical residency, I decided that wasn't the direction I wanted to go. Then, I worked for the Cleveland Health Department and ran their sexually transmitted disease (STD) and heroin/methadone treatment programs for two years, beginning in 1977. During that time and with my own money, I bought a computer that cost $150,000. I would use it in my clinic, which was one of five clinics in the City of Cleveland's Health Department. That started a big legal fight within the Health Department. They told me I had to take the computer out, which I thought was crazy. We went through some legal stuff about whether or not an employee could give the city such a gift. They actually asked questions like that, and all I was trying to do was to help people get well.

"Finally, I told them, 'If I put this $150,000 computer in this clinic and it works, you need to understand that there are clinics just like this in Philadelphia, Houston, Detroit, and Atlanta, and I can make a lot of money selling this system to those cities.' After several meetings, the city's legal department decided it was not illegal for me to give the city an expensive computer, but one of the city-fathers said, 'Our problem is that in the future, you might be the one making money off this system.'"

Wilfred continued, "Isn't that just crazy? But for some perspective, you have to understand that this was a time when Dennis Kucinich, the youngest mayor of a major American city, was in office in Cleveland. Kucinich is the guy who ran for President on the Democratic ticket in 2004, along with Al Sharpton and all of those other Democrats, in the last election. In those days, Kucinich ruled Cleveland with an iron hand like the Nazis ran Germany, and it was administration that told me I had to take the computer out of the clinic. That's when I quit. That scenario was so stupid that I couldn't believe it!"

That's also when Wilfred Anderson founded Anderson Systems, a computer company, which became involved with the U.S. Department of Defense contracting, and he sold computer systems to the Army, Navy, and a manufacturing firm. Wilfred said, "Every computer sold for about $150,000 back in the late 1980's. One of the companies that I was doing business with wanted me on-site, so they furnished an office and a secretary for me right there in the manufacturing plant. My company also had a U.S. Navy contract that paid me a monthly maintenance fee of $4,000, and since I had virtually no expenses, I was doing quite well financially.

"Finally, I figured that I needed to use my medical license, so I decided to see only people with sexually-transmitted diseases. I thought I would only see about four or five patients a week, and my plan was to have my own medical office in the building with Anderson Systems. That way I could write off the medical practice as a tax expense and have my computer company and a small-scale medical practice there in the same building.

"The Navy was actually financing that operation because they were paying me for my computer services. The computer company was paying me to set up my medical laboratory and clinical area, and they were providing office space for me at no charge. My computer business just took off, and, after awhile, it got to the point that I could bid on a $10 million dollar computer contract. However, the banks in Cleveland wouldn't loan me the money. It's interesting to me that I was competent enough to secure a $10 million dollar contract, but the banks weren't willing to finance it for me. Essentially, I had to come out of the defense-contracting business because I didn't want to spend my time with a lot of smaller contracts, knowing that I could do a lot more and a lot better than that."

Wilfred explained, "Here's what ultimately happened. I was a 30-year old, single, black male in Cleveland, and I would bounce into a bank and say, 'I need $3 million dollars for an Air Force contract,' and they looked at me like I was crazy. But that was back in the 1980's, and that's when I closed down the computer contracting business and began to run the medical clinic in Cleveland full-time until I closed it in 1998."

He continued, "I have been in private medical practice since 1982, primarily treating STD's. No other clinic in the country that we were aware of was set up solely to treat patients like we did. In theory, half of my medical practice that I treated for STD's was male. We treated groups of people. With us, it was one plus one equals three, because STD's affect more than just the couple that was involved. Our office was working with a ghetto-population in Cleveland. In truth, it was a public VD clinic, and we saw up to 500 people a week. I was the only doctor, and we had three nurse practitioners, but we ended up making a major impact on STD's in the Cleveland community."

How did you do that, Dr. Anderson?

"By sheer force of will. We approached people differently than other clinics. We didn't relate to them like they had some deadly disease. Ours was not what most people think an STD clinic was like. Everybody knew each other here, and I validated the health of my patients. We used a different approach because, when people walked into my office, we tested them for everything. Everything. When they went into a regular doctor's office, just having a discussion about STD's was a major discomfort, and it was like pulling teeth for the clients. Our office treated people with respect and concern, and the Center for Disease Control noted that in the area of the city that I controlled, the VD rate dropped dramatically. We were much more direct with our methods of treatment, and our desire was to cure whatever the patient had."

Wilfred continued, "People knew who I was in this community because I had helped so many of them and their friends. Our clinic became something of a social phenomenon, especially among the black, middle-class in Cleveland. A number of people named their children after me because they knew they couldn't have gotten pregnant if I hadn't treated them.

"In our building, we had a medical practice, a very sophisticated microbiology laboratory, a pharmacy, and all of it was obviously automated and integrated with our computer systems, which was another reason I wanted to set up the clinic originally. I never planned on having the number of patients that we ended up treating. We finally got to the point where we could automate the process and then market it to other physicians and hospitals. Blue Cross even came to us and asked us to help them develop their own automated billing system. Our office ended up with eight computers and four people running them."

Dr. Wilfred Anderson doesn't practice medicine any longer. He commented, "Since I had previously sold computers to the U.S. Defense Department before establishing my medical practice, now I set up computer systems for different businesses and organizations in Cleveland. For example, a company may need 50 computers and a couple of servers for their operation, so they will employ me to come in and set up a system for them."

* * * * * * * * * *

Wilfred Anderson, now widowed, has one son, Alexander, who graduated from Shaker Heights High School in Cleveland in 2004. It is easily apparent that Alexander is the joy of his father's life. "Alexander played football and went to the state finals by high jumping 6'5" his senior year," Wilfred stated with pride. "After Alexander graduated from Shaker Heights, he was on schedule to go to West Point, but the Army's medical board cut him because of his allergies to peanuts, of all things. West Point had bent over backward to get him there, and we went through a number of appeals, but, by the time everything was resolved, it was too late for him attend West Point in the fall semester.

"My son Alexander is the best thing that I have ever done in life," Wilfred confessed. "He is a kid who is an excellent athlete that scored in the 96th percentile on the math portion of the SAT and made a combined score of 1400 on the SAT. Alexander was exactly what they wanted at West Point, but his allergy situation prevented him from getting in. Now Alexander is considering the Air Force Academy and Michigan."

Currently, Alexander works for his dad's computer company, Anderson Systems. Wilfred spoke about his son, "He is a valuable asset to my company. Alexander wants to design artificial intelligence systems, but first he has to decide where he is going to college next fall."

* * * * * * * * * *

Frank Brunson was one of Wilfred Anderson's closest friends when they grew up on Vining Circle off Pio Nono Avenue in South Macon. Brunson now lives in St. Petersburg, FL, where he is in his second career as a claims adjuster for Assurance Solutions since retiring from Sears after 20 years. He recalled, "Like Wilfred, I had finished nearly all of my academic requirements at Ballard-Hudson, so I primarily transferred from Ballard-Hudson to Willingham out of curiosity. Then I went to Lincoln University in Pennsylvania and later earned a master's degree in mental health at Fort Valley State University. Brunson, like Anderson, was the product of well-educated parents, and his dad was the principal of Maude Pye Elementary School in Macon.

Brunson said about his friend, "Wilfred has been highly successful in life. Growing up, he wouldn't necessarily talk about business with you, but he had an amazing business mind. This was in an era before African-Americans became very business-oriented, but the more you were around Wilfred, the more you began to realize that he might be a genius. He was such an unassuming guy that his bright mind just sort of sneaked up on you. Wilfred could talk about subjects that we considered weird, but he thought it was perfectly normal. I always thought he was a Wiley Coyote-type, always thinking up new and different ways to do things.

"Wilfred would make up goofy games to play in his backyard, and we would all compete," Brunson recalled, "and he always won, not because he was the best athlete, but because he could figure out a way to do something that none of us thought about. He had a huge back yard that was fenced in by a concrete block wall. The game would be to race across his backyard while trying to avoid his big, boxer bulldog. The dog wasn't rabid, but it still had foam on its mouth, and the dog would chase us when we ran. Wanna guess who got caught by the dog? We did! Wanna guess who never got caught? Wilfred. He would also have us race along the top of the fence in his backyard. The fence had Cherokee roses growing on it, and we got cut and scratched. Wilfred figured out a way to avoid the roses and beat the rest of us."

Like most high school students, Brunson and his friends had no idea what they wanted to do with their lives. Wilfred, on the other hand, knew exactly that he wanted to do, which was becoming a doctor. Frank stated, "I see three things as being the major factors in the success of Wilfred's life. First, he was very bright. Wilfred skipped a grade in kindergarten and was just barely 17 in his senior year. Next, he just saw things differently from the rest of us, and, third, I consider him to be a risk-taker. We were all pretty conservative guys, but Wilfred was

Dr. Wilfred Anderson

one who got out on the edge. Simply going to Willingham as the first African-American student was a risky endeavor. On the other hand, that didn't really surprise me that he wanted to go to Willingham. He also took a risk when he quit practicing medicine and went into the computer business for himself. I always thought it was risky for him to relocate to Cleveland, OH."

Brunson concluded, "Willingham was a great experience for both of us. In fact, after Wilfred and I went to Willingham and enjoyed it, our sisters followed us to McEvoy, Willingham's sister school."

Another of Wilfred's friends was Roger Rawls, who graduated from Ballard-Hudson in 1965 and later from Tennessee State University in Nashville. Rawls, who had a 20-year career in the United States Air Force, spoke about his friend Wilfred. "I played in the Ballard-Hudson Maroon Tiger Marching Band and primarily knew him through the band. Wilfred was a clarinet player and a very good one. No one was more surprised than I when Wilfred didn't report to Ballard-Hudson for our senior year. I found out that he had transferred to Willingham. We saw each other a few times when we were in college since we both went to school in Nashville, TN.

"Wilfred was brilliant when it came to computers," Rawls recalled. "He would talk about computer applications back in those days, and what he said was so far-fetched that it sounded ridiculous to the rest of us. Then, low and behold, what Wilfred had talked about originally that sounded like something out of a science-fiction magazine became a reality. Wilfred always had amazing brain power and was one of the smartest guys I have ever known. He could take an idea and run with it and could turn it into a reality. Since he worked for IBM right out of college, he was on the front end of that computer wave. He became famous for tearing down a computer and rebuilding it better. I know that he taught his son, Alexander, about computers as well."

Cecil Bentley grew up in South Macon and graduated from Willingham in 1966. A long-time newspaper editor and prolific writer, Bentley now lives in Athens. He wrote the following article in the *Athens Banner-Herald,* January 6, 2001, about his association with Wilfred. The following quotes from Bentley were included in a four-part series entitled, *The Long Walk,* which commemorated the 40th anniversary of integration at the University of Georgia.

> *As chief justice, Earl Warren was considered by some to be the "chief villain" of a Supreme Court that unanimously declared segregation in public schools unconstitutional in 1954. The Court's decision allowed a black girl named Linda Brown to attend a white school in Topeka, Kansas. And, arguably, it was the first step on the long walk of the civil rights movement.*

> *Georgia Gov. Herman Talmadge, reflecting the view of most segregationists, called the Court's ruling ''a mere scrap of paper,' and it was 10 more years before the Brown vs. Board of Education decision impacted public schools in my hometown, Macon.*

> *Alphabetical seating placed me directly behind Wilfred Anderson, the first and only black student to attend Willingham High in the fall, 1964. Several students had planned to transfer from all-black Ballard-Hudson to all-white Willingham that year, but on opening day, only Wilfred came.*

> *Several things about Wilfred impressed me. He really understood trigonometry and was willing and able to help me learn it, too. He was a great athlete, but ineligible to play because of transfer rules. He was a sharp dresser, knew a lot of good jokes, and was a great musician, who helped an already awesome school band get better.*

> *What impressed me most, though, was his poise, patience, and perseverance. Unquestionably, those character traits allowed him to endure the daily insults and helped me and my school make it through a tumultuous year without a major incident. He made the long walk much easier for all those who followed.*

And certainly, Wilfred did just that since many others followed him to Willingham.

* * * * * * * * * *

One of those who followed Wilfred Anderson to Willingham/McEvoy was his own sister, now Carol Anderson Dorsey. Probably few people in this world know and understand Wilfred like Carol. She spoke proudly about her brother and said, "I am one of Wilfred's two sisters. He was two grades ahead of me in school, although he was only one year older. Wilfred is, quite simply, the most intelligent person I know, and I know a lot of smart folks. Since childhood, he has always had an uncanny ability to figure things out. His passion to know things made me and his other siblings sometimes think he was 'nuts.' Why would any 8-year old want to spend hours and hours with a microscope, or outside at night in the really, really cold weather with his eye stuck to a telescope lens?

"Still, he managed to avoid the nerd label by playing sports, having fun with the neighborhood kids, and getting into the required amount of mischief," Carol recalled.

Dorsey remembered the time when Wilfred was in high school and their dad suddenly, and permanently, lost the sight in one eye. "Many medical experts during the 1960's were handicapped by the lack of diagnostic procedures that are used today, and they could not find out what was wrong with our dad. Wilfred was the person who figured out that dad had a tumor on his optic nerve. A few years later, when the CAT-scan was developed, they found the tumor on our dad's optic nerve, just as Wilfred had said. Before and after Wilfred became a physician, he advised against 'medically accepted' practices and recommended alternatives that would be contrary to the advice of a friend or family member's physician. Many years later, all the things that Wilfred recommended for us to do medically have since proved to be the answer and are now seen as main-stream medicine. For example, Wilfred was always against the practice of combining medications unless it was absolutely necessary. With Wilfred, this went from having a passion for knowledge and developing solutions to displaying courage.

"Wilfred has always been ready and willing to stand up for what he believes is right," Carol declared. "No other black kid in Macon, GA, stepped up to integrate the previously all-white Willingham and McEvoy institutions. Wilfred, like his siblings who followed as pioneers, learned from our dad what the Bible taught, 'To whom much is given, much is required.' We were taught this same creed by our dad's example and by the way he fought, nonviolently, for social change and civil rights."

Carol Anderson Dorsey admired the courage that Wilfred demonstrated when, as a 16-year old he willingly left all of his friends, teachers, and the only high school he had ever known. She said, "My brother sacrificed the usual joys and kudos of the senior year in high school, and he did it with such courage and grace. Wilfred did this in the racially-charged, Southern, all-white, male environment in the 1960's. The best part is that he actually changed some people's minds about the value of blacks. With Wilfred, you had the makings of a man who dealt effectively with people from all walks of life. This is not to say that Wilfred got along with, or made friends with all of the people with whom he had contact. Wilfred has always done a great job of determining when the price of 'getting along' with someone is trumped by his values and principles.

* * * * * * * * * *

Dorsey recalled life around the Anderson house while growing up. "When we were all young, Wilfred, who couldn't have been more than eight, would order these big albums of classical music. He would play them very loudly on our family's stereo (Can you picture the 1950's stereo monstrosity?). Then, he would yell at all of us to 'Come, sit, and listen!' We all hated it, but somehow, we were drawn into it, and would hang off the sofa arms or roll around on the carpet, while Wilfred waved his arms like a musical conductor and admonished us to 'Listen to this part right here!' I remember that my favorite piece was *Peter and the Wolf* by Sergei Prokofieff. Wilfred would narrate the action in this invisible play, and at seven, five, and three years old, we were alternately bored and thrilled."

She continued, "Wilfred was a local chess champion in high school; he worked in a bomb-building factory one summer, and he was extremely popular with girls. I remember when he went on a Boy Scout trip to Mexico for several weeks in a dilapidated old bus that broke down intermittently. Our parents would get Wilfred's collect phone calls that were surprisingly upbeat while sharing the latest 'tragedy' involving the bus."

One of Carol Dorsey's greatest impressions of her brother is that he almost never harbors anger or a grudge. She said, "Wilfred is seldom angry, but if he is, he doesn't entertain it for long. He has the gift of total forgiveness, and he uses it well. Wilfred is generous with all that is his, and he has a tender heart surrounded by an immense intellect. Wilfred has helped our parents with thousands and thousands of dollars over the years, and he paid all the costs for my younger sister's private college education. He did these things without complaint or even comment, because I did not know for years afterward that he sent my sister to college. Whenever she needed anything, including spending money, she simply asked, and Wilfred quickly complied. Raising his son Alexander is another one of the best things he's done, along with being a great brother and son.

"When Wilfred became the proud father of a son in 1986, he tapped into a wealth of tenderness that was pure sweetness to watch," Dorsey said. "Wilfred often traveled—just he and Alexander—from the time his son was a toddler. Wilfred fed and cared for the little guy as if he had been doing it forever. Throughout Alexander's life, Wilfred has been like a combination dad/professor. Alexander scored a perfect score on the math part of the SAT because he and Wilfred had been 'computer buddies' since Alexander was old enough to stand up."

Dorsey understands that her brother has a tendency to get very excited about helping or solving your problem. "Because he knows he's right, he can get very loud, especially if you don't jump on his suggestion immediately. Due to years of experience, we all know that Wilfred is right 99.99 percent of the time, so we frequently say, 'OK, for goodness sake! Just calm down. We'll stop putting the diaper cream on the baby, and we'll use the athlete's foot cream on his behind! And we do it just because you said so, and then, 'Voila!' The diaper rash miraculously clears up.

"We have learned that Wilfred's initial excitement and loudness comes from his anger over the ineffective and sometimes risky advice that other health care professionals have advocated," Carol stated. "He has set his jaw in more than one hospital when visiting a family member and informed the attending physician that a different, more effective course of treatment is mandatory. After explaining himself in detail, the other physician is usually impressed, and the new course of action is almost always more effective. I call Wilfred every time I need to know anything that's really important, and he is always available, and he's always happy to help. Even if you call him in the middle of the night, he never complains. All Wilfred wants to know is, 'What do you need?'"

Dorsey maintains that her brother was born well before his time. "Wilfred was not simply smart like other kids who skip grades and graduate early. When he was just a young boy, he had a grown man's scientific mind, coupled with an entrepreneurial spirit and a warrior's courage. Life for him was both a

The Anderson guys: Dr. Wilfred and Alexander

burden and an adventure. Wilfred intuitively, and sometimes painfully, found a way, with no guide or instructions, to relate to other children when he was a child. His ability to withstand pain and injustice of overt, covert, traditional, and modern racism as a black man born in 1948 in the South and not allow it to dampen his spirit, his passion for knowledge, his generosity, or his ability to love others have made him successful in life. I love him, and I am blessed that he is my brother."

When the question was asked, "How will Wilfred Anderson be remembered?" Carol Dorsey did not hesitate. "All of the people in Wilfred's life, and there are many, will be consumed with a sense of real loss when he is gone. We all know that there is something about Wilfred that defies understanding or description. It's as if, in losing him, we will lose some important knowledge or some more good advice that would have saved us from unknown problems or peril. We will lose the loud, laughing, never-as-funny-as-he-thinks-he-is guy who will share anything with anybody - from a silly joke to a beautiful picture of a sunset. Wilfred e-mails everybody pictures of nature. Wilfred shares everything from his money to a welcome in his home, from a hand to hold at your bedside to a consultation with your doctor, and he simply does this out of the goodness of his heart."

Estizer Anderson knows that her son Wilfred has experienced success in life. "Wilfred, has been successful his entire life because of his determination. He has always had great self-confidence, just like the rest of our children. They all learned to love themselves first, as well as loving others. Personally, I have been blessed with long life. I have control over my faculties, and even though I have osteoporosis, I can still take care of myself. I have just kept on going, and before I knew it, I was 86."

So, the question is asked, "Wilfred, what does the future hold for you?"

He replied, "I know that I don't want to spend any more winters in Cleveland. After 30 years of the cold weather, I will probably look to relocate to some place warmer. I am in the process of building up Anderson Systems, and I enjoy working with my son."

If Wilfred's future is anything like his past, then he will be extremely successful in this next stage of his life, regardless of his vocation.

Rags to Rides

William Bradshaw
Class of 1968

"Do unto others as you would have them do unto you."
                                                    –The Golden Rule

"There's no right way to do the wrong thing."

T
he question begs to be asked, "Does anybody not named Bradshaw own an automobile dealership in the state of South Carolina?" That's a fair question since William Bradshaw, Willingham High School, Class of '68, owns seven dealerships (stores in the auto industry) in the Palmetto State and one in North Carolina. Life is good for William and Annette Brantley Bradshaw, residents of Greer, SC.

Things weren't always so bright, smooth, and affluent for Bradshaw, according to an old South Macon friend, Ed Bissonette, owner of Central Kia in Macon. "I went to Bruce School and Willingham High with William and have followed his career in the automobile industry with much interest. We all were fairly poor, but William probably grew up poorer than the rest of us.

To William, poor or not, South Macon was the only place on earth. "Growing up where I did was great. We had fun, and I have wonderful memories of my childhood. We lived in a little house on Hudson Avenue off Houston Avenue behind Powell's Pharmacy, and our rent was $75 a month. I didn't realize that we were that poor, because all of us were pretty much alike. Of course, we all thought that Lanier and Mark Smith were in the high-dollar sections of town, a little better off financially than the rest of us, but I didn't feel like we were deprived or lived in the ghetto. My neighborhood was near Pendleton Homes, a public housing project, so we thought the houses across Houston Avenue in Lynmore Estates were fairly up-scale compared to ours. My recollection is that we lived in solid neighborhoods in a solid side of town; we grew up happy with good friends, good churches and schools, and good relationships in South Macon."

William Bradshaw, the second of four children, was born in Dublin, GA, but was raised in South Macon. "My dad (now deceased) was a truck driver, who didn't make much money and was gone all the time, trying to make a living for us. Unfortunately, we didn't get to see much of him. My mother was a homemaker and raised four kids. My mother — at age 85 — is a saint and lives in Dublin. One thing that stands out in my mind is that my mother would have to go borrow from these small loan companies. She would borrow $100, $200, up to $500 just to pay back the other loan company that was hounding her to pay them off. It was a vicious cycle. They were probably charging her ridiculous rates, and I remember her staying on the phone and getting hammered by loan companies. She was 'borrowing from Peter to pay Paul,' and that made a lasting impression on me. I remember thinking, 'I don't want to be poor and get hounded like this.'"

Thus, William started working to make money to buy clothes, toys, or whatever. Among other jobs, William had a morning paper route when he was 12 years old and confessed, "I cut enough grass, as a kid, to last a lifetime. I used to sell bottles and knock concrete off bricks for a penny a brick, but I was trying any way I could to make a little money. I knew our family didn't have enough money, and that really motivated me."

During William's junior year at Willingham, his plans did not include going to college. "I was going to work when I graduated, but I ran into Roger Greene, a teacher at Willingham, who got me thinking that college was what I ought to do. Though I had not taken the proper courses that would prepare me for college, I decided to try it anyway. Somehow, even with my combined SAT score of 725, and having taken virtually no math courses, I was able to get into Macon Junior College, a brand new school. I struggled during my first couple of years there, but I stuck with it. I suppose I had to work harder because I came to college less-prepared than other students. After two years there, I went to night school at Georgia College at Milledgeville's Warner Robins extension on the Air Force base. My classrooms were actually barracks on the base."

In those days, William would work full-time at Wilson Electric Supply Company during the day, which he had done for four years as a student at Willingham and Macon Junior College (now Macon State), and go to school at night in Warner Robins. That's where he met another man who was a big influence on his life. "Mr. Ed Chase was my accounting teacher," William recalled, "and was also the top-ranking civilian employee at Robins Air Force base. He was the comptroller at Robins Air Force base and taught accounting in college as a hobby. I had Mr. Chase every semester and was in at least five of his accounting courses. I made pretty good grades in his classes, so he met me after class one night and said, 'I want you to apply for a job with a friend of mine. He has a Chevrolet dealership in Warner Robins and needs an office manager.' I was just turning 21 that month (February, 1971) and told Mr. Chase that I wasn't qualified to do that job. Somehow, he convinced me to apply, and I got the job with Bob Richards Chevrolet."

The irony here is that William's family had never even owned a new car, and he had never been in a new car dealership until he applied for that job. Three interviews later, he was hired by Bob Richards to be his 21-year-old office manager.

William had only one semester left to graduate from college but thought he needed more time to work at his new job. "I dropped out of school for a semester," William recalled, "because I knew I was going to have to really dig in and learn at my new job. I was working 80-hours a week but was planning to finish college in the fall. I kept thinking I would go back the next semester or the following semester, but, by then, I moved to Augusta, GA, in 1972 as the office manager for the same dealer in a larger dealership. I never did finish my last semester of college. Only one semester, but I never got around to getting it done.

"On the other hand," William said, "I had gotten into the car business and really enjoyed it. I worked hard to learn as much as I could and thought, 'This is something I want to do.' I was making a good living and began to think that I would like to own a dealership. It was 1973 when I set my goal to become a car dealer by the time I was 30."

He continued, "Since I didn't have family with any money, plus, I had no savings and had no idea about the cost of getting a dealership, I still knew that this was what I wanted to do in life. However, things began to work out, and that's when I met the next important mentor in my life, Mr. Ed Sherwood. I first met Mr. Sherwood when he purchased the Warner Robins dealership from Bob Richards. I had heard that Mr. Sherwood had helped people get their own stores, and, in 1974, he called me in Augusta to ask if I could recommend an office manager to him. He truly was fishing to see if I might be interested in working for him, so I went to Greenville, SC, and interviewed with Ed Sherwood.

"I may have been a little bold back then," William confessed, "because during my interview, I said, 'I want to be a dealer one day and own my own store. I don't know all it takes to do it, but that's my goal, and I want to do it by the time I'm 30.' Mr. Sherwood said he couldn't promise me that would happen, but he also told me that he had helped others get their own dealership. He told me I should come and join him, so I did. I worked for the Sherwoods from 1974 until 1979, first as an office manager and then as general manager of two different dealerships. In 1979, I approached Mr. Sherwood about backing me to purchase my first dealership. He agreed, if I could find the right one to purchase. After several months of looking, I found a small dealership in Greer, SC, that had been losing money, so it was cheap enough to buy, relatively speaking. In 1979, Ed Sherwood and his son Larry became my partners, and we opened up that small, struggling dealership in Greer, SC, and have been there since."

William recalled those early days and said, "Annette, my wife of 10 years, and I used every nickel we had. With the money we made on the sale of our home, along with our savings, we were able to raise $40,000 to put into the deal. It took an additional $80,000 to have one-third ownership, so Mr. Sherwood loaned us $80,000, he put up the rest, and we paid him back one percent over the prime lending rate, which, for a while, was over 20 percent. We were paying Mr. Sherwood a huge interest payment every month, but in time we made some progress, and I began to pick up some other small stores that were cheap or weren't doing very well, and we would be partners."

Before long, William was able to buy out Ed Sherwood and continues to buy other dealerships, as well. In 2005, William now owns eight dealerships which generate over $240,000,000 in sales in a single year, and Bradshaw Automotive has over 400 employees.

So, a lot of people depend on you, don't they, William?

"They do," he replied, "and I don't always think about that, but it truly means that over 400 families depend on the job we do and the type of business we run. It's a good feeling to know that you have the opportunity to be involved in doing something good and positive in your community and involving that many families."

Do you have plans to open any more stores?

"I do," he said, "but even though we have not been aggressively looking for dealerships to purchase in the last five years, we have opened three stores in that time period."

William's original dealership began with Oldsmobiles and Cadillacs but now includes Chevrolet, Buick, Hummer, Cadillac, Saturn, Honda, Acura, Infiniti, and Hyundai. Today, Bradshaw Automotive Company includes the following dealerships and locations:

- Breakaway Honda, Greenville
- Bradshaw Acura, Greenville
- Saturn of Greenville
- Saturn of Spartanburg
- Bradshaw Infiniti, Greenville
- Saturn of Asheville, NC
- Bradshaw Hyundai, Greer
- Bradshaw Chevy/Buick/Cadillac/Hummer, Greer

"Part of the reason I haven't been as aggressive recently is because of my work with the National Automobile Dealers Association (NADA), which has been pretty time-consuming. This year, however, we're looking to buy land in Birmingham, AL, for a Saturn dealership, and, within the next two years, build a Saturn dealership in Athens, GA. When we find opportunities that make sense for us, and we can do business without spreading ourselves too thin, then we'll do it.

"It's amazing to think that all of this came from the $40,000 that we squeezed out back in 1979. I bought out my partners in the late 1980s, and with a lot of borrowing, I was able to add franchises and expand our business along the way. Obviously, I was not averse to using other people's money."

* * * * * * * * * *

William Bradshaw is a man who remembered those who have helped him along the way. One such man is Roger Greene of Macon, who became a mentor during William's high school years. "Mr. Greene taught Distributive Education at Willingham," Bradshaw recalled. "That was a program for boys who, in all likelihood, weren't college-bound and figured to go to work when they finished high school. Mr. Greene taught me a lot, including something as small as how to tie a tie, but the biggest thing that he did was convince me that I could and should attend college. In high school, I wasn't very motivated or focused on my future. My family would have been considered working-class, and like a lot of families, we barely lived paycheck to paycheck, so I had no intention of attending college."

He continued, "In the tenth grade, I signed up for Distributive Education Clubs of America (DECA) so I could get out of school early and go to work. I realize I signed up for DECA for the wrong reasons, but the program had a major impact on my life. More specifically, Mr. Roger Greene had a major impact on my life. He must have seen something in me that I didn't know existed, because he took a real interest in me.

Roger Greene remembered young William Bradshaw very well. "During William's junior year, I encouraged him to run for president of DECA, which he did, and was elected. Our DECA Program was very strong because we sought to teach business and marketing skills to our students. Those skills would enable the students to move easily into the workplace if they chose not to attend college."

DECA had an employee/employer banquet in May of William's senior year, and, though he had never really considered college, William met the president of Macon Junior College, the banquet's keynote speaker. The college president hinted to William, "Why don't you come to school with us in the fall?" That was encouragement enough for William to give it a try, and, since he was interested in accounting, he asked Roger Greene about the possibility of enrolling at Macon Junior College.

Greene said, "Like many young men in those days, William was from a poor family, but it was clearly evident to me that he had great potential and leadership qualities. We both attended Houston Avenue Christian Church where William and his mother were faithful attendees. I remember that she was a role model as a parent. In those formative years, I also remember William as a Christian-minded young man who was faithful in the church. He had such good personal qualities which later served him well in the automobile business."

Greene stated humbly, "I don't know how, why, or what it was that I said to William that really influenced him. I really wish I knew how to do that with everybody. To show you the type of man William has become and how grateful he is, he called me several years ago when he was in Macon for a reunion and took my wife and me to lunch. Then he told me about the things I had done that had influenced his life in a profound way."

In addition to Roger Greene, William also grew up under the leadership of Rev. Bob Porter, pastor of Houston Avenue Christian Church. Rev. Porter was the Bradshaw family's pastor and remembered his first meeting with William. "I met William when his family first came to our church back in the 1950's. William was a quiet, reserved young man and was extremely well-behaved. He was always dependable and attended Sunday School, worship services, and youth meetings with regularity."

With pride in his former parishioner, Rev. Porter stated, "After William graduated from high school, his mother would frequently update me on how he was becoming successful as a car dealer. Mutual friends of ours have said that William probably has one of the largest businesses of its kind in the entire Southeast. All of us who knew him growing up are so proud of William's success and are pleased that he has become such a fine Christian man."

One of Macon's best known and most highly-respected automobile dealers, Barney A. Smith, Jr., has known William Bradshaw since their early days in South Macon. "William and I started the first grade together at Charles H. Bruce Elementary School in 1956. We were friends over the next several years through grammar school and high school. One of William's greatest strengths is that he has an extremely strong work ethic. He kind of waded into the automobile business as an office manager and then took a very successful plunge at a young age as an entrepreneur.

"Even though we have lost personal contact in recent years, I have heard many positive things about William's business accomplishments, since we work in the same industry. He became what is known as a 'chain dealer' in the automobile industry through the acquisitions of several stores.

"There is no question that William is a totally self-made person. He had no family connections to help him get established in the automobile business, but he did have a couple of very strong dealers, Bob Richards and Ed Sherwood, who provided him with some opportunities to succeed. William put all of his finances on the line and risked his family's financial security early on, but he was able to make it work."

Barney continued, "William's life is a true rags-to-riches story. He came from very humble beginnings but was not willing to settle for the status quo and took the appropriate chances to make his life better financially. He has been a tremendous success in life, and it is obvious that William has a burning desire to succeed in life. He has this unquenchable thirst to have a better life than the one he had as a young man in South Macon, and the fact that William has been married to Annette, his high school sweetheart for well over 30 years, speaks volumes to me about his character in this day and time."

* * * * * * * * *

Greenville Technical College is the largest community college in South Carolina with over 14,000 full-time students, 40,000 students who gain additional training from Greenville Tech, with four campuses and 42 buildings. The college started with only one building and 800 students, but today, over 54,000 people are educated in the course of an academic year. William has become closely affiliated with the college, due in part to his admiration for Dr. Thomas Barton, Jr., the school's president. Dr. Barton opened Greenville Technical College over 42 years ago when he was only 31 and is the only president the college has ever had.

William stated proudly, "Dr. Barton is one of the most amazing people I have been around. Had he chosen to go into business instead of education, there's no telling how much he would be worth today. Dr. Barton is an entrepreneur and an amazing motivator. He just happens to be doing it in public education."

Dr. Barton can't say enough good things about his friend, William Bradshaw. "William is the epitome of leadership. He either came into the world that way or learned it at an early age. I've never seen anyone who could motivate people to follow him like William. The first time you meet him, you immediately realize that he has something special. The Lord just placed something inside William that other people don't have. He is simply outstanding in every way, and William isn't nearly finished yet, because he's still a young man. He has unlimited energy, and I have never heard him complain about anything in any meeting that I have been in with him."

In the past 20 years, William has developed some very close ties with Greenville Technical College and served as both finance chairman and chairman of Greenville Tech's Foundation Board. Dr. Barton continued, "William headed up our capital fund-raising campaign where we had a goal of $15,000,000. That is quite an ambitious goal to raise that kind of money in one year, but with William's leadership, we got the job done. Because of his excellent work, we were able to buy a 600,000 square-foot mall that could be used for education, and we have seven universities renting space from us in that mall.

"William is positive and charismatic in his personality, and his people-skills are unbelievable," Dr. Barton said. "He runs his business in the same way he took over the leadership of our foundation that raised the incredible amount of money for the Technical College. He just took over and accomplished a goal that many thought was unachievable. I believe it is William's desire to help as many people in as many ways as he can in his lifetime. He is just strong, strong, strong when it comes to leading people and motivating them for a common cause."

Though he does not consider himself to be a public speaker, William was asked to give the commencement address to the graduating class of the Greenville Tech's automotive students, a huge honor and quite a thrill for Bradshaw. For the past four years, William has been a Platinum Level ($20,000) sponsor for Greenville Tech's annual golf outing and fund-raiser and was inducted into Greenville Tech's Institute for Entrepreneurial Studies in 2000. This prestigious honor was bestowed on five Greenville, SC, business leaders.

When William speaks to young people today, he gives them sound advice regarding important truths about life and business. "One thing that I have learned throughout the years," William said, "is how important certain people can be to the success of others. No one can become successful on their own. I consistently encourage young people to be willing to accept help when it is offered, and they need to be willing to open the door when opportunity knocks. I challenge students to set goals and make wise use of the opportunities that are before them.

"When I was 23 years old and had been in the automobile business nearly two and a half years, I made one of the biggest decisions of my life. Without any money, and with a family that had no money, I decided that I was going to be an automobile dealer. I didn't know a lot about the business at that time, and I certainly didn't know how I would go about achieving that goal. I just knew that I loved what I was doing, and I saw some great opportunities there. Thus, I set a goal that I wanted to be an automobile dealer by the time I was thirty, and, with hard work and the help of others, it became a reality."

William said, "I worked extremely hard to learn everything that I could – not just about my own job – but about every department of the dealership. I began learning about other automobile dealers who were willing to help young people like me by backing them financially to get their own dealership."

William's philosophy of business is treating people like family, which is true for both customers and employees. This mode of operation has served him well throughout the years and has earned him numerous awards, both personally and professionally. William's commitment to give back to the community which embraced him is quite obvious. He is very active in and supportive of numerous civic and service organizations. Showing no signs of slowing his professional pace, William's resume reads like a *Who's Who* in both the automobile and civic worlds. He has donated numerous automobiles to charity and local causes.

TIME Magazine named William Bradshaw, President of Bradshaw Automotive Company, in Greer, SC, as a finalist for their 1997 Quality Dealer Award. This recognition was announced at the National Automobile Dealers Association convention in Atlanta, GA. The convention was attended by more than 20,000 individuals involved in the automobile industry, and while the award recognized dealers for exceptional performance in their dealerships, it also recognized their distinguished community service.

* * * * * * * * * *

Ed Sherwood was one of the three most influential men in William Bradshaw's life. Ed's son, Larry Sherwood, was a Chevrolet dealer for 30 years and said, "William is a great friend, and I've known him since 1974 when we were 23 years old. He came to work with me in Mauldin, SC, and took a real cut in pay to join Sherwood Chevrolet, but he had a goal of one day becoming an auto dealer. My dad had been successful in helping worthy young men like William to realize that dream. William had enough insight and was willing to join us for less money so he could possibly have that opportunity 'down the road.' After doing a great job as general manager of the Mauldin dealership, William got his chance to have his own dealership in Greer, SC, and the rest is history. He and I have remained friends and business associates since those days.

"William is the same now as when I met him. He has the ability to analyze an opportunity and determine the probability of success before committing to it. This significantly increases his chances of success. William is sincerely appreciative of everyone who has worked with him along his path to success. He has built friendships that will last a lifetime, and we are all so proud of him and his accomplishments."

Sherwood continued, "William is a man with the highest integrity, but he remains humble and thankful for the opportunities he has had. While his business has grown enormously, he has continued to maintain a wonderful family, some of whom are involved in his businesses. I think his success lies in his ability to set goals and work tirelessly toward achieving them. William involves his employees in those dreams, surrounds himself with top-notch people who can produce, he treats everyone well, and believes in himself."

Larry Sherwood stated, "William is one of the most successful and admired men in the entire automotive industry, which is significant, but anyone who knows him knows that he is deserving of his success. We are all very proud of William."

Few people in a business know their boss like the administrative assistant. Betty Urso has been William Bradshaw's secretary and assistant for 18 years and has known William and Annette for the past 31 years. They met when the Bradshaws moved to Mauldin from Augusta, and Betty and William worked together for Sherwood Chevrolet. When William bought his own dealership, Betty Urso joined the Bradshaw family of dealerships and became his secretary. Urso said, "William just has a knack for bringing out the best in people. He is a master negotiator and mediator, as well as an outstanding businessman with high standards of excellence in his business and family life. William is a leader who encourages people to do their best in whatever it is they undertake. He is also a great family man, and he adores his three grandchildren."

In the highly-competitive world of automobile sales and service, William Bradshaw has developed a reputation for honesty, loyalty, compassion, and kindness. According to Urso, "William cares deeply about people and tries to help anyone he can to make their lives better through training, scholarship-funding, and providing the best advice possible. William is easy to work with and is considerate of those he comes in contact with."

Without question, William Bradshaw is creating quite a legacy, beginning with Greer and greater-Greenville, while extending into surrounding states. "His legacy," Betty Urso concluded, "is his gift of time, talent, and resources to our community, his church, business, and his family. William is a leader, both locally and nationally, and is the kind of person that will make a difference for the betterment of all people, both now and in the future. His passion is to do the right thing in all facets of life, and his business ethics are 'straight-up.' William is a great listener, and he has the love and support of Annette, his children, his son-in-law, and his grandchildren."

Tony Hill and William started working together 25 years ago in Greer. Today, Tony manages the three Saturn operations for Bradshaw Automotive.

"William is my best friend, which is fairly unique since we work together and are such good friends. I think the reason that situation works is that we both see eye-to-eye in business. We believe in giving a dollar's value for a dollar spent.

"One of William's major strengths is that he is interested in customers for the long-haul, and he has an ability to set long-range goals. We are interested in having people become customers for life by growing one customer at a time. I relate that to growing a garden where you plant a seed, water, cultivate, and fertilize it. Then it will grow into a mature plant that produces something of value. We try to cultivate our customers any way we can so they will continue to be our customers.

"William is a well-rounded, deep thinker who thrives on new challenges, but, above all, he has the uncanny ability to see things from every perspective, and that prevents him from stepping on other peoples' toes. Our motto is to do your best today and do it with honesty and integrity. He tells us that we may make some mistakes—some big mistakes, but they should be made from the head and not from the heart. Having the right heart is important in what we do for a living. I have always been impressed with William's tenacity in pursuit of his goals and his unique ability to forecast the future. He has amazing business sense and is fair and honest."

Hill has long been impressed with the growth of Bradshaw Automotive. "To show you how William's business has grown over the years, he started out in Greer by giving away 15 hams to his employees at Christmas. This year he gave out over 400 hams, and he drives to every store, hands each employee a ham, shakes their hand, and thanks them for what they do for this business. I just can't say enough good things about William.

"Unfortunately, many people today measure success only by the dollar, which is just one part of the measuring stick. William has been a success because of his pursuit of the challenge, his burning desire to be the best, and the way he treats everyone – both the customer and his employees. The first 25 years with William have been a heckuva ride, and I'm looking forward to the next 25."

In recent years, William Bradshaw has become increasingly involved in his industry's national organization. Andrew Koblenz, the Industry Affairs Chief Operating Officer of the National Association of Automobile Dealers (NADA), said, "William has served as a member and then chairman of the Industry Relations Committee of NADA over the past four years. As the lead staff member for the I.R. committee, I have worked closely with William during this period.

"William does so many things well," Koblenz noted. "He is thoughtful, appreciative, and constructive in his approach to problems. He listens to people on all sides of an issue before he decides how to proceed, and he is unbelievably reliable. If William says he will handle something, you can consider it done. He is known for improving everything he is involved in. William is not afraid to address problems that may be unpleasant or difficult to tackle and is one of the most impressive people that I have had the pleasure of knowing."

Koblenz concluded, "William is caring, thoughtful, giving, and is concerned for and interested in people. Working with him is a pleasure, because he values your opinion and causes you to feel that you are making an important contribution to what ever project you are working on."

Robert Davis is an employee of Bradshaw Automotive and first met William in 1979 when Bradshaw became a Cadillac-Olds dealer. Davis said about his boss and friend, "William is a great conciliator. While his business acumen is impeccable, I think one of his greatest strengths is his ability to achieve his goals without creating a rift. He allows both parties to feel satisfaction with the process and the results. It is obvious that William is gracious and has a great reputation."

Davis continued, "Much of William's success comes from his attention to details and his remarkable memory. William is a man with great drive and ambition. His successes are a result of his intelligence, energy, a commitment to his goals, and his deep moral convictions, but perhaps the best thing I can say about William is how devoted he is to his family."

When Bradshaw purchased the dealership in Greenville, SC, employee Larry Frank figured that he might be fired. "You never know what will happen when new ownership comes in," Frank stated. "I had talked with another dealership who offered me a job with a very good financial package, but when William and I talked, he told me that I needed to prove myself to him, because he didn't know me and didn't know if I could handle the job. I took that as a challenge and decided to stay with him. I wanted to prove that I was the man for the job. That small dealership which was losing money was turned around quickly, and we made money for his shop.

"William's advice to me has always been, 'I want you to do what's right. Never, ever let money become more important than doing the right thing. We are about integrity, and we'll do what is right by the customer.' Being with Bradshaw Automotive is an easy place to work, and I've become like a part of his family. I tell our new employees that William is just like us. He will occasionally come around the shop to just sit and talk with us."

Frank concluded, "I once went to William to ask him to help me get a loan. I figured I would go to the bank and work out the details. Well, William had the banker come to see me at the shop. That's just the way he is. For William, life is pretty simple. As the owner, he just allows his employees to be successful, and he doesn't micromanage what we do."

Ray Williams, Jr., has been William Bradshaw's attorney and friend for over 25 years. Williams has been highly impressed that Bradshaw's dealerships didn't happen as a result of good fortune or a gift. "William was able to negotiate and purchase dealerships and then operate them successfully. All of his dealerships are extremely well-run and are financially successful. William's successes in business have resulted in the stable employment of over 400 individuals with well-paying jobs.

"William makes a great impression on people," Williams said. "He is always courteous to everyone, whether it is a secretary in my office, an employee in his dealership, a customer, the president of a business, or anyone else. He shows everyone the greatest respect. Most businesses assume the character traits of the people who run them, and William's courtesy and service-mentality are reflected in the conduct of his employees. His people have a desire to serve and satisfy the customer, and that has resulted in customers choosing William's dealerships over others."

Ray Williams continued, "William is a man that always says what he will do and then does it. He also expects others to do likewise. This trait causes those in the community to feel comfortable in dealing with William. People like to do business with William because they can trust him."

* * * * * * * * * *

Anyone who spends time or has a conversation with William Bradshaw quickly finds out how important his family is. William Bradshaw and Annette Brantley were married in 1969, when William was 19 and Annette was 17. They have two children—Wes Bradshaw (28) and Angie Donovan (31). Wes is the general manager of the Greer dealership, while Angie's husband, Bill Donovan, is the general manager at the Honda, Acura, and Infiniti dealerships in Greenville, SC. The Donovans have three children—Caroline (6), Carson (3), and Ellie (2).

Bradshaw Automotive: Owner William Bradshaw

Angie Donovan spoke affectionately about her dad, "He is just the finest man I will ever know. Dad is a confident risk-taker, is remarkably positive, and has the ability to see the best in every situation. He is able to inspire those around him to be better, simply by the way he lives his own life. My father is very generous, both with his wealth and his heart."

One lesson that Angie learned from her dad was never to worry about something that you can't do anything about. She continued, "My dad always smiles, and he never seems to be bearing the weight of all the pressure that he must feel. He claims to be able to sleep at night, despite the enormous responsibilities that are his. Dad encourages others, and he is generous with his praise. His positive attitude inspires others to be the best they can be, and he never misses an opportunity to help someone. My dad is a giver, both to those he knows and loves and to people that he has never even met."

When considering why her father has been a success in life, she replied,

"My father has never let go of his hopes and dreams. He has never let setbacks keep him from trying again. My father is passionate about the things he believes in and is a positive-thinker. He is patient and knows that the goal he has set is worth all of the effort that is required to achieve it. He is powerful, yet sensitive; he is determined and strong-willed; yet he is gracious and humble. He has the ability to push beyond what is comfortable, but he never considers failure to be an option."

To Angie Donovan, her dad is unparalleled as a father and grandfather. In her words she asked, "Have I mentioned that William Bradshaw is the best grandfather a kid could ever know? His grandchildren love him dearly, and, despite how busy he is, Dad always makes time for them. They are truly blessed to have such a decent, loving man to look up to, and so am I. I truly cherish every day with my dad, and I don't take a second spent with him for granted."

Angie's husband, Bill Donovan, has a unique place in the Bradshaw family since he is an employee of Bradshaw Automotive, is William's son-in-law, and is father of William's three grandchildren. Bill showed obvious admiration and respect for his father-in-law/boss when he said, "First and foremost, William Bradshaw has unconditional love for his family, which I believe is his first priority. He loves and cares for his family like no one I have ever seen."

He continued, "When William is talking to you, you are his primary focus. In business and in life, William is always looking for a 'win-win' resolution, regardless of the situation. People in our area know William for his professionalism in business and his involvement in the community."

In his words, Bill Donovan knows William to be a 'gadget king.' "William just can't pass up any gadget," Bill laughed. "He can't even walk past a yo-yo; he just can't help himself. William has to pick it up, run the yo-yo through its paces, and brush-up on his tricks. He is actually pretty good at it, too!

"I think William is successful in business and in life for many reasons," Bill said. "He is excellent at measuring risk and forecasting results, but, above all, William is the most ethical businessman I know. When you combine these attributes with his genuine care for those who work with him, you will find a package that is rare in any industry. In William's life, he loves best, understands best, and leads best."

Brantley Dunaway is William Bradshaw's nephew. Brant (the son of Annette's sister Sharon) is not in the automobile business (He is a producer of feature films) but has immense love and respect for William. "William was the best man in my wedding and has been a beacon and a role model for me. I don't know anyone else quite like William Bradshaw. He is unbelievably humble, and it would take the life experience and knowledge of an artist, a scholar, a theologian, and a poet - all wrapped up in one - to answer why William has been successful. Many people admire him because of his business successes. I simply admire the man."

Dunaway told of a poem that he learned in college. "From the moment I first read it," he said, "and to this day, I instantly think of William. It truly describes William Bradshaw to me."

The True Gentleman
By John Walter Wayland (Virginia, 1899)

> *The True Gentleman is the man whose conduct proceeds from good will and an acute sense of propriety,*
>> *and whose self-control is equal to all emergencies; who does not make the poor man conscious of his poverty,*
> *the obscure man of his obscurity, or any man of his inferiority or deformity;*
> *who is himself humbled if necessity compels him to humble another;*
> *who does not flatter wealth, cringe before power, or boast of his own possessions or achievements;*
> *who speaks with frankness but always with sincerity and sympathy;*
> *whose deed follows his word; who thinks of the rights and feelings of others, rather than his own;*
> *and who appears well in any company, a man with whom honor is sacred and virtue safe.*

"I feel that if I could be only half the man he is," Dunaway concluded, "then I will have achieved something extraordinary. I am blessed that William is my uncle."

Annette Brantley Bradshaw recalled that she and William started dating when he was 17 and she was 15. She said, "We were so young then, but William really hasn't changed much in all these years. He was very kind and caring in those days and is the same today. He cares deeply about his family, his employees, and their families."

She continued, "In business, William is a very good decision-maker; he has very strong business ethics and a deep passion for his profession. From the time William went into the automobile industry, he has always treated others the way he wanted to be treated. William has become successful because he set specific goals early in his career. He knew where he wanted to be at different stages in our lives.

"I think William will be remembered by his family and friends as a man who proved anyone can make it in life if they work hard and devote themselves to being a success. He will be remembered in the business world as a man who worked hard to make this world a better place in which to live, both for himself and for others."

* * * * * * * * * *

William and Annette attend Taylor's First Baptist Church in Greer. His opportunity for service there is restricted because of his increasing involvement in NADA where he will be Vice-Chairman during 2005. In 2006, William will become Chairman of NADA, which will probably require about 80% of his time. National Automobile Dealers Association is an organization made up of 20,000 dealer members and is led by 63 directors and over 400 staff employees.

"Some of my success was just good fortune and the blessings of God," William confessed. "When a door opened, I had to walk through it, but a couple of times you look back and wonder, 'How did I get where I am?' I'm not the smartest kid on the block, and if they tested me, I probably wouldn't have been in the top half of the class. I wasn't a great student growing up, at least through the first ten or eleven years of high school, because I was focused on simply getting out of school and going to work. I wasn't involved in sports and wasn't in the inner circles socially, but when I ran into Roger Greene at Willingham, he got me pointed in the right direction.

"About this same time, I met Annette, and we began to date. She had a very positive impact on my life. Next I met Mr. Bob Richards who hired me and gave me a great foundation and education in the automobile business. At this point, I had decided that I wanted to be successful at something, and, by pure coincidence, I was lucky enough to get into a business that I love. I wasn't looking to get into the car business necessarily; I was going to school and planning on becoming a CPA. There I was, a semester away from a degree in accounting, when I just lucked into the car business. I didn't feel like I was even going to work each day because it was so rewarding. I became a student of the business and tried to learn as much as I could about this industry. I plugged away, but had I not run into Mr. Ed Sherwood, who was willing to be my mentor and my financial backer as well as being like another father to me, who knows what would have happened?"

Even with all of the financial and personal successes that William has achieved, he is convinced that the best things that he has done in life relate directly to his family. He stated, "I have been married 35 years to a wonderful lady who has supported and encouraged me all along the way. Together, we have raised two wonderful, very productive children who are very good people. They have made their mother and me extremely proud. Our daughter Angie, the mother of our three grandchildren, is a wonderful daughter, a great mother, and I'm so proud of her. Our son Wes is a fine young man who works with me in the automobile business and runs two of our stores. Wes and Angie are both super people with good hearts, good habits, and good values. They are both good citizens and are leaders in the community."

Regarding his own success in life, William continued, "With the help of my wife and family, my mentors, and our dedicated employees, I have been able to achieve a level of success in my chosen field. Receiving recognition as a *TIME Magazine* Quality Dealer in 1997 really meant a lot to me, as well as being elected to a leadership position in NADA, our national association."

William spoke with conviction, "I've been blessed in my life, and we got some breaks from the Good Lord. I make an effort to give back to the community and do things in our industry that benefit other people. For years and years, I wasn't involved because I was working so hard to make a living, pay my bills, and get out of debt. I did that a long time and felt a little guilty, because I was around others who were doing a lot more in the community than I was. In the last few years, I got my feet on the ground financially, and we got the debts paid off. We got the right people in place in our business where I could finally do more to give back to the community."

When the question was asked, "William, how do you hope to be remembered?" his reply was classic. "This may sound corny, but I just want to be remembered as someone who made a difference in life. I want to make a difference in my family, in my business with my employees and customers, in my community, and our industry."

William concluded, "Today, I would tell young people that there are great opportunities ahead for them, so it is vitally important that they make the right choices in their lives when they are young."

William Bradshaw certainly made the right choices.

The William Bradshaw family: William, Ellie Donovan, Annette, Wes, Caroline and Carson Donovan, Angie and Bill Donovan

Trust Me

Richard A. (Rick) Bennett
Class of 1970

*"And you shall love the Lord your God with all your
heart, soul, mind, and strength; The second is this:
You shall love your neighbor as yourself."*
                                                    –Mark 11:30-31

Rick, Bill Jr., and Terri Bennett grew up in a family where Mama was in charge of having fun, and Daddy was in charge of everything else. Bill and Fay Bennett made sure their three children knew that they were their parents' first priority. Middle child Rick, said, "We had great balance in our family. Bill, Terri, and I knew from the beginning that we were important."

Rick Bennett grew up loving baseball. After playing at Willingham High School for Coach Billy Henderson, he enrolled at Mercer University in Macon and started for two years at third base for the Bears. Mercer was coached in those days by the legendary Claude Smith. Bennett, a terrific player, confessed, "I was not the best student at Mercer, but I loved baseball and was having a great time."

Rick's dad, the man who had the greatest influence on his son's life, told Rick, "You could improve your hitting if you increased your upper body strength." So Rick, along with his older brother Billy, Key Chambers, a friend from church, and Mark Stevens, a high school friend and Mercer baseball teammate, all got jobs at the Blue Bird Body Company in nearby Fort Valley.

The four young college guys awoke daily at 4:45 a.m. to make the 25-minute trek down I-75 to work at Blue Bird, a massive plant which manufactured the yellow school buses used all over the world. Work-day for the four Maconites was from 6 a.m. until 3 p.m., five days a week.

Billy Bennett's job was to put the red tail-lights on each bus as it left the assembly line, and his job was not bad. Rick was assigned to be an apprentice for a fellow who ran an air hammer and 'bucked rivets' for eight hours a day. His was a demanding, physical job but was exactly what Bennett's dad had in mind for his son's summer job. Mark Stevens's job was to do the final sanding on each bus before it was painted yellow.

Key Chambers had the enviable task of walking around for eight hours with a small paintbrush and a Dixie cup filled with yellow paint. His job was strictly cosmetic, touching up nicks and scratches with his paint brush before the "Yellow Hounds" rolled off the line. In Rick's view, "Key Chambers had the 'plum' job!"

The college boys from Macon would gather each morning during their break to rest and talk. None of them was enjoying what he was doing, primarily because all were getting up in the middle of the night to drive to work. Bennett recalled, "Mark Stevens would walk up to the rest of us during a break after sanding buses for four hours. When he pulled off his goggles, he looked like a raccoon. Mark was covered with dust, except where his goggles protected his eyes. It was hilarious."

Rick ended each day exhausted from lifting the big, heavy, lead bucking-bar and running the air hammer. The fellow that Bennett was assisting had a beam that held up the roof which he considered his office space, since no one on the assembly line actually had an office. The man had a plaque that he proudly displayed for all to see which noted that he had driven three million rivets at Blue Bird. "That was a truly amazing feat," Bennett remembered thinking, "but that's not exactly the kind of plaque that I have in mind to display on my wall at home or in my office some day."

One by one, Billy, Key, and Mark all found jobs in Macon which had more reasonable work hours. Rick finished out the summer at Blue Bird. He got strong and fit from the physical work that he performed in the summer of 1971. Rick also never played another game of organized baseball.

After his freshman year at Mercer, Rick saw Eddie Creech, a former Mercer shortstop who had a great high school career in Atlanta prior to his stellar baseball and basketball careers at Mercer. Creech had signed a pro baseball contract with the Montreal Expos and was in their minor league system. He stopped by Mercer in the off-season and was working out with the Bears in the fall of 1972.

According to Rick, "Creech was an amazing baseball player. He could hit for average, hit for power, he had a great arm, and was awesome in the field. I played third base beside Eddie and saw him go deep in the hole between short and third, glove it, and fire a bullet to first base. He was phenomenal and was the best baseball player I had ever seen in person."

So Bennett asked Creech, "What do you think, Eddie? How long will it take you to get to the majors?"

Creech responded, "I'll never make it."

Rick remembered thinking that if Eddie Creech couldn't make it in pro baseball, there was no way he would ever play. Bennett knew instantly that his days of pursuing the dream that many young boys in the South had of playing in the majors were over. Period. Done.

However, Rick's summer at Blue Bird Body Company in Fort Valley helped him realize several things. One lesson was that an education was extremely important, and two, baseball was not going to be his ticket in life. Those realizations ultimately moved Rick Bennett out of baseball and into the real world.

Another life-changing event in Rick Bennett's life was when his older brother Billy was injured in a serious automobile wreck. Though Billy survived the crash, his long period of recuperation either caused or allowed Rick to learn about commitment and duty. Billy was scheduled to begin work at Bateman's Grocery on Pio Nono Avenue in Macon when the wreck occurred. Rick's dad felt a sense of responsibility because Billy was supposed to go to work at Bateman's on a Monday, but, due to the wreck and subsequent injuries, it would be impossible for Billy to be there. Thus, Mr. Bennett called on his under-age son Rick to take Billy's place at Bateman's. It was there that Rick first learned about obligation and hard work.

* * * * * * * * * *

Rick Bennett is a man who understands trust, and even he wonders when it all really started. When did he learn to trust people so quickly and completely? Whenever it was, wherever it was, Rick became a guy who believed in others and trusted them from the beginning. He continued to trust others until he was given a sound reason not to trust them.

Rick grew up in the Sussex Drive/Canterbury Road area of South Macon and attended Joseph N. Neel Elementary School. Cherokee Heights United Methodist was his home church until he turned 16 and was invited to Mabel White Memorial Baptist Church by Mary Alice Grimes, a neighbor. Mabel White was an easy place to like in those days because it was, according to Rick, "A target-rich environment for an awkward, nerdy, 16-year-old guy like me."

The pastor at Mabel White in 1968 when Bennett first visited there was Rev. James W. (Jimmy) Waters. Evangelism was the primary message in those days, and when Bennett was presented with the Gospel, he immediately responded to it and became a Christian. In retrospect, Rick remembered, "My personality and virtually everything about me changed from that time forward. Where I had been shy, timid, and somewhat reserved, I became more confident, upbeat, and more positive about life."

Rev. Jimmy Waters became a great influence on Rick Bennett's young life in many ways. Rick said about Jimmy Waters, "He taught me lessons about life that were timeless and unchanging, and he became a mentor to me. I was dating his daughter, Deborah, at the time. One night, when I walked in their home to take Deborah on a date, her dad tossed the keys to his brand new Thunderbird, complete with a Georgia State Patrol siren, lights, and accompanying bells and whistles, to me and said, 'Why don't you take the new car tonight?'"

Bennett thought, "Wow! Talk about trust." From that moment on, Rick Bennett learned a life-lesson about trust. He decided that you start off giving others the benefit of the doubt and allow them to prove that you can't trust them, not that you can.

In retrospect, Bennett considered, "Due to the less-than-desirable piece of junk that I was driving in those days, Deborah's dad was probably loaning me the Thunderbird more for her protection than he was showing his trust in me."

Bennett notes how 'trusting experiences' shaped his life in such a profound way. In fact, Rick's business methods today demonstrate that he delegates responsibility and authority to others. "I allow people to get their work done, and I trust them to do it in the manner that we agreed it would be done. That doesn't change until they prove that they either can't or won't do the work."

* * * * * * * * * *

In the fall of 1972, Julie Blair, also from South Macon and Mabel White Baptist Church, began to attract the serious attention of Rick Bennett. Julie graduated from McEvoy High School, the sister-school of all-male Willingham. She was in her first year at the Georgia Baptist School of Nursing in Atlanta. By now, Julie and Rick had a serious dating relationship going on.

Rick's best friend and Mercer baseball teammate, Mark Stevens, considered transferring to Georgia State University in Atlanta where Mark's older brother, Larry Stevens, had attended. Thus, Rick, Mark Stevens, and fellow South Maconite and Willingham graduate, Ben Hinson, lived together in a rental apartment in Forest Park, and all three began their junior year in college at Georgia State.

Rick talked to Georgia State's baseball coach about the possibility of playing there but decided that those days were over. Clueless about what to major in at Georgia State, Bennett finally declared a major in accounting without even knowing what accounting was. Mark Stevens's brother Larry already had a good job with Price-Waterhouse (PW) as an accountant. Larry wore a tie to work, had a desk by himself, and actually brought home a sizeable paycheck. With this in mind, accounting sounded like the right direction for Rick Bennett.

Rick entered the academic world of accounting for a couple of reasons — one, because he knew and respected Larry Stevens, and two, because he was good in analytical subjects and thought math was easy. He later learned the great myth regarding accounting. Rick said, "The myth is that people think math and accounting are interrelated. The truth is that they have very little to do with each other. Basically, if you could add, subtract, divide, and multiply, then you could be quite good in accounting. Advanced math was not important in the accounting world."

After a lackluster academic showing at Mercer University, Rick transferred to Georgia State University and graduated with honors with a Bachelor in Business Administration degree and a major in accounting. With marriage just around the corner for Rick and Julie, his primary focus was getting a good job, and PW had jobs available. Rick was looking for a career which had two things — good pay with opportunities for advancement. Plus, the job wasn't dealing with bucking rivets.

Bennett remembered, "Price Waterhouse in Atlanta was aggressive in the recruitment of young accounting majors. Larry Stevens invited me to lunch and introduced me around. He was responsible for guiding my early career in accounting."

In those days, you could take the CPA exam in May if you were going to graduate in June. Rick took the CPA exam which is considered by many people to be the most grueling professional exam of all. It took two and a half days to take all four sections of the exam. At this point, Rick and Julie were engaged, but after completing the CPA exam Rick picked Julie up at her nursing school and immediately said, "Darlin, 'I don't know what I'll do, but one thing I won't be is a CPA. I'll never pass that test, but don't worry, I'll sell something, and we're still getting married.'"

When the results came back, he had passed two of the four parts. Of course, Price Waterhouse was interested in their accountants passing all four parts, so in November, Rick took and passed the rest of the CPA exam, which was a very big deal. Then he went to work with PW and was involved in mergers, acquisitions, selling businesses, and doing audits. He worked for Price Waterhouse LLP from June, 1974 to 1980.

While at PW, he met Ken Thrasher, also a native of Macon, in August, 1974. Bennett said, "Early in our PW careers, Ken and I were basically considered 'grunts' which meant we were expected to work as long and as hard as management deemed necessary. Seventy-five hour weeks were commonplace in those days. You simply did what you were told to do for as long as they told you to do it, and if you got tired, then you could go home and sleep some and come on back to work."

Rick and Julie were married on July 20, 1974. Most of his accounting jobs at that time were out of town, which meant he was on the road 30 weeks a year. Meanwhile, Julie worked double shifts at the Georgia Baptist Hospital in Atlanta. Rick said, "For the first three years of our young marriage, we weren't at home together very much. Our lives were about work, sleep, and work some more, which was placing a lot of stress on both of us."

As a result of frustration and exhaustion, Rick went into Ed Pease's office, closed the door, and said to his boss, "I've always heard and have been told to never give the company an ultimatum, and I'm not giving you an ultimatum, but something's gotta give. Something has to change, because I can't travel this way any longer."

Pease called the tax office at PW about Bennett, and they found a place for him there. They had a spot and it involved very little travel, so Rick moved into the tax department of Price Waterhouse in January, 1977. Though he wasn't traveling, Rick still worked 13 weeks in a row—seven days a week, 10 hours a day. Bennett remembered asking himself, "Why am I doing this?"

The busy season for the tax business runs from January through April 15. According to Bennett, "That's when the accounting firms load you up on work." But he got through it and the job got easier. Now he was considered a 'tax senior,' though he really didn't know much about tax accounting. His friend, Ken Thrasher, joined him in the tax department soon after the busy season was over.

It was in the tax department that Bennett and Thrasher met Bob Medlin, Tom Burns, and Lofton Odom. All were tax seniors with PW in Atlanta in July,

1977, and they would frequently talk with each other after hours about, 'How do we do this tax thing?' The answer was that PW had a 'catch-up program' for guys like them where one would be trained for six months. Rick got an 'unofficial' master's degree in tax in those six months where all of his free time was consumed by studying tax digests.

Rick recalled, "After working together for the next three years, these five guys developed a bond that was different from other friendships at our firm. We were all about to become tax managers, and during this process Price Waterhouse wanted you to believe that the best job in the world was to be a partner in the firm, and the way you became a partner and became successful was by making the firm the first priority in life."

Bennett and Thrasher began to think, "The firm might be in the running for third on our list of priorities, but it will never be first." Rick and Ken were first and foremost 'family guys.' Additionally, Rick and Julie's first child Russell was born in 1977.

Rick recalled that Bob Watson of PW was in charge of the tax department in those days. "Bob was a man of extremes, and he had some of the best and worst traits that a man could have. If Bob Watson's life was a 'round of golf, his scores would be either triple bogey or birdie.' Watson trained Ken and me while we were tax managers. We were his people. Additionally, Bob encouraged us to become partners with PW, which was a 'carrot of sorts.' But as our work load increased, the carrot was beginning to get stale."

Watson taught Rick and Ken how to take care of clients and told them that sitting in their offices behind a desk was not the way you do that. Bennett and Thrasher would respond, "Bob, you don't understand. We have work to do."

Watson would respond, "That's why you guys, who are now tax managers, have seniors working below you. Delegate your work to them and expect them to do it. Trust them." Thus, Bob Watson became another guy in the life of Rick Bennett who taught him to trust people.

Bennett recalled, "Bob was about to drive us crazy because he was so adamant about us getting out into the workplace where our clients were. For the most part, we couldn't even go to the office if Bob was in town. If we did, Watson would say, 'Getcha butts outa here! Go see your clients. Go sit and talk with them about business and about their lives.'" So Rick and Ken learned to get out of the office and delegate more of their work to their underlings and trust them to perform.

It was in March, 1980, that Ken and Rick decided that one could only see his clients just so much without becoming a nuisance. Years earlier, Watson started taking Bennett with him to entertain their clients while playing golf. In the middle of the 'busy season' when their CPA's were working ridiculous hours, Bennett and Watson were leaving the office at 11 a.m. for Cherokee Country Club to have lunch and play golf with PW clients.

Ken and Rick also played tennis at Stone Mountain Park, which was near their homes, because Bob Watson wouldn't let them back in the office. One day, when they were sitting around after playing tennis, Bennett wisecracked, "You know, Ken, we could be working two jobs since we can't go to the office."

Soon, Rick Bennett followed Watson's lead and began taking CEO's and business owners to lunch and to play golf. Thus, he learned even more about his clients as he developed personal relationships with business owners.

* * * * * * * * * *

It was in April, 1980, that Rick Bennett and Ken Thrasher decided to 'take the plunge' and establish their own CPA firm. They had already been successful in the accounting world, but they knew they were destined to do this one thing. They determined from Day One that in their new company, family would be the No. 1 priority in their personal and corporate lives.

September, 1980, was the date that Bennett Thrasher (BT), a professional corporation of Certified Public Accountants and Consultants, was founded. Currently, BT is ranked among the largest CPA firms in Metro Atlanta (actually ranking as the second largest single-office accounting firm in Atlanta) area with eight partners and approximately 75 total personnel.

Bennett stated about their company, "First, every employee is mandated to take care of their family before they come to work. If an employee is preoccupied at work because of family issues, that employee will be less than effective while tending to their clients. Thus, if an employee must deal with a child or spouse before work, the time they arrive for work at BT isn't nearly as important as the fact that they have taken care of their family situation. A 10-hour day may run from 8 a.m. until 6 p.m., or it may be from 11 a.m. until 9 p.m. Working hard and doing the right thing, along with making family a priority, is vitally important at Bennett Thrasher."

BT is great place to work, according to their many employees. Because of the great trust that is built from the top down and the respect that is shown for each employee, the obvious result is loyalty within the firm. Certainly, there are 45 to 60-plus-hour weeks with deadlines and pressure, especially from January to April 15, but BT works extremely hard to meet the needs of their work force with support from the owners and support staff.

Rick spoke of the importance of hiring the right people who have the right attitudes about work and life. "We have to deal with people's attitudes. Chuck Swindoll is a Christian author and pastor who has written extensively about controlling our attitudes. Swindoll said, 'We can't keep things from happening to us, but we can determine how we will react to what happens.'"

One of the early lessons that BT employees learn was taken from a very short but meaningful book entitled *A Message to Garcia* by Elbert Hubbard. Bennett said, "While a prospective employee would be waiting in the lobby for an interview or an application, I would hand them a copy of *Garcia* and ask them to read it while they waited.

"*A Message to Garcia* is a book about a young lieutenant in the Army who was given an assignment by his commanding officer. He was instructed to deliver a message to General Garcia who was 'holed-up' in Cuba. There was no way to either radio or get communications to the general; so young Garcia took the message in an oil-skin pouch, secured it next to his heart, saluted his commanding officer, and delivered the message. The book wonderfully describes the type of employee that Bennett Thrasher looks for, and many prospective employees are not interested in that type of environment," Bennett said.

Rick Bennett, the co-managing shareholder along with Ken Thrasher, continues to work hard but in less obvious ways. "I average 37 calls a day at my office, and 24 of them are client calls. To both Ken and me, our clients are the masters of our time even today."

Rick and Ken are interesting partners, and both bring different skill-sets into their business. Thrasher said, "I have known Rick for almost 30 years since our rookie days at Price Waterhouse in 1974. Other than our wives, we probably know each other better than anyone else on earth. We worked together as audit staff, and we both transferred into tax together in 1977. We left PW in 1980 to form our partnership. It was just by chance that we both happened to have grown up in Macon. The rest, as they say, is history."

Thrasher continued, "Today we are a firm with more than 70 employees. I know Rick as a business partner, as a husband to Julie, and as a father to his three children. He is also a good friend, although we spend very little time together outside of business, except for going to the gym at lunch for the past 22 years."

Rick agreed with Ken and said, "We are very different from a style and personality standpoint, but we are very close on fundamental values such as faith in God, family first, and the importance of people and relationships."

Bennett said, "If you ask us both a question, I'll give you an answer in 10 minutes. Ken will take the time to analyze the data, but our answers will be the same most of the time."

"Rick goes by feel, while I am more thoughtful and calculated," Thrasher observed. "Rick's strengths are his integrity, character, intelligence, and people skills. He is the quintessential people person. Rick loves people and thrives on his relationships with the people in his life. He genuinely cares about people; they are important to him, and he wants the people around him to be satisfied. Rick is very giving of his time, and he is unimpressed with social status."

Ken continued, "Rick is goal-oriented, ambitious, he gets things done, and because he is a man of action, he can be impatient with processes that inhibit action and results. Rick has been as good a business partner as I could ever hope for. He respects my abilities and strengths. In fact, I believe we have thrived together because of the mutual respect we have for each other. We both recognize our own weaknesses, and we have 'played off' of each other's strengths. Rick has been honest with me, and we are committed to open, frequent communication."

Thrasher recalled a funny story about when he and Rick started their partnership. "Money was tight in those days. Rick drove an old Toyota that he had to jump-start, and it was missing a hubcap or two. I had a VW Rabbit that also had hubcaps missing, and the body was damaged on one side. When we went to see clients, we had to park strategically so the good side of our cars would show. Rick had to park on a hill so he could pop the clutch to get his car started. Those were the days."

* * * * * * * * *

Rick Bennett remains the consummate family man, and he and Julie have now been married for 29 years. They have a son, Russell (26), a graduate of the University of Georgia; a daughter, Natalie (23), a senior at Georgia State University; and Taylor (29), a graduate of Vanderbilt University. Taylor Wright is a story within herself.

Partners in fly fishing. Ken Thrasher (L) and Rick Bennett.

Taylor stated, "I first met Rick and Julie when my family moved to The Forest subdivision in Stone Mountain, and I was in the fourth grade. We lived directly across the street from the Bennetts, and I used to babysit for Russell and Natalie. One of my earliest memories was of Halloween when Julie would dress up as a witch and sit on her front porch. She played a cassette of scary sounds and waited for the kids to come by to trick-or- treat. My mom was diagnosed with cancer soon after we moved to The Forest, and she died four years later when I was 13. Rick and Julie were very supportive, and I looked to them for guidance."

Taylor continued, "Russell and I went to the Westminster School in Atlanta which was about a 35-minute drive from Stone Mountain. When I got my learner's permit at 15, Rick said that I would drive to school. I was so nervous about driving his shiny, new, black Jaguar, but he insisted. He must have been nervous, but he never showed it. I could not believe that he trusted me to drive his car.

"When I was sixteen," Taylor said, "I moved in with Rick, Julie, Russell, and Natalie, and very shortly afterwards, I went to work in Rick's office helping with anything that a 16-year-old could do. I think that every younger member of Rick's family who has ever lived in Atlanta has worked at Bennett Thrasher at some point in their lives.

"I can't remember exactly when I felt that I was part of their family," Taylor recalled, "but there were little things like Russell or Natalie introducing me as their sister that made me feel special. I remember an article that was written in the paper about Rick. At the end of the article, he had said that he had three children. I was just overwhelmed."

Taylor completed her high school education and was accepted at Vanderbilt University in Nashville, TN. She won a Walter Wattels Fellowship which meant she was able to go to London to study and work for a year. While in England, she was assigned to Airline Claims at Lloyd's of London and met Nigel Wright, a nice English boy, who happened to be a claims defense attorney from London. They fell in love, were married in 1999, and Rick Bennett gave the bride away.

She continued, "Rick has always been the person to whom everyone turns for advice. He must get as many personal calls at work as he does business calls. He helps everyone. Rick is also the person that everyone wants to talk to, whether it is in a board meeting or a family reunion. You will always see several people that want his opinion, his advice, or just want to talk to him. Rick treats everyone the same way. He could discuss your great aunt's infected bunions as easily as he could discuss your tax situation, and one of his major strengths is that he always makes people feel at ease.

"I think that one of the reasons Rick is so successful on so many levels is that he always tries to do what he says he is going to do. That is one of Rick's many 'life-isms.' He is so honest and always talks straight to people. One of his favorite sayings, when faced with an extended curfew question, was that 'nothing good ever happens after midnight.'"

Today, Taylor and Nigel have two young daughters, Henrietta and Amelia. Thus, Rick and Julie Bennett now have two granddaughters. Taylor concluded, "Seeing Rick with my two little girls is the sweetest thing. He loves children, and when I found out that I was pregnant with our first child (Henrietta), Rick was so excited. Today, Henrietta calls him 'granddad.' Rick is such a great person"

The Bennett family's original reaction to Taylor and her dilemma was a result of their Christian background. Julie remembered, "When I was growing up, my family had helped a lot of people who were in need, so coming to the aid of a young teenager was nothing new for us."

Ken Thrasher had these words about his business partner, "Julie and Rick have successfully raised three children with God's help, and in my book that is as great an accomplishment as any human being can achieve. Taylor was brought into their family as a 16-year-old at a time when they easily could have passed on that responsibility. I think Rick will always be remembered as a man of faith, a family man, and a good businessman/CPA/ business advisor. He is a true professional who genuinely cares about people."

* * * * * * * * *

Rick had always wanted a place to go to get out of Buckhead (a suburb of Atlanta). He recalled, "Buckhead wasn't all there was in the real world, so we bought a 110-acre farm near Monroe, GA, in 1989. At the time, Russell was 12,

Taylor was 15, and Natalie was 7."

Russell and Natalie loved the farm though it was extremely primitive. In the beginning, the house, which was built in 1827, only had a wood stove for heat. Rick continued, "As we began to add on to the original structure, one day I told the bulldozer operator to just push a section of the house away so we could expand the old house. That's the kind of shape it was in."

The end result was a great place for the Bennetts to be a family while getting away from the city. It was a place where Rick and Julie could go, relieve stress, and forget about business for a while.

Julie remembered, "We bought horses soon after we got the farm, and Natalie and Taylor found that they really enjoyed their rides. Horseback riding became Rick and Natalie's special time. Rick's whole demeanor changes whenever Natalie's name is mentioned.

"His love for her is exhibited through a full-body smile. Natalie has Rick's personality. She is always concerned about other people and is very trusting in her interaction with others."

Rick told about the day a man showed up at the door of the farm house. "The guy had a long, unkempt beard, was disheveled, and quite scary in his appearance. He was our next-door neighbor and looked so bad that I decided that someone 'had to try to look that bad.' But the man politely introduced himself to us; he told us that the previous owner of the property had allowed him to hunt there for years, and would we allow him to continue to hunt there?

"While I was talking with him, Julie was strenuously shaking her head, 'No!' I told him, 'I'll make a deal with you. You can hunt on the property, but you have to keep other people off the property. I can't have my son in the woods if other people are out there hunting.' He assured me that no one else would hunt there."

So, it was a deal, but when he left, Julie was in disbelief and railed, "I can't believe you are going to let a total stranger hunt on our property! What are you thinking?"

Rick replied, "He's done nothing wrong. I know he doesn't look like much, but I don't have any reason not to trust this man. Plus, I don't know how to hunt, but he does. I'm not a fisherman, but he is. And neither Russell nor I know how to call and hunt turkey, but he does."

To Rick and his son Russell, life on the farm was about as good as it could get, and a friendship was started that day at the Bennett's farm, because Rick's philosophy was to trust people until they proved to him that they shouldn't be trusted.

Hunting soon became a major part of Russell's life. Rick and Russell would frequently drive to the farm after a Friday night football game so they could rise early and hunt on Saturday mornings. When Russell turned 16, he got an F-150 pickup truck that he drove to 'preppy' Westminster School.

Rick said, "Russell would wear camouflage, flannel shirts, and boots to school. He became known as the 'Buckhead Redneck,' but he couldn't care less. In fact, several of his buddies at school soon adopted the same 'dress code,' drove pickup trucks, and began to spend time on the Bennett farm as well. Russell and his friends began to learn what was real and what was not."

Today, Russell is a real estate developer with Richport Properties. He also works as a conservation planner with the Georgia Land Trust. He and his wife, Sarah, a high school counselor, were married in May, 2003, and now live at the farm near Monroe. Natalie is an artist, a journalist, and is completing her degree at Georgia State University. Nigel, Taylor, and their two daughters have relocated to Atlanta where Nigel practices law.

* * * * * * * * *

Rick currently spends an inordinate amount of time with meaningful charities and benevolent ministries. He is on the Board of Advisors for the Shepherd's Spinal Center in Atlanta. According to Bennett, "As one of the world's finest hospitals and clinics of its kind, their function is not just to keep the patient alive but to get them back into the community."

He is on the Board of Governors for the Vinings Club, where he exercises religiously three-days a week and is involved in The Bridge.

Bennett said, "The Bridge is an organization of the Foster Care system of Georgia. It is a secure facility that specializes in intense counseling. The Bridge is expressly for kids who can't be in a private home. It is located in the southwest section of Atlanta and is a 'common sense' program that has taken the children's' psychological care system by storm. The youngsters there have no reason to believe that anybody loves them, and they have very good reasons to believe that nobody loves them."

Rick related the story about a boy (14) who had been in 30 foster homes. Bennett asked the question, "Why would this kid think that anybody loves him?" At The Bridge, they accentuate the positive and eliminate the negative. This 14-year-old had major anger management issues and had bitten 13 people. He got mad and bit them hard."

He continued, "The boy had not gotten angry and had not bitten anyone in two weeks, so they had a celebration for him with a cake and all of the trimmings. At The Bridge, they celebrated his two weeks of doing well, and, in my mind, this method of handling problem children has proven to be 100-times more effective than the punishment of an act of transgression."

According to Bennett, the concepts and philosophy of The Bridge are sweeping through the United States rapidly. He related, "Instead of punishing bad behavior, they are celebrating a win. In the past, when he would get attention for biting someone, now he gets attention for not biting. In short, it's 'do right and have a party.' I believe in The Bridge, so I give my time to this ministry."

Rick Bennett is a family man. According to their friends, Rick and Julie have a solid, committed marriage that is based on truth and mutual trust.

Rick concurred, "Julie trusts me completely, because how many women would send their husbands all over the world to play golf like Julie sends me?"

He continued about his wife, "Julie always expects the best from me. She has been the most significant influence in my adult life. She has always known when I could do better, and she has always been able to tell me the truth."

The Irish Rovers: Rick Bennett (2nd from left) and friends in Scotland.

Julie Bennett spoke about Rick, "He has always treated everyone he meets with respect. Rick is fun-loving, competitive, driven, smart and confident. Those who know him speak of his willingness to help other people, and they appreciate the way he listens to what they say. I think people will always remember Rick for his integrity and his passion for life, his family, and his friends."

Interestingly, it is Ken Thrasher and Julie Bennett who are most similar in personality. Rick said, "Both Ken and Julie are analytical in their approach to a problem. They both use lots of data and will go through a methodical process to reach a conclusion. I usually go by instincts and intuition."

Rick said, "If I tell Julie that my shoulder hurts, I'll wake up the next morning, and she will have a list of six things that she has researched in medical books. She'll ask, 'Does it hurt when you do this?' Then I'll call the doctor and tell him I'm having these symptoms. He'll ask me, 'What does Julie say?' And 99 times out of 100, he will go with Julie's diagnosis."

Rick's church and his Christian faith have always been major parts of his life. His closest friendships in life were developed at Smoke Rise Baptist Church in Stone Mountain. These 11 men, affectionately known by some as the Irish Rovers, vacation together, dine together, and are basically each others' best friends. The Irish Rovers range in age from 51 to 78 and claim to be "each others' hobby." Their wives are glad that their husbands have such good friends and consider them 'the most harmless guys ever.'

One such friend is John Edgar. Edgar said, "I met Rick and Julie about 25 years ago. We became good friends and worked on the church's finance committee together when Smoke Rise was in the process of building a 1600-seat sanctuary from 1983-1986. Rick was instrumental in arranging the outside bank financing for the building program. The sanctuary, which is located at the base of Stone Mountain, is now a wonderful Christian testimony for all of Metro Atlanta and Georgia."

Edgar continued, "Rick is a brother to me. He is a best friend that I trust with everything I have. I know him as a confidant in good times and bad times. He is a man who knows how to listen.

"On the lighter side, Rick is also a very keen competitor. We have a group of guys who have taken trips to Scotland and Ireland to play golf. We normally invite about six to eight guys on the trips. On one particular trip, we had a new fellow along from Mississippi. He was a left-hander named J.D., and he was really a great guy. Unfortunately, he was about as competitive as Rick. One night over dinner, J.D. looked over at me and said he wanted to challenge me to a 9-hole golf match. He wanted me (as a right-hander) to play left-handed, and he would turn around and play right-handed on one of the shorter courses in Castle Rock, Northern Ireland.

"As I began to tell J.D. how inept I was trying to do anything left-handed, Rick, also a right-hander, jumped in and accepted J.D.'s challenge. They agreed on a 50 quid bet, and that night they both went out to the parking lot to practice. They were trying to hit balls over the road into the ocean. Rick was swinging lefty, and J.D. was swinging righty, so we named the competition the 'Lefty-Righty Open.'"

Edgar recalled, "The next afternoon after our regular matches and after quite a few pints, Rick and J.D. went out to the short par-3 course for their match with the rest of us close behind. The match was on.

"J.D. won the first hole on the par-3 with a '7'. After four holes, Rick was down by three holes with only five holes left to play, but the scene was set for Rick to rise to the occasion. He got back into the match by winning the next three holes. Now, they were all even with two holes to play. They halved the eighth hole. So while the rest of us were laughing and heckling, Rick and J.D. were hooking up for a huge finish."

John Edgar continued the story, "Well, as we all knew he would, Rick was beginning to get his left-handed swing into a pretty good groove. He had the honor on the ninth and last hole, and he laced a wicked 7-iron (left-handed, mind you) right onto the green. J.D. was whipped right then and there as he barely got his tee shot off the tee box. It was a great match and a great comeback."

Edgar offered a word of advice to future opponents of Bennett. "If you ever play golf with Rick, he never takes a practice swing. Rick's opinion is that practice swings only slow down the game. However, if he ever swings and misses the ball, be sure to charge him a stroke, because he'll try to convince you that it was only a practice swing."

* * * * * * * * *

As a founder and chief executive of Bennett Thrasher, Rick and Ken have been in business together for nearly 25 years. In Thrasher's words, "Rick takes care of the people. They know that he will tell them the truth and be honest with them."

Bennett concluded with great passion, "I have no question about *who* I am in life. I've got it. Not only do I know *who* I am, but I know what my purpose is for being on this earth. With me, people know exactly who I am and what they are getting with me.

"But the best things that I have ever done in life deal with my wife and my children. A great moment in my life and my family's life was when we invited Taylor into our home, and helping with The Bridge has brought incredible fulfillment to me. Of course, when we established our business —Bennett Thrasher—we were truly creating more than just a business. We were developing a ministry for our lives."

Rick and Julie Bennett have lived very full and meaningful lives to this point. They have been married for 30 years and are active members of Druid Hills Baptist Church in Atlanta.

Rick concluded, "I am a man who has been truly blessed."

Riding horses at the farm. Julie, Russell, Natalie, Taylor and Rick Bennett.

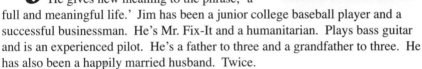

Angel Flight

James Alvin (Jim) Lambert
Class of 1964

*"I can do all things through Christ who
strengthens me."*
                    –Philippians 4:13

Jim Lambert has been a lot of things in
life and is about as unique as they come.
He gives new meaning to the phrase, 'a
full and meaningful life.' Jim has been a junior college baseball player and a
successful businessman. He's Mr. Fix-It and a humanitarian. Plays bass guitar
and is an experienced pilot. He's a father to three and a grandfather to three. He
has also been a happily married husband. Twice.

"If I'm asked 'What is the best thing that I have ever done in my life?', it
would be that I have married both of my wives, Ann and Brenda," Jim stated.
"I can say, with no qualifications, that I have been so blessed to have had two
wonderful marriages. Sadly, many people are unable to say they have had one
wonderful marriage."

Jim Lambert graduated from Middle Georgia College in Cochran in 1966,
and then made what he considered an academic *faux pas* by attending Georgia
Tech for a year. "To say I didn't do real well at Tech would be understating it,"
Lambert laughed. "Then I went back to Middle Georgia College and took some
courses before transferring to Georgia Southern in Statesboro."

While a student at Southern, Jim met a pretty, blonde, talented, freshman
pianist from Savannah named Ann Womack. They dated from 1967 until
Lambert went into the Army and were engaged in 1970. "I wouldn't marry Ann
until I got out of the Army, but when I found out that I was being discharged
on August 4, she quickly set the wedding date for September 5, 1970, in
Savannah."

With his BBA degree with a major in management from Georgia Southern
College in 1969, Jim and Ann Lambert moved to Marietta where he began
his business career as an adjustor for Georgia Farm Bureau. Their only child,
Meredith, was born in 1973.

The summer of 1976 proved to be a time that would forever change the
Lamberts' lives. Ann Lambert was diagnosed with lupus, which attacked and
basically destroyed her kidneys. She went on dialysis shortly thereafter and led
a relatively normal life, playing piano and working in the music ministries of
her church. Ann had a kidney transplant in 1990 and became a patient in ICU at
Emory University Hospital for seven months.

Jim recalled, "I walked into her room one morning in January, 1991, and Ann said, 'Take me home. If I'm going to die, I don't want to die in this hospital.' I remember Dr. Whelchel, who was one of Ann's wonderful doctors at Emory, was making his morning rounds with several interns, since Emory is an excellent teaching hospital. I told him, 'Doc, Ann's ready to go home.' And he said, 'She is? Well, maybe soon.'"

Jim told him, "'No, now. She wants to go home now.' And maybe for the first time in Emory University Hospital history, a patient was dismissed from ICU to go home. We didn't even use an ambulance. I picked her up, and we drove home to my parents' house in Macon, where a hospital bed had been set up for Ann. We couldn't stay at our house, because the dirt road that we lived on had been scraped to be widened and paved, and when it rained, the road was so bad that ambulances couldn't get out to our property."

Ann Lambert went into a coma for two days before she died on February 7, 1991. "What I learned from Ann's illness and death is that as sick as she was, and she was really sick, she never complained," Jim said. "Not once. Ann was really committed to getting well, and we all believed that she would make it.

"Ann was an amazing musician and was totally dedicated to church music. I have asked, 'Why did this have to happen to somebody like my wife?' but I've never gotten an answer. All through her illness, Ann never lost her wit or her mind, and she was always so thankful for our daughter, Meredith."

When their pastor married them in Savannah in 1970, he asked Jim Lambert and Ann Womack to take wedding vows which said, 'For better or for worse; for richer or for poorer; in sickness and in health; to love and to cherish, until death do us part.' Both took their wedding vows as seriously as a couple can take vows.

While Ann was at Emory, Jim would bathe and feed her each morning; then drive to Macon and run the Allen & Lambert Insurance Agency during the day. Next, he would pick up Meredith from school, and take her to his parents' house. Then, he would drive back to Emory, where he would spend the night in the lobby near ICU, and continue the same routine the next day. Jim learned that there was no good or easy way to get to Emory from Macon. He would frequently make the trip twice a day if the hospital called to say Ann had taken a turn for the worse. He put 58,000 miles on his vehicle in six months, going back and forth to Emory.

Jim remembered those long, arduous days at the hospital. "While Ann was in ICU, she and I had the pleasure of sitting and talking every morning and evening. No television or other distractions. We also met a lot of different people there and would run into them later. Sadly, when I would ask how their loved one was doing, the answer was usually, 'They died.' Those were some very difficult days."

Jim recalled, "I'll never forget walking outside with Meredith after Ann died. My head was down, and it was spinning with details that had to be handled soon. The funeral arrangements. Visitation. Insurance. What to do with Meredith. I was pretty much having a pity party, but, as we walked out of the house, Meredith, who was 17, spun me around and said, 'Dad, Mom just died. You and I didn't. We've got to keep living, so you need to get your act together.' And so I did."

* * * * * * * * * *

Jim Lambert was single for a year and a half when he encountered a friend from his past. He and Brenda Stokes grew up together at Mikado Baptist Church. Jim said, "I had no intention of remarrying, because I never dreamed that I could find someone else that I could care about as much as I had cared for Ann."

Lambert had written some insurance in the past for Ralph Stokes, Brenda's dad, who had owned a number of laundromats. While they were working out the details of the insurance policy, Jim asked him about his family, and Ralph told him that Brenda, who was two years younger than Jim, had been single for eight years. "I asked him if she was dating anyone, and he said she wasn't," Jim recalled. "I asked her out around Christmas, 1991, and somehow I knew that night that I would marry her. On our first date, we went to dinner at Richard's Restaurant and then to see *Father of the Bride*. We were both very patient in our dating relationship because of the horror stories that we had heard about blended families. We knew that our children needed to be compatible, and they were."

Brenda recalled her first actual date with Jim. "Jimmy likes to tell the story of our first date, though we both recall it in different ways. He laughs and said 'He got me out of my clothes on the first date.' I saw it like 'If this man comes back after this first date, then he's a keeper!'

"We had been to dinner and a movie and were enjoying catching up with each others' lives. We were sitting in my den with my daughter Christy when we heard screeching tires and a thud. Christy and I jumped up, thinking about our 70-pound golden retriever Rex, who liked to chase cars. As we opened the door to the garage, Rex ran into the house with blood pouring from his nose onto my white kitchen floor."

Brenda continued, "At that point, I took off toward the bedroom while taking off my clothes, since I wasn't about to get dog blood on my new outfit. We spent the next three hours trying to stop a nose-bleed on a very large dog and cleaning the blood from the kitchen floor and garage. After Jimmy left our house in the wee-hours of the morning, I thought, 'Well, we've run him off.'"

However, the story has a happy ending since Jim and Brenda have been together since that first, unforgettable date. Brenda said, "Jimmy is my best friend. We love to do things together, whether it's attending church, working in the yard, riding the tractors, building a new fence, playing with our grandchildren, snow-skiing in Colorado, or enjoying our condo at the beach. He has taught me the beauty of flying in a small plane, though I don't like it as much as he does.

"He is a wonderful father, grandfather, friend, and Christian man, and I am so glad that we came into each other's lives. I plan to retire this year from the nursing profession and look forward to spending time with my wonderful husband for many more years to come."

Jim acknowledged, "I don't consider Christy and Brad, Brenda's children, to be my step-children, and likewise, Brenda considers Meredith to be her own daughter. We are really blessed that our families get along so well."

Jim Lambert and Brenda Stokes Whitfield were married in 1992 and now have three children between them. Dr. Meredith Lambert Voyles, a veterinarian, is married to Kevin Voyles and lives in Daphne, AL, with their daughter, Cameron. Christy Whitfield Spurlin lives in Atlanta, is married to Pearce, and is the mother of Riley and Pearce, III. Brad Whitfield was recently married to Dana Lyles, and they live in Savannah.

* * * * * * * * * *

As long as Jim can remember, he has always had two passions in his life. Certainly, one passion has been his family, while the other passion is his love for flying. "I have always been infatuated with aircraft. My dad worked shifts and carpooled to Warner Robins Air Force Base, but sometimes my mother would have to take him to work, and I would ride with them. I was fascinated with the airplanes at the Base, and at 16, I got a job at Lowe Aviation as a line-boy washing, parking, fueling, and cleaning the airplanes.

"I love piloting a plane," Lambert confessed. "There's nothing quite like being up above the clouds on a beautiful day. I truly love to fly, but if I was forced to make a choice between flying and being a grandfather, I choose grandchildren every time. Brenda and I now have three beautiful grandchildren, and we couldn't be more proud."

Family has always been vitally important to Jim. "My parents, James and Allene Lambert, who are still living in Macon on Lake Tobesofkee, and my brother Ronnie, now retired from Georgia Power and living in Vidalia, have always been highly influential in my life. We have always had strong family ties, and so has Brenda's family. We still remain close now that our children are grown, and they have children of their own."

When he was 18 and a freshman at Middle Georgia College, Jim got his pilot's license. He joined the National Guard in 1968 and became an aviator in the Army. "I knew that I never wanted to fly for a living," Jim said, "but it has almost become an obsession. Today, I have logged over 4,000 flight hours."

Lambert got out of the National Guard in 1976 when Ann developed lupus, and actually quit flying from 1976 to 1989, since there were more pressing issues going on in his life. "I am a strong believer that God has a plan for our lives. While working with the youth group at Tattnall Square Baptist Church, I met Jerry Stephens, who owned Reeves Paving Company. We began to talk about flying and found out that we were both pilots. Jerry told me about his plane and invited me over to see it. The bug got me again that instant. Larry

Benton, another friend at Tattnall Square who was taking flying lessons, and I went in together and bought an airplane.

"As part of the master plan for my life, while Ann was in the hospital at Emory, I met a young couple from the Carolinas in the ICU waiting room. They had a baby that had to be transported back and forth from their home. That's a long haul by car, so they found out about a service called Angel Flight which carries patients that can't afford transportation on a commercial airliner. Then six months after Ann died, I came across an article in *Air Flight in USA*. There was a listing called 'Angel Flight – Georgia,' so I pursued the idea of flying people who were in need, and actually became part of 'Angel Flight' in 1993."

Jim continued, "We at 'Angel Flight' have really been taxed since 9/11 with many more requests than in previous years, due to the government regulations of commercial flights. Today 'Angel Flight' transports patients that meet four criteria:

1. Patients must be ambulatory, and able fly in a small, non-pressurized aircraft;
2. Their doctor must give them permission;
3. Their treatment cannot be administered locally;
4. There must be a financial need.

"'Angel Flight' is the most meaningful thing that I do. I used to wonder what my purpose in life was. Now I know, and because of my passion for flying and with my ability to fly an aircraft, I have found that my purpose is to serve others. As pilots, we aren't paid for 'Angel Flight,' other than getting a tax break. We volunteer our time, and we pay for our own gas and plane maintenance, but we are richly rewarded in other ways for the services that we provide."

Lambert remembered flying a young girl to Shands Hospital in Gainesville, FL, to be treated for a yet-to-be-determined disease. "I flew her to Shands three or four months in a row. This little girl, who was confined to a wheelchair and couldn't talk, loved to fly. Now, anytime I think I'm having a bad day, I think about her. That's why I have entitled the talk that I give to civic clubs and churches 'The Story of Angel Flight - Why I Never Have a Bad Day.'"

* * * * * * * * * *

Jim's background is similar to many other young men who grew up in South Macon. He attended Charles H. Bruce School before entering Willingham High, where he graduated in 1964. Jim attended Mikado Baptist Church, pastored by Dr. E.C. Sheehan, until 1963, when his family joined Mabel White Baptist, whose pastor was Dr. Jimmy Waters. "I'm blessed today because my parents made me go to church with them. They took me to church; they didn't just send me. My parents also encouraged me to play Little League baseball, along with other activities at school and church.

"Growing up on Beddingfield Drive, I had a great childhood. I had some outstanding teachers, both at Bruce School and at Willingham. My third grade teacher, Mrs. Trapp, encouraged us to always do our very best. It didn't matter to her if I made an 'A' (average) or a 'G' (good), as long as I did my best. She was always excited about school back then, which made a bunch of third graders excited about school, too."

Leonard Pridgeon, one of the all-time great teachers in Willingham's 12-year history, taught chemistry and physics. "I always thought I wanted to be an engineer – I'm not sure why – and Mr. Pridgeon kept you pretty disciplined in your preparation for his class. He demanded the best from us. Charles Bird taught English at Willingham, and, for any teacher in an all-boys' school to be able to get a bunch of guys to enjoy Shakespeare was a chore. He taught me that it was possible to actually enjoy subjects that you really didn't care a whole lot about. I remember that I was in his class when we heard that President John F. Kennedy was shot in November, 1963.

"The teacher with the greatest influence on my academic life, though, was Mike Garvin," Jim recalled. "He was a great math teacher who not only knew the material but wouldn't accept less than your best. If you tried to give him excuses, he could make your life miserable."

Jim remembered, "I was a bit unique in high school in that I was involved in sports and in the band. I enjoyed Jim Littlefield, our band director, and learned discipline from him. He was creative and brought pride to the band like the coaches brought pride to our teams. I was encouraged by him to learn different instruments, which for me were the trombone and percussion. When I was young, I took piano lessons, so I already knew how to read both clefts."

Growing up in South Macon in the Lambert household was a wonderful time for Jim. "We didn't realize it at the time, but everybody in our neighborhood was fairly equal economically. Nobody had a lot of money, but then nobody was real poor either. We lived on Beddingfield Avenue near the corner of San Juan and Moreland Avenues. There was a vacant lot that remained undeveloped until I graduated from high school. We turned it into our own athletic complex, because we played football, baseball, and even basketball there. One of our parents put up two goals on one end of the lot so we played full court. The children in our neighborhood, and there were a lot of us, played together, and all of the families knew each other. We walked to school thinking it was such a long way when, truly it was three blocks. Later, we rode our bikes to school."

Jim reminisced, "Mr. E.P. Hight, one of our neighbors, was a railroad man whose grandchildren were about our age and would come visit all summer. We played the world's greatest Monopoly games that lasted for weeks. Since there was no air conditioning back then, we played Monopoly on their screen porch, and we never put the game away. Monopoly was a rainy-day and a night-time activity. Growing up in our South Macon neighborhood couldn't have been any better."

Lambert's biggest disappointment during his days at Bruce School was when the football team forfeited three games because of an ineligible player. "Frank Jacobs was our coach, and we were 3-0 at the time. We won our last two games and finished the season un-scored upon but didn't get to go to the Pony Bowl, which was the Bibb County-equivalent of the Super Bowl for elementary schools. Weir School, whom we beat, went to the Pony Bowl in our place and lost to Pearl Stephens. We were crushed because we knew we had the best team in the city."

He continued, "Being in the Willingham band and going to out-of-town football games are great memories. My memories of Willingham days are good ones. I was very well-prepared for science and math in college, primarily because of Mike Garvin and Leonard Pridgeon. Another great high school memory was in football, because we never lost to Lanier, and we split with them in baseball."

During his high school years, Jim had the opportunity to meet guys from the other side of town. "We had to go to Morgan Field or Willingham Mill Field to play Pony League and Babe Ruth League baseball. Wayne Slaton and I were the only Willingham guys on our team, so we got to know a lot of Lanier boys. I didn't see much difference in us, but we never did things with them socially. A few Willingham boys pledged Lanier-dominated fraternities, but my dad wasn't about to pay for me to be in a fraternity. To me, South Macon was like a separate town, because we went to church and school with people in our community. Our neighborhoods did things as a community."

Jim remembered people and experiences from his formative years in South Macon which greatly influenced his life. "My parents taught me Philippians 4:13, which says, 'I can do all things through Christ who strengthens me.' There were lots of things that Ronnie and I couldn't do as we grew up, but seldom was there something that we couldn't accomplish. I learned a lot from James Johnson, who managed the A & P Grocery Store on Houston Avenue. He taught me about customer service and how to treat people. I learned about cleanliness, discipline, and being fair with people."

Little League was a big deal in South Macon neighborhoods back in the 1950's and 60's when Jim played for his dad's team. Jim recalled, "My dad was a tremendous Little League baseball coach. He was always kind of quiet and was not thought of as a motivator, but he could always get the best out of his players. He knew how to coach, and he knew how to draft good players."

Jim's baseball experience continued at Middle Georgia in Cochran. "Coach Buddy Gleaton was my coach when I was a freshman. He was a gymnast and knew nothing about baseball. Coach Gleaton wore penny loafers and no sanitaries (long white under-socks) with his baseball pants. Now that was a good look! We made up our own signs. If he was coaching third, we looked to the first base coach for our signs. Then, we had Coach Dave Harris for one year. He was a great coach but left Cochran to coach at Kennesaw State where he later became their Athletic Director. When Ann and I got married and moved to Marietta, we attended Roswell Street Baptist Church with Coach Harris and his wife, who coached at Kennesaw."

David Luckie was a friend, teammate, and fraternity brother of Jim Lambert. They met in high school through mutual friends, Luckie from Ft. Valley High and Lambert from Willingham. Both played music, majored in business administration, and were excellent athletes; so they had much in common. Luckie recalled, "Growing up, I always thought that Jim Lambert was an over-achiever. Here are two examples: First, he is left-handed. When several of us began playing acoustic guitar in the 1960's, Jim simply turned the guitar around (guitars are generally tuned for a right-handed player) and played it upside-down and backward, and he actually played it very well."

Luckie continued, "Second, when we were playing fraternity flag-football at Georgia Southern, he and I were the defensive safeties. Jim covered one side, and I covered the other. In a tight, crucial game where we were decided underdogs, Jim came through with an over-achieving play. On the last play of the game - which was tied - the other team threw a long pass towards Lambert. He was not as fast as the receiver (nor did he have the same moves) and was clearly beaten on the play that would produce the winning touchdown for the other team. Remember, this is flag football - no tackling was allowed.

"All Jim did was tackle the receiver which drew an obvious pass interference penalty flag. He certainly would not get beaten by the receiver for a touchdown. This quick-thinking on Jim's part placed the ball on the two-yard line, where our opponent had one play. We held, and the game ended tied. We celebrated, since we were not supposed to win."

Luckie concluded, "Since we are all a little older now, I have come to realize that perhaps Jim Lambert is not really an over-achiever at all. He is really an achiever. Jim has achieved most everything that I know he wanted to achieve in life. He is a pilot that owns his own plane and makes volunteer emergency flights for others, and he is happily married with a great family. He is a successful businessman with his own company, and he has done many other things of which I am probably not aware. Jim has certainly been an achiever and has done it with a great attitude. I just wish he would learn to play the guitar the right way!"

* * * * * * * * * *

After graduating from Georgia Southern in 1969, Jim earned his Master's Degree in Insurance from Georgia State University in 1976, while working for Georgia Farm Bureau for ten years. He went into the insurance business for himself in 1980, in a partnership with The Marion Allen Agency of Fort Valley. He started Allen & Lambert, Inc., with the financial help of Marion Allen. They remained partners for several years before Lambert bought out Marion Allen's interest. The name was not changed, primarily out of the utmost respect for Marion Allen. Also, it kept his company's name first in the phone book. Today, the agency employs eight people, and is one of the premier agencies in the greater-Macon area.

In the past year, Lambert and a couple of partners purchased the franchise rights for several Zaxby's Restaurants. Their first restaurant opened in August, 2004, in Savannah. Several more Zaxby's are in the planning stages and should be open in the next two years.

Jim met Currey Gayle, originally from Perry, GA, in 1967, and they have been friends in the insurance industry since 1970. Currey now lives and works in the Metro-Atlanta area and said, "I was invited by a college friend, Joe McDaniel, to go on a vacation camping trip to Vogel State Park near Blairsville. I knew the other guys on that trip, but I had never met Jimmy and his brother Ronnie. Our evenings were spent around a campfire playing guitars and singing folk songs by artists like the Kingston Trio and the Brothers Four. Jimmy played bass and primarily sang background, thankfully. It was a very memorable trip and one where I made some life-long friends. We later became Kappa Sigma fraternity brothers at Georgia Southern and were in each others' weddings."

Gayle said, "Jimmy's strengths are in his convictions and principles which are the same now as they were almost 40 years ago. He has always lived according to his Christian beliefs, and you never doubt where James Alvin Lambert stands on an issue.

"I have always felt there were basically two kinds of people in this world — givers and takers. Jimmy has always been a giver. His selfless, generous ways earned him recognition as the 'Agent of the Year' by the Professional Insurance Agents of Georgia in 2002. This award was won, in part, for his involvement in his profession, church, and community. Jim's connection with 'Angel Flight' is one of his interests of which he is most proud. His desire is to help others in need in any way he can."

Gayle recalled a story from their past. "Jimmy's first wife, Ann Womack of Savannah, and my wife Pat were about the same age and size. One year, not long after we were married, Jim and I went Christmas shopping at a local boutique in Atlanta. We had no clue regarding size or how something would look on our wives. We selected a clerk that we thought would wear the same size as Pat and Ann and asked her to try on some outfits to see how we liked them. We liked what we saw, bought the same outfits in different colors, and our wives had no idea how we could become such great shoppers for women's clothes.

"Jimmy Lambert is the consummate friend," Gayle concluded. "He is the type of person that is only a phone call away if you need him. I know that Jimmy's parents are extremely proud of him as a son, husband, father, and grandfather. His parents' strong moral and religious convictions were instilled in him at an early age. However, the characteristic that stands out most about Jimmy is his love for his God, family and friends."

Bobby Jones concurred with Currey Gayle about the kind of man and friend Jim Lambert has become. Jones is the owner of the Bobby Jones Agency of Cotton States Insurance in the greater-Athens area. Bobby and Jim became business partners in 2004 when they opened a Zaxby's restaurant near Savannah. About his long-time friend and business partner, Jones said, "Jim's strengths and assets are his easy manner, extreme loyalty, and the way he treats everyone with respect. He is the consummate family man and has always demonstrated that he is a loving father, loyal husband, and a true friend to the rest of us."

Jones and Lambert have known each other since their days as Georgia Farm Bureau insurance agents in the early 1970's. "I will always remember how dedicated Jim was to his first wife, Ann. She suffered for an extremely long time, but Jim never wavered in his faith or in his loyalty to her as her primary care-giver. I can't remember one day that Jim complained about his responsibilities to Ann and Meredith."

Though Jim has done most things right in his life, Jones felt that marrying Ann, and then Brenda, may have been the best things Jim has ever done. "Without them, Jim probably wouldn't have amounted to very much," Jones joked. "As successful as Jim's professional life has been, his personal life may have been even better. I feel that the key to Jim's success is the way he approaches his daily life and his loyalty to his employees and customers. His faith in God has carried him as long as I have known him, which goes back over 30 years. To use an appropriate cliché, Jim 'walks the walk, and talks the talk.'"

Jim Lambert, without question, has become a success in life, but it hasn't come without a cost, a financial cost. "When Ann died," Jim said, "we received a medical bill for $1,200,000. That's one million, two-hundred thousand dollars, which is a lot of money for a boy from South Macon. We were covered by Medicare for Ann's renal failure, and we had private insurance, but, because of the experimental medicine that was practiced on her, our bill was still $400,000. I did have some money in the bank though, and I paid Emory the entire bill in full, but in 1991, I had no cash. I was, in every way, starting over."

Lambert wisecracked, "I've become good at hiring people. It only took twenty-five years to finally get the right staff. I remember being at Georgia Southern and thinking that if I ever made $10,000 in a single year, I would have it made. Little did I know! I truly have been so blessed – financially, and in every way."

That attitude of 'being so blessed' is the benchmark of Jim's life. In 1999, Lambert discovered that he had leukemia. Specifically, he had chronic lymphocytic leukemia which, in the words of his oncologist, "If you have to have leukemia, this is the best kind to have." From March, 1999, until December, 2003, Jim never had a single treatment for leukemia, but his doctor ordered a round of chemotherapy the week before Christmas, 2003, due to some abnormal platelet counts that had trended downward. "Other than the chemotherapy," he said, "I have never felt bad a single time and have had no side effects from the leukemia.

"I have enjoyed every stage of my life – from growing up in South Macon attending Bruce School and Willingham, to my time in the military, and then being married to Ann and Brenda. However, I have never experienced joy like being a grandfather to Riley, Cameron, and Pearce, III. That is the greatest joy in the world. I've always said that I wasn't going to be a doting granddad, but I lied."

* * * * * * * * * *

At age 58, Lambert shows no signs of slowing down. His days start at 6 a.m., working out regularly at the Wellness Center. Jim has invested in a Zaxby's Restaurant and speculates in real estate. He has stayed busy as a member of the Macon Exchange Club since 1981 and plays bass in the Praise Band at Forest Hills United Methodist Church. His hobbies include keeping up his and Brenda's 40-acre spread in Monroe County and regularly flying to their condominium at Orange Beach, AL. "When I fly there, it takes about an hour and twenty minutes. If you drive, it takes roughly six hours. Being a pilot has its benefits."

'Angel Flight'—Pilot Jim Lambert and friends.

Jim and Brenda have had many opportunities to travel, due to incentive trips that he has won through the insurance industry. "We have been to China, Hawaii, Prague, Vienna, Canada, Boston, and on an Alaska Cruise just to name a few."

With a high level of self-motivation, Jim Lambert has risen to the top of his profession. He was named Professional Insurance Agent of the Year in Georgia in 2002. Jim was selected as the winner of the Macon Exchange Club's Book of Golden Deeds, the highest honor given for contributions to the club and the community in 2002. But perhaps the notoriety that means the most to Jim was being honored at the American Cancer Society's Hope Gala Ball for the cancer Survivor Volunteer of the Year in 2001. Jim's wife Brenda won the Cancer Society's Volunteer of the Year for a lay person, as well.

Dr. Meredith L. Voyles, Jim and Ann Lambert's only child, was born in 1973. Mirroring her dad's positive attitude and deep faith, Meredith probably knows Jim Lambert better than anybody in his life. She and her dad experienced some long, difficult days during the illness and subsequent death of Ann in 1991. Meredith stated, "My dad's best qualities are his determination, compassion, strong work ethic, and his devotion to whatever he is doing. He is especially passionate about flying and grandchildren. There's no doubt that Dad is a very good businessman, but much of that has to do with the personal touch that he gives to his clients. That's simply because he cares so much about people."

She continued, "He has made a personal impact on many people's lives, many of whom don't really even know him well. Dad's involvement with Angel Flight has given him the opportunity to minister to people who are in deep need. He truly cares about helping to make life easier for those families that he flies to various destinations. The way my dad stayed by my mother's side when she was so sick for so long, as well as running an insurance business while raising a teenage daughter, tells a lot about his character."

Meredith experienced a strong, committed family life while growing up, and humor was always a big part of the Lambert household. "My mom could tell the funniest stories, especially when they were about my dad. There was a time when my dad, who has always been quite a handyman, was cleaning the shower. There was a lot of mildew that had built up in the shower, and regular cleanser couldn't clean it, so he decided to use gasoline. Mom walked back to the bathroom to see how he was doing and found him passed out from the gas fumes. That was highly unlike my dad.

"My mom also told stories about the way my dad would get me dressed for church. She always had to be at church early because she played piano and had to rehearse with the choir, so my dad would get me ready to go to church. Not knowing any better, he always put my dresses on backwards, which meant he had the buttons in the front. After church my mom would see me ill-dressed and was mortified. Dad didn't seem overly concerned," Meredith smiled.

"As a father, I couldn't have asked for anyone better. He has provided me with everything I could ask for, yet he taught me to appreciate what I had. My dad is an example of how I want to live my own life, both professionally and personally. He is totally devoted to the Lord and his family. My dad's priorities are in order."

Meredith concluded, "My dad's attitude – 'he has never had a bad day' – has helped make him very successful in life. He realized a long time ago that someone somewhere else is having a much worse day than you."

Well said, by a grateful daughter.

At Orango Beach, AL. Jim Lambert, Brenda holding Cameron, Meredith and Kevin Voyles.

Born in England; Raised in South Macon

Michael Verdon (Mike) Cheek
Class of 1962

"Do unto others as you would have them do unto you."
–The Golden Rule

Mike Cheek officially retired from the day-to-day corporate world on December 31, 2004, and began receiving retirement checks from numerous corporations that he has faithfully served throughout his 38 years in business. "I reminded myself of my grandfather, because after retiring, he religiously went to the mailbox every two weeks to get the checks that he needed to feed his family and pay the bills. Though my first retirement checks were direct-deposited, just the sobering impact that my retirement years had now begun brought back fond memories of my late grandfather and grandmother and the significant impact that their values and love had on my development."

Mike has become a highly successful businessman and a world traveler, but he is, above all else, a family man. "There are several passions in my life these days, but none is as important as my family. Runell and I have been married for 40 years and have two wonderful, grown daughters. We are extremely proud of both, and both have matured into beautiful women. Both are married to great guys, and each has blessed us with grandchildren. We see both of their families as often as possible, and Runell talks with both daughters on a daily basis.

"Our older daughter, Kelly, who graduated from Queens College in Charlotte, NC, is married to Tom Johnson, and they live in Athens with their two children, Jordan (10) and Kathryn (8). Tom and I also own seven Wendy's Restaurants, five in Athens, one in Greensboro, and one in Winder. Our younger daughter, Andrea, who graduated from the University of Kentucky, is married to David Zaepfel, and they live in Austin, TX, where David is employed and is making excellent career progress with Dell Computers. They have one son, Nolan, (30 months old and already 3' 4" tall!) and are excitedly expecting a daughter soon."

Mike continued, "Runell and I have an outstanding relationship with both sons-in-law. I golf with them at every opportunity. Last summer, I took Tom and David to Scotland for a week of unforgettable golf. It was a great bonding experience for us. As parents, there is nothing more important than maintaining a strong relationship with our children and their families, and we are truly blessed to have such a relationship."

Runell and Mike Cheek are now legally Floridians by living in Naples the majority of the year, but their second home and their hearts are in Georgia – Athens, in particular.

Mike's second passion is his service at the University of Georgia, where he was named a Distinguished Executive-In-Residence at the Terry College of Business in 2004. In this role, he is lecturing on subjects such as Business Ethics, Leadership Development, and, from a marketing perspective, Global Branding. This forum enables Mike to share with students some of the fabulous business and personal lessons he has experienced in his many successful years in the corporate world.

Mike said, "This volunteer role allows me to share the best business practices and, in a small way, give back to a great university that has meant so much to me and my success." His experiences as a Chief Operating Officer for over 15 years, and, specifically for the last four years as the global president of the largest division of a major international corporation, have been invaluable in his lectures to young business students at UGA. Mike led an organization with annual revenues of over $1,400,000,000. This background in international and domestic brand-building provided him with the credentials to present and address key discussion issues with the future business leaders of tomorrow at the Terry College.

Mike is a great believer in the role and power of 'brands' in the global market and has been successful with consumers around the world, building on the equity of some great marquee brands with which he has been associated such as: Coca-Cola, Diet Coke, Sprite, Jack Daniel's, Southern Comfort, Finlandia, and many Carnation brands such as Coffee Mate, Friskies Pet Foods, and others.

As he reflected back on his rewarding career, Mike recalled, "I am much further along in life, professionally, than I could have ever dreamed during those great high school days at Willingham. I remember the tough times my dad had as a butcher while working at Piggly Wiggly and other places. He never made more than $100 a week. While we were somewhat disadvantaged economically, the good news is that we never knew any better."

"In the business world, I have traveled to countries and locations which I never thought I would either see or experience. For the last four years, I have traveled globally about half of the time, making at least two trips per year to Asia-Pacific, along with about seven trips per year to Europe. I have been chairman of Finlandia Vodka Worldwide," based in Helsinki. "I've made numerous annual trips to the United Kingdom, where I have served on the board of directors of a public company. As a result of significant international travel, I have accumulated over three million air miles."

He continued, "I have always believed and demonstrated that it was important to visit different countries and to experience the consumer behavior by better understanding their lifestyles and culture. In so doing, I have seen a great deal of this vast world, and one can never tell in advance what they might see or hear. For example, a few years ago, I was in China on a business trip, and we visited a large Sam's Hypermarket. The store was absolutely huge with a few thousand shoppers rushing around on four or five levels. In the midst of all of that confusion, I overheard music coming through the store's sound system, and when I could hear it better, much to my amazement, blaring out in English was the song, 'Who Let The Dogs Out?' Until that moment, it was my belief that one would only have expected to hear that song in heart of Dawg Country back home in good old Georgia. Of course, with all of my extensive global travel, I must also confess that I have tasted some unusual cuisine, not all of which I enjoyed."

Mike's third passion is his personal, physical well-being, and now that he is retired, he intends to take even better care of himself by walking, bike-riding, and playing golf. He stated, "I have been very fortunate in that my weight has not varied more than five pounds over the past 30 years, and I plan to maintain that good behavior. My dad died at 52, and my late-brother, Darrell, had an aneurism at 43, and later died at 50. To compound this misfortune, Darrell's wife also died at age 50."

Mike confessed, "With the unfortunate loss of my brother and his wife, Runell and I are honored that their two children view us much like they would their own parents. Darrell's daughter, Melanie, is married to Jim Guest, and they live in Atlanta where they have two lovely children, Andrew and Allison. Darrell's son, Mark, is a graduate of the Medical College of Georgia, and is a doctor of Internal Medicine, practicing in Tampa. Runell and I love Melanie and Mark and their families as if they were our own."

The fourth and most fun passion for the Cheek family is following the Georgia Bulldogs. "We have been season ticket holders for 20-plus years, and with a home in Athens, we make the football games a big event with our family and friends. I remember fondly the Herschel Walker-years in Athens. Runell and I only missed three games during his career and that was due to a business commitment. However, we were able to see all three of those games on television. Even today, we try to make all of the home and away games, if possible. Go Dawgs!"

Mike Cheek was born in England in 1944. "My mom was a war bride, and we came to America in 1946 on a small Argentinean ship following two rough, horrible weeks on the North Atlantic, I was told. When we arrived in the States, we took a train to the Southeast and landed in Winder, GA. It's interesting that today, my oldest son-in-law and I own a Wendy's in Winder, GA, which is about 500 yards from the same train station where we disembarked. Today, I still have first cousins in England, and we make return trips there periodically. We took our daughters when they turned 10, and we will be taking each of our grandchildren when they reach that age. Therefore, since Jordan is now 10, we will be taking her for a visit in 2005. We want them to understand the history, background, and appreciate the culture of our ancestors. These trips will be very educational for the grandkids and will be great fun for Granddaddy and Mimi."

Mike grew up in the Jefferson Hills section of South Macon and attended Glenwood Hills Baptist Church until he began to date Runell Short. Her family was actively involved at Mabel White Baptist, so Mike tagged along. With the church being a focal point of his life, one of the joys of adulthood has been Mike's participation in the churches in the cities where they have lived. A church-related high-point for Mike was serving as the chairman of the Administrative Board for two years, and also heading up a $3 million fund-raising campaign at Sandy Springs United Methodist Church. "This was one of the most rewarding experiences in my life. Being part of something that will have eternal, lasting benefits for other people has become very important to me. Our family's church involvement has been a key foundation for our life and our base of friends throughout the years."

* * * * * * * * *

Mike played baseball and basketball in high school, but golf was, by far, his favorite sport. "Our golf team was made up of Raymond Baggarley, Buzzy Leverett, Jim Pritchett, Jerry Leverette, and Bobo Olson, along with me and several others. Our home matches were played at Bridgewood, which could be described as something akin to a blue-collar course, on Hartley Bridge Road. Our team was invited to a golf tournament at Idle Hour Country Club in Macon, which was by far the nicest golf course in this area and was unlike anything we had ever played. Compared to the other teams, we showed up looking a little bit out of place, but we had a great time and competed aggressively to the best of our ability."

Cheek's best friends in high school were Jim Pritchett and Jerry Leverette. They called themselves 'the Cheverretts,' a contraction for Cheek, Leverette, and Pritchett. "We thought we were pretty cool, and we did just about everything together. One of my great memories from high school days was playing baseball in a summer league for the Giants in the Babe Ruth League at Willingham Mill Field. When I was a 15-year old, our South Macon team won the City Championship by beating our arch-rivals, the Lions, who were also from South Macon and were led by Pete Gaines, Mark Bowen, and others. It was a great lesson, demonstrating that one doesn't have to be the favorite to be the winner."

Basketball at Willingham, however, was a different matter. "I remember that we had a woeful basketball team when I was in high school," Mike recalled. "Coach Martin Allman got so disgusted with the varsity at one point that he moved Johnny Higgison, Bobo Olson, and me from the B-team to the varsity in mid-season for the remainder of the season. I wore size 13 shoes as a ninth grader, and the school didn't even have a pair of size 13's. In fact, Charlie Wood Sporting Goods didn't have Converse All-Stars that size in stock, so one of the ministers at Glenwood Hills Baptist Church, who had big feet like me, loaned me his 13's. We had to travel to play LaGrange. Their team was one of the best in the state and included the tall, talented Mahaffey brothers. They beat us something like 54-19. Johnny, Bobo, and I scored 15 of our 19 points that night."

Growing up in South Macon and especially during his high school years, Mike learned about ambition and developed a will to succeed. "I developed self-confidence and really believed that I could make something of my life. As I reflect back on my younger years, there were three life-threatening, life-changing situations that happened to me. They also convinced me that God had a plan for me. The first situation occurred when I was a baby. I was born in England in 1944, and World War II was still raging. My mother related the story to me that each night the Germans would launch 'buzz bombs' across the English Channel. They were directed at a large American military base near our small town. As the bombs began to explode, sirens would blast to signal that residents should leave immediately for safety in a nearby shelter. My mother would take me in her arms and run while praying. She was never quite sure if we would be killed or not."

Mike continued, "The second life-threatening episode in my life happened when I was three. After we arrived in America, my appendix ruptured. If my parents had not used good judgment and taken me to the emergency room, I would have died within an hour. After life-saving surgery, I spent two weeks in intensive care.

"Then at 16, I was on a trip to Lake Sinclair near Milledgeville, GA, with Runell's family and friends. While swimming, I was stricken with severe leg cramps. Her dad heard my screams and the screams of others and immediately dove in and pulled me to safety at the last possible moment. Otherwise, I certainly would have drowned that day."

Cheek said, "With those near-fatal events, I became convinced that God surely had given me a second chance, and I made a commitment that day to always strive to do my best and to succeed as a person, as a responsible citizen, and later in life as a husband, father, grandfather, and friend. Material things weren't nearly as important to me as becoming successful in life."

Mike gives the credit to his mom for being the driving force in their home. "She was very bright, and she pushed and motivated me to achieve and make something positive happen in my life. My mother was truly a remarkable woman who, in her early 20's, married my dad, an American soldier based in England. After I was born, my parents soon decided that our futures would be best spent in the United States, so they made plans to move to Georgia after the war ended. My mother became one of tens of thousands of 'war brides' that came to America to begin a new life in a new country. She didn't know if she would ever see her immediate family again, but she was full of hope that she would have a better life.

"Leaving her family behind in England had to be the most difficult decision of her young life," Cheek stated. "The good news of this story is that although my dad was never financially able to send my mom back to England to see her family, she was finally able to return to England for a lengthy visit nearly 30 years later. My dad was also a great guy, though he lacked the education and opportunity to achieve what I believe he truly wanted to accomplish in life."

Mike continued, "As I approached graduation from Willingham, I was determined to graduate from college, and I would be the first in my family to do so. However, I also knew that my parents didn't have the financial resources to send me to college, so I knew the ball was clearly in my court regarding the funding of my college education. Somehow, I was lucky enough that the Willingham family in Macon, who owned the cotton mills, found out about me and my financial dilemma. They offered me the opportunity to attend Georgia Tech at their expense and become a textile engineer. They also paid my expenses for my first year in junior college. However, I quickly determined that engineering was not the career path that was best suited for me. Although it was a difficult decision considering my lack of financial resources, I went to Mr. Willingham and told him, 'I just can't do that. I'll pay you for the money you invested in me, but I'm just not interested in becoming an engineer.' He told me 'No, let's just consider this as an excellent investment and money well-spent on you. I admire you for making that decision and telling me. You will make a difference in life.'"

Jerry Leverette and Mike had both applied for early-admission and got accepted at Auburn, but the out-of-state tuition expense was much too great to bear. Therefore, each decided to attend Georgia Southwestern Junior College in Americus. Mike had an outstanding two years as he was the starting catcher on their strong baseball team, as well as being a key reserve on the basketball team. He also was a solid contributor on the school's golf team.

After completing two years at Southwestern, Mike returned to Macon, married Runell Short, and began working for White Brothers Auto Parts. He quickly realized that his sales ability and leadership skills would most likely be his ticket to success. However, he also realized that nobody would hire a 19-year old salesman, so he transferred to Athens to complete his education at the University of Georgia, where he graduated with honors from the College of Business in 1966. He recalled, "The Rayonier Corporation provided a full-academic scholarship for me, which seemed like money from heaven. By this time, I had become super-motivated, academically. I graduated from Georgia on Saturday night and drove to Jacksonville on Sunday morning with Runell to locate an apartment. I was determined and ready to go!"

Through the years, the Cheek family moved often, a situation for which Mike gives maximum credit to his wife. "Runell encouraged my upward mobility in my business career, and I would never have had the professional success that I have experienced if she hadn't been so supportive. Unlike many of my friends and business associates, I never had to call home to clear it with her when I was considering a better job or career advancement (although I called her anyway). Runell had confidence in me that I would do what was the best and right thing for our family. She only worked outside the home while we lived in Jacksonville and before we had children. After our children were born, Runell was able to stay home with them, which was great, since I had to spend about 80% of my time traveling in the early days. She was working behind the scenes by providing a solid, stable environment for our girls. Later, when our daughters were out of school, Runell was able to travel with me, especially on international trips to such places as Australia, New Zealand, Finland, most of Europe, and other countries, which was great for both of us. Through our entire married life, Runell has been a great supporter and should get equal credit for our success, while I pushed up the corporate ladder. She truly made the most important contribution, which was taking care of the family."

Mike confesses that the things that have always been important to him in business are having the right values, believing in people, and understanding that people can and want to be motivated by effective leaders. "I have always held the opinion that leaders must be willing to do, or have done, the things that they are asking their employees to do." In the early days of his career as a salesman, Mike realized that his outgoing personality was important for his success, because that would usually get his foot in the door, allowing him the opportunity to sell his product. "I developed the reputation of never meeting a stranger, and thankfully, that came naturally for me."

Mike also determined quickly that leaders are made, not born, so he began to sense, even in the early days of his professional life, that he may have some unique leadership skills. "In business and life, leadership is about having a positive attitude, developing and communicating a vision, laying out a plan, and motivating people to buy into it. Equally important is establishing trust with each other. It's doing the right things the right way. Then it means that we do things right. That concept was abbreviated to 'Do the right things right. Then do things right.' Being a leader is seeing the magic in people, picking the right team, motivating them, and ignoring who gets the credit."

* * * * * * * * * *

The golf bug bit Mike Cheek when he was in his early teens, and when Mike's family moved from Albany to Macon in 1958, the only options for golf in town were Bowden Golf Course, a public course which was fifteen miles across town, and Bridgewood, a rugged, nine-hole course on Hartley Bridge Road. Little did Cheek know that one day he would be a member of the Valhalla Golf Club in Louisville, KY, which hosted the 1996 and 2000 PGA Championships, along with the 2004 Senior PGA Championship. He has also served in a major leadership position by being a Vice-Chairman of those three tournaments and will do so again in 2008, when Valhalla hosts the most exciting of all golf events, the Ryder Cup. In addition, he is also a member of the historic Royal Dornoch Golf Club in Dornoch, Scotland, which is almost always ranked in the top 15-20 courses in the world.

Mike's extensive travel in business has afforded him the privilege of seeing the world with his golf clubs in tow. His work experience has included the Coca-Cola Company, where he was the Senior Vice-President of Marketing and Sales for the Fountain Division, as well as serving the company as Senior

Vice-President of Sales for the Wine Spectrum of Coca-Cola earlier in his career. Prior to his eight years with Coke, Mike worked from 1966 to 1975 for the Carnation Company and four years with the Ernest and Julio Gallo Winery in Modesto, California. More recently, his experience included Chairman of Finlandia Vodka Worldwide, and President of Brown-Forman Global Spirits, where he was based in Louisville, KY.

Working hard and making a difference have characterized Mike's life. His resume, which contains memberships and service opportunities locally, nationally, and world-wide, is rivaled only by the numerous awards that he has won in the business and civic world. Listed below are just a few of Mike's memberships and organizations:

- Past-President of the Atlanta Chapter of the Bulldog Club
- Past member of Valhalla Golf Club of Louisville, KY
- Member of Collier's Reserve County Club, Naples, FL
- Member of Athens Country Club, Athens, GA
- Member of The Presidents Club at the University of Georgia
- Member of the Atlanta Classic Foundation

Other awards are:

- American Cancer Society's Dr. Louis Berger Memorial Award in 1999
- National Association of Beverage Retailers (NABR) Industry Executive of the Year in 2001
- WABBI Unity Award
- Inducted into the Sky Ranch Hall of Fame, 1997
- Industry Executive of the Year, selected by retail leaders in 1996
- Recipient of the Terry College of Business (UGA) Distinguished Alumnus, 1995; a Distinguished Executive in Residence in 2004.

There were many influential teachers and adults that helped shape the life of Mike Cheek. Coach Billy Henderson is at the top of his list. "Coach Henderson was always positive and had such a 'can-do' attitude. His sense of urgency and the discipline that he personally lived by and expected others to follow really impressed me. Coach Henderson was a giant of a man to me. He had outstanding personal values and ethics, and he was a role model for me and many others. The unwritten rule at Willingham was that Coach Henderson was always in charge. He expected the best from us, whether it was in a P.E. class or on the baseball field. There was no question that he dedicated his life to helping young people grow to become leaders and responsible citizens."

After Mike began dating Runell Short, his home church soon became Mabel White Baptist, which was pastored by Rev. Jimmy Waters. Of his former pastor, Cheek said, "Rev. Jimmy was a true leader and a man of God. He was a great family man, and he always had time for others. Like Coach Billy Henderson, I consider him to be one of the role models who had a significant impact on my life.

"Rev. Waters was fond of telling the story about the time I was cheering loudly at a Georgia football game. A photographer from *The Macon Telegraph* took a photograph of me screaming for the Dawgs. Of course, my mouth was wide open. The photo appeared in Sunday morning's paper, and, when I ran into the pastor at church the next day, he told me, 'Mike, I will expect you in the choir next Sunday after seeing the way you could yell and get excited at the football game!' I told him, 'Reverend, I don't think so. Cheering and singing in the church choir are two different things. I can cheer fine, but I sure can't sing a lick.' He was such a great guy."

Cheek continued, "Joe Swain was a long-time coach in South Macon in some of the junior sports and sandlot leagues. He was a tough but fair coach, and he gave so much of himself to help mold the lives of young boys like me at such a critical time in our lives. I'll always be indebted to Joe Swain.

"I had many great teachers that were especially meaningful in my years at Willingham, but four were special," Mike said. "Mrs. Mary P. Smith, my American History teacher, was tough in the classroom, and she always challenged me to do better. I liked her a lot and never wanted to disappoint her. Coach Mike Garvin was a smart math teacher who pushed us hard, but his classes were also a lot of fun. He was a man who led by example. Mrs. Joyce Clary taught Spanish and was my supervision (home room) teacher when I was a senior. She was such a dedicated teacher and really worked hard. Mrs. Clary set high standards in class and pushed us to achieve and to grow academically. And, of course, Mr. Leonard Pridgeon, who taught chemistry and physics, was a brilliant teacher. Like the others, he pushed me to develop my intelligence. He was a mild-mannered teacher, but everyone knew that he was in charge in his classroom, and was he intelligent!"

Mike grew up and attended elementary school in Albany, GA. When the Cheek family – parents Verdon and May Cheek and Mike's brother, Darrell, all of whom are now deceased - moved to Macon, they settled in the Jefferson Hills subdivision. "I remember the fun and the competition of playing football and baseball in our neighborhood.

"There was a special culture at Willingham as I entered the new school in 1958. I remember our principal, Mr. Fred Johnson, the excellent coaches, and the top teachers there. We had a lot of fun at Willingham. I enjoyed the daily morning trips up the hill to McEvoy, and then the frantic race to school as we tried to beat the opening bell. Some of my contemporaries back then were Jim Pritchett, Jerry Leverette, Johnny Wires, Gary Digby, Bobo Olson, Tommy Reid, Randy Wheeler, Pete Gaines, Mark Bowen, and many others.

"One of my favorite memories from high school was the time Randy Wheeler, a bunch of other seniors, and I went to Lanier in the middle of the night and raised the Willingham Ram flag on their flag pole. It was just before the biggest high school football game in the area – the Willingham-Lanier game, which we won, by the way."

Mike reminisced about his playing days on the varsity baseball and basketball squads, "In basketball, I will always remember those road trips in the middle of the winter to Columbus, Moultrie, LaGrange, and Albany. Coach Allman was our coach, and I enjoyed watching his sideline demeanor. In baseball, I was never blessed with a lot of speed and had the dubious distinction my junior year of drilling a sharp single to right field, only to be thrown out at first base by the right-fielder. I'll never forget the concerns that I had returning to the dugout and seeing that frown on Coach Henderson's face.

"Overall, I had a terrific high school experience and learned a great deal in my years at Willingham," Mike said. "I was taught that I had to use my God-given intelligence, but I also had to work hard if I was going to succeed. At school, I was taught discipline, learned about ambition, and developed a will to succeed. I learned values from my parents, but I learned motivation at school."

* * * * * * * * * *

From Mike's nearly 40 years in business, he made friends locally, nationally, and world-wide. Ron LaRocca is a sales and marketing consultant and has been self-employed for the last 14 years. He works with small and medium-size companies that sell consumer products through grocery and hardware/home center stores. LaRocca said, "I met Mike Cheek when we moved to Atlanta in 1980, and became next door neighbors. Our families instantly bonded

The Cheeks with President George H. W. Bush, Kentucky Derby 2000.

and have been friends ever since. Our wives and children really connected with each other as well. Even after the Cheeks relocated, we maintained our ties with them. They remain some of our closest friends, though we have been separated by distance for a long time. Mike and Runell celebrated their 40th anniversary, along with his birthday, in November, in Athens, and we gladly attended."

LaRocca observed, "Mike is bright, cordial, a great listener, and is very generous with his time. Not only is he a very good businessman, but he immediately impresses people with his sincerity and personality and makes friends easily. Mike is a great dad, husband, friend, and is an outstanding businessman. He is just a great guy to be around, because he is always so positive, and, if you ever need Mike for anything, he is always there for you. Mike Cheek is a '10' in my book."

Ralph Aguera, who serves in Trade Relations for Brown-Forman, recalled, "I first met Mike in the early 1990's when we both worked with Heublein, and again in 1999 when we worked for Brown-Forman. Mike is the best I have ever seen when working with people. He is smart, honest, he gets things done, and has unlimited energy. Mike treats people like a personal friend and always finds time to talk to each client. People know Mike as a kind and compassionate person who is extremely successful in all that he undertakes. He is a true and natural leader."

Aguera obviously knows Cheek well enough to comment on the sports-passion of his friend. "No one loves golf more than Mike Cheek. I truly believe he remembers every shot he has ever hit. For example, in 1992, he played in the Greater Hartford Open Pro-Am, and 10 years later, he asked me if I remembered his approach shot on number 17. I told him, 'I was having problems remembering the year, 1992.'

"The best things I can say about Mike Cheek are that he is dependable, honest, is a true leader, a great teacher, and a super speaker. It goes without saying that Mike has a wonderful family, but professionally, he rose to the top executive positions with Coke, Heublein, and Brown-Forman companies. Every occasion with Mike is an uplifting experience. His drive, loyalty, leadership, and motivation are the things that have made him successful in life. Macon, GA, should be extremely proud to have Mike Cheek as one of its favorite sons."

Another colleague at Brown Forman, Angelo Lucchesi, has been impressed with Cheek's ability in business. He said, "Mike Cheek is a man's man. In business, he understands markets and people. His greatest strengths are his ability to communicate and his availability to all those that work with him. Mike deals openly, directly, and fairly with people."

Lucchesi continued, "Mike will be remembered fondly for restoring dignity to our company and by his fair, even-handed leadership. Whatever position in business Mike was responsible for, he always took it to a higher level and restored some much-needed dignity."

Lucchesi poked fun at his friend's addiction to golf. "Anyone who knows Mike knows what an avid golfer he is. When he has a bad round, it's never his fault. It's always the clubs' fault, and he has been known to buy a new putter on occasions.

"He is such a good husband and father who has provided well for his family," Lucchesi concluded. "Mike is a very proud grandfather, and I am proud to call Mike Cheek my friend."

David Sliney met Mike Cheek in the late-1970's after Coca-Cola purchased the Taylor and Great Western Wineries where Sliney worked as regional manager. Cheek was hired by the newly formed subsidiary of Coca-Cola, The Wine Spectrum, and was recruited to be the Director of Sales for the new Coca-Cola venture.

Sliney said, "Since I was now part of field management, I began to be involved in meetings that Mike called for the 'field sales team.' In early 1980, he appointed me to run the premium sales division of the company, and moved me to Atlanta to our headquarters. At that point, we interacted nearly every day. Coca-Cola sold our company in 1983, and our careers went in different directions. However, since we both remained in the Wine and Spirits Industry, we stayed in contact with each other. I left the industry in 1990, so our contact was minimal until Mike's retirement last year. Since then, we have reconnected and communicate by email, talking about our golf games and football."

About his friend, Sliney observed, "It is obvious that Mike has a great many strengths and assets. What makes him unusual is that he could put them all together to create a most effective environment for those who come in contact with him. I have always felt that humor played a critical role in being an effective manager. Mike was a master at humor while maintaining his commitment to whatever the task may be. He led from a position of strength in that he was always well informed about the subject at hand, because he usually had first hand experience in that subject. Mike was keen in using his people wisely on various subjects, and he seemed to know whom to depend on for a specific task, or who could provide valuable input.

"Mike has always been very goal-oriented. He had the unique ability to not only present his goals, but effectively convince the organization that we could and would achieve them. Furthermore, Mike created an atmosphere where it was both exciting and extremely rewarding. It never seemed to concern Mike about making a goal. With him, it was only a question of how long it would take."

David Sliney said, "It was clear that Mike's strong presence and posture positioned him as a senior executive at Coca-Cola. However, one of Mike's great strengths is that he always maintained the human side, which those of us reporting to him could relate to. He came from the same background as most of us, starting at the bottom from humble beginnings, and he never lost sight of that as he grew in importance professionally."

Observing Cheek's strengths, Sliney said, "Mike had this unique ability of not only knowing his people personally, but relating to almost everyone who worked under his authority. Our organization consisted of almost 200 people in sales, plus a distributor network of some 200-plus companies, yet Mike knew most of them extremely well. As a result of his personal contact, combined with his enthusiastic commitment to our objectives, Mike created an organization of people and distributors who fully embraced our plans. It made us the most effective sales organization in an industry which was previously dominated by the Gallo Wine Company."

Mike Cheek has always been consistent in his dealings with people since his early days in South Macon. Sliney's belief is that Mike will never change in that area. "It is another reason for his great success," Sliney commented. "Mike was always honest and hard-working, far beyond what most people would have been committed to, and was always oriented toward change. He is obviously goal-oriented and incredibly enthusiastic, whether it is a sales goal or a Georgia football game, and people love him for it. People follow Mike Cheek, because they can trust him. Thus, they go with his direction and enjoy the success that accompanies it.

"While I worked with Mike in the wine industry, the industry leader was always Gallo. No one ever challenged them, nor did anyone ever think Gallo could be successfully challenged. Mike proved the industry wrong. Not only did he challenge them, but we, as a company under his leadership, became the new leaders in the wine industry."

Part of Mike's charm and success has always been his Southern humor. His contemporaries considered him to be a master at negotiating with his ability to use his Southern expressions well. Sliney recalled, "I am especially fond of one expression that I have used many times after hearing Mike use it. We were in a meeting with a major distributor, and it was clear that we were only agreeing to disagree. The tension in the room was getting out of hand; both sides had dug in and were being overly critical of the other. Mike had been sitting back, listening and allowing his managers to argue our position. Finally, when it appeared that the meeting needed to end before someone made a major mistake, Mike interrupted and said, 'You people are trying to pick fly-dung out of pepper.' The entire room stopped talking, looked at Mike, and everyone started smiling. Mike had broken the tension and let everyone know that they had lost track of the subject and the objectives. At that point Mike took control of the meeting. The outcome was a great success for everyone involved."

Contemporaries of Mike have been impressed, not only by his enthusiasm for life and professional competency, but also with his strong moral background. They see the same consistency and high standards in his personal life that they observe in the workplace. Sliney continued, "I think Mike is as great a father and husband as he has been a friend. He is always talking about and is actively involved with his family. Mike certainly has a successful family and personal life. Despite the successes that he has enjoyed, Mike has remained the same guy who grew up in Macon, GA. It is very rewarding to see Mike as the same person that he was before he experienced success in business. He really hasn't allowed success to change who he truly is. Mike's family has never forgotten where they came from, and they have always been appreciative of what they have.

"In business I had a great time with Mike, and as a result of his training, I enjoyed a very successful career," Sliney concluded.

Donald Price is a general contractor in Sandy Springs, a suburb of Atlanta. He and Mike Cheek got to be close friends when both were actively involved at Sandy Springs United Methodist Church back in the early 1980's. Their families have remained friends throughout the years, and the Prices have visited the Cheeks who have lived in Connecticut, Louisville, Naples, and Athens, among other places. Price joked, "Mike has had more houses than most people have had cars."

Price told the story of the time he and his wife invited the Cheeks to join them for the weekend at their White County, GA, mountain cabin. Runell rode up early with the Prices, and Mike was to join them later in the evening. Price said, "Since Mike had never been to our cabin before, I drew up a detailed map so he could come directly from Athens and join us. After we arrived, I realized that I had given Mike the wrong highway number where he was supposed to turn off the main highway, so I immediately took a huge piece of plywood that was four feet by five feet and made a sign with an arrow. The sign said, 'Turn here, Mike!' He soon arrived at the cabin; I apologized for the mistake, and asked him about the sign. Mike countered, 'What sign?' The four of us had to get in the car and drive him back to the intersection to convince him there was, in fact, a sign with his name on it. Mike followed the wrong directions and got to the right place. So much for Mike Cheek's observation skills."

On another occasion, Price was recovering from ankle surgery during football season. "I was still on crutches and Mike talked me into going to Clemson with him and Runell. He wanted to go early so we could park close to the stadium, and I wouldn't have to walk far. Sure enough, we went so early that we were practically the first ones there. Mike told me he was going to get a game-day program. I told him, 'Mike, they haven't even printed the programs yet!' That's how early we were."

Price continued, "All kidding aside, Mike's success has not come without hard work, intelligence, and good business sense. Mike looks into the future and sees things the rest of us don't see. I have observed his keen business acumen and his intuitive observation of market conditions, and I have never talked with any of his employees who were not totally committed to Mike as a boss and especially as a person. They go out of their way to express their respect and admiration for Mike. He gets the best out of people by making them feel important and appreciated, and he does that better than anyone I know. Mike is totally genuine, and everybody knows that his word is his bond."

In conclusion, Price said, "I am happy to count Mike as one of my friends. His positions in business have gotten progressively larger through the years, but Mike has remained the same person that I met over 20 years ago. Mike Cheek is truly worthy of his amazing success."

* * * * * * * * * *

There is seldom pretense among college friends, and the same was true for Cheek. Likewise, college friends know stories about each other that can be highly informative which need to stay within the confines of the moment they occurred. Philip L. Pitts and Mike Cheek were close friends during their days at the University of Georgia, and both were in the graduating class of 1966. "I first met Mike in Athens in 1964 when we had several classes together and became good friends," Pitts said. "We were both married and enjoyed getting together to grill some dog bones from Kroger, as well as going out to dinner at the Chicken

Shack on Broad Street in Athens. In those days, we could get a complete dinner for $1.00 to $1.25. Our other favorite place to go for a 'Glorified Steak Walking through the Garden' was The Varsity in downtown Athens. That was the local lingo for a hamburger (steak) with onions (walking) with lettuce/tomato (through the garden)."

Cheek was working part-time in the business school and helped with registration each quarter in Stegman Hall at UGA. Pitts recalled, "Mike became the most popular person at the Business School during registration, because he had early access to the IBM cards that were needed to register for classes. He knew which professors were teaching certain classes at specific times. If you were good friends with Mike, he could 'pre-register' you with the best professors on campus and do it from his sportcoat's inside pocket. Loosely translated, he could place you with teachers who gave good grades if you so desired. He could get you registered before the doors opened for registration."

During their senior year, Pitts and Cheek were both interviewed on campus by nearly 50 different companies. They both accepted jobs that took them to Jacksonville in June, 1966. Pitts recalled, "We caravanned from Athens to Macon and visited Mike and Runell's family, and then drove to Jacksonville the next day. We both found apartments several blocks from each other in Jacksonville, where Mike worked for Carnation and I worked for Esso.

"There was a time," Pitts said, "when Mike was stocking those little red Carnation evaporated milk cans on the shelves at a Winn-Dixie when he ripped the seat of his pants. Mike was thoroughly enjoying being on an expense account for the first time in his life, and he was eating so well that he outgrew both pairs of slacks that he owned. In short, Mike's expense account had allowed him to get too big for his britches. When he ripped his pants, that didn't slow him down a bit. The Winn-Dixie manager gave him a butcher's apron; Mike wrapped it around his waist in reverse and kept on working."

Pitts added, "As Mike began his career, he was a man on a mission and wasn't letting anything slow him down. He has been a go-getter since I first met him, and that drive has taken him to the top in his professional career. We have been great friends for 40 years. Mike is what you picture in your mind when you read Dale Carnegie's book, *How To Win Friends & Influence People*. He has more friends than you can imagine and has more connections than the railroad. I am honored to have him as my friend."

Jim Donnan, the former head football coach at the University of Georgia, is now a college football analyst for ESPN radio and television. Donnan, who lives in Athens, met Cheek through the Georgia football program. Donnan recalled, "Mike was a supporter of the Georgia football team when I moved to Athens, and I met him through his son-in-law, Tom Johnson, who was affiliated with the Athens Touchdown Club."

Donnan spoke about his friend, "Mike Cheek is as sincere and genuine as anybody you will ever meet. He has the unique ability to meet people very easily, and he knows how to put people around him at ease. I know that Mike has worked hard throughout his career and laid the groundwork for his success in business.

"Mike always loved going to the Ole Miss and Kentucky games, since he lived in Louisville for a while. He also enjoyed standing on the sidelines with our team. When he was on the sideline, Mike was a guy that I never had to worry about because he was always so positive; he enjoyed being around the team and was such a good influence on our players. When we started our gala banquet for the football team, Mike was very generous, and he donated a weekend package to the Kentucky Derby for our silent auction. His gift really helped us a lot, because that package was valued at $7,000 to $8,000.

"Mike is a very competitive guy. I have played golf with him a good bit, and he really wants to do well when we play. He's also very compassionate, too. He does a lot of things in the community that most people don't know about. He's a great family man, a great citizen in the community, and anybody would be glad to have Mike Cheek as a friend. We need more people like him in this world."

Mike and Runell celebrated their 40th wedding anniversary in November, 2004. Today, the Cheeks are truly enjoying the good life as they divide their time between Athens and Naples, FL. Now that Mike has retired, he can anticipate endless rounds of golf, Bulldog football and basketball, lecturing at the University, traveling for pleasure, and spending time with his grandchildren and the entire family.

"There is no limit to what one can achieve, as long as you don't care who gets the credit."

That statement says it all about Mike Cheek. He has lived his life and has led others with this belief as his foundation.

Mike and Ruvell Cheek on their 35th wedding anniversary in Louisville, KY.

And Starting at Quarterback for the Willingham Rams...

M. Eddie Battle
Class of 1960

Things don't happen by themselves.
–Billy Henderson

Being a quarterback brings with it some built-in issues. First, they get more credit than they should when their team wins, but they also get more blame than is due when their team loses. If those platitudes are true, then Eddie Battle received zero-credit and a ton of blame the first year he quarterbacked the Willingham Rams in their inaugural season in 1958. Their record? 0-7-3. That winless record was misleading, though, because Willingham was a first-year school with no seniors on the squad. Bibb County's Board of Education permitted rising seniors, though they lived in South Macon, to graduate from Lanier.

"To be honest," Eddie stated, "I wasn't the least bit excited when they called us into the gym at Lanier in the spring of 1958 and told us that if we went to certain elementary schools and still lived in those same neighborhoods, then we would be going to the new school in South Macon next fall. I didn't want to go to the new school, because I liked Lanier, I liked ROTC, I never minded cleaning my rifle on Fridays, or wearing the military uniform to school."

Battle's high school coach, mentor, and life-long friend, Billy Henderson spoke about his protégé, "Eddie Battle was a pioneer of sorts and a great leader who helped put Willingham High School on the map. He was our first quarterback and a co-captain at Willingham in 1958-59 and 1959-60. Eddie was an outstanding athlete who played football, basketball, and baseball, and was the first Willingham athlete to play in the Georgia High School All-Star baseball game at Ponce de Leon Park in Atlanta."

Henderson said, "Eddie is one of those 'fringe benefits' in my life as a coach. Being a teacher and a coach, you love all of your students and players, and many of them maintain contact with you even into adulthood. Eddie Battle is one of those people. I talk with him on a regular basis, and he drives to Athens to visit with me about once a month."

Eddie lived in the Rocky Creek Road neighborhood of South Macon until he was 14 and played elementary school athletics at Cynthia H. Weir School. His family—parents Hardwick and Hazel Battle, along with his sisters, Jan and Joy—moved to Hartley Bridge Road in South Bibb County when Eddie was 15. Battle said, "I grew up in blue-collar, working-class neighborhoods that were filled with good, honest, hard-working people. It was a great place to live, and I had a lot of close friends when I was growing up. Some of my friends and high school teammates in those days were Tommy Edwards, Gary Hall, Larry Jackson, Billy Lyles, Joel Dickens, Johnny Goss, Randy Wheeler, Pete Gaines, Larry Tucker, Pete Henderson, Catfish Walker, and my best friend, Charlie Partridge, who was killed in an automobile accident in 1970. I don't see many of those guys very often.

"When Willingham was founded," Eddie recalled, "one of the strongest areas of our brand-new school was the athletic program. Though we didn't win a football game that first year, we laid the foundation for Willingham's success in the following years. Willingham gave a lot of boys the opportunity to play sports that may never have even gone out for the team at Lanier. Many of my teammates and I had never seen a college football game in person until my junior year when Coach Henderson drove a yellow hound (school bus) to Atlanta to the Georgia-Georgia Tech freshman game at Grant Field in Atlanta on Thanksgiving Day."

Colista Raffield and Eddie Battle were high school sweethearts in the early years of Willingham and McEvoy. Eddie left Macon after graduation and attended Newberry College in Clinton, SC, on a football scholarship. Missing his girlfriend, family, and home, Eddie returned to Macon after his freshman year, married Colista in 1962, and enrolled at Mercer University. He graduated from Mercer in 1965 with a Bachelor of Arts degree with a concentration in science, and he taught biology and physical education for two years at his high school alma mater.

Then, with children making their way into the Battle household, Eddie left teaching and coaching, went in to the sporting goods business for several years, and then went to work for Macon, Mine and Mill selling industrial supplies for the next 18 years. The Battles have two sons, Chip and Chris, who both live in Macon. They also had a daughter, Beth, who died at age three from leukemia. Today, they have seven grandchildren.

* * * * * * * * * *

Most people who grew up in South Macon were keenly aware of the enormous influence of two men, both giants in that section of town. Rev. Jimmy Waters and Coach Billy Henderson took on gargantuan leadership roles in the South Macon community. Rev. Waters, affectionately known as "Brother Jimmy," was a leader in the Christian community and pastored both Billy Henderson and Eddie Battle at Mabel White Memorial Baptist Church. Rev. Waters became one of South Macon's most respected voices for morality and decency.

Neither Waters nor Henderson had to talk Eddie Battle into going to church or going out for football. Eddie was interested in everything they were selling, coaching, or preaching. He explained, "Dr. Jimmy Waters was the pastor at

Mabel White Baptist Church for 31 years and was a dynamic preacher who was always easy to talk to."

"Coach Henderson's influence covered more than football skills. He sacrificed so much to help others. People will never know the things Coach Henderson did without any fanfare or personal glory. When young men needed some direction in their lives, he was always willing to try and help them in any way he could. If Coach Henderson had gone into any other profession, other than high school coaching, he would have been a millionaire, but money meant nothing to him. He was interested in giving back to the community at large and the South Macon community in particular. He was primarily responsible for giving pride to a section of town that was primarily made up of middle-class families that had never much of an identity."

In addition to Billy Henderson, Eddie had several teachers who also motivated him to be successful. "William Bell, my senior English teacher who later became a high school principal in Macon, was a good disciplinarian and an excellent teacher. Leonard Pridgeon taught chemistry and physics and was an outstanding teacher. He seemed to really care about his students and wanted us to get a great education so we would be prepared for college. I remember Mr. Lloyd Newberry who was the principal at Willingham when the school opened. Coach Mike Garvin was a very good math teacher, and was right out of college; so he related well to high school guys. Even though I never had Coach Johnny Stallings as a teacher, he had one of the best defensive minds in football and was a great inspiration to me. I still consider him a friend today."

Mike Garvin remembered Eddie Battle from his teaching and coaching days that began at Willingham in 1959-60. "I have had the privilege of knowing Eddie from many different perspectives. I first met him when he moved into my neighborhood when he was about 10-11 years old. He became a playmate of my two younger brothers, McKenna and Minter, for several years. Eddie was an interesting person even then, running through the neighborhood full-steam and barefooted. I next encountered Eddie when he was in my homeroom at Willingham and was the quarterback on the first Willingham football team. This was really the beginning of a long and enduring friendship.

"When Eddie joined the Ram's football staff in 1964," Garvin recalled, "he became the first person that I had helped coach and then coached with. He and Colista honored me by giving me their sons to coach as football players at Mount de Sales and to teach in various math classes. Eddie and Colista were first-class parents, and both Chip and Chris were outstanding students and excellent football players."

Garvin closed, "The relationship that began some 50 years ago still continues today. We both serve on the Board of Directors for the Macon Sports Hall of Fame, and we continue to make and share memories. It has been my privilege to see Eddie develop as a person of high moral character with leadership qualities who serves the Macon community."

Willingham's first quarterback, Eddie cut his football teeth in grammar school playing for Cynthia Weir School. "When I was 12, I also played football in the Santa Claus Bowl in Lakeland, FL. That was a big deal for me in those days, because we were able to travel and play football against a team from out of state. Cloyd Hall and Lynn Zoller coached our team.

Eddie Battle, the baseball player, was the first athlete from Willingham to make all-state in any sport. Playing in the high school all-star game in Atlanta in 1960, he made the South squad which was coached by Willard Nixon, a former major leaguer who played for the Cleveland Indians and Boston Red Sox. "In that game, I remember having bursitis so bad in my right elbow that I could hardly throw it back to the pitcher, much less to second base.

"I always loved baseball," Eddie claimed, "and I was privileged to play in the first Little League in town, Macon Little League, and it was located on the Mercer campus. Jerry Modena, Larry Jackson, Robert Towe, and Jimmy Carr also played in that league. After Little League, my friends and I would walk to Memorial Park on Second Street to play in the citywide sandlot baseball program. We were the Beddingfield Booger Bears, and we won the city championship one year. I also remember walking to Porter Stadium from Rocky Creek Road to watch the Lanier Poets play football on Friday nights."

* * * * * * * * *

Eddie Battle spent large blocks of time with his sons when they were growing up, teaching them how to play ball and to love sports. Currently, he spends as much of his scarce leisure time as possible watching his seven grandchildren, who are involved in athletics, piano, and academic endeavors. The entire Battle family takes an annual vacation together.

Chip and Chris Battle spoke with great respect and admiration about their dad. Chip, the older son, said, "My dad's greatest asset is my mother, his wife of 43-plus years. He is kind, fair, and loyal to his family and friends. He has been a faithful son and has cared-for and honored his mother and father.

"My dad's nature is to give you the shirt off his back," Chip said, "and he'll give you his time, if that's what you need from him. His reputation has been to give to others, even if it has been very difficult financially for him. For example, he went through some extremely rocky times years ago when he was in the sporting goods business. He chose not to consider the bankruptcy-path, because he wanted to pay the debts that he owed. It took years of working more than one job to pay off that debt while trying to raise a family. I've admired him for that, because he didn't take the easy way out that so many people can legally take these days. I believe he's been blessed ten-fold for doing what he thought was right in his heart though it was not the easiest avenue available to him legally."

Chip continued, "My dad has a good name and reputation. I think he's still known by a lot of people as Willingham's first quarterback under Billy Henderson. When I tell people my name, many of them will ask, 'Are you related to Eddie Battle? I always liked him.' I believe people will remember my dad as someone who never spoke an unkind word about anyone and was always encouraging to others. Even while running a business, and with all of the employee challenges that go along with it, I've never heard him say anything unkind about another person.

Colista and Eddie Battle.

"When Chris and I were early teens, we got strong enough that we could wrestle with our dad and came close to winning, or at least he let us think we could win. One afternoon on Fairfax Drive, we were wrestling with him in our living room (apparently, our mom must have been preoccupied), and we were giving him a three-count. Dad decided he wasn't quite through with us, but Chris and I must have been tired of wrestling, because we jumped off him and ran out the front door. We jumped over our wrought iron railing, over the flower bed, and into the front yard, thinking we had gotten away from him. Little did we know that he was on our heels, and he jumped over the same railing and was in the front yard right behind us. I'm sure that was a sight for the neighbors. Chris and I both couldn't believe he could still move like that. I don't remember us wrestling much after that episode."

Eddie once took his sons quail hunting near Marshallville, GA, before they were teenagers. Chip recalled, "The owner of the farm was burning off one of his fields, and I remember he had the largest new Ford 4-WD farm tractor I'd ever seen. They had used it to harrow around the field before the 'burn' to keep the fire from spreading. Chris, Dad, and I stood and watched the field burning, and then went on our quail hunt. We were using the property owner's hunting dogs and were having a great time finding a lot of birds, and we weren't very far from where the field was being burned. After spotting and shooting at a few coveys of quail, I remember the expression on my dad's face when he looked behind him and saw thick black smoke in the woods, and it was blowing our way—fast. The wind had picked up and was blowing the fire over the dirt road. The fire went across the fire breaks and into the woods where we were hunting. The fire was spreading fast through the pine trees, and black smoke was billowing through the tops of the trees. I don't think I've ever seen that look in my dad's eyes since then. He shouted, 'Drop your guns!' He grabbed our hands, and we started running as fast as we could. I don't remember how long it took to get out of the woods, but I remember making it to a pecan orchard where we were finally safe. Once we got out of the burning forest, we could hear our ammo going off in our shotguns and vests that we had abandoned while we were running. We also saw the burned-out shell of what was the farmer's brand new Ford tractor."

Chip continued with his Eddie Battle-memories, "My dad would take Chris and me fishing on the weekends at Coley Lake, which is now Oak View Golf and Country Club on Hartley Bridge Road. He would go out there on weekdays and feed the fish so they would come to a certain spot in the lake at a certain time to be fed. When we got there, we would have a field-day-type free-for-all, catching as many fish as we could. There was also a place where we could drive an old jeep around, and we would take target practice. One Saturday, we decided to go behind the dam and fish in a pool where the lake overflowed. My dad called that spot 'Rattlesnake Hollow,' and he was right. We were cautiously walking down a steep embankment when my dad spotted a huge rattlesnake. He owned several high-quality guns, but for some reason, he had this really old single-shot shotgun that was held together by grey duct tape. We were carrying fishing tackle and poles while we walked down this steep embankment, which was slippery because of the thick pine straw. I remember that my dad shot the rattlesnake and then slipped down on the pine straw. When he fell, the single-shot, duct-taped old shotgun broke in half where it originally had been taped together. Dad started scurrying around trying to pick up both halves of the gun and quickly put it back together, because he saw another rattlesnake just a few feet away. He put the raggedy old gun back in one piece and took another shot at the snake. I don't remember ever going back to the pool of water behind the dam after that incident, and I don't remember ever seeing that old gun again."

Chip Battle realizes that his dad has left a good reputation, along with a great family name and reputation, for him and Chris. "I can't fathom what a better father would be like. I'm very proud of him, and I can say with pride that Eddie Battle is my father. I know he loves me no matter how imperfect I am. He loves his wife, parents, children, and grandchildren, and he tells us often. I believe my dad's spiritual gifts are wisdom, giving, and service. He does things for people and never wants credit and avoids having his name attached to it. Dad gives and serves from his heart."

As previously noted, Eddie was the first athlete at Willingham to earn an athletic scholarship to college. At Newberry College he was a promising baseball player until he hurt his elbow. Chip added, "My dad then transferred to Mercer, where he majored in biology, and was intending to go to medical school after graduation until I, being the first born, interrupted those plans."

It has always been obvious that Eddie Battle loved sports, both as a player and as a spectator. His sons can't recall their dad ever missing a midget football game or a Mount de Sales game when they played. "He was never the type of dad that complained or officiated from the sidelines. He didn't yell at the officials or talk about missed plays or bad calls," Chip recalled. "He always said, 'It was a good game.' He complimented you on the things you did well, and would let you chastise yourself on the mistakes that you knew you made. He always kept games and sports in perspective. Dad taught us that sports were important, and if we committed ourselves to playing, then we should give it 100%, and if you were in the game, then you were in it until the end. There was no quitting, just because things got difficult or intense. And he taught us that you always play the game to win; that's why you keep score."

Chip concluded, "I think his wife, his moral compass, belief in God, the drive to help others, and his work ethic have all contributed to his success in life. He loves his church, Mabel White Baptist, and I know he always enjoyed a close relationship with Rev. Jimmy Waters, and many others for a long time."

Chris Battle, the second son of Eddie and Colista, likewise has great memories about his dad and said, "God puts people in our lives for a reason. Having the father that I have is an example of God's love for me, and Him not giving me what I really deserve. I remember that the Bible says, 'To whom much is given, much is required.' My dad has been given many talents and skills, and he has used those skills well. My dad's strengths are that he sees everyone as decent and honest, and he will keep that opinion until they prove themselves otherwise. He is a man who has his emotions under control, and I have never heard him yell at me, unless it was to hit harder or to run faster in football.

"Many people will remember my dad as a very good athlete and a leader in high school," Chris said, "but I think he'll be remembered more for being such a good husband, father, grandfather, and friend to a lot of people. He has been a great example of a godly, faithful husband to my mom and a wonderful father to Chip and me. The older I get, the more I realize how smart my dad was when I was growing up. As a father, he always spent time with us. As boys, we enjoyed the outdoors, and he enjoyed being there with us. Whether we were hunting, camping, or playing ball, Dad enjoyed spending time with us. We grew up in a great neighborhood, and though we didn't have a lot of material things, the older I got, the more I realized how rich I was in things that were truly important that you can't put a price on. I have a father that rarely missed a ball game and always encouraged me to do my best."

Chris continued, "Today, the best things that I could say about my daddy are that he loves spending time with his grandchildren and doing things for them. He also loves doing things for others, and he appreciates the type of parents that he had while growing up. Dad doesn't believe he is better than anyone else. He has always been honest and compassionate toward all people.

"My daddy has always bought, sold, and traded unusual things like Army jeeps and even an old fire truck. One of my best memories was during the big snow of 1973. He had bought several old Willis Army jeeps, and I remember riding around with him during the snow and helping pull people out of ditches. We had snowball fights with anyone we could find. I think he had more fun than Chip or me. There was also a standing joke between my dad and mom that she wouldn't allow him to go to an auction unsupervised because of all the stuff he would buy. Some of it we needed, and most of it we didn't."

When Eddie Battle was a senior at Willingham, a young Mike Garvin was on the coaching staff. Chip and Chris Battle both attended Mount de Sales Academy in the 1970's when Mike Garvin was the football coach and a math teacher there. Chris recalled, "Daddy told me stories about Coach Garvin, and how Coach Garvin had given him the worst paddling in his life. I take it as a great honor to have played football under one of the men that coached my daddy in high school. Of course, my daddy also thought it would be good for me to play for Coach Garvin, and as usual, he was right."

Though Eddie Battle only coached at Willingham for two years, he continued to influence young lives by coaching Little League baseball teams in the summer, even when his own sons were too old to play. Chad McDaniel, now the Sports Information Director at First Presbyterian Day School and the school's cross country and track coach, vividly recalled playing for Eddie. "I have fond memories of Coach Eddie Battle from Vine-Ingle Little League baseball. As a 'career right fielder,' (since nobody hits it to right in Little League), I could generally be seen kicking a dirt hole in the ground, chasing butterflies, or picking dandelions. In those days, I frequently prayed for balls to be hit in any direction but mine. Things were not much better at the plate for me. When Coach Battle told me not to swing until the umpire called a strike, I replied, 'But then the ball will already be in the catcher's mitt.' Instead of replying sarcastically, or making me feel stupid, Coach Battle calmly explained to me the strategy behind making the pitcher throw a strike.

"Throughout my life I have shared many entertaining Little League stories with numerous friends, and most have asked me why I continued to play (and I use that term loosely) Little League baseball. It's a great question, since I once went an entire season without a hit. Coach Battle was the major reason why I enjoyed my time in Little League, and I firmly believe he is the perfect example of how youth league coaches should conduct themselves."

Chad continued, "As a high school coach, I see too many coaches and parents of young children put a high premium on winning at the expense of everything else, and they rarely focus on developing a love for sports or teaching skills to those (like me) who are not extremely talented. Without Coach Eddie Battle, I wonder if I would have ever felt like a part of a team or developed such a great love of athletics later in life. I know that my experiences on other teams pale in comparison to my two years with Eddie Battle, and it says a great deal about his character that he picked me for a second season, having seen my ability the year before.

"As a high school cross-country and track coach, I have been accused many times of allowing any kid who has a pulse to be on my team. It's absolutely true. I see myself in those kids. The amazing thing to me is that Eddie Battle was an excellent athlete, and he still understood that the kid without talent deserved to be coached, encouraged, and treated as a vital member of the team. This most important lesson I will carry from my experiences with Coach."

Certainly, nobody on earth knows Eddie Battle like Colista, his wife of 43-plus years. "In high school, Eddie was always a gentleman who just loved sports, and he is still the same today. Even though he no longer participates, he finds great joy in playing with his grandchildren and going to their games. His grandson Michael loves the Georgia Bulldogs, and Eddie enjoys taking him to see the Bulldogs play.

"I feel that the one thing that stands out about Eddie," she said, "is his 'grace under fire.' There have been many occasions throughout our marriage where a crisis would come, either at home, church, or with our children. Eddie was always the one who could think rationally and act calmly. One specific time, when we were members at Tattnall Square Baptist Church, there was to be a serious matter to be brought before the deacons. Eddie was a deacon then, and they would not have their meeting until Eddie was able to be there. I think they felt like his presence could calm a volatile situation. He has always been a peacemaker and believed that arguing and being contentious served no purpose. The Bible verse, Matthew 5:9, says, 'Blessed are the peacemakers, for they shall be called the children of God.' That verse is meant for Eddie."

Colista knows firsthand what a giving person Eddie has always been. "He loves to surprise people with gifts. A favorite habit of his is to buy a case of a friend's favorite item and give it to them at Christmas. One year, he gave apple butter; another year, it was banana nut bread, and still another Christmas, he gave them a new barbeque sauce he had found."

On a light note, Colista recalled the time Jim Lambert, who is a pilot, needed to get in some flight time; so he offered to fly Eddie to Alabama to pick up a truck that Eddie had purchased. They met at the airport, the plane was checked, and they took off. They were barely airborne when the tower called Jim and told him to turn around and come back, because his plane was on fire. Eddie said that they were both very calm; they turned the plane around, and landed it, complete with a full array of emergency vehicles and a fire truck. The mechanics fixed the problem, said that it was safe for us to go, and off we went to Alabama."

Like his influence on a young Chad McDaniel, Eddie Battle has always related well to young people. Though they disagree, Colista has always believed that her husband should have stayed in coaching because he was so good at it. Eddie not only related well to athletes but to youngsters in general. Colista recalled, "One of the best times of our life was when Eddie helped Key Chambers, minister of music and youth, at Tattnall Square Baptist Church. The youth group loved Eddie, and he helped Key by driving the church bus or van."

Just as Eddie was highly-respected as a coach and teacher, he was also revered for his leadership in church and at Tattnall Square Academy. Colista said, "Under Brother Jimmy Water's leadership, God used Eddie in so many ways. Eddie became the chairman of deacons, he actively served on Tattnall Square Academy's board of directors for 13 years and was chairman of the board more than once. Eddie served on the church's building committee that oversaw the building of the education building that was named in honor of Jimmy and Annette Waters."

As an example of Eddie's commitment to serve and lead, when he was chairman of Tattnall Square Academy's board, the school's headmaster was out for an extended period of time, due to surgery. Eddie was there at the school every day providing leadership until the headmaster could return.

"I remember one particular incident that shows Eddie's level of service to Tattnall Square and to that congregation," Colista recalled. "There was a lady who was in failing health, and her daughter wanted to move the lady out of state so they could be closer to each other. The older lady called the church and asked for the pastor to come visit her because she was so upset about the prospect of leaving her home. The pastor was not available, but the lady was told the minister of music was available, and he could come instead. 'No,' the lady answered politely, 'I want Eddie Battle to come visit me.'"

As a father and husband, Eddie has demonstrated a strong faith in God, which has been the guiding force in his marriage to Colista. She said, "The greatest tragedy of our lives was losing our daughter, Beth. I was so lost in my own grief that I could not help Eddie with his. This was our most difficult time together, but time is a great healer, and even though we will never forget losing our daughter, we have learned to move on.

"Eddie has always been very supportive of me and all that I try to do. He loves his sons and enjoyed coaching them as they grew up. He especially loves being with his sons and their families now, whether it is swimming at our house, going to the beach, or spending time in the mountains. Each summer, as a family, we spend one week at Hilton Head, which is a very special time for all of us."

Colista continued, "Two years ago, Eddie's best friend, Wayne Bevill, passed away. He and Wayne had been friends since high school, and in some ways, they were closer than brothers. I am so glad that Eddie was able to be with Wayne in those final weeks before he died. Many afternoons after work, Eddie would go to Wayne's house where they would sit and talk and eat banana split ice cream.

Eddie Battle has become very successful in business by building swimming pools. His company, Astro Pools, Inc., which he bought in 1986, has a reputation for building the best pools in the Middle Georgia area. He continues to work hard to assure customers that they will get the best pool that can be built. His company designs and constructs high-quality gunite pools. Eddie commented, "I may have 11 pools being built at the same time. It takes about 30 days for us to complete a pool if the weather cooperates."

Without question, Eddie has done many important and meaningful things in his life—as a coach, a friend to many, as a Christian businessman, and as a first-rate husband and father. However according to Eddie, "The best things that I have done in my life were marrying Colista Raffield and accepting Jesus Christ as my Lord and Savior."

Many South Maconites will always remember Eddie Battle as Willingham High School's first quarterback. He would prefer to be remembered as a good husband, father, and grandfather; as one who treated people fairly and with respect; and as someone who made a contribution in life by helping others.

"Don't figure how you can't; figure how you can."
–Rev. Jimmy Waters

The Battles: Eddie, Chris, Colista, and Chip

A. R. Willingham School for Boys to Johns Hopkins University

Danny L. Strickland
Class of 1966

"Whatever you do, leave things better than you find them."

"**C**onnie Stafford and I, along with several other boys who were good students at Willingham, got a call from Phillips Exeter Academy of Portsmouth, New Hampshire," Dan Strickland recalled. "At the time, we didn't know that it was one of the top prep schools in America. I guess they had some diversity targets in mind back in the mid-1960's, and wanted to help some poor Southern boys get a top-flight New England education. I remember that Connie and I listened to their representative's presentation, and they offered us scholarships to go there for high school. We turned it down because you had to wear a tie with your uniform. We found out years later that President George H.W. Bush actually graduated from Exeter, but what did we know back then?"

Without realizing it at the time, 'Danny' Strickland, was also being observed by many for his academic and athletic abilities. The leading scorer on the 1965-66 Willingham Rams basketball team, he began to draw the attention of colleges who wanted a tough, hard-nosed, though quite small (5'9", 150 pound), shooting guard.

Willingham's football, baseball, and track teams were strong in those years, playing and beating the top teams from all over Georgia, but the basketball program could never quite measure up to the other sports' successes. In 1966 during Strickland's senior year, Billy Beale and Tommy Mixon took over the basketball coaching responsibilities, and for the first time in school history, Willingham's basketball fortunes improved dramatically and had the school's first winning record.

"We had a very good team that year," Mixon recalled. "Our starting lineup was full of athletic types. Bobby Goldsby (6'6") went on to play basketball in college. James Holland (6'5") played college football at Georgia Tech, while Darrell Parker (6'1") also played baseball and football at Tech. Durwood Sauls (6'1") played football at Auburn, and Danny Strickland (5'9") went on to Johns Hopkins and played there. Danny had a very good senior year, and we beat Lanier twice. That was the first time we had beaten them in years."

However, as good as Strickland was in basketball, his ticket for a college education would ultimately be in the classroom. The educational gauntlet was thrown down early in Strickland's career. Dan said, "I started off making all 'G's' in elementary school. 'G' equaled 'Good' in those days, so my mother knew that I was capable of high achievement from the very beginning.

"Growing up, I went to Charles H. Bruce School, which was about three blocks from my house," Strickland remembered. "We lived between Tela Place and San Juan Avenue. My granddad was a carpenter, and my dad was a painter. They built a garage apartment in back of my grandparents' house. We were living there when my father died. After that, my mom ran a nursery in the downstairs portion of the garage apartment. Later, after my granddad died, we moved into the front house with my grandmother and rented out the garage apartment for $60 a month to help with living expenses.

"My mom, Louise Strickland, was an amazing woman," Dan said. "She grew up in South Georgia. Her dad, Walter Angus Tapley, was a character and he married my grandmother when she was 15 and he was 31. He was the nicest man in the world and was so meek and mild-mannered. My granddad ran the main hotel in a small town. At various times, he was a hotel operator, an undertaker, and a carpenter.

Strickland's dad, Lloyd M. Strickland, died from a brain tumor when Dan was seven years old. "Back in 1956, there was no MRI or neurosurgery, so they simply relieved the pressure and hoped for the best. My grandfather died not long after that, so I was raised around a bunch of women," Strickland noted. "In addition to my mom, grandmother, and sister, we virtually lived next door to my aunt Dot and cousin, Dorcille, who is like a sister. My mother never took a job outside the home, because she wanted to be there to raise me and my sister, Arlene, who was thirteen months younger. My mother was an excellent seamstress and sewed for people and businesses. She would sew numbers or names on uniforms or letter jackets for Charlie Wood's Sporting Goods in Macon. I remember that she would have rush jobs to do and would stay up all night sewing. I didn't like that, but she was grateful for the work. She was truly a nurturing figure to my sister and me.

"My parents had been married 10 years before I came along," Strickland said. "My mother followed my dad around while he was in the Army in World War II. He was stationed in Baton Rouge near a naval facility for a while, and she went to look for work in the shipyard. When she was asked what type of work she could do, her reply was, 'Which type of work pays the most money?' Mrs. Strickland was told that welding was the best-paying job at the base, so she told the officer, 'OK, then I'll weld.' She welded ships and sewed patches on soldiers' sleeves to help make their financial ends meet."

Strickland recalled, "Like the rest of our neighborhood, we had very little money. I was born at the clinic in Macon. Our electricity was turned off several times, because my mom couldn't pay the power bill, but for some reason, we never felt poor. Everyone I knew was like us. In our neighborhood, we didn't throw baseballs away when the stitches broke. We just taped them up and played on. If the ball went down into the gutter, you went down there and got it. I remember getting a basketball at Christmas one year when I was 10 or 11, and before the day was over, my ball was punctured. It wouldn't hold air, but I didn't get another basketball. I made a goal in the backyard with a very small backboard and would shoot at night using the light from the back porch. I made a net and shot with my ball which wouldn't hold air. I would shoot it, the deflated ball would hit and stop, and I would hustle after it and shoot again."

Growing up in South Macon, it was common knowledge that Lanier was the school with money and influence. Stratford Academy was a very young school in the 1960's and it was private, which precluded most South Macon boys from attending. Strickland said, "Somehow, I knew that there was a difference in the two sides of town. Our South Macon stores seemed to close and go out of business more often than stores in other parts of town. There didn't appear to be any sense of prosperity in South Macon, but it didn't seem like a bad part of town. It was just different. Our houses were different. If you rode around town, you always saw bigger, nicer houses in the other parts of Macon. Heck, I didn't even know where most of the nice parts of Macon were."

* * * * * * * * *

"My experience at Willingham was a very good one overall," Dan recalled. "I only made one 'B' in high school and was involved in a number of activities. I was president of the Key Club, co-editor of the sports section of the yearbook, and was into just about everything. I also worked very hard in school. Athletically, I did pretty well as an All-Star pitcher in South Macon Little League, in Pony League, and Colt League at Morgan Field. Actually, I usually played with a baseball glove that I borrowed from Danny Purvis, a neighborhood friend. Socially, I remember being somewhat awkward since our family had no car. Thus, I would ride with my aunt or walk. I rode to high school with Bo Hardison and paid him 50 cents a week for gas. I usually caught a ride to ball practice with Durwood Sauls.

"At Willingham, I hung out with three distinctly different groups. One group was the 'cool guys and the jocks' like Tommy Hinson and Brad Henderson. Then there were the 'bad boys' who, in those days, were in high school fraternities and partied quite a bit. They also got into a lot of trouble, sometimes serious trouble. I also hung around the 'nerdy guys' who didn't have many friends. For some reason, I seemed to fit in a little bit with each group. Later on in life, I learned that kids are usually the average of their twelve closest friends, and, if you get in with the wrong crowd, then you are pretty much stuck there unless you change schools or move so you can join in with a new and different crowd. I'm not sure why I ended up where I did."

Strickland reminisced, "If I had my high school years to live over again, I would have played varsity football. Coach Johnny Stallings of Willingham seemed to make it his life's passion to get me to try football at Willingham. He all but promised me that I could have a starting position if I would just come out for football, but the harder he tried, the more I resisted. I really don't know why I didn't play varsity football, but I played touch football in P.E. and fraternity football on Sunday afternoons at Baconsfield Park. We played tackle with no pads. I don't think my lack of size had anything to do with me not playing for Willingham. I really enjoyed my high school sports career a great deal. In addition to basketball, I was a sprinter, long jumper, and pole vaulter in track. My senior year, I vaulted over 13'0" and finished fourth in the state."

Several men were influential in Dan Strickland's life at Willingham. Billy Beale was the head basketball coach and really encouraged him. "Coach Beale would let me borrow a key to the gym so I could go shoot on weekends. He was the one that taught me about athletic discipline, and, since my dad died when I was seven, he was sort of a father figure to me.

"Tommy Mixon was my baseball coach," Strickland recalled, "and he taught me toughness. He was also an assistant coach in baseball. James Holland and I would play two on two against Mixon and Beale, and they just physically beat up on us. He taught me aggressiveness, and a couple of times, when I would have a big offensive game, it was simply because his expectations were so high."

Mixon, who later became a baseball scout for the Los Angeles Dodgers, recalled coaching Dan Strickland at Willingham, "Danny's best sport was basketball, and he was a quiet type of leader. I remember that he was hard-working and highly motivated. Danny had tremendous skills as a shooter, was our leading scorer, and played tenacious defense. He played both baseball and basketball at Willingham and worked as hard as any kid that I've ever coached. I always loved his appetite for competition, and the bigger the game, the better he was. We had a very good basketball team Danny's senior year, and he was very instrumental in our first winning season and beating Lanier, our city rival, for the first time in years."

Another man who greatly influenced Dan Strickland as a young man was Carson Wallace, whose son, Ron, was an outstanding football player at Willingham and later at Florida State. Carson Wallace was a minister who also owned a furniture store in downtown Macon. He was on Macon's City Council and helped Strickland get his first car in his last year of college. Strickland said, "I found a car that I liked and thought I could afford, so I applied for a loan but didn't get it. E. Raymond Smith Motors wouldn't approve me for the loan since my job was only for the summer, and my mom didn't have any steady, documentable income. Since I needed to buy some inexpensive furniture for my apartment in Atlanta, Mr. Wallace asked me to come to his furniture store office. I remember that he picked up the phone and called E. Raymond Smith. I was just sitting in his office while they were chatting about lamps. Then Mr. Wallace said, 'I have this young man who is a good friend of mine, and he wants to buy a car from you. I want you to give him this loan and give him your best rate.'

"Carson Wallace helped me when there was no real reason for him to do so except to do a kind thing. I was overwhelmed at the influence that he had and how he used it for good. He was very smooth and extremely impressive, and, because of what he did for me that day in his office in Macon, I guess I have now done that same thing for over 100 people. And it's simply because I got help when I needed it from Carson Wallace. Just a phone call to the man, and it was done."

Having teachers taking a personal interest in Dan Strickland during his teenage years certainly helped jumpstart his academic career. Leonard Pridgeon taught chemistry and physics at Willingham and in Strickland's words, "Mr. Pridgeon was the one that got me into science. He was so cool and reserved as a teacher. He wore those old-style, academic-looking glasses, and he was quite a scholar. I would grade papers for him during a free period. Mr. E.J. (Erasmus Jerome) Hancock was a science teacher who was extremely colorful and had a wild delivery in class. He loved science, and his enthusiasm for what he taught was infectious.

"Coach Mike Garvin was one of my favorite math teachers because of the way he made math fun. I also remember having two women who taught me at Willingham. One was an English teacher named Doris Sagers, a very tall lady who taught me to like English. She introduced us to interesting, unconventional material in class, and she drove a Corvette to school. She read Bob Dylan's writings to us and was totally cool. Another teacher I liked, who was interesting and taught me a lot, was named Carol Seabrooke, my social studies teacher. She was interesting, and I learned a lot in her class. I also think I had a bit of a crush on her."

When Dan was a senior at Willingham, he won the math award for the highest score on a standardized math test. However, he had no idea where he was going to college after graduation, but he applied to NC State, Auburn, and Johns Hopkins in Baltimore, MD. Dan chose Johns Hopkins University because his mother's sister married a man from Baltimore, and he could live with them without paying for room and board. In short, Dan went to the best school he could find that was willing to provide a full scholarship.

"Johns Hopkins is obviously a tremendous school. I went there for two years as a chemical engineering major and played basketball," he recalled. "I did well academically and made the Dean's List and achieved a 3.9 GPA while majoring in chemical engineering. I rode into the city with my uncle at 6 a.m. daily. My classes were usually at 9:00 a.m., and he would pick me up in the afternoon. Johns Hopkins' baccalaureate program had around 5,000 students, but their chemical engineering program changed during my second year there. Their focus became geared more toward graduate school, and they stopped granting specialized engineering degrees and just provided degrees in engineering. I really wasn't interested in that, because I wondered how I would get a job with such a general degree. They certainly weren't going to change it just for me, so I transferred to Georgia Tech."

Dan continued his sterling academic progress and graduated Summa Cum

Laude from Tech in 1970 with a BS in Chemistry and a 3.8 GPA while working 40 hours a week in the school's aerospace engineering department. He worked with professors there and organized events for the department while taking a full load of classes. He also did research for some of the chemistry professors and was a resident advisor in one of the dorms. Always one to provide for his mother, Dan made enough money to send some home to help her with her own living expenses. During his senior year at Tech and without any clear direction for a career, he considered architecture (he was accepted into Duke and Tech's graduate programs), law, (he considered a combination law and MBA degree program from Harvard and Stanford), and the PhD program for chemistry at Tech.

Strickland's plans for graduate programs screeched to a halt with Viet Nam and military service looming large. "I had number 126 and found out that those under 200 would probably be drafted. I had interviewed for several companies and went to work with Procter and Gamble. Some of their employees were getting occupational deferments if they could demonstrate that their job was considered in the national interest. My job qualified since we were removing phosphates from detergents, so P&G filed for my deferment, but we missed the cut-off deadline by one day because P&G had sent it by the slowest means (registered mail). Soon, I received greetings from President Nixon in 1970. P&G appealed for me, but we lost the appeal, 3-2. We appealed to the state board of Ohio where P&G was based, but lost that appeal, 3-2. They said, 'Don't worry. We'll appeal to the President's appeal commission,' but we lost that appeal, 2-1. So, one Friday, I received a notice to report for induction the next Tuesday.

"I hadn't told my mother since I knew she would be upset, and I hoped not to go. I was shipped off to Fort Leonard Wood, MO, which we affectionately renamed, 'Fort Lost-in-the-Woods.' I called my sister and asked her to call my mother to tell her that I was officially in the Army."

Dan continued, "Twenty guys died from meningitis while I was there. It was awful. I had orders for Viet Nam infantry training at Ft. Polk, LA. Amazingly, these orders were changed, and I went into their Science and Engineering Program. My first duty was at Ft. Deitrich, MD, where I worked in biological warfare research. We worked on anthrax and Venezuelan equine encephalitis. While we were there, the U.S Government decided that biological warfare was immoral, so we worked extensively on defensive weapons. President Nixon changed our focus to a cancer research center, and I was reassigned to the Redstone Arsenal at the Marshall Space Flight Center in Huntsville, AL. My roommate from Georgia Tech, Larry Russell, worked there as a civilian – I believe his project was to create the big arm on the original space shuttle. I spent a lot of evenings over at Larry's house. I got out of the Army after a year and a half as the country moved to a volunteer Army. My situation was also considered a hardship, since I was the only remaining male in my family."

Dan then went back to work with Procter and Gamble in their products research group. Strickland said, "In my 18 years at P&G from 1970 to 1988, I worked on every product category they had except for food items. We covered products like Tide, Cheer, Era, bar soaps, shampoos, paper products, feminine protection, Pampers, Downy fabric softeners, Bounce Sheets, and Attends, the first adult incontinent product. I felt very domestic!"

He continued, "In 1983, I went to Brussels, Belgium, and worked at the European Research Center where I worked on household products, Crest, shampoos, Pantene, Prell, and Vick's Mentholatum before moving to London in 1986 to be the Director of Research and Development of the European Health and Beauty Care Division of P&G. I loved it there."

In 1981, Dan was married to Denise (NEE Gardonio), whom he met while working for P&G. Their son, Brandan Lloyd Strickland, whose middle name came from Dan's father, was born in 1982, and was one year old when they moved to Europe. Brandan quickly fit into the European routine, picking up French and Spanish in his early years.

While at Procter and Gamble, Strickland met Tim Fealey who worked for P&G for 29 years. Fealey's last role was VP of Strategic Planning for Food and Beverage Worldwide. He is now retired but continues to work as a technology strategist, along with various other pursuits. "I first met Dan Strickland after I joined P&G in May, 1972. Dan had joined the company two years before, and, from 1974-76 and again in 1979, I worked directly for him. After 1981, our career paths went in different directions, yet we kept in touch. He was my mentor. and we became good friends and colleagues. We are still close friends after all these years. Despite the passage of time, and though we have had minimal dealings in recent years, re-establishing contact is just like when we would meet and work together every day.

"Dan is a true professional and is dedicated to getting the best from himself and the people around him," Fealey said. "He is analytical to the extreme, focused, and brings a sense of determination and persistence to do the right thing as he executes his responsibilities. He is excellent at reading people and is a great team leader who builds consensus effectively. Dan has personal and professional charisma and this aura of trust which helps him get the best from his people. He is results-oriented and is a courageous leader who is dependable and direct; so he works well with management that is similarly focused.

"Dan Strickland has a direct coaching-management style and leads by example. His values and principles are embodied in the phrase 'he does the right thing,' and he leverages this in earning the trust of those around him. Dan's striving for excellence in results creates the environment in which individuals, groups, and departments grow and produce good things for his company. He is highly competitive and really likes to win, as well as making his team and his company winners."

Fealey said, "Dan will be remembered with high regard for his competence and effectiveness as a professional manager in the consumer products industry.

He is already remembered as an individual who is high-energy, fun-loving, sports-oriented, humorous, and an all-around great guy. People just like to get to know him and be with him. Dan Strickland makes the world around him a brighter and a more enjoyable place."

Fealey has seen both the focused, as well as the lighter side of his long-time friend and said, "P&G was generally recognized as the 'home of the memo,' which was the vehicle of choice to communicate purpose, goals, plans, actions and roles, and responsibilities for any key project. Dan took this process to an entirely new level of craftsmanship. He would 'niggle' structure, word-use, phrasing, and sentence design until people would almost cry in frustration. But Dan would also be vindicated by a hand-written note or personal call to the memo-writer for a job well done. Dan used the memo-process as a learning and training vehicle to sharpen the thinking and communication skills of our employees and to show how the written communication left an impression with the reader that was important."

Fealey recalled about Strickland, "Dan had a marvelous sense of humor. He worked for a very good guy who was not too fashion-conscious and who bought the cheapest shirts he could find. Some of the shirts he wore had old-fashioned epaulets on the shoulder that were similar to a military shirt design. To celebrate the promotion of his boss, Dan designed military stars from cardboard, covered the stars with aluminum foil, and presented them to his boss at the celebration. The two foil-stars made him the two-star general of Procter and Gamble's Research and Development. His boss wore the same shirt with the foil-covered stars for the rest of the week! Dan had that special quality that made it possible for him to get away with actions that others could not pull off. He was able to communicate his respect and regard for his superior, but he could do it in a fun way."

In those days, there were inter-divisional rivalries with sports teams within the various divisions of P&G. Fealey said, "For several years Danny had played on these teams with much success, but with no championships. Eventually, winning a company championship became a goal of his. He recruited some of his teammates, got a new team manager, and developed a game-plan to win a championship. This new strategy was to make it a requirement in our annual personnel recruiting efforts to attract proven running backs and strong forwards to fill some weak spots on his teams. Thus, recruiting top-quality personnel took on a whole new flavor and interest, but Dan's effort was very successful. Good people were recruited who met the company's and the team's requirements. Within two years, Danny Strickland had his coveted Procter and Gamble championship!

"Competition aside," Fealey continued, "Dan has developed his subordinates into the best possible professionals, and I am convinced that this will be his professional legacy. He has been a good, reliable, and trusted friend. Throughout the years and with all of the success that he has experienced, Dan has retained his basic character and goodness. He has become a role model for the rest of us, and he makes life more enjoyable and much brighter for those around him.

"A positive 'can-do' attitude, seeking a 'win-win' consensus, striving for the best possible outcome, and avoiding internal battles have made him successful in business and in life," Tim Fealey concluded. "Dan Strickland is a man who leads by example. He brings a spirit of 'life is an adventure, and we all should enjoy it to the fullest' to everything he does. His personal outlook is reflected in his mannerisms and communication style. His speech is fast and punctuated with references and stories that make his points interesting. He is a bundle of high-productive energy, while his mannerisms reinforce his drive and desire to make others be more effective and productive. Danny leaves the impression of someone who wants to live life to the fullest while being as successful as possible, but he does it with humility and humanity."

1988 was the year designated as the beginning of an upward, professional spiral in the area of Research and Development in the life of Dan Strickland. He was recruited back from Europe by Kraft Foods in Chicago to become their Vice President of Technology Development. The Philip Morris Company later bought Kraft and merged it with their General Foods business, and there was a huge integration between these two major companies. Strickland worked for Kraft General Foods, now renamed Kraft, from 1988-1993.

Bob McVicker, now deceased, was Strickland's first boss at P&G. McVicker left P&G to become the head of R&D at Kraft and a few years later, recruited his protégé. He had given young Strickland great tutelage on how things are done in the area of Research and Development. Dan was VP of Strategy and Development at Kraft and was responsible for a $50 million budget. At Kraft, he recruited approximately 200 managers and scientists to upgrade their organization. With his background in chemistry, Strickland was primarily responsible for developing fat replacement technology for products which included natural and processed cheese, frozen dinners, ice cream, salad dressings, and margarine that had all of the taste but significantly lower levels of fat and calories. He also established a Consumer Fundamentals program that gave consumers input into the product development process.

Dan continued his ascent in the field of R&D when he was recruited in 1993 to go to work for Johnson and Johnson. He moved to Princeton, NJ, to become the Executive Vice President of Worldwide Absorbent Products and Materials Research for J&J's consumer sector. Dan headed up J&J's worldwide research and development activities and oversaw $260 million budgets supporting $3 billion in revenues and 1,000 employees.

During those four years, Dan was out of the country about 50 percent of the time, since he managed 13 research centers around the world. His travels and work took him from New Jersey to places like Montreal, Sao Paulo, Düsseldorf, Manila, Sydney, Hong Kong, India, and Tokyo. His primary functions with J&J were in R&D, strategy, engineering, and quality.

"I married late the first time, and we were divorced after six years," Dan recalled. "Then, I met Christine (NEE Lonergan) in Chicago when I worked at Kraft. We were married in 1993 as I moved to Johnson & Johnson. I went to work with General Mills in 1997 in Minneapolis as Senior VP for Innovation Technology and Quality and worked there until April, 2003."

Lydia Midness, currently Vice President of R&D for Cereal Partners Worldwide, worked for Dan at General Mills and commented about his strengths and assets, "Danny is a born leader. He has a very positive outlook on life and shares that with those around him. He can quickly identify an individual's strengths, and he encourages them to excel at whatever they can. He is very strategic in his thinking and planning skills.

"Danny is a highly creative individual who is constantly innovating. Over the course of his career, he has led significant change through innovation. Sometimes, the change was difficult, but through his special leadership style, he was able to bring about positive change. Danny has a strong work ethic, is highly intelligent, and has an excellent memory. Danny has a great gift as a storyteller, which he uses in all types of situations to get his point across. All of those things make him an exceptional leader."

While working with Strickland at General Mills, Midness saw that Dan was always concerned about the well-being of others around him. "He has been known to be very kind and generous to those who are less fortunate, often helping employees, friends, and family behind the scenes. He is fully committed to what ever he does; he's a humanitarian, and is loyal to his friends, family, and employees. His positive outlook on life makes him successful in life."

After a highly successful six-year stint with General Mills, Strickland took his family and moved to Atlanta when he went to work for Coca-Cola as their Chief Innovation and Technology Officer. "Coke and I have been a great fit," Strickland said.

No one knows better than Bud Johnson about 'perfect fits' in the corporate world. Johnson, a former Navy pilot in the Korean Conflict, corporate recruiter, and business consultant, now lives in Scarsdale, NY. He raved about Dan Strickland and the amazing skill-sets that he possesses. "Our business relationship developed into a deep friendship nearly 20 years ago. I first knew Dan when he was in London with Procter and Gamble as their Associate Director of Research and Development. P&G had acquired Richardson/Vick's whose most famous product was Vick's Vapor Rub. He was the master at understanding Health Care and Hygiene. It was a funny situation at first because Dan had inherited 100 German engineers whose only language was German with no interest in learning English, but he saw to it that the company prospered. This was a massive, multi-million dollar operation, and Dan was a key player.

"In his years with P&G and General Mills, Dan dealt with mega-businesses," Johnson said. "He had an amazing knowledge of advertising and product development, and he understood the mind of the consumer. Dan not only knew what product to make, but with his background, he knew how to make it. I recruited Dan from P&G to Kraft Foods because Kraft, whose direction and profits were going sideways back then, really needed someone creative and innovative. About all they were doing in those days that worked well was cheese and frozen foods. Dan was instrumental in the creation of many, many products that tasted great, but wouldn't make you fat. After Johnson & Johnson, which was the most respected

Dan Strickland's children: Sophia, Savannah, and Brandan.

name in feminine hygiene, recruited him away from Kraft, Dan's genius led to the creation and improvement of their feminine protection, tampon products, and incontinent products. While at J&J, he pretty much wrote the book on innovation and improvement."

Johnson continued, "Dan Strickland is such a bright guy, and he's fun as well. He has an amazing sense of humor, and people enjoy working with him. He is just way ahead of the competition in the realm of R&D, and when it comes to the packaging of products, Dan sees it in the total area of its environment. Most people see products. Dan sees price, appearance, packaging, and the entire process. He is the focus-person that is interested in the total food experience for the consumer.

"There aren't many people who can turn around a $100,000,000 operation and make it more profitable, but Dan Strickland can," Bud Johnson said with conviction. "He has no peer in this industry. Steve Sanger, former Senior Vice President of Innovation, brought Dan to General Mills. Dan determined that consumers needed to feel good about eating Cheerios, which was the top product line at General Mills. The country was moving swiftly toward the wellness and health craze. Thus, Dan struck the chord, *Eat Cheerios. Lower your cholesterol.*" He also made food more fun, like the creation of Gogurt...yogurt in tubes for kids."

Johnson continued, "Dan's background has been creating a solid foundation due to his association with these major corporations. Dan learned something important at every place he has been. When Dan arrived at Coca-Cola in 2003, he had been working for years on the way products taste while making them healthier for the consumer. And Dan Strickland is the only guy I've seen that knew how to unlock these products that have become so popular. Cokes' newest product, C2 Coke, features the great, original taste of Coke with only half the calories and half the carbs of regular Coke. That's Dan."

When asked why Dan Strickland is successful, Johnson answered, "Because he's innovative, he's a super problem-solver who brings analytical disciplines to his work, and he has a keen awareness of how to get to the end point. He's a brilliant leader. Dan sees dots that others don't see, and he knows how to connect them. He creates new ways to think that are always ingenious and, for all that he has done and accomplished, he did much of it while inheriting other people's baggage. He can strip away what needs to be removed until he gets to what needs to be kept. Dan asks, 'What does the public want that will enhance their lives?'"

Johnson said, "At Coke, Dan's office, which is bigger than some buildings I've been in, overlooks the Georgia Tech campus. Dan acknowledges that much of his success has to do with his roots at Georgia Tech, and he also credits his modest beginnings in South Macon as being motivation for success in his life. Sure, he has a keen intellect, but he also has a strong desire to improve. He is such a fierce competitor who loves to win. Many guys hate to lose. Dan loves to win.

"It was apparent early on that Dan is a man of very high integrity," Johnson concluded.

* * * * * * * * *

As far and as fast as South Macon's Dan Strickland has climbed the corporate ladder and has been an international force in business, his family has continually become more and more important to him. Dan's son, Brandan, now 22, is a senior at the University of Wisconsin in Madison. Dan spoke proudly about his son, "Brandan was a 4-sport letterman at Carmel High School in Chicago. When I was with General Mills in Minneapolis, I would fly down on Friday nights to watch him play football. I saw almost every football game he played. He had a 12-yard average per carry in football and was class president. In college, he was IFC president, and his three-man basketball team was the school's intramural champion."

Christine and Dan now have two girls, Savannah Belle, who was born in Princeton, NJ, in 1996, and Sophia Louise (middle name from Dan's mom) who was born in Chicago in 1998. Today, both girls attend the highly-selective Wesleyan School in Atlanta. The Stricklands live in an Alpharetta neighborhood that looks like the homes were airlifted in from Charleston, SC. Their home backs up to the Chattahoochee River for a magnificent setting.

"Wesleyan is clearly the best school in our area of the city," Strickland said. "It is a Christian, non-denominational school that prides itself in the screening of its teachers. Their faculty and staff are people of character and faith, as well as strong academic credentials. Wesleyan has unbelievable facilities like an indoor pool, an indoor tennis facility, and a baseball field that looks like something a professional team would play on. And though it's a small school of 1,000 students (grades K-12), it looks like a college campus. We feel really blessed that our girls were able to get into Wesleyan. My wife is totally happy with the school and our neighborhood. I think every day, 'What a difference from where I started!'"

Dan Strickland is equally happy to be back in his native Georgia and working at Coca-Cola. At age 56, he is now the Senior Vice President of Coca-Cola and became a member of the Executive Committee in December, 2003. As the head of Research and Development at Coke, he is responsible for all innovation and other technical matters.

Steve Heyer, the recent President and Chief Operating Officer of Coke, brought Dan on board over two years ago. Heyer had served as the COO at Turner Broadcasting prior to joining Coke, and said, "I was searching for the best innovator in the world and through the search process, Dan Strickland's name was on our short list. With his strengths – imagination, great judgment, and balance – he was unquestionably the right man for this team. Dan operates as a collaborative, innovative force for positive change at Coke. He is just the absolute best at what he does. He is everything we were looking for and much more."

Heyer continued, "The thing about Dan, personally, is that he is genuine and kind. And his sense of humor draws people to him. He is a role model in this industry. When Dan came to work here, he was instantly embraced for his creative ideas and style. His responsibility is to create new consumer products for Coke. C2, our mid-calorie Coke, Studio Red, and Heart-Wise, a Minute Maid Juice product, are just some of Dan's creative product lines. And he focuses on more than just drink products. He has us moving with more of a consumer and user-friendly focus, whether it is with coolers, packaging, or vending. He studies where we need to be, whether it's in America, Japan, or elsewhere."

"Dan Strickland is just a great fit here at Coke," Heyer concluded. "He is absolutely phenomenal in this business and on top of that, he is a wonderful guy."

Dan often sounds more like a marketing representative for Coke than the head of Research and Development. "Coke is the best known and most recognizable brand in world. It is the most successful consumer product in history and the most valuable brand in the world. Coke sales are over $24,000,000,000, but that's mainly just the concentrate syrup. The value of our retail sales is over $100,000,000,000 a year. Consumers in more than 200 countries enjoy one billion servings per day of Coke products."

Dan said, "Coke has been a powerful system since 1886, but it got complacent. Steve Heyer ran Turner Broadcasting prior to Coke and began to put his team in place. He believed that innovation is most important value-creation mechanism there is. My work is to help create new things with value. The future of our company must be based on innovation. Steve and I had lunch, and 30 minutes into lunch, he asked me, 'When can you start?' He basically set the deal with me that day. Steve doesn't know how to do these technical things that must be done, but he appreciates the people who do know how. It's a privilege for me to work for the most important brand in the whole world."

Dan explained, "What I do is what Coke needs. Steve Heyer told me, 'Dan, if you fail, then I fail.' Our area does all of the technical things at Coke, and I am responsible for creating the environment and the processes that go with creating new packages, products, and even new ways of working. For example, when you stand in the lobby at the movie theater by the fountain, we want to know, 'What is your experience with Coke?' When you go to a vending machine, or to a grocery store, 'What's your experience with Coke?' Innovation is finding the places and things that are important to people and being innovative to meet their needs and wants."

Strickland continued, "There are things that Coke can do around the world that no one else can do. We bring prosperity to small villages in Africa. We do water treatment. Some people in certain parts of the world drink Coke for the nutrients. Creating the new Lime Coke or Vanilla Coke is easy stuff to do. Beyond our products, we see ourselves as a company that makes the world a better place."

Dan is on the Executive Committee of Coca-Cola, the most senior group in the company. It is easily apparent that Coke has been a great situation for him. Dan has demonstrated throughout his career that people like to go where they know that their work is important. He concluded, "We're on a worthwhile mission here, and I love what we're doing."

* * * * * * * * * *

Apart from work, Dan stays active and involved doing things that primarily involve his wife and children. He said, "When you think about your kids, you want them to have more opportunities than you had growing up. They don't realize it right now that they are growing up leading privileged lives. My daughters dance, swim, take piano, and do gymnastics. My son lives in Wisconsin and is involved at the University. I get to play some golf with my son and friends on some amazing golf courses. I'm also on the Board of Directors at the Fernbank Museum of Natural History here in Atlanta. Christine and I have been married for eleven years now, and life is good."

When asked, 'What is the best thing that you have done in your life?', Strickland said without hesitation, "I took care of my mother. I have traveled extensively in my career so I wasn't always able to be near my mother. When I lived and worked in Cincinnati, I rented a house close to P&G in an older section of town where a lot of senior citizens lived. It was about a mile from my work. When I moved to Europe a year later, I moved my mom to Jacksonville, FL, so she would be near my sister. After my dad died in 1956, she never remarried, because she thought we wouldn't like who she married. I realized that I could never pay her back for all of the sacrifices that she made, and she didn't want me to try. My mom died on December 10, 1996. It broke my heart that I was on a trip in the Philippines when she passed away. I was lucky to be able to take care of her."

"As I reflect on my life, I think of guys who died in Vietnam and I think, 'But for the grace of God, there go I.' I make a great salary, my kids go to great schools, I have an amazing life, and I often wonder how I could be so lucky."

Strickland concluded, "The older I get, the more I understand how all of us are more fortunate than we ever realize. I have always liked Rudyard Kipling's quote that speaks of 'being able to walk with kings, while keeping the common touch.' That tells me that I need to keep balance and perspective in life. I would like to be remembered as someone who always tried to do the right thing. I have always wanted to leave things better than I found them, and I have never forgotten where I came from."

Dan Strickland family: Dan, Sophia, Savannah, and Christine

Dr. Lawyer

William C. (Skeet) Heard, M.D., J.D.
Class of 1966

*"Those who wait upon the Lord will renew their
strength; They shall mount up with wings as eagles;
they shall run and not be weary; They shall walk,
and not faint."*

–Isaiah 40:31

Skeet Heard's life and career were cruising
along quite well, thank you. "My Ear, Nose, and Throat practice was
almost an exclusive ear surgery practice," Heard recalled. "In my
medical practice, I had a specialty within a specialty as I rebuilt the middle ear
for problems caused by disease and hereditary deformities. In May, 2000, on a
Saturday morning when my wife and our three children had gone to our place at
the beach in Florida, I found myself doing a job around the house for my wife.
Our tomato plants needed staking, because they were growing so large, and not
realizing that I could buy tomato stakes, I thought I'd rip a piece of plywood into
tomato stakes. I was using a circular saw, and suddenly, I cut off two fingers
on my right hand. Dr. Guy Foulkes, a remarkable hand surgeon in Macon,
reattached my middle finger, but he couldn't do the index finger."

Suddenly and painfully, Dr. William C. (Skeet) Heard's life would never be
the same again.

"The reattached middle finger worked well," he said, "but later, I would
have no propioception in it, meaning I couldn't sense pressure with the tip of
my finger, which would make it unlikely that I could operate on ears again. My
life turned upside-down that day. While I was in the emergency room after
the accident, I remember that I was kind of joking around, but the attending
physician was pretty stoic. I asked the doctor if I would be able to play golf
again, and he told me if I needed my right hand that badly for golf, then I didn't
need to play golf again!"

Heard continued, "Somehow, I imagined I could still operate again. I
figured I could rehab the hand. A company even made special instruments for
me to use, but the problem was that I couldn't feel pressure in my fingers. The
insurance company told me not to try operating again, so in September and
October, 2000, I worked in the office doing non-surgical procedures. But I
wanted to fly the plane; I didn't want to just to ride in it."

Realizing that he had no control over what had happened to him back in
May, Skeet Heard came to the conclusion that he did have control over how he
would respond to the catastrophe that had occurred. "It was then that I realized I
had had twenty years at the very top of my profession. I had done surgeries that

allowed people to hear again and had improved the quality of life for many. I was a professor at a top medical school, where I taught other young doctors. It had been a great run."

So, he retired.

"That lasted about one week, because I was in my wife's way," Skeet laughed. "Plus, you can only play so much golf and cut so much grass. My daughter, Heather, told me, 'Dad, you've always talked about going to law school. Why don't you try that?'

"I had taken the Law CAT as a junior in college," Heard said, "so I thought if I do OK, that will be a sign from God, since He doesn't close one door without opening another one. I took the LSAT and did OK, but not as well as I wanted, so I prepped for it again and did well enough to turn down an Ivy League law school."

His wife made two requests of him – "You can go to law school, but we aren't leaving Macon," Skeet recalled. "I enrolled in Mercer's Walter F. George School of Law in 2000, graduating *cum laude* and editor of the *Law Review*. After I completed law school, I suppose I became somewhat of a valued recruit in something akin to a basketball draft. I was entertained by law firms, and the one I really liked was an Atlanta firm, Alston and Bird, which just happened to be (the legendary golfer) Bobby Jones' old law firm. I liked the people there, I worked in Atlanta, and they provided an apartment for me during the week. Later, I tried commuting to Atlanta for two years, but the amount of traveling that was required – Detroit, Cleveland, Los Angeles, was just too much for this 50-year old body to stand. I found myself missing my son's ballgames.

"Alston and Bird was a great experience for me. I had already validated myself with my experience in medicine as a surgeon. I, then, turned around 180 degrees and was validated in a whole new profession in a nationally-elite law firm. I just closed my eyes and thought how neat my life has been."

But with the extreme demands of commuting to Atlanta and across the country, Skeet spoke with his Willingham High School friend, Tommy Hinson, in the fall of 2003. Hinson, a senior partner with the Macon law firm of Westmoreland, Patterson, Moseley, and Hinson, LLP, told Heard that they had a place for him; so he signed on to practice law in Macon. "I like my new career, and I have enjoyed the new challenges. Law isn't medicine; it's different. Do I enjoy it? Yes. I love the challenge, and it keeps me mentally sharp and on my toes. I like the type of law that I practice, because I come in contact with some very bright minds on the other side of legal arguments."

Heard confessed, "Law isn't my first love; medicine is. Being an otologist was great. I remember one situation when a lady came to me with a severe hearing loss. We did a stapedectomy on one ear, and when the packing was removed, she walked down the hall crying. I said quietly, 'She can hear a MPOC.' Someone asked me what that meant, and I said, "She can hear a mouse peeing on cotton." The lady turned around quickly and said, 'I heard that!'"

* * * * * * * * *

Skeet Heard grew up in the Jefferson Hills community of South Macon and attended Charles H. Bruce and Agnes Barden Elementary Schools, but he graduated from Jessie Rice School. His family attended Glenwood Hills United Methodist Church. After graduating from Willingham in 1966, Skeet attended the University of Georgia and graduated in 1970 with a BS in chemistry and a minor in zoology. He graduated in the upper 20% of his class at the Medical College of Georgia in 1974.

Kay Field and Skeet Heard were married in 1974, and they have three children, Heather Pritchett (27), Hilliary Heard (24), and Bryan Heard (20), a junior at Mercer. Skeet's mother, Mrs. Marion Heard, still lives in Macon, though his dad became estranged from the family when Skeet was a freshman in Medical School.

"My mother was a nurse, and I fell in love with medicine through her influence. When I was very young, I had a disorder of my hip called aseptic necrosis of the femoral head, which occurs after an injury. Basically, the ball of the hip joint dissolves, much like Bo Jackson's injury. What happens is the hip will reform, so from the age of four until the fourth grade, I was in a non-weight bearing sling with crutches. I was a patient of Dr. Walter Barnes, the first orthopedic surgeon in Macon, who was another person that had a big influence on my life. Medically, Dr. Barnes really knew what he was doing. He was stately, authoritative, informed, and just had an air of confidence that I picked up on even when I was a kid."

Skeet's mom was an operating room supervisor, and she would talk to him about people like Dr. Milford Hatcher and other surgeons whom she worked with and thought were exceptional. "I think it became evident to me when I was six or seven years old that I wanted to become a doctor, primarily because of the influence of my mother and Dr. Walter Barnes. I can't remember having any thoughts of ever wanting to do anything else."

Thankfully, Skeet's hip got well as the femoral head grew back, and he began a normal childhood. He began playing Little League at South Macon as a ten-year-old and picked up the game of golf, eventually playing on the golf team at Willingham. The only physical problem that he experiences today is arthritis.

Along with becoming a doctor, Skeet decided along the way that he also wanted to be a surgeon. "I think I decided, and this may sound silly, that I wanted to be a surgeon based on a book I read titled, *The Intern,* by Dr. X. He was a surgery resident at Belleview Hospital in New York, and, later, I think he was actually identified. He wrote the account of his residency there, and I really thought that was neat because, to me, surgeons were the epitome of being a doctor. When I was in medical school, most internists didn't really do anything that was invasive. To me, surgery was like flying the plane versus serving drinks in the back. That's when I decided I wanted to be a surgeon and become a vascular surgeon."

His first surgical rotation during his internship year, also at MCG, was on blue surgery, the oldest surgical service at Talmadge Hospital in Augusta.

"It had more patients than any other service at the hospital. From July 1 to September 30, I never got home. It was constant work, 16-20-hours a day, and those were the off-days. When I was on duty, it was 24-hours a day, and that was every third night. In October, I rotated into plastic surgery, but it wasn't cosmetic surgery. It was reconstructive surgery: burns, rebuilding mangled and torn body parts, and those were some very tedious, tiresome processes. It was worse, because I was the only intern on the service. There was a resident with me doing the 'scut work,' so by the time I got to November in my intern year, I was exhausted."

He continued, "I rotated onto Ear, Nose, and Throat, and my chairman looked at me the first day and said, 'Golly, you look tired. Why don't you take a couple of days off?' I replied, 'I think I only have a few days for vacation.' He said, 'This isn't counted as vacation. Take a couple of days off and then come back and we'll have fun.' I hadn't heard that kind of talk in medicine before."

ENT at Talmadge was being offered for the first time as a service. There were no residents, so Skeet was the only resident physician on that service. "I got to do everything which was kind of a dream for me, and I was performing procedures that were actually beyond my training. I fell in love with the ENT service and my attending physician, Dr. Ed Porubsky. He told me, 'I want you to be one of my first residents;' so I started in January that year and was one of the first to finish at the Medical College in ENT. Under Dr. Porubsky's guidance, that program grew into one of the premier ENT programs in the nation."

Dr. Ed Porubsky is currently listed as a Professor and Chairman of the Department of Otolaryngology, Emeritus, at the Medical College, where there is also a Chair named after him. Dr. Porubsky stated, "I retired, but I'm still working. I knew Skeet Heard when he was a med student and later interned in general surgery at MCG. Though MCG is the 12th oldest Medical School in America, we just started the ENT program when Skeet was there, and he was the second resident in that program."

Growing up in South Macon, Skeet had never lived a life of financial privilege. "I strongly identified with Skeet," Porubsky recalled, "because I, too, was poor when I grew up in Cleveland. My dad was a truck driver and my mother was a secretary. Skeet and Kay were just married when I met him, and there came a time when he chose to take a year off between his internship and his first year of residency to work and make some money to clear out debts that were beginning to accrue. Then, he came back and completed his requirements for graduation. I greatly admire Skeet's determination and resolve because those traits have helped make him a success, both as a doctor and a lawyer.

"In one sense, growing up without financial means may have ended up helping Skeet become a better doctor. He was always very bright and conscientious, but his drive and desire pushed him to become a top student and an excellent doctor. I think when you are poor, you have a tendency to appreciate your accomplishments, because you have earned them. Skeet used that as motivation for his success. Certainly, nothing was ever handed to him on a platter, and, after the serious injury to two of the fingers on his right hand, he changed directions and continued on with a successful career in law."

* * * * * * * * * *

Kathleen Neal was a neighbor of the Heards in Jefferson Hills and taught Skeet when he was a student at Jessie Rice Elementary. He recalled about Mrs. Neal, "She was an avid Civil War historian and taught us about the major battles. She was a tough, hard-nosed teacher. Miss Atwater taught me when I went to Bruce School and then taught my child at Stratford. She was a very young teacher in those days and was just a nice person."

Skeet continued about several of his teachers who had meaningful influences on him, "E.J. Hancock was a sport! He had a great love for science; it was obvious that he really enjoyed teaching, and I picked up on that. He had a way of bringing out the best in his students. Mr. Hancock created a science fair and brought people from Mercer University's science department over to Willingham to critique our projects. Then, he would get our science projects entered in the Georgia State Science Fair. That was quite a big deal for many guys from our class that went on to the State Science Fair. We did quite well, and it was strictly because of Mr. E.J. Hancock.

"I remember that, as a school, we sometimes weren't the most respectful and best-behaved students, but the core students at Willingham were as bright and well-mannered as any that I have run across anywhere. With guys like Dan Strickland, George Balkcom, James Collins, and others, they were some of the brightest guys you will ever find."

As with most of Willingham's high-achieving, college-bound students, Leonard Pridgeon had quite an impact on Skeet Heard as a scientist. "Mr. Pridgeon taught basic chemistry at Willingham and was such an outstanding teacher that I took chemistry in college as a freshman and did well in it, simply because of the strong foundation that he had built. That foundation was important because medical school was so competitive. You basically didn't have any place to relax in the four-year curriculum, so I couldn't do poorly in a freshman chemistry course and expect to get in med school."

Coach Mike Garvin, one of Skeet's math teachers, was remembered for his organization as a math teacher. "I don't know if Coach Garvin was a great math teacher or not, but he was always there working problems and showing you how things went together. His leadership with young men in and out of the classroom demonstrated the kind of leader he was.

"Of course, Coach Billy Henderson was a master motivator of young men," Skeet recalled. "In our neighborhood, when I was in the sixth grade, there was a Saturday bowling league on Pio Nono Avenue, and Coach Henderson was always there. I remember him telling those kids that he was waiting on them when they got to Willingham. In that environment, I don't know if he was recruiting or not, but he walked up to me one time and said, 'You'll play offensive line for us.' At a school that was just founded a few years earlier, it was quite impressive for the head football coach at a AAA school to interact with grammar school guys like that.

"Dave Hill, probably more than any of the other coaches, was very much like me. He encouraged me, and he was even my golf coach for one year."

* * * * * * * * * *

Kay and Skeet Heard.

Reminiscing about his childhood, Skeet remembered playing baseball every day in the summer, from sun-up to sun-down, in a field behind Cecil Bentley's house. "At the end of the day, if there was a Little League game that evening, then you came home early enough to get ready to go play baseball again. Our days were just consumed with playing baseball, which was the heartbeat of our summers. There is no telling how many games Cecil, Darrell Parker, Jack Evans, and I, along with a bunch of other kids, played.

"The home where I grew up was a place where there was always order," Heard said. "My parents always knew where I was, though I may have been gone all day long. We had dinner at 5 p.m., the television was turned off, and we conversed at the table. These days, I can't tell you, other than Thanksgiving and Christmas, when all of my family has sat around the table and eaten a meal together."

Skeet has nothing but good memories of growing up in South Macon. "Our baseball teams at Willingham were always very good, but I really remember that great run of football victories that we had against our biggest rival, Lanier. Our football program was excellent, and it made us all proud when we beat Lanier. It wasn't just the poor kids of South Macon versus the gentry of Macon, though there may have been some undercurrent of that. I have a feeling that many of those boys at Lanier who lived in the mill villages were about as bad off as we were.

"I had no real opinion of South Macon when I was young, but in high school, our boundaries were exceeded by where we could go on our bicycles. I knew that there was a rich section of town, and I knew I didn't live in it. I never thought I was disadvantaged, but I knew we weren't wealthy either. I did know that going to Ben Jones Clothing Store on Cherry Street to buy a bunch of nice shirts wasn't going to happen to me. In the tenth grade, when I began to meet people outside my sphere, that became one of the driving forces, not to acquire

196

wealth, but I believe I spent a large part of my early life trying to get beyond South Macon."

Skeet spoke passionately about his educational experience at Willingham. "Academically, I have made the statement often that I paid tens of thousands of dollars to educate my children at Stratford, and they got a lesser education than the public school education that was provided for me. What good is it to speak French if you can't find Paris on a map, or Latin, if you don't know the history of the Roman Empire? Today's schools do a good job with the humanities, but not with history, geography, and science. My Willingham High School education was one of the best educations around."

Heard recalled one high school experience when representatives from Phillips Exeter Academy from Portsmouth, NH, visited with many of the top academic students from Willingham's class of 1966. "None of us had any idea that it was one of the top prep schools in the country, and here they were in Macon, GA, trying to recruit the best students in our class. I found out a few years ago that President George H. W. Bush graduated from Exeter Academy."

Athletically, Skeet's favorite sport at Willingham was golf, though he enjoyed and took pride in the athletic reputation and success that his high school enjoyed statewide. "We played in Region 1-AAA against the best teams in the Central and South Georgia area. Later on, I met guys from those schools that we played, and they all said how much they hated to play against Willingham."

Socio-economically, Skeet saw a dichotomy in the makeup of his high school. "I saw this division more in terms of achievers and non-achievers," he said. "There were many at Willingham who were destined to go to work and start a family. There were others who were going into the military after high school, and there were others who would go to work on the base in Warner Robins. Then, there were those who were going on to further their education and were destined to move upward, leave home, and find a life beyond Macon. There was another world out there, and many of those boys wanted to find it."

* * * * * * * * * *

Jack Schroder is a partner and senior counsel in the Health Care Regulatory section of the Alston & Bird law firm in Atlanta. Skeet worked in that area immediately after graduating from law school. Schroder recalled, "My first encounter with him was one of my most memorable. First, there's that thing about his name. Here I am in the first 30 seconds of an interview for a potential lawyer in Atlanta's largest law firm, and this guy in a suit and tie is telling me with a straight face that he'd rather be called 'Skeet.' Of course, if he'd merely followed-up by telling me he was from Macon, I'd have understood!"

In a mere five minutes, it was established that Schroder and Heard were the same age. "I'd been practicing law over 25 years," Schroder said, "and here he was looking for a job as a summer associate which was a position normally held by a '20-something.' Furthermore, he tells me he'd been practicing medicine for more than 20 years, but he now wanted to start at the bottom of the heap as an associate, competing with kids 30 years younger. Having dealt with doctors all my life (my father was one), I was skeptical to say the least, but Skeet, as he would later do time and again, went straight to the heart of the matter. 'I'm ready to be an intern again,' he said. 'I know I've got to swallow my pride and follow orders in order to learn.' He got the job, and that's exactly what he did."

Skeet knew early-on that he wanted to try cases, but he had never cross-examined anyone in a real hearing before. Schroder recalled, "After a particularly long and tiring day, I told Skeet he could cross-examine the opponent's star, expert witness, who was scheduled to take the stand at 8 a.m. the next day. After a 30-minute lecture on how one should cross-examine, I sent Skeet off to prepare, admonishing him to craft every question so the witness could only answer it in one word – 'yes.' That way, the witness wouldn't be able to circumvent the truthful answer by prevaricating with medical double-talk."

Schroder continued, "You should have seen Skeet Heard in action. After pulling an all-nighter, his questions were devastating, incisive, and honed with his usual surgical precision. Our client was absolutely delighted with Skeet's performance, and their vice president, a fellow physician, congratulated Skeet, thinking he was a time-worn veteran in the art of cross-examination. Walking out of the hearing room, I noted to Skeet with pride that out of 40 questions, the witness answered 39 of them with a one-word answer – 'Yes.'"

Adam Milani, Associate Professor at Mercer University's Walter F. George School of Law, teaches Legal Writing. "I first met Skeet Heard when he was a student in one of my classes. He was obviously older, and better dressed, than the typical law student, but I could tell that he had bonded with his younger classmates. That had to be challenging, given the difference in age and life experience between him and the other students. They treated him as part of their group, but also with respect, because of what he had done before law school.

"The thing that impressed me most about Skeet as a student was that he really wanted to learn how to be a lawyer. That's not true of all students, even the good ones. After you've been teaching for awhile, you recognize that some of the students who frequently stop by the office to ask questions are primarily doing so because they want to get a good grade. They hope that the professor will give them the 'right answer,' and they can spit it back out to him and get a higher grade. Skeet wasn't like that."

Milani continued, "It was obvious from the type of questions he asked that Skeet wanted to know not only how the concepts that we were discussing in class applied to the current assignment, but also how he would use those concepts when he was a practicing attorney. It's a pleasure to work with students like that, and my job would be a lot easier if there were more students like Skeet.

"Another thing that struck me about Skeet was how comfortable he seemed in his role as a student. After being a successful doctor whom others looked to for answers, it must have been a dramatic switch to be a student again, especially in a completely new subject area where he was actually older than me and some of the other professors. Skeet's main goal, however, was to learn how to be an effective lawyer. He realized that even the younger professors could help him toward that because they had training and experience in the profession he was now entering as a novice. He approached us in that way, and that, too, made him a pleasure to teach."

Dr. Arthur W. (Buster) Browning lives in Jacksonville and was Skeet's roommate in Medical School in Augusta. Dr. Browning remembered his long-time friend as being confident, self-assured, and extremely bright. He said, "Skeet learns from others, he knows what he knows, and he admits when there is something that he doesn't know. He has the ability to laugh, show compassion, and make hard decisions in life."

Browning continued, "Skeet has always been a true and trusted friend. He was a very bright and competent doctor who had such compassion for his patients, family, and friends. Skeet always kept his eye on his goals in life, and he achieved them. He has been successful because of his ability to keep and expand on those things that he has obtained, whether it was wealth, friends, or knowledge. I will remember Skeet Heard as a smart, family-oriented man who enjoys the finer things in life."

Skeet and Kay Heard's middle child, Hilliary, is a recent graduate of Southern Methodist University in Dallas, TX, where she was a track and cross country athlete. Hilliary said, "What makes my dad successful as a lawyer is that he is very, very intelligent and is the hardest worker I know. I remember when he quit his practice as a doctor and became a lawyer. He started at the bottom and worked his way upward. Our family went on this great island vacation, and there he was sitting in a lounge chair with his laptop. He was trying to get some vacation time in, but he was also going to work because that's just the way he is. That work-all-the-time ambition was more prevalent back then, but he continues to work a great deal, and it's simply because he loves learning. Dad enjoys it, learning is fun for him, and that's just his thing. I'm different because I'd rather go to the beach and simply have fun."

She continued, "Though my dad has many outstanding characteristics, his best quality is his work ethic. Also, he sometimes appears to be tough on the outside, but inside he is very kind and caring. In his medical practice, for example, he did a lot of community service. One day a month, my dad treated children at the Crippled Children's Clinic, which was a great way for him to give something back to his community. Children came to the clinic in buses and vans to get medical treatment, and he loved doing that.

"I was in high school when dad had his accident, and it was very hard on all of us for about three years. Obviously, Dad was a little depressed because the accident was such a shocking thing, but I do remember that he bounced back quickly as far as work was concerned. It never occurred to him to sit around and mope. He promptly came up with a plan regarding what he was going to do to keep our family stable. At that point, every member of our family, including my mom and dad, were in school at the same time. My dad was paying a lot of tuition without a lot of money coming in, so it was kind of tough."

Hilliary laughed about her dad's unique relationship with her. "My mom and dad love all three of us, but my best connection with my dad has been through sports. I have been an athlete and a runner since high school, and now I help coach track and cross country at First Presbyterian Day School. My dad comes and watches me coach two sports that he never played at a school that I didn't attend.

"From my dad, I learned the lesson that when life gets tough, then you have to be tougher. That's an important lesson, because life is always tough. He has lived by that premise, and he always taught me that lesson; so when tough times came up in his life, I watched him power through it."

* * * * * * * * * *

Currently, Skeet Heard is still a member of several medical societies. He also has a clinical medical professorship at the Medical College of Georgia that deals with legal issues in the medical profession. "I enjoy that connection a great deal, because I am able to use both my medical and legal training to assist young doctors."

Looking back on his career as a physician, he said, "As an ENT surgeon, I wasn't dealing with life and death issues, but I could deliver something to a patient that was very important to them, and that made people's lives much better. Sometimes, I ask questions like, 'Why am I here? Why have I been so successful and had such a good life, when a guy that grew up in my neighborhood in South Macon ended up in jail?' I do know that God gives us all talents and abilities, and it's so important what we do with them. I've been very lucky, I suppose, because I was born with some sense. Especially at this stage in life, I think it's important that we all ask, 'Whose opinion do we value in life?' It's also important that we understand Who it is that is watching over us."

Though Heard doesn't have the excessive amount of time away from the office that he briefly enjoyed when he realized he could no longer practice ENT surgery, he still finds time for golf at the Idle Hour Club in Macon. He also enjoys family time and taking trips with his wife. "Being married to Kay may make me the luckiest man anywhere. We met when I was a senior medical student in Augusta, and she put up with me when I was doing an internship and was gone all the time. We have been married for over 30 years, and she is my best friend. Kay has been my rock and is my anchor to reality. She has such stability and is the one that I turn to for advice, because she has such a level-head and is so even tempered."

Skeet Heard has lived a life that he probably never dreamed about when he was growing up in Jefferson Hills in South Macon. Doctor, lawyer, husband, and father. His life has been quite a ride. An interesting, but a very good, ride nonetheless.

Skeet, Heather, William Jackson, David, Mary Evelyn,
Mary Collier and Charlton Pritchett, Bryan, Hilliary,
Josh Carson, and Kay Heard.

My Grades Dropped, and Mama Made Me Quit

Bennie Frank (Ben) Hinson, Jr.
Class of 1970

*Jesus said, 'I come that you might have life, and
have it more abundantly.'*
–John 10:10

Ben and Vicki Hinson have moved in some powerful and influential circles with some of the most recognizable people in the free world. They dined on barbeque with President and Mrs. George W. Bush at 'the ranch' in Crawford, TX, and were presented at the White House Christmas Party in Washington. Twice. Ben has shot sporting clays with VP Dick Cheney at Reynolds Plantation. Governor Sonny Perdue, Senator Saxby Chambliss, and Ben have hunted quail together in Albany. Ben laughed, "I remember thinking, when Vicki and I went to the White House for the first time, 'Boy, this is a long way from Canterbury Road.'"

Walking in those circles can be somewhat intimidating if self-confidence is lacking. Thus, when Ben was asked if he ever felt frightened or anxious in any of those situations, his answer was easy. "Picking up Coach Billy Henderson's daughter for her very first date was way-more intimidating than anything else I have ever done," Ben claimed. "In the eighth grade, the girls asked the boys to the FHA Valentine dance at Porter-Ellis Community Center, so I put on my one suit, my folks drove me to the Hendersons', and I knocked on the door. That was pretty scary for an eighth grader. Coach Henderson invited me into their house on Westbury Drive. So, there I was, just me and 'The Coach.' Since that time, I've been in some pretty intimidating situations and have walked into some significant offices with high-powered, imposing people in intense circumstances, but those situations were nothing compared to taking Fran on that first date. Everything else in life has been a snap."

Though he was born on Walnut Street, Ben Hinson became a true and loyal son of South Macon. From attending Joseph N. Neel Elementary School to living on Canterbury Road, approximately one-half mile from Willingham (and even closer to McEvoy), Ben's roots grew deep in South Macon soil. Much of his connection with, and deep affection for, Willingham came from his respect for his coach, Billy Henderson. Ben said, "Billy Henderson was a giant. We didn't realize what an incredible blessing it was to have had him as our coach until we went off to college. Playing intramurals at Middle Georgia College in Cochran, we would sit around and relive our high school football glory days. It was easily apparent that Willingham guys revered Coach Henderson highly. We would have done anything he asked us to do; we didn't want to embarrass him with our actions or let him down. Our friends in college who played for some good high school coaches with really good records and a lot of wins couldn't have cared less about their coaches. To them, their high school football experience was like having a mean, ornery math teacher that you somehow just survived, and, thankfully, it was finally over."

Ben said, "Of all of the situations in my life, other than coming to faith in Jesus, the most important circumstance in my life that helped make me what I am today was when my parents decided to buy a house on Canterbury Road instead of on Ingleside Avenue. That totally changed my life and my future. Otherwise, I would have gone to Lanier High, and that probably would have been a good thing, but I would have never learned at Lanier what I learned at Willingham. That situation was simply the providence of God, because Willingham wasn't even a school back then. In fact, there was not even a plan for a school to be on Canterbury Road. It's amazing how little things are part of God's larger plan for our lives, and we can see it more clearly with the advantage of hindsight. Moving to Canterbury Road was the first important circumstance in my life.

"Then, Mr. Shaffer, my wife's daddy, brought his family to Cherokee Heights Baptist Church because he thought it was too far to drive from North Macon all the way out to South Macon to hear E.C. Sheehan preach at Mikado Baptist Church. See, my family went to Cherokee Heights, so Vicki and I met in church. Little things in life really matter."

* * * * * * * * * *

Bennie Frank and Grace Culbreath Hinson had three children—Martha Ann, Ben, and Jimmy. "Mama finished high school and then attended nursing school for three years at the old Macon Hospital," Ben said. "Daddy graduated from Chester High School in Dodge County when it went through the eleventh grade, joined the Army when the war began, and served in the South Pacific with the Army Air Corps. He ended up living in Macon and working at 'The Field' (Warner Robins Air Force Base) for his career. Mama joined the Army after nursing school and served in the nurse corps, mainly at a POW hospital in Jacksonville. A guy in Eastman offered Daddy a scholarship to attend Georgia Tech, but my grandmother was worried about him going that far away from home, so he never went to college."

Ben graduated from Willingham in 1970, the school's last year of existence. He attended Middle Georgia College from 1970-72 and graduated from Georgia State University in 1975 with a BBA in Hospital Administration while working 90-hours a week for Metro Ambulance Service in Atlanta. Ben married Vicki Shaffer from Macon on June 14, 1975, and they have two children, Brittany (25) and Shae (23).

"Clearly, my parents have been the most influential people in my life because they taught us, not just faith in, but a complete injection of faith in Jesus

Christ in our everyday life. The faith that they taught and demonstrated was not a piecemeal-approach to faith in God, but it was like a blanket-effect. Then, I heard a guy say that sometimes in our lives, we aren't just covered by God's love like a blanket, because it's more like a quilt. A quilt has so many different pieces of fabric sewn together without any gaps. I decided that Jesus was more like a quilt covering me where there were no gaps in His love and protection for us. The way that particular truth was manifested to me was in the total, unconditional love that came from God and from my parents."

Ben continued, "Mama and Daddy encouraged Jimmy, Martha Ann, and me to always do our best, and they expected nothing less. They demanded honesty, and, if you were dishonest, or, if you broke your integrity, then you decided to do that. We weren't allowed to decide to be dishonest or not, but no matter what we did, whether we were a success or a failure, there was an all-inclusive love in our home.

"We never took tests in school and made a 90, or even a 70, and have our parents ask, 'Why didn't you make 100?' I heard a story once that said, 'As White, Anglo-Saxon Protestants, if our son comes home with a 70 on a test, we rail on him and ask, 'Why didn't you do better than that?' See, we take ownership in our kid's grades. But a Jewish father would say, 'A 70? Is that teacher a fool? My son, I know that you're better than a 70!' That's the way my parents were, but not because we were never wrong. My daddy never spoke those words of the Jewish father, but we knew that he was always in our corner, and we could always come home. That's a lesson my parents taught us about Jesus. Nothing you do can ever break that relationship between the Father and His children. Things may break the fellowship but not the relationship. There were times when I was disciplined sternly, and my daddy would be really upset with me, but he was still my daddy, and he was the first person that I would go to if I needed advice or needed to talk. My parents taught us that particular truth from the Bible, and it was at the core of the relationship that I developed with Christ. Sadly, we sometimes teach our children that they have to earn our love and respect, and, somehow, that translates over to their thinking that they have to earn their relationship with Jesus, and that's not the way it is with Him at all."

Ben Hinson has always been one to learn life lessons in the routine, mundane things of life. Ben learned some important lessons from his parents when he played Little League baseball for the 'A'-team Indians in South Macon. "My birthday was August 16, and the cut-off date was August 1, but they let me go to tryouts as an eight-year-old. I must have had the best baseball day of my life and got drafted by the 'A' team Indians, where I played for five years. In my first four years, I played two innings—not two innings a game or two innings a week. I played two total innings, one inning in my second year and one inning in my fourth year. I never batted once. I just stood in right field and watched Barney Smith, Jr. just smoke baseballs over the fence, the scoreboard, and nearly into Houston Avenue. I finally played as a 12-year old, but in the first four years of riding the bench, I never missed a single practice or game, and my parents never missed a game. Not once did I hear them complain about my coach, or to my coach. And here's the drill. I was on the team, the good kids played and the rest of us sat on the bench. It was a thrill for me to coach third base and to be a part of the team. The lesson I learned is if you can live with that, everything else is easy. Some kids made fun of me, but I didn't care. I was the guy who just did what I was supposed to do, and I did it without complaining."

* * * * * * * * * *

Ben and Vicki Hinson took faith, perseverance, and a strong work ethic into their first, major life-changing career opportunity. "When we started our ambulance service in 1977," Ben recalled, "the thought suddenly occurred to us that we were two 24-year-olds starting an EMS business and borrowing a lot of money. People were going to call us, and we had to be ready to save their lives. That's a big deal, and, at the thought of us opening our own business, others believed we were just two confused kids. However, we never thought we weren't going to make it. On the other hand, though, if we failed completely in the ambulance business, I knew that we could still go home. It was that safety net of Mama and Daddy beneath me that allowed us to walk that tightrope."

Ben reminisced, "I saw my first ambulance in Atlanta when I was about four, and I thought it was the greatest thing in the world. Growing up on Canterbury Road, with all of those woods between our house and the Westgate Mall, we would spend hours a day playing army, digging foxholes, and I was always the medic with a helmet and a red cross on it. My mama stitched some canvas around two pieces of bamboo for a stretcher, and even then, I loved the idea of helping people who were hurt. I didn't know what I wanted to major in when I went to college, so my mama mentioned hospital administration, and I thought, 'The business side of hospitals? Let's give that a whirl.' So, I visited with Damon King, the administrator at The Medical Center of Central Georgia hospital, and he encouraged me to study hospital administration. I went to work at the Medical Center in September, 1971, as an orderly on weekends and was working sixteen-hour days. I worked every weekend for an entire year, including Christmas, Thanksgiving, New Year's Day, and I loved every minute of it."

Hinson remembered moving from his job as an orderly to working in the emergency room at the Medical Center. He also recalled the thrill he experienced when someone invited him to ride as the third person to assist on an ambulance. "Another night, someone called in sick," Ben said, "so I was told I would ride as the attendant and sit up-front on the ambulance. I'll never forget that our first call was from someone off Log Cabin Drive who was suffering from back pain. We picked the guy up, and on the way to the E.R., a call came across our radio urgently asking, 'How many ambulances do you have tonight?', and we already had two trucks running calls. They said, 'That'll never cover this wreck.' There was an awful wreck on Gray Highway that we worked for hours, moving people to the hospital, going back for others, helping injured people, and the 'EMS-bug officially bit me that night.'

"I had a friend, Mike Flanders, who was with me at the Medical Center and told me to look up Metro Ambulance in Atlanta because they had great-looking ambulances there. Actually, their ambulances had mag wheels, and that was the total reference that I had to begin my career in the ambulance business. So, I looked up Metro Ambulance in the phone book, and it took me three hours to find 392 14th Street, NW, in Atlanta. I told them I wanted a job; the man told me to come back tomorrow and ride along to see if it would work out, and so I began. Soon, I was working 90-hours a week and going to school full-time. Ricky Bennett, Mark Stevens, and I were rooming together in those days, and Mark, being an old 'fire-dog,' couldn't hear enough rescue stories from me. I worked at Metro through June, 1975. I confess that I took a couple of quarters off from school – some were my decisions, some were the dean's decisions! Literally, I would be wearing my uniform and the ambulance would drop me off for class where I would take a test, and the ambulance would be waiting for me outside the building. I remember sticking my briefcase behind the seat in the ambulance, jumping in, and going off to work a wreck. Then, I'd work four hours and go back to class. I learned a lot about EMS work during those years."

After Ben graduated from Georgia State in 1975 and Vicki's dad had died, Vicki's mother asked Ben to come back to Macon and help in their family business. Ben recounted those days, "I did accounting, tax returns, and learned a lot about that business, but I had ambulance in my blood. I learned that three things could happen regarding EMS and my involvement in the ambulance business. One, I could go to work at The Medical Center. Imagine this, 'I'm 23, and I'm going to the largest hospital in Middle Georgia to apply for the job to run their ambulance service.' It was kind of like, 'What do you mean work here? I want to run this operation.' So I applied at The Medical Center, but that didn't work out."

He continued, "Next, I applied for a job with the state to become a state-employed bureaucrat doing planning, grants, and other bureaucratic things. Thank God that didn't work out. So, the only other option was to open my own ambulance company. It still amazes me that I went to the C&S bank and talked a guy into loaning me the money to get started. The ambulance was going to cost $6,000, so I borrowed $6,000, not thinking that there might be other start-up costs involved. Then, I went to Atlanta and bought a used ambulance and an old, worn-out wheelchair-equipped van, so I ultimately borrowed $9,000."

Mid Georgia Ambulance was officially off-and-running on June 1, 1977. "We started off in a converted service station on Vineville Avenue. We chose to open June 1 because the phone books went out in June, and I couldn't afford to advertise. I thought I'd just take the natural 'bounce' from being listed in the local phone book. Also, my brother, Jimmy, was finishing his freshman year at Mercer, and I knew he would work cheap. We started out, just the two of us, in khaki pants and blue uniform shirts. Jimmy and I wore khaki, because we both happened to own a pair of khaki pants. Twenty-eight years later, our medics still wear khaki and blue uniforms."

For the first 48 days, Mid Georgia Ambulance didn't have an emergency ambulance license, so they could only run non-emergency calls. Then, they found out that Medicare wouldn't pay unless they had an ambulance license, and to do that, they had to run emergency calls. Hinson said, "We got our first license on July 18, 1977, and we're still trying to get this thing going."

Those in the EMS industry are fully-aware that Ben Hinson has moved his ambulance service to a status that few privately-owned services in America enjoy. Mid Georgia Ambulance, from its humble beginnings with two ragged vehicles and the two Hinson brothers running all of the calls, has burgeoned into one of the top-rated EMS agencies in America. With over 165 employees, including over 100 medics and over 25 state-of-the-art ambulances, Mid Georgia has won local, area, and national acclaim for its high-quality EMS care. From 2001-2003, Ben served as president of the prestigious American Ambulance Association and has been on state and national committees that determine policy for EMS certification.

From the early days of 1977 when Ben would ravage the drink machine to buy supplies or pay employees, Mid Georgia Ambulance now operates with a budget of over $10,000,000. In 1992, Ben created his own billing service and wrote the software for Hinson Systems, which now claims over 40 EMS agencies as customers. Hinson Systems does billing and accounts-receivable for EMS services in Georgia and North Carolina, managing over $120 million in revenues each year.

With an EMS service that ranks with the best anywhere, Hinson, historically, has tried to keep things as basic as possible. Ben's simple philosophy of EMS is, "Arrive on time—with a big smile—and clean sheets. If we do those things well, we're going to be fine."

Leon Jones, Bibb County's newly-elected Coroner and a medic at the Medical Center of Central Georgia, has known Ben Hinson since their high school days at Willingham. Leon stated matter-of-factly about his long-time friend, "This guy bought a worn-out wheelchair van and a worn-out ambulance that had over 200,000 miles on each one. When Ben started Mid Georgia Ambulance, he was so poor that the paramedics and EMTs had to buy some of their own supplies. Yellow Cab was dispatching for him, but look at him now! He has a fleet of new ambulances in Macon, Columbus, Adel, and Montezuma, started a billing company for other EMS agencies. Ben is a man of hard work, determination, and faith."

Jones recalled, "Ben's biggest asset in business is that he doesn't mind taking chances. One of the things that I have admired the most about Ben throughout the years is that he has given people opportunities to redeem themselves when others have given up on them. Ben is a great family man, a go-getter in business, and is an opportunist in the best possible way."

Leon smiled when he recalled one incident that happened at Willingham in 1969. "On the lighter side, I was one of the few blacks in what once was an all-white school, but Ben didn't look at my skin color. He looked at me as an individual. I was pretty skinny in high school, and for some reason, I thought I had to make a name for myself. So, I found the biggest white boy in school, and I hit him. Thankfully, Ben pulled him off me."

Leon concluded, "Ben Hinson has earned the reputation in business of being fair and reasonable with all people. Much of that is because of his Christian beliefs which have served him well in life and in business. Ben has been successful because he is a person who puts Christ first in his life. He is dedicated to his family and his profession; he is honest, and when he gives you his word, you can count on it."

* * * * * * * * *

Though he was not a great student in high school, few people loved the Willingham High School experience more than Ben Hinson.

"The education I got at Willingham served me extremely well," Ben recalled. "I get frustrated when I hear people say that they didn't get a good foundation for college. On the other hand, I was one who didn't let class work interfere with my high school experience. I enjoyed every minute that I was there. My teachers were good, and I had some great friends, many of whom I still see today."

Charles Crowe taught psychology and was at Willingham only a few years. Ben said, "He really engaged his students and involved us in the classroom. He taught us lessons about business and life that I still remember to this day. Tommy Hooks was a Willingham graduate and taught English. During the height of the Viet Nam confusion, when people were asking, 'Should we be there?' Tommy Hooks said, 'The immature man wants to die for a cause; a mature man wants to live for one.' As an eighth grader, that stuck with me. I remember how everybody wanted to go 'kill a gook,' and then come home in a casket as a hero. How foolish. We were just kids."

He continued, "Charles Cook, as a math teacher, was great. I loved Mary P. Smith's American history class, and I had Leonard Pridgeon in chemistry, but he scared me to death every day in class. The top 10 percent of our students in his class did extremely well, but since I didn't fit that mold, his class wasn't my favorite.

"Harold Watson was a great math teacher. Part of his responsibility at school was to sit in the office and write passes to class for people who were late. He knew I lived within sight of the school. I came in late one morning and he asked, 'What is it this time, Hinson?' I told him, 'We had a big rain last night, and it washed out the bridge between my house and the school, and I had a hard time getting here.' He said, 'Just go to class!'"

Mr. Watson said something in class one day that helped the academic light to come on for Ben. Watson said, "You know, what I'm trying to teach you in math are things that you'll use one day." Ben thought, "Like, doing what?" Watson continued, "Like Ben's dad, for example. He buys electronic radio parts for the missiles for the United States Air Force, and you have to know math to be able to do that.' That was the first time I ever heard anybody say what my dad did was important, which meant a lot. It was also good to see how a subject actually related to life.

"One of the most influential people on me while I was at Willingham was not a teacher at all. He was Willie Goolsby," Ben said. "Willie changed my understanding of the racial issue because he showed that he was just another guy. He was doing what I was doing. Willie was just like me, and our similarities were so much bigger than our differences."

Though Hinson always tested well on standardized exams, his grades in class seldom reflected the same. "I was in a math class with a bunch of really smart boys—the bright guys like Ricky Bennett, Richard Tumlin, and Greg Gay. I have no idea how I got stuck in there, because my academic career was less than stellar. We were tenth graders, and the class was mainly seniors. Our daily routine was to report to Mr. Watson's room, he would call the roll, and then we'd go to lunch. After lunch, everybody went outside for a break, and a bunch of guys were always out there smoking in a designated area (which was in another era!). Then, we would report back to Watson's class.

"Mr. Watson would frequently write on the chalkboard with one of those little mechanical chalk holders. Everyday he would pick up his chalk holder, hit the bottom of it, and say, 'Gentlemen, what do we have today?' One day, I went to class early and got all of the chalk dust from the chalk trays and poured it in his mechanical chalk holder before replacing the chalk. He came in and said, 'Gentlemen,'... and he hit the bottom of chalk holder. A huge puff of chalk dust went up in the air and then covered him with yellow dust. The entire class got totally quiet. No one moved, and Watson said, 'Ben...' He had a t-square, and he wore me out with it."

Hinson recalled seeing his former coach, Jesse Duckworth, a few years ago (Duckworth has since passed away in 2001). "We greeted each other, and Coach Duckworth immediately said to me, 'Ben, five for a 'D' and 15 for an 'F.' What he was referring to was if you were a football player in those days, you had to take your report card to the coaches, and you had to wear your gym shorts. It was quite simple. If you made a 'D,' you got five licks with a paddle. An 'F' would get you 15 licks. The lines were clearly drawn, and there was no confusion about what was expected from us as football players."

Growing up, Ben lived so close to both Willingham and McEvoy High Schools that he always had a place to play and children to play with. "Our neighborhood included Coach Billy Beale's and Coach Billy Henderson's kids, and we had access to a gym and playing fields, so how could growing up be any better than that? I could go 100 yards over to McEvoy and play tennis or go a half-mile to Willingham and play a pick-up baseball game. Our games were played on the Little League field at Willingham. We had huge ball games in our yard. My best friend, Sammy Patterson, his older brother, Doug, and the rest of us had some tremendous football games in their backyard. There was a strategic sapling in their yard that we would use to scrub-off a defensive player, kind of a pick-play. Our neighborhood was made up of families with husbands who just came back from the war, every house seemed to have a couple of kids, and we were all within three or four years of each other."

* * * * * * * * *

"Ben, did you ever think Willingham was different or less than other schools?"

"That never entered my mind," he said. "Maybe it was because I went to church at Cherokee Heights, and there were only a few Willingham/McEvoy families at Cherokee, so I was in among Lanier and Miller people. I learned they were just like me. Still are. I went to the Shoney's on Riverside Drive as quickly as I'd go to the Shoney's on Pio Nono. That didn't matter to me. Yes, there were some jerks at Lanier, but there were some jerks at Willingham, too. I think I would have enjoyed ROTC at Lanier."

Hinson had an interesting observation about Lanier after Willingham and Mark Smith were founded. "When you take as much energy and excitement out of a school as they did when Willingham/McEvoy were built in 1957-58 and then remove those students and families that became Mark Smith/Lasseter in 1965, then Lanier became a different school than it was in the 1960's. Don't get me wrong; Lanier was a great school for a long, long time, but it was also the only school in town, basically, for white kids. There used to be a parade down Cherry Street to see the Lanier football team off when they left on the train from the terminal station to go play in Miami. Everybody, it seemed, went downtown to send them off.

"As the new schools, but especially Willingham, emerged," Ben stated, "that changed things for Lanier because many of the hard-working, committed families left for the new school. Houston Avenue, in front of Bruce School on the way to Fincher's, became downtown South Macon. That was the heart of South Macon back then."

When asked how he rated his experience at Willingham socially, athletically, and academically, Hinson replied, "Well, it was the only one I ever had, and if each of those areas was not a 10, it was my fault, because a 10 was there to be had. Athletically, for me, it was about a six because I was so slow. I wrestled for a year and flirted briefly with cross country. I went out for cross country one day and didn't go back the next. Johnny Stallings was the coach and saw me in the weight room the next day and asked, 'Hinson, what happened to you yesterday? I missed you at cross country practice,' and I said, 'Coach, my grades dropped, and Mama made me quit.' An eighth grade kid looking at his coach and telling him that!"

"My life is way better because I grew up in South Macon," Ben stated matter-of-factly, "because I was able to grow up without some of the pretense that other people have. There was not a lot of 'society' going on where we were in South Macon, so those things didn't matter. I have friends who grew up in other parts of Macon who were so disenchanted with the social status that they spent much of their life fighting against it. There were others who were so impressed with society that they spent their life trying to achieve it. To me, it was all neutral."

* * * * * * * * *

Jimmy Hinson spoke about his older brother and said, "Obviously, I have had the pleasure of knowing Ben all my life. I am fortunate in that I had him as a role model, mentor, sounding board, protector, and most of all the best big brother the Lord has ever blessed anyone with. Ben doesn't know the meaning of the word 'can't.' He is the eternal optimist; he thinks big and reaches even bigger. Ben runs in some circles that we didn't even know existed as children growing up. He has the uncanny ability to walk into a room and fit in with whoever is there, making them feel warm, needed, and important. Ben is an encourager, and he inspires those around him to exceed their own expectations."

Observing his brother's willingness to encourage and help untold numbers of people, Jimmy commented, "One instance that comes to mind was a high school student that Ben taught in a youth Sunday School class at Ingleside Baptist. The young man shared his disappointment with Ben about not getting into MIT, so Ben talked to him to make sure he truly wanted to go to MIT. The next thing you know, they flew to Boston and walked into the Admission's Office that sent the boy's rejection letter. Ben and the boy obviously made convincing arguments, because this young man has now graduated from MIT. In short, Ben does not know 'quit.' If he believes in you, knowing that you believe in yourself, he will help you with everything he has."

Jimmy continued, "Everywhere he goes Ben tries to encourage others. I don't think there is a town in America that Ben can go to without calling someone he knows and sharing a meal together. Not only does Ben give of himself, but he and Vicki have instilled that same value in their children. Ben and Vicki work with people to help them get better.

"I think Ben will be remembered in many ways," Jimmy said. "He will primarily be remembered as someone who is a giver and cares about others. Ben's personality is such that people just want to hang around him because of the respect they have for him. Conversely, Ben also has the conviction to fire someone when it is the right thing to do for the good of the whole. This may clearly be the toughest task of all for any businessman, but he has the ability to communicate the reasons 'Why' and to be able to do it with love and compassion. That's a very difficult balance to find."

Ben Hinson has always been known for his self-deprecating sense of humor which seems to genuinely disarm those around him. Jimmy remembered the

2/2

story when they were young and had gone squirrel hunting near their grandmother's house. "On the walk back to the house," Jimmy recalled, "we encountered an old barbed-wire fence that was 12-inches off the ground at it lowest spot. We took turns stepping over the wire, but Ben decided to show how cool he was by jumping over the 12-inch high fence. Unfortunately, he only elevated eight inches, caught the inside of his ankle on the barbed wire, and demonstrated the same athletic ability that kept him off the basketball court. And with the inside of his ankle laid open, he picked himself up, laughed at himself, and walked back to the house for medical attention."

At 'The Ranch' in Crawford, TX. Ben Hinson, Laura Bush, President George W. Bush, and Vicki Hinson.

Jimmy continued about his brother, "Ben has established an EMS service that has had a far-reaching impact on thousands of people. God has blessed him financially, which, in turn, has allowed Ben to share with others. His ambulance business speaks to his very core. He picks people up in order to help them get better. Everything he has done in his life reflects that fundamental principle. Ben is a caring and loving brother, son, husband, and father, and every place that he has been is better off because he passed though."

As a father, husband, and friend, Ben sets an extremely high standard in the eyes of his brother. "Ben would be a tough standard to measure against. Certainly, he is my only brother, and I am truly blessed to have shared a bedroom with him in my formative years because he helped shape my view of life. I got to watch him closer than most anyone. Ben's love of his Lord is a great example to those around him as is love for Vicki, the true love of his life."

Ben Hinson would be the first to say that the foundation for his life was laid by his parents, Bennie and Grace Hinson. Jimmy attended Joseph N. Neel during elementary school and knew of the influence that Coach Billy Henderson also had on Ben. Jimmy said, "Coach Henderson expanded on the foundation in Ben's life, and Ben has been smart enough to find mentors for different aspects of his life. In business, religion, or politics, he has always sought others who could teach him more. His desire for knowledge, along with the support and encouragement of his wife, has given him the ability to continue to run the race the Lord has laid out for him, and in that vein, he moves at a very fast pace. Ben uses a familiar cliché that says, 'If you don't want to run with the big dogs, then stay on the porch.' He lives life to the fullest, guided by his spiritual beliefs as his True North. Ben is special, and South Macon can be proud of this son."

* * * * * * * * * *

Ben and Vicki Hinson have two of the finest children anywhere. Brittany and Shae Hinson both graduated from First Presbyterian Day School and from Samford University in Birmingham. Brittany is a Child Life Specialist at Children's Healthcare of Atlanta, while Shae is completing a two-year term as a missionary in Peru. Both have experienced, along with their parents, the highs and lows of starting and running an ambulance service. Shae commented, "Before I had any idea of my dad having success in life, I just knew that we had happiness in our family. We didn't take vacations when I was young; we just went to the park on Saturdays and did things together as a family. One thing I remember is that we always had peace at home, and we had it all the time. Our home had peace when we were broke or when we had plenty, and the reason that we had peace was Christ in our parents' lives."

Shae and Brittany both recalled, "When we were young and we had so little money, we would go to the post office with Dad on Saturdays in hopes of Medicare checks being there. We would hop in the car, stop by the Farmer's Market to get boiled peanuts, turn on Larry Munson, the voice of the Georgia Bulldogs, and listen to the game. Then, we would go to the post office. We had a key, and we would rush into the post office and check box number 2710. My dad has that same box on display in his office today. There's a lot of sentimental value there, as well as a reminder of what used to happen when things were tough at Mid Georgia Ambulance. If we saw some large envelopes with certain logos on them, we knew that there were checks inside, we could make payroll, and we could have food on our table. We would sprint outside with the checks in our hands and smiles on our faces."

Shae continued, "The first two years that my dad started Mid Georgia Ambulance, he either worked or was on call 24/7. If he took any time off, he was still in town to run calls if he was needed. Dad and Mom were only 24 years old when they borrowed the money to begin their business. People thought they were crazy to try and start an ambulance service. Dad told me he prayed 'that by the time he turned 30, he wanted to know for sure that this is what he should be doing with his life, and if it was God's will that he should be in the ambulance business, he just wanted to know for sure.'

"Just when Dad was ready to declare bankruptcy on the day before his thirtieth birthday, he got a letter from a local hospital saying, 'We believe in what you're doing, and we want to finance you and help get you going. That was confirmation that this was what he should be doing with his life. It was like God was putting him to the test to see if he would be faithful. And he was."

Like his Dad many years prior, one of Shae Hinson's best memories was running an ambulance call. "We had lights and sirens on our old station wagon, and I ran calls with dad from home," he recalled.

"I remember that Mom and Dad would play games with Brittany and me, while teaching us truths from the Bible at the same time. They would ask if we wanted to play a game called 'Faith.' I remember being on my parents' bed, and Mom or Dad would ask if I had faith in them or not. Then, I would run and jump, and they would always catch me. That game taught Brittany and me about faith and trust because, if we had faith in our parents and could trust them, then we could trust God even more.

"Dad also taught me about trust when I was three or four years old. We were sailing on our friend Howard Armstrong's catamaran when I asked Dad what this orange thing was that I was wearing. He told me it was a life jacket, and if I fell in, it would help me float. So I just flipped right back into the water in the middle of Lake Lanier because my dad said it would keep me afloat. I trusted my dad because, if he said it, it was the truth. That's a lesson that he taught me about God—that He would do what He said He would do."

When Shae was a senior at First Presbyterian Day School, Ben would come to practice nearly every day. Shae commented, "In my four years of football, he may have missed a total of 30 practices, because he loved me and he just liked being around football. It was a reminder of his high school days at Willingham and playing for Coach Henderson. My granddaddy was my Dad's father-figure; Coach Henderson was his mentor."

Shae recounted a story Ben told him, "One morning at 5:30, Dad's phone rang and he heard a voice bark, 'Hinson?' and Dad jumped out of bed and said, 'Yes, sir?' It was Coach Henderson, and he said, 'Whoever is gonna whip you today has been at the office for two hours already.' And Dad replied, 'Yes, sir, I'm on the way!' I don't know if that motivated my dad to become an early riser or not, but he gets up very early every day, now.

"One thing I learned from my dad was a simple statement, 'Remember who you are.' My grandmother, Grace Hinson, would tell me the same thing, and it wasn't just, 'Remember that you're a Hinson.' It was more like, 'Remember that you're a child of God.' Dad's other statement for me was also simple, 'Do the right thing all the time.'

"In our home," Shae said, "my mom was amazing. Dad worked so much when we were young, and she set the tone for our home. Times were certainly difficult, but she held things together. It has been a cool thing to see that my parents are best friends. Dad has always had friends in his life – Tim McCoy, Bob Lane, Howard Armstrong, and many others, but my mom is his best friend. There was never a single time that I feared that my parents or their marriage was in trouble. Not once. I never saw them disagree, which is amazing. Recently, my parents were in a drama at Ingleside Baptist Church, and, as a married couple, they had a serious disagreement in the drama. It was very strange to see my parents in that scenario, even though it wasn't real. They have been model parents for Brittany and me.

Brittany Hinson couldn't agree more with her younger brother. "One of my dad's greatest strengths is relating to people. He can relate to almost anyone, anywhere, anytime, and loves his interaction with them. My dad is a man who seeks after the Lord first and loves his family with his whole heart. Dad is a passionate person, a strong leader, strong supporter, hard worker, a great businessman, and just generally a great person to be around."

Brittany Hinson said, "I think the best thing that he has done in life was marrying his best friend, my mom. Then, as a couple, they have raised Shae and me to seek the Lord first and live life to the fullest. I have heard my dad say many times that 'God gets all the glory for the successes in his life.' It has been amazing to see how Dad has gone after his goals, even though they were lofty at times, like starting a company when he and Mom were 24 years old. The partnership that my parents share in the decisions of life, along with the joys and the trials, keep them both motivated and spurred on to continue to seek the Lord throughout their journey in life."

Like others who spend time with Ben Hinson, Brittany observed, "Dad seems to always think outside of the box. I feel this is a huge part of his success in life. His wisdom brings great ideas to the table, and then his creative thinking develops a great way to implement those ideas effectively. My dad lives life to the fullest and gives his best in whatever endeavor he is involved. Our family motto is 'Make a memory,' and Mom and Dad have lived this out with Shae and me in so many ways. My favorite childhood memories are:

- Having friends at our house all the time when I was in high school. They came to see my parents as much as they came to see Shae and me, and I loved that my friends loved spending time with my parents,

- Mission trips with Mom, Dad and Shae. I love seeing a heart for the world grow in my dad and our entire family from our first mission trip until now,

- Dad's commitment to our family first and giving up many different important business meetings or events to be at different events for Shae and me,

- The ability to laugh at life, enjoy it to the fullest, and continue to seek new challenges.

"Living as an example of Christ, loving others, and serving others are things that are most important in my dad's life," Brittany concluded.

Hinson's pastor at Ingleside Baptist Church, Dr. Tim McCoy, has known Ben on two levels. Dr. McCoy said, "First, it's been my joy to have been his pastor since 1989. In fact, Ben was on the Pastor Search Committee that the Lord used to bring me to Ingleside. Second, Beverly and I count Ben and Vicki as good friends. Ben is curious, innovative, creative, and he's always exploring new ideas, options, and possibilities. He's not afraid to be outside the box and rarely settles for the status quo. Ben is willing to take a risk and venture down a path few others would even consider.

"Ben is a gentleman in the very best sense of the word. Almost anachronistic in his devotion to manners, customs, and courtesies more common in Southern culture decades ago, Ben sets a high standard in terms of the gracious and winsome way he relates to people. He is tenacious, and he's not a quitter. I have seen Ben stay strong and resolute during times of prolonged challenge and difficulty. He is reaping the good fruit today of perseverance in the past."

Dr. McCoy continued, "Above all, Ben is a devoted follower of Jesus Christ. His faith commitment is the primary and unifying theme of his life. Whether it's in business or politics as a husband, father, or friend, every facet of Ben's life is under the umbrella of his allegiance and devotion to Jesus Christ."

Having served on numerous church-related projects and ministries, the pastor had this to say, "Ben has a keen and incisive mind, but, when dealing with people, Ben follows his heart. Again and again, I've seen Ben's heart of concern, compassion, and generosity lead him to relate to people in ways other tough-minded business people might not understand. Ben has a tough mind but a very tender heart for people - especially those in genuine need of help."

Ben has truly developed a heart of concern and a love for missions in recent years. With his son, Shae, serving as a missionary in the mountains of Peru working with the Peruvian people and training pastors, Ben has become more keenly aware of mission opportunities world-wide. Dr. McCoy continued, "Though Ben's business, professional, and political achievements have certainly been significant, the personal investment Ben has made in Christian missions may have the greatest eternal impact. He is generous in his financial involvement in missions, and he has been even more generous in the time he invests. Ben is the point-person for our entire overseas mission efforts at Ingleside and regularly goes to serve alongside the many volunteers he helps recruit. I have seen this man, who is at home with governors and presidents, serve missionaries, their families, and those who need to know Christ in far-flung places around our world. This humble and sacrificial 'missions-spirit' not only burns brightly in Ben but lives in his children as well.

Dr. McCoy succinctly described Ben Hinson, "Ben is a loyal friend— enough said."

* * * * * * * * * *

Two hobbies began to obsess Ben Hinson in recent years, though this obsession is in a positive way. Ben confessed, "Quail hunting at Wynfield Plantation in Albany is something that I have become passionate about. I try to hunt about 20 times in the fall and winter. One avid hunter who has observed Ben's hobby up close is United States Senator Saxby Chambliss of Moultrie. Senator Chambliss said, "Ben Hinson did not grow up hunting quail, but I was with him when he first hunted a few years ago at a South Georgia plantation. Ben was like a duck taking to water when he experienced his first quail-covey flush! He was obviously a good athlete, because his good hand-eye coordination made him a good shooter immediately. His love for the outdoors is something we have in common, and we have shared many jeep rides, the fun of watching the dogs work, and the thrill of many covey-rises."

In the past 10-12 years, Ben has become increasingly intrigued with the political world. When Saxby Chambliss decided to run for a seat in the United

States Senate in 1994, Ben was among the first contributors to the Chambliss election fund. Since those early days, Hinson has campaigned tirelessly for Chambliss, President George W. Bush, and for countless other conservative and Republican nominees.

When quizzed about his hobbies, other than hunting and politics, Ben responded, "I really like to read, but I have a hard time taking the time to do it. I am also fascinated with technology. When computer games first came along, people enjoyed the game, *Thermonuclear Wars.* With me, I played *Thermonuclear Medicare,* because I was fascinated with the intrigue, the intellect, the thought process, and with writing the programs. Others played the game; I was trying to develop something I could use. I like to create stuff. I figured out how that video game could help me change Medicare. I try to be creative and look to do things, not just differently, but better."

Ben confessed, "I have a hard time just sitting still." No truer words were ever spoken. His schedule is jam-packed with meetings, both locally and nationally. He has served on too many boards and committees to name, and he has always been deeply involved in his church. Today, he is an overseer at Ingleside Baptist Church. He served on the board at FPD from 1993-97 and claimed, 'That was the best board work I've ever done, anywhere.' He stated that the board he worked with was an incredibly bright and gifted group of people. Ben said, "Our board saw the great work that Headmaster Henry Middlebrooks, school founder, and his faculty and staff had done and the solid foundation they had laid (Middlebrooks was a former coach and math teacher at Willingham.) Then, we saw the leadership of the board moving the school to more fully embrace the founding ideals and to offer the best possible education in a completely, unapologetic, Christian environment."

Conversations with Ben Hinson will invariably gravitate toward family matters. Ben commented, "I see things that are named for people and wonder, 'Why would you want something dead named after you? I've got two people – Brittany and Shae - who are alive, who have my name, and that's good enough for me. Aside from my relationship with Jesus, which is the core of my life and the most important One, marrying Vicki has been the best thing that I have ever done. After that, it's just been 'hang on for a great ride.'

"Personally, I would like to be remembered in several ways. First, when people look at my son's and daughter's lives, let them say, 'You must have had a good daddy.' I want to be remembered as a man who was passionately, crazily, blindly in love with his wife. But above all, I want to be known as someone who loved Jesus with all of his heart."

Hinsons in Peru. Ben, Vicki, Brittany,
Shae, and Katie Hagen.

Officers of RAM Club, 1960, present principal, Fred Johnson, with a $300 check. Pictured (L-R) are: Bobby Cass, Tommy Edwards, Jimmy Hallman, Jean Moore, Tommy Reid, Mr. Johnson, Billy Henderson, and LeRoy Mann.

Llyod Newberry 1st principal at Willingham High School. 1958-1959

1958 - First football team captains with Head Coach Billy Henderson. Left: Charles Partridge and right, Eddie Battle.

Several members of Willingham's only state championship team - 1969 Baseball. L-R, 1st row: Coach Billy Henderson, Gary Curtis, Andy Durden, Donnie Fussell, Billy Beale Jr., and Coach Edgar Hatcher. Back row: Richard Tumlin, Jimmy Clanton, Charlie Price, Mark Stevens, and Allen Redmond.

1957 Pony Bowl Football Captains (L-R): Pete Gaines, (St. Joseph's) Grover Bradley (Alexander 4), Tee Carstarphen (Alexander 3), and Bobby Bryant (Bruce).

1962 Willingham vs. Lanier: Pete Gaines (WHS) Grover Bradley (LHS), Tee Carstarphen (LHS), and Bobby Bryant (WHS).

South Macon Little League All-Stars, circa 1960. 31206's
representatives are: Dan Strictland-front row, left; Skeet Heard-
front row, center, Darrell Young-second row, 4th from right.

Willingham Track Team, 1961 (L-R) Mack White, Randy Wheeler,
Terry Duffy, Jimmy Hallman, Tommy Reid, Ronnie Wimberly,
Tony Wilkes, and Clint Tucker.

Willingham and McEvoy Senior Superlatives, 1960. First WHS
graduating class: (L-R): Johnny McCoy, Lynda Adams, Beverly
Moseley, Joe Maddox, Marcia Cason, Charles Partridge, Helen
Newton, Jeweldine McCrary, Eddie Battle (kneeling), Mike
Willoughby (seated), Steve Carter, Sharon Stokes, Larry
Jackson, and Lurlene Garrett (seated).

1960 Class Officers-1st graduating class (L-R): Front row-Beverly
Moseley, Lynda Adams, Sharon Stokes, and Lurlene Garrett.
Backrow-Charles Partridge, Jerome Chapman, and Eddie Battle.

Something That Doesn't Draw Criticism is Either Perfect or Dead.

Morris Alan (Mark) Stevens
Class of 1970

"A leader is someone who motivates and moves others to produce results."
—John Maxwell

Mark Stevens is a pianist. He can only play two songs – "Near The Cross" and "Silent Night"—but he really plays them well. He has also been a master of ceremonies, sound technician, a deacon, an actor, and a pirate. Mark has even worn a pink sports coat on more than one occasion. Mark Stevens is a man of many talents and skill sets, but, of all the things Mark Stevens is today and has been in the past, being a banker and a leader are at the top of the list.

Mark Stevens has been very good at just about everything he has undertaken as an adult, and the primary reason is that he has the ability to surround himself with very good people. His leadership skills have been superbly developed since his high school days at Willingham. As the starting catcher on the only State championship team in Willingham High School's 12-year athletic history, it was easy to spot who the team-leader was on the field.

Ben Hinson, a long-time friend who would room with Stevens at Georgia State, recalled Mark's behind-the-plate demeanor. "Mark was the fiery, always-hustling little catcher who would get so excited behind the plate. After a great pitch, Mark would take about five little 'crow hops' toward the mound and then absolutely burn the ball back to the pitcher with about as much speed as the pitcher had just delivered. The pitchers would be taking cover because they knew Mark was gonna be firing it back to them."

Stevens wasn't always a catcher in baseball. He considered himself to be a third baseman. Mark remembered the first day he attended baseball practice at Willingham and was walking toward the baseball field. He recalled, "Coach Tommy Mixon walked up beside me and said, 'I heard that you're a catcher.' I really wasn't, but he slapped a catcher's mitt against my chest and said 'Let's see what you can do today.' I became the starting catcher in the ninth grade that day. Coach Mixon taught me how to catch. Coaches Tommy Mixon and Jimmy Hammond had a lot of confidence in me."

Tommy Mixon remembered his young protégé. "Mark was always a leader, even back in his high school days. He was totally dedicated to whatever the task was. He was always industrious, enthusiastic, and very bright. When I told Mark that he was our catcher in baseball that day, he never questioned my decision. I told him that he was the guy we would build our state championship around, and that's what happened. Mark had a great arm and was a very good receiver who just worked hard to be the best, and he really got the job done."

When asked where his leadership ability came from, Mark wasn't quite sure. He is convinced, though, that he learned from several men that he has greatly admired for years. One of those early mentors for Stevens was Willingham's varsity baseball coach, Billy Henderson.

"Mark was the catcher for Willingham's baseball team in 1969," Henderson recalled. "We were playing Therrell High out of Atlanta in a best-of-three series to see who would be AAA state champs that year. Mark caught all 14 innings of a double-header that day at Luther Williams Field in Macon, and he must have been about to drop from exhaustion. Therrell had a pitcher named Larry Waites, a big, strong left-hander who faced us in the first game. Waites went on to have a long, successful career pitching in the big leagues."

Henderson said "We were locked up in a pitcher's duel in the first game – Jimmy Clanton, our ace, was pitching against Waites, who was so good we could barely touch him. But late in the game, there was a close play at the plate, and Waites knocked Mark upside down trying to score. Mark's teammate, Gary Curtis, was a guy that never backed down from a physical confrontation and came to Mark's aid. Curtis and Waites got into a shoving match and thankfully for us, the home plate umpire threw them both out of the game. What a break for us! If Waites had not been thrown out, we may still be playing today.

"We went on to win that game, 2-1, and then took the second game as well to win Willingham's one and only state title. That was a proud moment for all of us, and Mark was our 'quarterback,'" Henderson concluded.

"Coach Henderson had such an ability to motivate young men to do more than they ever believed they were capable of doing," Mark said. "I am a prime example of that. I learned a lot from Coach Henderson by the way he related to people. He had an uncanny knack for instilling confidence in those around him. I apply the same principles that I learned from him in baseball to banking. And as the catcher on our state championship baseball team in 1969, I learned the lesson about never giving up. To be successful, you can never give up.

"As an example of how he instilled confidence in us, Coach told us never to enter a room full of people and feel like you were a stranger. He told us to walk in and introduce ourselves to somebody. Go up and shake their hand with a strong grip, look them in the eye, and tell them your name. I still do that today," Stevens said.

"Coach Henderson told us that when you work hard, run, train, and struggle, you're 'putting money in the bank; you're making a deposit.' He said, 'We have a game this week, and we're gonna need to make a withdrawal from the account. So your hard work right now is really a deposit, and you'll need to make a withdrawal on Friday when we play.' I have told my daughters and my employees that story that I learned from Coach Henderson way back in the 1960's."

Another extremely influential man in Mark's life was Dr. James W. (Jimmy) Waters. Known in the greater-Macon community as 'Brother Jimmy,' Dr. Waters had a tremendous impact on Mark since Stevens' teenage years and would later become Mark's father-in-law, pastor, confidante, and close personal friend. Deborah's mom, Annette, according to Mark, "has been like a second mom to me. She is one of the most charming women that I have ever known."

Jimmy Waters said of his son-in-law, "Mark is like my own son. He is bright, hard-working, and is a great family man. He understands the 'church' and has always been supportive of its programs and ministry. You won't find a man any more loyal than Mark Stevens. His loyalty stretches from his family, friends, and church to his bank, community, and civic responsibilities. Mark is as solid as they come, and I'm proud and happy that he married my daughter, Deborah. He's just the best son-in-law you could ever want. Mark loves my daughter and granddaughters and is a good husband and father. He comes from good parents. One of Mark's greatest attributes is that he can get along with anyone. He has the right kind of personality and temperament to lead a bank. He knows banking and he knows people. I have always been confident that Mark would be a success in whatever he chose to do in life."

Mark recalled several reasons that he has always had such great respect and admiration for his father-in-law. "Brother Jimmy has such a spirit of excitement about everything he did. He was enthusiastic about life. I learned a million quotes from him, but one in particular always stuck with me and helped shape the way I live, lead, and do business. He told me, 'Something that doesn't draw criticism is either perfect or dead. Anytime you're doing something good, you will be criticized.' And he was right."

(Author's note: Dr. Jimmy Waters died in February, 2004. His funeral took place at his home church, Mabel White Memorial Baptist Church. He was buried in a private ceremony at Riverside Cemetery in Macon.)

Stevens has always spent time around highly motivated men like Billy Henderson and Jimmy Waters. Their styles of leadership and the way they interact with others are easily seen in Mark Stevens' leadership style as well. But as influential as Coach Henderson and Jimmy Waters were in Mark's life, the greatest influences on his life were his parents, James and Elise Stevens.

James Stevens was a firefighter with the Macon-Bibb County Fire Department, while Elise Stevens worked part-time in the admitting office of the Macon Hospital, now The Medical Center of Central Georgia. According to Mark, "My mom kept a perfect house. It wasn't a showplace or anything, but our home was always clean and well-kept. I never remember our house being a mess. My dad has always been the one who has most significantly shaped my life. As with most firemen, he had a second job where he drove a truck and delivered freight on the days when he wasn't at the fire station. My dad never complained about having to work two jobs to be able to provide for us. And he is one of the finest Christian men I have ever known. I have never heard him say a single curse word – not one. My parents raised us to work hard and be responsible in everything we do."

As the son of a fireman, and the son-in-law of the chaplain for the Fire Department, Mark has always had a deep love and respect for these civil servants. Jim Hartley, Chief of the Macon-Bibb County Fire Department, has known Mark Stevens for many years. "He is the son of James Stevens, a retired Macon-Bibb Fire Department Captain, whom I spent several years working alongside. One of Capt. Stevens' duties was to act as a Relief District Chief when the regular District Chief was off duty, and Mark regularly 'rode the car' on Fridays. He liked to ride along with his father on Friday nights when he didn't have to work the following day. The District Chief's car was housed at Fire Station No. 6 on Pio Nono Avenue. I was a sergeant at the time and was assigned to Engine No. 6 in the early 1980s, so I got to know Mark through our Friday nights at the fire station."

Hartley said, "Mark is the quintessential Southern gentleman. He is so kind and humble. I've never heard him speak an unkind word to anyone. He later became my banker, and he could even turn me down for a loan with a smile on his face! I think what I like most about Mark is his idealism and positive outlook on life. I believe that people love to be around him because of his positive spirit, and his leadership style is visionary. Mark has the ability to get people excited about ideas with his boyish charm.

"I think it goes without saying that Mark married well," Chief Hartley said. "His wife, Deborah Stevens, is one of the finest people I've ever met, and Mark's mother-in-law and father-in-law aren't bad either. I dearly loved his father-in-law, Jimmy Waters, who was a real friend to the Fire Department. I believe that Deborah, Jimmy, and Annette Waters all had positive, profound influences on Mark's life."

Chief Hartley vividly recalled a story, with a fireman's detail, involving Mark in 1983. "One Friday night, the fire phone rang at Fire Station No. 6. We received a fire call to go to Central (formerly Lanier) High School on Napier Avenue. As we approached the school from Clisby Place, we saw smoke pouring from every crack and crevice of the building. A glow emanated from the center of the roof. We had a working fire on our hands. I was the officer in charge of Engine No. 6 that night, and I transmitted a working fire on the radio and ordered the plug man to catch the hydrant. We laid a supply line to the center of the curve on a street nearby and spotted the apparatus. We laddered the roof with a 14-foot ground ladder and pulled a 1 and 3⁄4 inch attack line to the roof.

"I remember looking down at Mark as I reached the roof level with the attack line, Hartley said. "His eyes were as big as saucers. I advanced the line along the roof to where smoke and hot gases were escaping through a rapidly spinning turbine vent. As Mark pulled slack, I kicked the turbine top off the vent pipe. Orange and blue flames immediately shot out like a blowtorch about six-feet into the air. I opened the nozzle and placed it in the vent pipe. I remember looking back at Mark who was standing on the top rung of the roof ladder. Now his eyes were now as big as plates! But thanks to Mark's assistance, we saved Central High School.

"We soon discovered that vandals had started the fire in the principal's office, but our quick action kept damage to the building and its contents minimal," Hartley concluded. "As for Mark Stevens, I am honored to call him my friend."

* * * * * * * * * *

Apart from growing up in the home of a firefighter, Mark was raised in a solid, Christian home. James and Elise Stevens always made sure that the needs of their family of five were met in every way, especially spiritually. "My folks took us to Sunday School and church on Sunday mornings and didn't just drop us off," Mark recalled. "The church was always very important in my family. I became a Christian when I was eight years old. My pastor in those formative years at West Macon Baptist Church was Y.Z. Gordy, who was a great man and a wonderful preacher and pastor. We went back to church on Sunday evenings for Training Union and evening worship and were there again on Wednesday nights for Prayer Meeting. My parents made church attendance a priority. They were developing a strong foundation in my brothers and me for our Christian lives. Deborah and I have trained our children the same way."

The church has been such an important factor in Mark's life that his first date with Deborah Waters actually centered around the church. Deborah was attending Georgia College and State University in Milledgeville, GA. Mark's friend, Rick Bennett, encouraged Mark to go out with Deborah, so Mark called her up and asked her to go to Mercer University's Homecoming basketball game. Deborah told him she couldn't go because Mabel White (where her dad was pastor for 31 years) was having a revival, and she was responsible for 'packing a pew' for the revival. However, Mark was persistent enough that he went to Mabel White and helped her pack the pew. Then they went to the basketball game.

Mark Stevens grew up in South Macon on Dixie Avenue and went to John W. Burke School. At Burke, Mrs. Lucille Comer taught Mark in the seventh grade and was one of his favorite teachers because of her happy, positive, and upbeat manner. He would continue to gravitate to teachers and leaders with those traits. At Willingham High, Mary P. Smith was his American history teacher. "I liked Mrs. Smith's style of teaching and her compassion. She truly cared personally about her students. She even had a desire to see those 'non-interested students' learn American history even though they sometimes gave her fits! When I run into Mrs. Smith these days, it is always so good to see her and remember old times. Another excellent teacher of mine was Mr. Leonard Pridgeon who taught chemistry and physics. I was not a great science student, but he was a great science teacher. His courses in high school made the same courses easy in college.

"I am proud to be from South Macon. We had a great neighborhood with a lot of children my age. I learned how to play baseball at a place that we called Palmer's Field that was owned by Rick Palmer's granddad. My brothers, Larry and Neil, and I used to play ball there all day long in the summers. When it was time for supper – we called it supper when you ate the evening meal – I can remember my dad calling my brothers and me to eat by putting two fingers together, placing them on his lips, and whistling real loud for us to come home.

"After I finished at Burke School, I went to Lanier Junior in the eighth grade and played baseball there," Mark recalled. "Coach Billy Beale of Willingham told my family that they needed me to play baseball at Willingham. My dad told him to 'figure out a way to do it.' And they did. I played Little League in South Macon for Fincher's Barbeque Rebels at old Hudson Field off Houston Avenue and lead the league with seven home runs. Phil Howard's dad was my first coach."

Baseball at Willingham was never better than the years when Mark was catching for the Rams. Certainly winning the 1969 State AAA baseball championship was one of the school's all-time great moments. Stevens had the opportunity to catch some of the top pitchers in the school's history. Mark said, "We had a bunch of pitchers during my years on the varsity at Willingham. Butch Barnes, Chuck Arnold, Doug 'Hunky' Furney, Chuck Beale, Wayne Hart, and Jimmy Clanton were incredible pitchers and just great baseball players. Just about all of those guys either played professionally or played in college. I loved being their catcher."

Stevens had some opportunities to play college baseball at Georgia Southern, Middle Georgia, and Georgia Military College, but he got a partial scholarship at Mercer, so he stayed in Macon and caught two years for the Bears. After Mark's second year at Mercer, he transferred to Georgia State University in Atlanta where he declared Hospital Administration as his college major. Mark roomed with two of his Willingham High School friends, Ben Hinson and Rick Bennett, at Georgia State.

By this time, he and Deborah were so in love that he came home every weekend. His weekly routine was to leave Macon early on Monday morning and go to class at Georgia State through Wednesday afternoon, come back to Macon Wednesday night and see Deborah, go back to Atlanta on Thursday morning and then back to Macon after Friday classes. In order to cut down on travel time, costs, and being away from Deborah during the week, after only one quarter at Georgia State, Mark sensed that some changes would need to be made in his educational direction.

Mark went on a tour of Europe that was led by Rev. Jimmy Waters in June, 1972. Mark proposed to Deborah in Hyde Park, London, England, and they were married on June 30, 1973. Both transferred to Mercer and graduated in 1974. Mark ended up with a BA in Economics, while Deborah's degree was in Elementary Education. He later graduated from The Banking School of the South at LSU and the National Commercial Lending School at the University of

Oklahoma, as well as the Georgia Banking School in Athens.

"In 1974, Tom Greene, a graduate of the University of Georgia, gave me my first job at the First National Bank in Macon in the computer room," Mark said. "Because my brother-in-law, Duane Griffin, also worked at First National, and because of First National's nepotism rule, I left and went to work for Glen Misinco at the C & S Bank. Later I went to work for Neal Ham at Central Bank in Macon, which was sold to and became First Union Bank. Neal Ham became my mentor in banking."

Neal Ham, retired from Security Bank of Macon, is now chairman of the board of Security Bank shares. Ham said of his young protégée, "Mark went to work for me as soon as he graduated from Mercer. I saw some qualities in him that I knew would make him successful. First, he was a very strong and committed Christian man and was very intelligent. He had a particular drive and an entrepreneurial spirit that I knew would benefit him one day as he started a new bank in Macon. After all, as bankers, we had started Security Bank from scratch and also took a struggling local bank, The People's Bank, changed the name to Central Bank of Georgia, and totally changed the image and saw it become a very successful local bank. I knew that Mark Stevens had what it took to lead people and cast a vision for what could be done in banking on a local, personal level.

"One important story that I recall about Mark happened in his first year of banking with me," Ham remembered. "He called me the first thing one morning and said he couldn't straighten up. Mark found out that he had a ruptured disc, and the surgery required a long, slow recovery. Central Bank's policy said the bank would pay his full salary for the first 90 days before the disability insurance kicked in. Mark's recovery took nearly six months, but he never missed a paycheck. He reminded me later that he was surprised that the bank had treated him so well since he was just a young banker with little seniority and was out of work for such a long time. But that instance helped shape the way Mark Stevens would treat his employees as he moved up the banking and financial ladder in years to come. Mark lives out the Christian life in the way he works and treats people."

In 1988, Stevens left to become the No. 2 man at a bank in Clayton, GA, (Rabun County) and lived in Sky Valley for the next two years. "We loved it up there in the mountains of North Georgia," Mark said. "Sky Valley is where our girls learned to ski. We were ready to build a house when Ed Loomis called me and said they were starting a new bank in Macon and would I be interested in coming to work back home. My friend, Barney Smith, gave Ed my name. I told him we were very happy in Rabun County, but he said if I changed my mind, I should let him know.

"I remember coming back to our home near Clayton and telling Deborah that Ed and I had talked. I also told her that I said that I was not interested. She told me that I should at least see what he was offering, so we met again on Saturday at the Cracker Barrel and drank coffee for three hours. After that meeting, I decided that we would leave Clayton, come back home to Macon, and help start the First Macon Bank from the ground floor. With the advantage of hindsight today, helping with the new bank start-up was invaluable as we began work on New Southern Bank which we opened in December, 2001," Mark said.

Having been in the banking industry since his graduation from Mercer University in 1974, Mark has developed a sterling reputation as an outstanding banker and an honest man. Steve Bridges, the former Banking Commissioner for the State of Georgia, has represented over 300 community banks and is now President/CEO of the Community Bankers Association. According to Bridges, "Mark called me to discuss the possibility of starting a new community bank in Macon just over two years ago, and the bank's charter was easily approved. Mark has done some teaching in the banking field for our lending schools and does an excellent job. He always gets great reviews from the students, not only because of the material that he presents, but because he is so accommodating and sincere. Mark really wants to give something back to the banking industry and especially to those who are just learning the business. Mark is a good lender and a very good banker."

* * * * * * * * * *

Since returning to the Macon/Bibb County area in 1989, Mark has been a leader in the community. He has served as president of the Macon Exchange Club and has helped that organization raise multiplied thousands of dollars for local charities. In 2002, Mark served as the chairman of the Cherry Blossom Festival (CBF) in Macon, one of the Top 100 Events in America, according to several periodicals.

Carolyn Crayton, the founder of the Cherry Blossom Festival, has known Mark Stevens for the past 20 years. About Mark, she said, "I have been blessed to know Mark Stevens for such a long time. He is one of the finest gentlemen that I have ever known. We have worked together at his church when Mabel White Baptist was the official host church for the annual Cherry Blossom Festival's visiting dignitaries and opening worship ceremony.

"He has held a leadership position on the Festival's Executive Board for eight years and has worked tirelessly to build the Festival's success," Mrs. Crayton said. "Mark served as Festival Chair and the CBF's Board Chair. For twenty years, he helped with the interdenominational worship service where his wife, Deborah, and daughters, Monica and Molly, sang each year. Mark has spoken on television and radio promoting the Cherry Blossom Festival, and we have had the opportunity to travel together while attending International Conferences to promote Macon. On each occasion, Mark has been the outstanding leader.

"As we have worked together," she continued, "I have witnessed his Christian faith. Mark always thinks of others before himself. I feel extremely blessed to have had the opportunity to work with him as one of his founding directors of New Southern Bank. It was thrilling to witness the total respect and friendship shown to Mark by banking officials as New Southern Bank was being formulated. Due to his outstanding leadership as the President and CEO, the bank's growth has been phenomenal.

"Mark is filled with commitment, dedication, passion, and love in everything that he does," Crayton concluded. "He is quite the gentleman, is very effective in whatever he undertakes, and always sees the good in people. I feel that his loving parents instilled the values of responsibility, love, and sincerity in their home. He is an outstanding leader, and he is greatly respected and admired."

There is little doubt that Mark Stevens is well-respected and highly-effective in both the banking world and as a civic leader. However, most local citizens are unaware of his interest in music and theater. "My wife, daughters, and son-in-law have been involved in local theater for a long time. I began to get interested in theater as well, and I guess I've had parts in at least ten dramatic productions at Theatre Macon and The Macon Little Theatre," Mark said. "I have played the commander in South Pacific and have had several speaking roles in local theater. I was a pirate in MLT's *Peter Pan*. How about that? A banker as a pirate! And I was the master of ceremonies for my church's *Gospel Night at the Grand Ole Opry* on several occasions."

Mark's older daughter, Monica, is married to Chris Kirby, the director of the highly competitive International Baccalaureate Program and long-time drama coach at Central High School in Macon. Monica, the director of counseling at Wesleyan College, has great memories of her dad when she was growing up. "My dad has always been a loving family man first. He is so honest, dependable, and loyal to the point of being 'Boy Scout-ish.' Dad is gregarious, a mama's boy, generous, and is quite the capitalist. Adjectives like *trusting* and *pragmatist* fit him well. He models himself after Andy Griffith and believes that Mayberry is a state-of-mind that is attainable for each of us. He is absolutely a kid inside."

Monica said, "My dad's strengths are his truthfulness and trustworthiness. He has always given me good, constructive criticism. I have always been impressed with Dad's tremendous work ethic. He really believes in the American dream – that we can all have what we desire if we will work hard to achieve it. He is equally proud of his middle-class roots and continues to embrace his middle-class values. Dad has always been so generous with his time and money.

"He taught me to have a good time and that life is for living and enjoying. In our family, as long as we work hard, we can play hard, too. Mark Stevens knows how to have fun, and he is extraordinarily creative, as well as being a great storyteller. My dad loves his parents and continues to work to please them. He also loves his in-laws as if they were his own parents and simply adores his two daughters.

"I have observed my dad in business and know that he is fair and firm, but he always maintains his very genuine, nice-guy attitude. Anyone who has spent much time around my dad knows that he is always positive and believes the best about people, but he is smart enough to be skeptical about anyone who might hurt or endanger others. I think Mark Stevens will be remembered as a loyal man who believes in the good of his country and its values. He will likewise be remembered as a successful businessman, as well as an avid fire-chaser."

Monica continued, "Mark Stevens has always been a man who has gravitated to people who are funny and who enjoy good times. He has had some limited, if not highly regarded, bit parts in local theater in Macon. Despite his business sensibility, Dad is extraordinarily creative. When I was young, Dad loved to play circus with me. My dad introduced me as Angela Richett (his name for me), the tightrope walker, and I was the star of the circus. He played the roaring, fierce lion that Angela tamed by waving her wand. Dad then submitted and became a gentle kitten. Sometimes, he played a racehorse appropriately named 'Kentucky Downs' and willingly offered rides, even on his bad back. Once I'd had enough, he'd slowly get up, only to have thrown his back out. Dad's left hip would cause him to angle to the left when he walked.

"My dad, the highly-successful banker, had a special set of characters that he created just for me. My lead character was named 'Possum Hollow' who wore one purple knee-high sock and another yellow and white striped sock on the other leg. Every night before bed, I experienced a new chapter in the saga of 'Possum Hollow.' When my sister, Molly, was a little girl, Dad created the story of Butterfinger John, who was Possum Hollow's cousin. We loved those stories he made up."

Mark has long been seen by family and friends alike as a guy who was creative, uninhibited, and who did funny, if not goofy, things. Monica recalled, "Once, during the middle of the night, I heard a thud that echoed throughout the house. My mom immediately screamed. I was about 12 years old and remembered thinking that my dad must have had a heart attack and died. Molly and I ran into their room and saw our dad on the floor. I was in tears, but my mom was laughing, not crying. He'd had a dream that he was playing baseball and upon awakening, he'd made the catch that saved the game. He sat straight up in bed, caught the ball, and landed on the floor. We died laughing that night, and all of us had a hard time getting back to sleep.

"I have always loved the creative stories my dad has told and the funny things he has done, but I will remember my dad primarily for having taught me to have fun and enjoy life. Life at our house has always been spontaneous and fun. Our creativity was always encouraged, and we were taught that we matter. No matter where we are or what we're doing, we can always find a way to laugh and have a good time. The same can also be said about my Granddaddy and Grandmother Waters and with the Stevens family as well."

Monica concluded with a tribute to Mark's parents. "Although my dad's parents don't have a lot of formal education, they are just amazing people, and I credit them with teaching him and shaping his life. All three of Grandmama and

Granddaddy Stevens' sons teach Sunday School, serve as deacons in their churches, have great marriages and successful children, and are in positions of influence in their jobs. They have all done well financially and are all generous men. The Stevens family may not be as well-known as the Waters family, but they are wonderful, honest, Christ-like people, and are just as admirable in every way."

Mark and Deborah Stevens have been married for over thirty-two years. Deborah said, "I knew when we first started dating that I would marry Mark. We dated for

Mark and Deborah Stevens 1973.

eight months and were both juniors at Mercer University when Mark asked me to marry him. We were also engaged for eight months."

"My dad was leading a trip to Europe that included my family, me, Mark, and others. Mark and I certainly got to know each other at our best and our worst on that fast-paced three week tour. Interestingly, Mark also had the dubious privilege of rooming with my (then) 13-year-old brother, Jimmy. What a blast we had!

"One cool morning when we were in Munich, Germany, Mark stepped out on the balcony in his underwear to check out the weather before getting dressed for the day. Young Jimmy proceeded to jump out of bed and lock Mark out of the hotel room. Then, he started laughing hysterically and jumped back into bed. Finally, Jimmy allowed Mark to come back into the room. That vacation, which was full of joking around and a lot of pranks, was great in that it began a lasting bond between those two. Jimmy considers Mark to be like his brother, and they continue to have a close friendship today.

"While we were in Europe, our tour ended in London, one of our favorite destinations. Mark and I found some time to be together in Hyde Park without my little brother tagging along. It was there when the magical moment occurred, and Mark asked me to marry him. We both agreed to have the initials H P engraved in our wedding bands as a remembrance of that very special trip and that very special day."

Deborah recalled a story about Mark that caused some doubts about his courage. "One cold, wintry night, we had a fire in our fireplace, and with the logs beginning to die down, Mark decided to go to the woodpile in our back yard to get another armload of wood. All of a sudden I heard scurrying feet and Mark yelling, 'Open the door! Hurry!' I ran to open the door and Mark breathlessly exclaimed, after dropping the firewood, that a bobcat was chasing him. We had a screen door on our back entrance and suddenly there was a small 'bobcat' with his claws stuck to the screen."

Deborah continued, "Anytime something exciting or disturbing happened in our neighborhood, I immediately called Key and Debra Chambers, our long-time friends and next door neighbors to come and help. There were times when Key, who was quite a character in his own right, would come to the rescue as the 'Caped Avenger' wearing thermal underwear and a red cape. Debra and Key showed up with their young daughter, Katie, who quickly helped us with our 'bobcat dilemma.' Katie immediately went to the back door, peeled the 'bobcat' off the screen, and in her youthful wisdom proclaimed, 'It's just a kitty!' Indeed it was. It was a Manx cat, a breed of cat without a tail! Out of the mouth of babes..."

Mark's daughter, Monica, described a vintage Mark Stevens' moment. "Years ago, Mom and Dad thought someone had entered their house at some point without their knowledge. They thought that person had maybe heard them get up to go to bed and then locked themselves in one of our bedrooms. Mom and Dad called Granddaddy Waters, who was the chaplain of every Peace Officers organization in Georgia, and then he called 911. Dad got out his shotgun and followed my Mom, who was in her robe, up the hallway to the locked bedroom. They were both afraid as they walked past the door that was locked. Courageous Dad made Mom walk first. He walked behind her holding onto her robe with one hand and a shotgun, which was pointed at her, in the other hand.

"The police arrived, pounded on the front door, and then forced their way into our house yelling, 'We have a hostage situation! Drop that gun, Buddy! Drop that gun! Drop it!' Dad didn't know what to do, because he didn't understand they were screaming at him. They aimed their guns at him and were about to fire, when Granddaddy Waters arrived, ran into the house, and shouted, 'Don't shoot! That's my son-in-law! Drop the gun, Mark!'"

Monica concluded, "The police investigated the house and saw that there was no one in the bedroom. Mom and Dad then realized that her brother, Jimmy Waters, Jr., had stayed there the week before, and must have locked and closed the door by mistake. A few years ago, my dad bumped into the officer who almost shot him that night. He told Dad that if he hadn't dropped the gun immediately, they were actually about to shoot him."

Mark Stevens has always had an affinity for fire trucks, and, subconsciously, he must have wanted to be a fire fighter. Mark's mom said, "His dad was a city firefighter, so Mark spent a lot of time at the fire station. The fire chief issued Mark a complete set of all the fire fighting gear, and he loved wearing it."

Mark has also loved chasing fire trucks, especially when he would hear a call on his scanner, and it was in his vicinity. Deborah recalled, "One night, as we were preparing Monica, Molly, and ourselves for bed, a fire call was heard on Mark's beloved scanner, 'Engine three, report to Tucker Road!' Since that was in our general neighborhood, we grabbed the girls in their pajamas, I

The Stevens family. Molly, Deborah, Mark, Monica, and Chris Kirby (Monica's husband).

grabbed my robe and flip-flops, and we jumped into our Grand Torino to go chase the fire truck. We had gone about a mile from home with the fire truck sounding its siren ahead of us when the car gave out of gas. Gave out of gas! There we were with two sleepy little girls in tow and me in my flip-flops and robe. We walked back home without even knowing the final destination of that fire call. But since I grew up as Jimmy Waters' daughter, chasing fire trucks and ambulances with Mark was really nothing new or unusual for me!"

* * * * * * * * * *

Mark Stevens, president and founder of New Southern Bank in Macon, has been on the ground floor of perhaps the most innovative, exciting new bank start-up in Macon's history. The bank's slogan reads *New Southern Bank. The bank you've always wanted.* And, if anyone in Macon should know what bank customers are interested in, it would be Mark. With three banking locations up-and-running in Macon, and with another branch scheduled to open in nearby Warner Robins, Mark has seen many of his personal and professional dreams come true.

He continues to give large amounts of time to Deborah and their daughters,

Monica and Molly, now a senior at Mercer. He and Deborah are very active at Mabel White Baptist Church, where Mark teaches an adult Sunday School class, and Deborah sings in the adult choir, as well as working with children's choirs. Mark has been president of the Board of Directors for the Macon Little Theatre. They own a house in Highlands, NC, and for the past five years have looked for opportunities to spend weekends there whenever possible. Mark plays a fair amount of golf and enjoys traveling with his family. They have been to all 50 states except North Dakota, and they have traveled to Europe with Dr. and Mrs. Jimmy Waters on several occasions, as well as taking a cruise to Puerto Rico recently.

Deborah Waters Stevens said it well for both of them when she claimed, "We have had so many happy memories throughout our 32 years of marriage that I could fill a book with them. I thank God for such a happy, Christian home that I had as a child and for the wonderful marriage that Mark and I have experienced together."

Mark Stevens—catcher, actor, creative story-teller, leader, and bank president who continues to live his life with enthusiasm, passion, and a sterling reputation.

A True Example of a Life Long Learner

Dr. Ernest Steven (Steve) Smith
Class of 1969

"Some people see things as they are and ask, 'Why? But I dream of things that never were and ask, 'Why not?'"

–George Bernard Shaw

Steve Smith was in a dilemma. "I was about to complete my degree in sociology at Georgia College but had no prospects for a job or career. Coach Billy Henderson was a man that I greatly admired and respected. He had been my coach when I was in high school at Willingham, and he asked me what I was planning to do when I graduated from college.

"I don't have any definite plans at this time," Smith replied.

Then Henderson posed the question that would change the direction of Smith's life forever. "Steve, have you ever considered a career as a teacher and a coach?"

My response was, "I'm not sure I am suited for teaching and coaching. They both require a lot of patience. Also, one of my greatest regrets in life is quitting football, a sport I truly love."

Billy Henderson had just become the head football coach and athletic director at Clarke Central High School in Athens in 1973 after coaching for 12 years at Willingham and three years at Mount de Sales Academy in Macon with Mike Garvin. Henderson answered Steve Smith's question when he said, "Mike Garvin was one of your favorite teachers and coaches, and he never played varsity football when he was a student at Lanier High School. But he has won three state football championships at Mount de Sales. Why don't you come help me coach at Clarke Central?"

* * * * * * * * * *

Steve Smith is a man who has come a very long way from having no definite plans for a career path to earning a Doctor of Philosophy degree and becoming the county school superintendent of the largest school system in South Georgia.

Ernest Steven Smith started his young adult life as a volunteer coach in Macon and served in both the public and private sectors of secondary education as a teacher and coach. His is the story of a young man who moved to Macon from Augusta as a high school freshman and immediately enrolled in Willingham High School, an all-boys' school - a foreign concept outside Macon's public schools.

When Borden's Dairy transferred Steve's dad to Macon in 1965, Steve moved with his parents, Ernest and Barbara Smith, and his brother, Stan (one year younger than Steve). The family began to look at various neighborhoods throughout Bibb County and found a house they liked which was located across the Ocmulgee River in East Macon, a neighborhood which would have put them in the newly-created Mark Smith High School district.

Dan Pitts, Steve's uncle and the head football coach at Mary Person's High School in nearby Forsyth, told Steve's parents, "You need to send your boys to Willingham. Billy Henderson is the coach over there, and he's a great one. Willingham is where they ought to be."

Thus, Ernest and Barbara Smith changed their minds and bought a house on Robin Hood Road in the Bloomfield area of South Macon in July, 1965. Without any idea of what would transpire over the next few years at this all-boys school, the choice of Willingham High School and the South Macon community was one that would shape Steve Smith's life and career forever.

When the Smiths moved to Macon, they found what appeared to be a cliquish community. Steve stated, "I remember thinking that to feel accepted and be a part of the school, you had to grow up and attend elementary school in Macon. I know I didn't realize it at the time, but my desire to be accepted as a new student in a new school probably gave me compassion for new students attending a new or different school. I had already experienced the loneliness and isolation of moving into a new town and trying to adjust to different surroundings. Later, as a teacher, coach, and administrator, I would do all I could to make new students feel welcome."

In South Macon, the Smiths discovered a working class community with a lot of young families like their own. Steve recalled, "We began visiting Pine Forest Baptist Church, which was within a mile of our new house, and liked the church, but Stan and I were invited by friends at school to another South Macon church, Mabel White Memorial Baptist Church. Mabel White had a dynamic youth group that was led by Hubert Wheeler, the music and youth pastor. Stan and I had found our new church home.

"Dr. Jimmy Waters, the young pastor at Mabel White, had a daughter, Deborah, who attended McEvoy, Willingham's sister school, and was in the church's youth group. It seemed like everything began to fall in place for us, and we began to develop close relationships with friends and church leaders.

"I met some guys - Mark Stevens, Billy Browning, Terry Sark, and Richard Merchant - who were all strong Christians and were leaders at Willingham," Steve said. "The stress of being the new guy at a new school was greatly minimized because of the friends I was making. Those guys demonstrated levels of friendship, character, integrity, and leadership that had a great effect on me. I became part of the Key Club, was sports editor of the *RAM-SCOTT* (the school's yearbook), and was involved in other organizations as the result of the new friends that I made at Willingham."

Adapting to the church's youth group was easy for Steve. "With friends like Don Shurley, Steve Mann, Andy Harrison, Bobby Rhodes, Darrell Merritt, Jimmy Bloodworth, Bobby Story, Key Chambers, and Jerry Hunnicutt, I now had a support system both at school and at church, and I had finally found my niche. I remember playing softball for the church's youth team, being involved in its youth ministry, and going on choir tours all over the Southeast. These events allowed me to develop some long-lasting friendships, many of which I still maintain today."

Steve recalled being a good student, but not spectacular. "I was greatly influenced by many of my teachers at Willingham. Robert Floyd, a bi-vocational pastor, was my biology teacher who also served as pastor of a small, country church in Ocilla, GA. He was somewhat notorious for his dreaded, daily five-question pop tests in biology. If you missed one, two, or three questions on the test, not only would you fail the pop quiz, but you could expect to get one, two, or three licks from Mr. Floyd's paddle. No conversation. No debate. No lobbying. Just, 'Bend over and grab your ankles.' Corporal punishment was not only legal in those days, but was pretty much a fact of life in the all-male classrooms at Willingham High. There was never any doubt about who was in charge, or who created the rules in Robert Floyd's classroom - it was 'Ocilla Bob' - and if you didn't like it...well, there's the door."

Smith added, "Guys studied for biology and for any other subject where they were held accountable by the teacher. In some classes, licks from a wooden paddle gave plenty of motivation, but in Leonard Pridgen's chemistry class, it was self-motivation if you were college-bound. In Mike Garvin's math class, if you were a slacker, you would get so far behind that you would never catch up, so the only alternative was to study Garvin's algebra every day."

Mrs. Mary P. Smith (no relation), an American history teacher, was one of the most popular faculty members of all time at Willingham. Affectionately known as 'The Rock' for her toughness and inflexibility (both traits seemed to be absolute requirements for women who worked in an all-boys school in those days), Mrs. Smith had a great interest in the Civil War and could make history come alive for her students.

Mrs. Smith recalled, "Steve had been given some letters by his great-grandmother that were written by his great-great-grandfather while he was serving in the Confederate Army. Steve brought those letters to class, showed them to me, and I took them to Dr. Spencer King, chairman of the history department at Mercer. Dr. King unfolded the old, old letters, deciphered them, pressed the letters out flat and smooth, made copies of them for the Mercer University Library, and gave us the historical accounts surrounding the letters. Those letters were a wonderful teaching tool in my American history class.

"I remember that Steve Smith was a good student with high character, strong morals, and a deep interest in American history. He was a leader in school even back in those days," she said. Obviously, Mary P. Smith made a lasting impression on Steve, because he recently wrote her a long, detailed letter thanking her for being such a great influence on his life, both personally and professionally.

Steve had a number of teachers at Willingham who greatly influenced him as a teenager. Math teacher and coach Mike Garvin and English teachers, Lenoir LaMounnt and Jerry Rogers, were several of the excellent educators and role models in Steve's life. He credits coach Eddie Battle for encouraging him to give football a try, even though young Smith - who had great speed - was not blessed with a football player's body and was quite late developing physically. While at Willingham, Steve wrestled on the varsity for coaches Garvin, Johnny Stallings, and Lloyd Bohannon while running the 440-yard dash and the 880 in track for coach Jesse Duckworth.

None of Smith's teachers, however, were more significant in his life than football coach and athletic director, Billy Henderson. With his charismatic personality and his ability to motivate young men, Henderson encouraged Steve to give teaching and coaching a try, and though Steve never excelled at football in high school, his early affiliation with Henderson through athletics would shape his life greatly.

Steve graduated from Willingham in 1969 and enrolled at Macon Junior College (now Macon State College). Upon completing his two-year program there, he went to Georgia College and State University in Milledgeville, where he graduated with a B.S. in Sociology in 1973. Steve wrestled with a career path as he graduated from college. Early in his college career, he pursued a course study with a concentration in veterinary medicine, but his struggles with chemistry and physics altered his path by his junior year. Sociology, with its focus on the study of people and relationships, proved to be of great interest to Steve and would later prove to be invaluable professionally.

"Frustration began to set in for me as my senior year of college was winding down," Smith recalled, "because I really had no direction for my life when I graduated from Georgia College. During this time, I went on a retreat to the FFA-FHA Camp in Covington, GA, with the youth and college students from Mabel White, and while I was there, it seemed like I 'wrestled with God' in the sense that I audibly cried out, 'What do You want me to do? Am I supposed to preach? Would you please open up some door for me?'"

That weekend, Smith found himself feeling desperate, a little frantic, and without any direction at a time in his life when his buddies all had good ideas about their futures. That's when coach Billy Henderson asked Steve the 'life-changing' question about considering education as a career, and Smith's educational journey was officially underway.

Though Steve was given an opportunity to work with Coach Henderson at Clarke-Central High in Athens, he also weighed another offer to teach and coach in Cochran at Bleckley County High before saying "Yes" to Henderson. Smith, and fellow Willingham graduate and ex-Marine, Carl Summers, drove to Athens every afternoon for spring football practice in 1973. Steve served as an assistant coach in both football and baseball; and he was the head soccer coach. He also started a wrestling program at Clarke-Central the following year.

Regarding his educational and coaching careers, Steve stated, "My greatest experience was working with coach Billy Henderson immediately after I graduated from college. It helped me establish the discipline, structure and work ethic that I would need to become successful in life. It was there that I was first exposed to 6 a.m. coaches' meetings, listening to Coach Henderson's theme song—*The Impossible Dream*—and hearing some disgruntled young coaches who weren't sold on Coach Henderson's new way of doing things at Clarke-Central."

It was common knowledge around Athens that several coaches at Clarke-Central resented the structure, work ethic, and 'driven manner' in which Coach Henderson did things. Smith, nonetheless, did what was expected of him and learned more about coaching football than he would ever learn anywhere else. He, likewise, remained loyal to his head coach despite the persistent negativism of those around him. Smith stated, "My experience as an assistant coach for Billy Henderson gave me instant credibility with other coaches and educators around the state." And sure enough, other schools began calling for his services.

The first to call was Henry Middlebrooks, headmaster of the newly-founded First Presbyterian Day School in Macon and a former assistant coach at Willingham. Middlebrooks called Steve about coming back home to Macon and helping the young school with their fledgling football program. Smith said, "One important lesson that I learned from Billy Henderson was that if anyone is interested in you, have the courtesy to go talk to them. So I did."

Steve recalled, "My first teaching and coaching job at Clarke-Central in 1973-74 paid me $6,800 a year plus a $1,000 coaching supplement for a grand total of $7,800, which I thought was pretty good. I left Clarke-Central and took the job at FPD in 1974, making $8,500 as an assistant coach in football, basketball, and track. I even tried to start a wrestling program, though the school, at that time, didn't have the money to purchase a wrestling mat."

It was at FPD that Smith became part of an outstanding young coaching staff that included Philip McLeroy, the first head football coach in the school's history, Rex Putnal (former UGA wide receiver), and brothers Brannon and Cam Bonifay (both former athletes at Georgia Tech). It was also at FPD that Smith first became active with the Fellowship of Christian Athletes national organization.

* * * * * * * * * *

"Fate would have a hand in more ways than just a career for me," Smith said. "After I left Clarke-Central to return to Macon to coach at FPD, I met my future wife, Linda Mock, at Mabel White Baptist Church. Linda was an attractive young woman from Bainbridge, GA, a wonderful community in extreme Southwest Georgia. She had relatives in the Macon area and was the daughter of a high school basketball coach in Bainbridge. Linda was a rising senior at the University of Georgia but had moved to Macon for the summer to work in her grandparents' business. After dating for a year, we were married on

July 19, 1975. Today, we are the parents of two sons, Brian (26) and Michael (22)."

With their first child on the way and a conviction that Linda should stay home with their children, Steve decided to leave coaching in 1978. In order to make more money, he went to work for Minnesota Mining and Manufacturing Company in Macon, where he made twice as much in sales at 3M as he did in coaching. On the other hand, he frequently went home feeling frustrated and unfulfilled.

In 1981, FPD called again to see if he was interested in returning to education. He was. Upon telling Linda that he missed teaching and coaching, she told him, "Steve, go where your heart is; go coach and teach again."

Thus, he left the private sector and went to work at First Presbyterian Day School. Throughout that year, his good friend and neighbor, coach Tom Simonton, encouraged him to come to Central High School (formerly Lanier) in Macon. In 1982, Steve went to work at Central as an assistant football coach for Simonton, became the head coach in wrestling and baseball, and served on staff for 18 years.

Smith taught history and government for seven years at Central. His mentor, Tom Simonton, was an outstanding role model and preached that they were teachers first; coaches second. Steve served in administration for 11 years while at Central as the Lanier 'A' building principal and later became the complex principal. Steve's coaching career ended in 1995 when he became the supervising principal of the Central High School Complex.

As a coach and teacher at Central, Steve was a major influence on a huge number of students. Robert Greene is part of a family that has been very close to Steve Smith and his family. Robert, an associate pastor at Vineville United Methodist Church in Macon, played varsity baseball for Steve. His mother, Cynthia Davis Greene, taught with Steve at Central, while Robert's sister, Katherine Greene Phillips, was both a student and a teacher under Smith's leadership.

Robert remembered the courage of Steve Smith, "One day at baseball practice, several of us were taking batting practice in the cage that was quite removed from the practice field. We heard some guys yelling to us, 'Hurry up, and bring your bat with you!'

"When we got there, Coach Smith had confronted a big man who appeared to be drunk, had a big stick, and apparently had been beating his wife or girl friend. Coach Smith got the man to stop the beating and was trying to talk the guy into putting the stick down. Before we knew it, Coach Smith had jumped on the guy, had taken the stick away from him, had the guy face down in the parking lot, and told us to call 9-1-1, which we did. The police arrived quickly and took the man away. We couldn't believe what we had just witnessed. Coach Smith never had any fear about jumping in there and helping that defenseless woman."

Cynthia Greene also has fond memories of Steve Smith. "By the time I actually met Steve, he was already a household name. He was the main subject of our nightly conversations around the dinner table. There was no doubt that his government classes were a highlight of Katherine's school day, or that the lessons Robert learned at baseball practice were every bit as important as the lessons he learned in a classroom. We all became very informed on the happenings in the state legislature, and we often spent time dealing with one of Steve's 'truisms' such as 'If it's to be, it's up to me.'"

Cynthia Greene recalled, "Steve often threw out meaningful aphorisms in his talks with his teams, in his classroom, or he had them printed on t-shirts to inspire winning attitudes among his players. Our family was grateful for the opportunities to discuss these life lessons that didn't seem 'preachy.' After baseball games, Steve would use those few minutes to talk to the team about good sportsmanship, fair play, or moral standards.

"The boys on Central's baseball team wanted to win big for their coach, and they did. I believe that our biggest thrill came when we beat the Warner Robins Demons, our fiercest rival, for the region championship. That win was unforgettable, and the guys ordered a plaque for Steve with the words inscribed, 'We came back with more than just the sand in our shoes.'"

Cynthia Greene continued, "Steve's young, boyish face belies his strength and energy. It is readily apparent that he believes in dealing with problems 'head on.' On more than one occasion, when there were issues or dilemmas, I would hear him say, 'Come in here and let's talk about it.' He would confront the situation and sometimes become a catalyst for a solution.

"Steve always had a big vision for our school and earnestly worked toward attaining a School of Excellence award for several years. That our school was not included in that award did not diminish his resolve to go for it again the following year. He was proud of the school's achievements, and he really wanted that distinction."

Former student/athlete Robert Greene remembered Steve Smith as a man whom everyone respected. "They might not necessarily agree with him, but they respected him, nonetheless. People have always been important to Steve, and he managed to find time for everyone, regardless of their lot in life. His ability to motivate players and students was also evident. He frequently placed motivational quotes and sayings around the dressing room areas at Central. My favorite Steve Smith-saying was, 'Losers make excuses; winners make commitments.'"

Smith was deeply committed to being successful in whatever venue he chose. He strived to be a success in sports as a player and coach and as a school administrator. According to Robert Greene, "Steve Smith is a man with a deep and strong Christian faith, and he instilled the right values in his players. He lived out his Christian faith in a secular setting, and his players respected him for that. It was a common occurrence for former players to show up at practice and seek Coach Smith's wise counsel. He remained friends with scores of his former players and students, and he had a knack for not only remembering their names, but he knew points of interest about their lives, which was pretty amazing."

Katherine Greene Phillips was in Steve's social studies class. She is now married to Ed Phillips, is the mother of three-year-old twin sons, and lives in Alpharetta. Smith influenced Katherine to the point where she became a social studies teacher at Central High School, mainly because he was such an interesting teacher.

After Katherine graduated from the University of Georgia, she got her first teaching job with help from Steve Smith. "He became my principal and was such a supportive leader for me when I was a young teacher. He encouraged me to persevere through my first year and apparently saw that I had the potential to become a good teacher. He has been important to my whole family - as a boss, a coach, and a friend. He became my hero.

"One thing I have always admired about Steve Smith is that he is absolutely fearless. There were many situations at our high school with students who were really dangerous (carrying weapons, fighting, etc.), but he would not hesitate to literally jump, run, or shove his way into the middle of things to stop the situation."

Katherine remembered Steve being almost 'omnipresent.' "He somehow seemed to have a knack for being in the right place at the right time. Maybe that's what heroes do because of their fearlessness. He was right there for me one morning when I had a wreck on the way to school. His was the first face I saw when I got out of my car which had just been totaled. I spotted him with his outstretched arms, and he made me feel like it would all be okay."

Katherine Phillips was saddened when Steve left Macon to go on to bigger things. In her words, "It was a real loss to the community of Macon. He cared deeply about Macon and its people, and it showed in the choice of his profession and in all of his actions as a teacher, coach, and administrator."

The things that Phillips liked most about him as a teacher and coach were, in her words, "The ways he inspired countless kids. As a principal, he inspired teachers and students to reach their potential, and he has always been such a model for us as a loving family man. He demands and commands respect, but he gives respect in return. Although he is highly educated, he is never seen as condescending or academic. He is a great leader who doesn't have to be seen as authoritarian to make people want to do well for him. I especially liked him, because he was such a funny, smart, and kind man who would do just about anything for anybody. He believes in the 'goodness of people.'"

Today, Steve Smith is seen by students, teachers, and administrators as a courageous and a compassionate leader. Pam Wacter, the daughter of Mary P. Smith, one of Steve Smith's most influential teachers at Willingham, became Central High's principal when Steve left Macon for the superintendent's job in Hawkinsville.

Mrs. Wacter said, "I have many special thoughts concerning Steve Smith. We have a special relationship with many twists and turns. He was, of course,

one of my mom's favorite students. Then, when he followed in her footsteps
by teaching American history, he taught my twin boys the same subject that my
Mom had taught him. He also coached Russ and Rod in baseball and continued
to model strong values and fine character for them. Our relationship broadened
even more when I became principal at Tinsley Elementary School. I had the joy
of working with his wife Linda, a superb teacher, and we were neighbors, so we
visited often as he and Linda walked their huge pup, Beau.

"Steve's greatest influence on me came when I was given the honor of
following him as principal of Central High School. He had such a strong and
contagious love for Central and that 'Central Orange.' His encouragement and
enthusiasm were extremely meaningful to me in my new position as principal. I
can now fully understand his loyalty to Central and his love for the students and
staff. I've caught his Central Charger Pride, too."

Wacter continued, "I have a funny story about Steve. Before he and Linda
left Macon for Hawkinsville, they stopped by late one Friday afternoon to visit
with me. He wanted to catch up on Charger News and tell me about his new
position as superintendent. Steve was well-dressed when he sat down in our
backyard swing. I was trying to warn him to stand up, but it was too late. Our
103-pound Chow, Harley, jumped into his swing and into Steve's lap. Steve
was shocked to have a 100-pound dog in his lap, but he never lost that cool,
professional demeanor."

* * * * * * * * * *

Leadership and the study of leaders have become something of a passion
to Steve Smith in recent years. "Regarding leadership," Steve said, "I have
been greatly influenced by the teachings and the ministry of Dr. John Maxwell,
the founder of InJoy Ministries. Dr. Maxwell teaches about the concepts of
being a servant-leader, and that is the great desire of my professional life. I
want to be known as a servant-leader by those whom I have a responsibility
to lead. To become a servant leader, you must not only have a passion for
what you do, but also for those you lead. The ultimate goal must be to use the
talents of the individuals you lead in order for them to become more successful
in accomplishing the goals of your organization. When the connection or
relationship between the individuals is strong, the groups will more likely work
as a team to accomplish their goals. You can move people to act as a team more
expediently through emotion. In other words, you must touch their hearts before
you can reach their heads and their hands."

With his reputation as leader growing rapidly, in 2000,and after 18 years
at Central High School as a teacher, coach, and administrator, Smith was
pursued by the Pulaski County (Hawkinsville, GA) Board of Education for their
superintendent's position. Steve said, "After years of furthering my education,
the time had finally come where I would have an opportunity to create and shape
school policy at the highest level. I developed an instant love for the people

of Hawkinsville. The fact that the Pulaski County Board of Education would entrust their school system to my leadership endeared them to me even more."

As the top individual in the Pulaski County school system, Smith finally realized how far he had actually come from the days when he was so unsure about what he would do with his life. Though, as a student, he never questioned that he would graduate from college, he likewise never thought he would go back to school either. After years of teaching at the high school level, Steve pursued his master's degree in social science education from Georgia College & State University in Milledgeville and said, "Now I have my master's. That ought to be enough education for me."

However, eight years later, Smith had second thoughts about his educational future and stated, "It looks like I'm going to be in this line of work for a while; so I probably need to go back and get more education. That way, I will be better prepared and will make a little more money." He earned his second master's degree, this one in Educational Administration in 1989, and the Specialist in Education degree in 1993 from GC&SU.

Steve never really considered pursuing a doctorate in education during those days. As people began to talk in his presence about doctorates, it seemed that most of the doctoral programs did not offer the type of degree that he was interested in pursuing. Finally, Steve decided to apply to the University of Georgia, Georgia Southern University in Statesboro, and Georgia State University in Atlanta just to see what would happen.

Georgia State was the first school to respond to his application. While Steve was playing in a church softball game one summer evening, Linda answered the phone and talked to Dr. Al McWilliams, a professor from Georgia State. Dr. McWilliams said, "Please tell Steve that he has been accepted into a cohort group where we will only take eight people into the program. However, we need to know within two days if he will accept this position in our doctoral program."

Upon returning home from the church softball game, Steve called the professor at 11 p.m. and hastily replied, "I'll take it."

Georgia State was the only school to offer the PhD program, while the others offered the Educational Doctorate degree. The PhD was an important factor for Steve's choice of schools. He was advised that if he desired to teach at the collegiate level, the Doctorate of Philosophy Degree in Education would make him more marketable. "I do have future aspirations of teaching prospective administrators at the college level and writing on the topic of leadership," he said. "My dissertation topic was Leadership and Teamwork, and I am passionate about helping school teams improve academic achievement through more effective leadership. I greatly enjoy teaching, and I believe that teaching is what God put me here on earth to do."

Steve was named the recipient of the J. Everett DeVaughn award for the most promising doctoral student in the department of Educational Leadership in 1999. He earned his PhD from Georgia State in 2001. Now, he is officially

Dr. Ernest Steven Smith, but to be in his presence, no one would ever be aware of his four advanced degrees. He considers himself a model of a life-long learner and hopes that others will meet the challenge to pursue higher levels of education.

* * * * * * * * * *

In 2002, the Lowndes County Board of Education in Valdosta pursued Steve Smith while he was in his second year as superintendent of schools in Hawkinsville. In fact, Vic Verde, the executive director of the Leadership Academy for the State Department of Education in Georgia, was very instrumental in the process of Steve Smith moving from Central-Macon to Hawkinsville and then from Hawkinsville to Lowndes County.

Verde said, "I met Steve Smith in Macon while I was training his leadership team at Central High. Steve had applied for and received a grant for the leadership seminar that I would lead. We worked closely with each other for two years, and together, we developed a true team-leadership program at Central. The thing that I admire most about Steve Smith is that he is a high-integrity guy with great character. He is certainly a 'people person,' which was evidenced because he knew kids' names. He also knew his staff personally and would ask questions about their family members and about previous conversations.

"It has been interesting to me to see how school systems have pursued Steve," Verde stated. "They all like him for the same reasons. He is an avid and fast learner, a good writer, an excellent speaker, has an unquenchable thirst for knowledge, and he represents his school or system extremely well. I think Hawkinsville and Lowndes County saw something unique in Steve. He had so many ingredients that made him attractive as a candidate.

"One thing that these school systems liked about Steve was that in anything he did, he became a leader, and he developed others around him to become leaders. He literally coached those around him," Verde said. "Steve is a rising star in Georgia education. People like him because he is dependable and trustworthy. He is forever getting feedback from his staff, parents, students, and board members, but perhaps the best quality of all is that he treats everyone he meets with dignity and respect. Anyone can express what he or she thinks or feels to Steve Smith. His future in education is unlimited."

After months of prayer and consideration of Lowndes County's offer to become their school superintendent, Smith accepted their invitation. He left Pulaski County for Lowndes County, the state's largest school system (over 9,300 students) south of Houston County.

Today, Steve says, "I see much of my responsibility as the superintendent as working with others in creating a shared vision for establishing the most conducive educational environment. I want to be a visionary leader who inspires others to work together for the benefit of the entire school system and community. Through our work, we can improve the human condition and make our world a better place."

Throughout the years, Smith has used numbers of creative approaches to help motivate teachers for whom he is responsible. He said, "I frequently show movies to our staff as a new school year begins, because I have always believed that a picture is worth a thousand words. I particularly like movies that deal with students and teachers. I search for thought-provoking themes that appeal to the emotions. Several recurring movies that became favorites of our teachers and staff were *October Sky, Dead Poets Society,* and *Mr. Holland's Opus.* Plus, I have always been sort of a movie buff. Some of my personal favorites, though I don't necessarily use them to motivate teachers, are *Dances With Wolves* and *Field of Dreams* with Kevin Costner, and *Brian's Song,* the story of the friendship between Gayle Sayers and Brian Piccolo of the Chicago Bears. Brian Piccolo died of cancer while he was a member of the Bears, and he had such a burning desire to succeed. In fact, we named our first son Brian after Brian Piccolo."

Smith spends the few leisure hours that he has playing his Martin HD28 acoustic guitar which his wife encouraged him to buy. Steve plays golf socially, does some hunting and fishing with Brian and Michael, and continues to watch high school sports. Though he played 30 years of competitive softball and has played tennis in a Volvo Tennis league in Macon, one of the great joys of his adult life has been hunting with his son, Brian, and watching his son, Michael, play baseball at Central High School.

Steve also has a love for outdoor photography and travel. His home and office are adorned with photos he has taken while on family trips throughout the United States and Western Europe. Smith said, "Photography inspires my artistic and creative nature. It helps me gain multiple perspectives on life and to recognize the true beauty in God's creation."

Steve Smith is a man with many strengths. His easy-to-get-along-with manner has made him a favorite with many of his teachers and subordinates, both past and present. Smith stated, "One thing that I take much pleasure in is that I still have great friends wherever I have served."

When asked about his academic and leadership strengths, Smith replied, "One of the greatest gifts that God has given to me is that of vision. I see great potential in others, especially when we all work together for the same goals. I have also been successful in helping others develop a shared vision. People achieve more as a result of this visionary approach and teamwork. Four key elements are involved in being a great leader. You must provide hope, establish trust, offer encouragement, and give praise. If we are to be effective leaders, then we must be merchants of hope, because hope is what leaders sell."

Cynthia Greene and Katherine Greene Phillips gave Steve a plaque with a quote by George Bernard Shaw that deals with vision and says,

Some people see things as they are and ask, "Why?"
But I dream of things that never were and ask, "Why not?"

It was the Greene family's opinion that Steve Smith's philosophy of life and education coincided with Shaw's verse. Thus, that framed quote hangs on the wall behind his desk.

* * * * * * * * * *

Greg Winters, an assistant district attorney of the Macon Judicial Circuit, played baseball for Smith at Central. "I first met Steve when I was in high school, and he was my football and baseball coach. Like many guys in high school, my first impression of him was not very pleasant. He was some 'old man' I would have to deal with while I was proving how much of a 'stud' (in my own mind) I was. However, I soon began to see Steve as someone who was really interested in how each kid was doing. This not only pertained to sports, but to school, family, etc."

Smith reminded Winters of his own father, who had been a high school coach for 30 years. "Steve knew when to be tough and demanding, but he also told us when we did a good job. He knew what to say and when to say it."

"While I was at Central, I began to hear rumors that Steve wanted to go into administration. I couldn't believe that he would want to become one of the pinheads, our term for administrators. To my dismay, he soon became the assistant principal and the head administrator at Lanier 'A,' a part of the Central High complex. I believe he felt that he could reach more kids at that level than he could as a coach."

With each step that he has taken professionally, Steve Smith has left an indelible mark. Winters recalled, "People's love for Steve was demonstrated when he accepted the job in Hawkinsville. A banquet was held in his honor at Central, and I was honored to be one of the guest speakers. Several individuals who spoke about Steve were Judge Bill Adams, Mrs. Leontine Espy (former principal), and others that Steve had influenced at Central. The common, recurring theme was how Steve made people better by challenging them in some way. Each of those challenges helped shape each person's life, including mine. It seemed as if he treated everyone like they were part of his own family. He wanted everyone's best and expected more than people were used to giving."

Winters recalled a funny story about Smith's days as a high school baseball coach. "One day, we were practicing baseball when some kids started throwing rocks and busted a window in one of our cars. This, of course, did not make us very happy, but Steve was going to save the day. He told some of us to load up in the back of a truck; we were going to find the culprits and turn them over to the police."

The coach and his players started out on their manhunt. Winters continued, "We were confronted by someone living in the neighborhood who wondered why an adult had several teenagers in the back of his truck wielding baseball bats. (Steve didn't know we had the bats!) The neighbor called the police and said, 'Some guys with bats are in our neighborhood chasing kids.' As we continued on our mission, we finally found the individuals that broke out the car window, but as we arrived, so did the police. They wanted to know why teenagers with bats in the back of a pickup truck being driven by their coach were chasing neighborhood kids. We thought Steve Smith was going to have a heart attack! He could barely speak, but he soon began a feeble attempt at an explanation. It was hilarious, and that's a memory about Steve Smith that I'll never forget."

There is little doubt that Steve has made lasting impressions on people wherever he has served. When asked how he wanted to be remembered, Smith replied, "I would like to be thought of as a servant-leader with a mission in life to serve others. In fact, my leadership style over the years has changed significantly from autocratic to servant-oriented. I have a real desire to be seen as a faithful Christian, husband, father, and son."

As a teacher, coach, principal, and superintendent, Steve sees himself as an effective leader who challenges the educational process and who inspires a shared vision with those around him. Smith said. "I have enjoyed the privilege of working for several great bosses. Each one helped me to grow as a leader. As an educator and being what I call 'a life-long learner,' I believe I have been wise enough to learn from those around me. I am a product of my experiences. I have observed the 'good, the bad, and the ugly' along my leadership and educational journey, and I have identified those traits that I want to avoid and those that I want to emulate. I had the advantage of having access to many extraordinary teachers, coaches, mentors, and leaders in my life. These are the people who have helped me succeed."

* * * * * * * * * *

Steve Smith has always been drawn to people of great character who have high standards of morality. He said, "There have been several people who have been particularly influential in my life because of their ethics, motivational abilities, and positive outlooks on life. My parents, Ernest and Barbara Smith, helped support me and establish my direction in life. They taught me that you only get out of life what you put into it. They have blessed me with a strong work ethic, an attitude of bringing out the best in others, and a tremendous desire to succeed. I owe my parents a huge debt of gratitude.

"My grandfather, Hamlyn Stevenson, was also a great influence in my life. He died when I was 13, but he helped mold my character. My uncle, Brady Link, helped me acquire an appreciation for music, but he also helped me develop a sense of fairness and compassion for others. He was not a formal teacher by trade, but he was very intelligent and was one of the best lay-teachers I know. I learned so much from him by the way he lived his life. He spent time with me as a young boy and taught me about hunting, fishing, and playing the guitar. He had the patience of Job."

Steve's first real boss, Dr. Mack Butler, a veterinarian in Macon, taught him much about life. "During that stage of my life, he was like a second father to me. We had many deep conversations about education, politics, religion, and an assortment of other areas of interest. Dr. Butler taught me to use my critical thinking skills when analyzing an issue. He inspired me to pursue my education as far as I wanted to go, but neither of us knew where it would take me."

Smith continued, "From a spiritual perspective, my pastor, Dr. Jimmy Waters, and my youth minister, Hubert Wheeler, were very positive influences. They impressed upon me the importance of my relationship with Christ and how that should be my top priority in life. Brother Jimmy greatly influenced my leadership style. I observed his leadership skills and learned to multi-task, which is essential for a school superintendent. He was the master of multi-tasking even before that term was coined.

"Professionally," said Smith, "there was no greater influence than the late William Bell, supervising principal at Central High, who became the assistant superintendent of Bibb County Schools. It was under his leadership that I became a true professional educator and realized, beyond the shadow of a doubt, that God had called me to be an educator. Mr. Bell saw potential in me well before I realized it myself. His inspiration has led me where I am today."

Smith made many friends at every juncture of his career and maintains friendships with people from Macon, Hawkinsville, and Valdosta. One of his close friends from Macon is Judge Bill Adams, judge of the State Court of Bibb County, who knew Steve through their work with the Middle Georgia Dugout Club which sponsored an All-Star game each spring after the high school baseball season ended. The game included seniors who had just graduated from public and private schools within a 50-mile radius of Macon.

"Steve Smith was an amazingly hard worker and was a very good baseball coach," Judge Adams recalled. "We put on the Middle Georgia All Star game for seven consecutive years, but when Steve left, no one wanted to take it on. Steve also hosted the Lem Clark Old-Timers game that was a big hit locally. Lem Clark was the long-time baseball coach at old Lanier High. A spring baseball tournament, which began in the 1960s, is still played in his memory.

In the Old Timers game, former athletes played and represented their alma maters at Charger Field (formerly known as Willingham Mill Field and later as Poet Park). Judge Adams concluded, "We had graduates from eight Macon schools from a prior era playing on the same day, and it was so much fun. Under Steve's leadership, we tried to play the traditional rivalry games which created a lot of interest. We had Willingham against Lanier, Mark Smith played Dudley Hughes, Mount de Sales took on Stratford, and Ballard Hudson faced Peter G. Appling."

* * * * * * * * * *

Mark Stevens and Steve Smith have been long-time friends since the 1970's. Their families have vacationed together, remained friends throughout the years, and have great mutual respect for each other. According to Stevens,

"I can best sum up Steve's character by a quote that I recall him using while addressing a youth group at Tattnall Square Baptist Church. Steve told me, 'Periodically, I make myself watch a documentary on Public TV, or I listen to classical music on the radio to teach myself discipline. Discipline is who we are and what we're about. Then, who we are becomes our character.' Steve's character has been demonstrated to hundreds of students. There is no doubt that Steve Smith was called to be an educator. His character is contagious, and he has dedicated his adult life to improving the quality of public education wherever he has lived."

Stevens recalled a story about Smith when they vacationed together one summer. "Deborah and I were traveling with Steve and Linda in the western part of the United States when Steve dropped his sunglasses on the side of the road while taking pictures of the Grand Teton Mountain range. Steve was lying in a prostrate position, because he thinks he's a professional photographer. He didn't discover that his glasses were missing until we had driven about 45 minutes into Yellowstone Park. I offered to buy another pair of sunglasses for him, but, of course, there was not another pair like them in the civilized world, in Steve's way of thinking. Therefore, we had to drive all the way back to the spot where he dropped his sunglasses. They were still there and were intact, but it threw our entire vacation schedule off track."

Like Mark and Deborah Stevens, Steve has scores of friends in Macon. However, he had especially close friends on his faculty and staff at Central High. Perhaps none had greater admiration and respect for Steve Smith than Erin Weaver. She began, "One of the first times I ever met Steve Smith was one hour before a statistics exam that we took to complete our specialist degrees. I knew that he was Linda's husband, and I'd heard he was quite a personable guy. Steve came into my office, introduced himself, and said, 'Teach me all you know about statistics. We've only got an hour!' I remember thinking that he must be kidding, so we studied for an hour, and he proceeded to get a better grade than me. That is where our friendship began.

"Steve was the one who talked me into leaving a faculty position in college and come to Central High to be a secondary high school assistant principal," Weaver said. "He just told me to think about it. I asked him if he was crazy. He told me that no educator could really understand a school system until they had worked in a high school."

Weaver continued, "Right, I thought. I'd been in the business of educating kids for 25 years at that point, but he was like water dripping on a rock – 'Come work at Central. You'll love it.' He had been my daughter, Molly's, principal, and she said he was so much fun. He saw the potential in everyone. Within a week, I'd had an interview with the faculty, been officially offered the position, and had given my notice to the college. It was indeed a leap of faith, but it was one that I have never regretted.

"Steve treats everyone with respect. It doesn't matter who he's talking to - the President of the United States or parents. He is the same guy. He's tickled to see a former custodian; he corresponds with his lunchroom managers, and he knows his students - their parents, grandparents, and their ministers," Weaver recalled. "Someone said that the kids at Central never had to wear ID badges when Steve Smith was there, because he knew everyone's name."

Weaver said, "Steve worked not only to teach the brains of the Central students and faculty, but he encouraged their hearts as well. He got together with Rev. Ronald Terry to hold a memorial service for the students killed in Columbine. He honored former Central teachers and administrators with a reunion at Christmas so that they would know they were still remembered for what they gave to Central. He even crowned the homecoming queen and king and attended almost every activity that was held at his high school.

"The morning our son, Mike, was killed, Steve and Linda Smith left Valdosta and were at our house in less than two hours. He was not only my former boss (you didn't work for Steve; you worked with him), but he gave the main eulogy at Mike's funeral, because he had also been Mike's principal, too."

Erin Weaver was named principal of Central High School for the 2004-2005 school year. She concluded, "I always think of Proverbs 17:17 when I think of Steve Smith. It says, 'A friend loves at all times.'"

* * * * * * * * * *

People in Hawkinsville and Valdosta know what an excellent 'school man' Steve Smith is. Bill Slade, an employee for 30 years and now the operations director for Pulaski County Schools in Hawkinsville, answered directly to Smith. "He is the nicest guy you'll ever meet. There aren't enough people in this world like Steve Smith. He just did a great job as our superintendent, and it's amazing what he accomplished in only two short years."

Slade continued, "Steve encourages you, and he backs you up. He really brought this community together in every way - educationally, in business, and he involved the entire community. Steve's a team player and is a great coach to those who answer to him. When he tells you something, you can take it to the bank. Steve lets you do your job and then compliments you when you do it well. If you don't do it well, then he helps you get it right."

Slade remembered taking Steve fishing with two school board members in the Gulf of Mexico several years ago. "It was windy and rough, so I asked him if he still wanted to go out and fish.' Naturally, Steve said, 'Yes,' so we went out about 20 miles into the Gulf. Man, it was blowing and rough, and when we got to our destination, Steve had turned green.

"He said, 'Bill, I hate to tell you this, but I need to go back in.' We turned right around and went back 20 miles to land."

Slade recalled, "Steve enjoyed fishing down here in Hawkinsville, but one day, he and his dad were fishing out at Sam Way's place. Somehow, they turned the boat over, and his dad was shouting, 'I'm drowning! I'm not gonna make it!' Steve shouted back to his dad, 'You aren't drowning, and we're gonna to be fine!'

The superintendent speaks
Dr. Steve Smith.

"They lost their big tackle box that day, and though Steve thought he could see it submerged in 15-feet of water, he tried to recover it, but failed. When he and Linda left Hawkinsville for Valdosta, we took up money and bought him a new tackle box and also gave him some money. We really miss him in Hawkinsville. Lowndes County got a prize when they got Steve Smith."

Hap and Grace Jones, two life-long fans of Hawkinsville High School and its athletic program, agreed with Bill Slade. "We didn't know Steve Smith before he came to Hawkinsville," Hap said. "The only thing we knew was that he was going to be the new superintendent of our school system, and the folks in Macon didn't seem too happy about him leaving. The comments we read in *The Macon Telegraph* made it sound like Hawkinsville was on the receiving end of something good. The folks in Macon had nothing but good things to say about Steve's character, his work ethic, and what he'd done for their school. So, we waited and hoped."

Jones continued, "After we met Steve and got to know him personally, we understood why Bibb County hated to see him go. He was fired up and ready to go as he jumped into his new position here. Steve immediately made himself available to the community and didn't meet a stranger. It was as if he and Linda had always lived in Hawkinsville. Steve was committed to making our school system top notch. He had the children's best interests at heart, as well as the entire school staff and community. He was unashamed to be a Christian, and that meant a lot to so many people here. It was refreshing to have an honest, hard-working person with such fine standards in a leadership role in our community."

The Joneses and other Hawkinsville residents began to hear reports that the Smiths might be leaving Hawkinsville. "Everyone hoped it was just a rumor," Hap Jones recalled, "but unfortunately for us, the news was true. Steve and Linda had become good friends of ours, and we hated to see them go. It was hard not to be selfish and ask him to stay, but this was a great opportunity for them, and we all knew it. Our hearts were heavy in Hawkinsville. Our loss was Valdosta's gain."

Jones concluded, "To show what kind of people Steve and Linda Smith are, they joined us at one of the Hawkinsville Red Devil football games last year when we were on our way to a State Class A championship. It was great to sit and visit with them again. There were plenty of hugs and handshakes to go around. It was obvious in the short time they were in Hawkinsville that they made quite an impression on the people in our town. They also made some life-long friends, especially in our family."

Steve Smith family.
Micheal, Linda, Steve, and Brian.

Citizens and leaders in Lowndes County/Valdosta know what an outstanding leader they got when Steve was hired to lead their school system in 2003. Bill Fuqua, chairman of the Lowndes County Board of Education for four years and vice president of the Citizens Community Bank in Valdosta, remembered his first meeting with Steve Smith. "Two years ago when the Lowndes County superintendent's position opened up, we received Steve's resume, but due to a death in the Pulaski County school community, Steve withdrew from the interview process. He felt compelled to stay in Hawkinsville to help that community heal. I thought that spoke well of his commitment to the people in Pulaski County. Later, Steve interviewed with us and accepted our offer to become our school superintendent. We have been thrilled to death to have him lead our school system. I have met a lot of leaders in my time, but Steve Smith is one of the greatest leaders in the educational system of Georgia."

Fuqua continued, "One of his great strengths is that he has never put himself on a pedestal. Steve has never lost sight of being one of the common folk. He feels as much at home with those who have sophistication as those who have led deprived lives. Steve reminds me of Andy Griffith because he is such a good, wholesome person, and he has the ability to reason and rationally achieve the correct solution in matters much like Andy Griffith did.

"When Steve came to Lowndes County, I felt like I benefited twice," Fuqua said, 'once, because we have the best superintendent in the state, and twice, because he and I have such a great friendship. Personally, I have been so impressed with Steve because of the way he handled a crisis when his son's close friend from Macon died this past year. Steve spoke at the young man's funeral service. Brian and Michael Smith are really blessed to have great parents like Steve and Linda Smith."

* * * * * * * * * *

Steve Smith is the first to admit that he has been influenced by a lot of people throughout his professional career. "Many coaches have cast a positive influence on my career," Steve said. "From the beginning, my first mentor as a coach was Joe McDaniel, the boys' basketball coach at Mount de Sales. Coach Billy Henderson suggested that I spend time with Joe and get to understand the relationship between coaches and athletes. I was not a student of basketball like Joe, but I learned a lot about how you treat people and motivate athletes. It was the result of this positive experience that I decided to give teaching and coaching a try.

"Certainly, I am forever indebted to Coach Henderson," Smith said. "He believed in me and gave me my first coaching job. He taught me that anything in life was possible if I trusted God and put my mind to it. I learned the words to *The Impossible Dream,* and I actually began to believe it. It may have taken a little longer to sink in, but Coach was right: You must dream it to believe it. He provided me with a wealth of knowledge about motivation and the price of success."

Smith said, "My uncle, Dan Pitts, retired head football coach at Mary Persons High School in Forsyth, and one of the all-time, great coaches in Georgia football history, gave me sound advice and helped to guide me through my coaching career. Tom Simonton, retired head football coach at Central, not only taught me about football, but also about teaching. We spent 16 great years together and became an outstanding team."

Steve concluded, "I have always been a student; therefore, I have tried to observe and model the behavior of the people I admire most. They are the ones who have shaped my life."

Steve Smith is a man who went from being a college student with no idea about what he wanted to do in life to Dr. Steve Smith, superintendent of Lowndes County Schools. He has become a respected leader who not only knows where he is going, but how to take others with him. Steve Smith - a great example of a life-long learner.

Willingham 'Gaines' 7-6 Win, City Title!

Dr. Turner Pearman (Pete) Gaines , Jr.
Class of 1963

*"Thou will keep him in perfect peace, whose mind
is stayed on thee, because he trusteth in thee."*
–Isaiah 26:3

Coach Billy Henderson can still describe in sequence the entire 82-yard, 24-play drive on a frigid Friday night in November, 1962. His account of perhaps the greatest win in Willingham's 12-year football history culminated with Pete Gaines' quarterback sneak from the six-inch line on fourth down. After Carlie McNeil tacked on the extra point with only 53 seconds remaining, the size 72-font headlines in *The Macon Telegraph's Sports Section* screamed, 'Willingham 'Gaines' 7-6 Win, City Title.'

Life was still sweet in South Macon as the Willingham Rams edged the Lanier Poets, their bitter, cross-town rivals, for the third consecutive year. And in South Macon, 'The Drive,' as it became known to blue-and-white Ram diehards, became something of a Willingham football staple. Staying true to hard-nosed, grind-it-out football, Willingham completed two of five passes on the night for 17 yards.

"Eighty-two yards in 24 plays, all on the ground, no fumbles, no penalties, and we ran almost twelve minutes off the clock in the fourth quarter!" Billy Henderson exulted with obvious joy and even a measure of disbelief though 42 years have passed. "It was the greatest drive I've ever seen or been part of. I remember in Saturday morning's *Macon Telegraph* that I singled out ends Jimmy Clay and Mark Bowen, tackles Emmett Jordan and Wayne Johnson, guards Raymond Bateman and Carlie McNeil, and center Buck Carroll for their blocking on the drive. We thought we had scored on third down when Floyd Evans ran it up the middle, but a 'Lanier referee' said, 'No,' and placed the ball on the six-inch line. Pete scored on the next play."

"That year, I began to see some of the inequities in sports," Gaines said, "because a lot of the people who did the real work were the ones who didn't get the proper recognition and press."

About 'The Drive,' Gaines recalled, "Lanier had quick-kicked the ball down inside our 20-yard line. During that drive, I remember that we didn't throw the ball a single time. We were running Floyd Evans up the middle and off tackle, and I was running the option until we finally got the ball down to the one. After Floyd Evans got it close, I got to sneak it over on the next play, Carlie kicked the PAT, and we beat them 7-6."

Pete Gaines was a high-quality athlete from the beginning, and he apparently had some way-above-average athletic genes in his family as well. Pete's first-cousin, Tommy Reid, was one of the best athletes to ever come out of South Macon. Pete said, "My mom was the oldest of the Reid children, while my uncle Richard was the youngest. Richard Reid was an all-time great athlete at Lanier High prior to his outstanding baseball and basketball careers at Mercer University. He was later inducted into Mercer's Sports Hall of Fame as an athlete and into the Macon Sports Hall of Fame for his years of success as a high school coach."

Despite Pete's outstanding achievements in sports, other members of his family had their doubts about his chances for success in athletics. Richard Reid said, "We always called him 'Little Pete,' not because his daddy was 'Big Pete,' but because he was so frail and weak when he was young. I remember watching him play Little League baseball and hoping the opposing pitcher wouldn't hit and break him in half. It was hard to believe that the sport Pete would excel in would be football. The entire Reid family was so proud of him when he went to the University of Georgia on a football scholarship. Pete was probably the smartest and most dedicated one in our family. I know it took a lot of hard work and studying for him to become a dentist."

Gaines said, "Tommy Reid and I grew up on Grenada Terrace in the heart of South Macon. Charles H. Bruce School was less than a quarter of a mile from my house, but being Catholic, Tommy and I attended St. Joseph's Catholic School in downtown Macon. However, we played a lot of ball on Bruce School's fields and courts."

As a 12-year old pitcher for Coach Neil Bowen of the Fincher's Barbeque Rebels in the South Macon Little League, Pete Gaines could 'bring it.' He was arguably the best pitcher in Macon's Little League history. Pete and Jim Pritchett both pitched South Macon's Little League All-Star team to the finals of the state tournament in Cordele. Gaines had pitched South Macon to a hard-fought 2-1 win over Ocmulgee Little League the previous week to win the district tournament. Woodrow Fincher homered against big Robert Richardson with Gaines on base. As a seventh-grader, Pete quarterbacked his St. Joseph's football team to a win in the Pony Bowl, the elementary school championship. Big, fast, smart, and competitive, Pete was unlike many young athletic prodigies who tended to peak physically at an early age. He only got bigger and better.

* * * * * * * * * *

As in most families in Macon in the 1950's and 60's, Gaines and his older sister, Cathy, grew up in a stable, hard-working, God-fearing household. "My dad grew up in Elbert County, GA, and worked on a farm. Due to his father's death, Dad had to drop out of school in the third grade to go to work. He later found a job with Happ Brothers in Macon as an elevator operator when he was only 14. My dad was not an educated man, but he was a very smart man. When Oxford Industries bought out Happ Brothers and moved the company to Atlanta, my dad became a vice president with them," Gaines recalled.

"My mom was from Macon and was raised Catholic. My dad, a Methodist who later became a Catholic, died on February 11, 1994. My mom had a stroke the day my dad died, and she passed away exactly one month later. They were married over 60 years," Pete said. "I was part of a very loving family, but my parents demanded a lot out of Cathy and me. They insisted that we work hard and respect authority.

"I remember how my mother always insisted on me dressing correctly and acting like a gentleman," Pete recalled. "At St. Joseph's School, we had won our small-school enrollment league championship and qualified to play against Alexander III in the Pony Bowl which was played on Thanksgiving Day. Bruce School and Alexander IV were the large school enrollment league champions and would face off in the other Pony Bowl game. I got ready to leave on my bicycle to go to over to Bruce School for pictures of the Pony Bowl team captains. That picture would appear in *The Macon Telegraph,* and, as I was about to leave the house, my mother asked, 'Pete, what are you doing?' I told her, 'I am going to Bruce to get my picture made for the paper,' and she said, 'Not until you put your shirt-tail in.'

"I complained and told her that I bet the other captains would have their shirt-tails out, but she insisted. If you look at the picture that was in the Macon paper, all of the other teams' captains - Bobby Bryant of Bruce, Tee Carstarphen of Alexander III, and Grover Bradley of Alexander IV - had their shirt-tails out, but not me. My mother had made me tuck my shirt in." (See that picture in the middle of this book)

"I used to give my mother a hard time because all of the guys in our neighborhood were playing ball barefooted, and I had to wear tennis shoes. I looked like a little preppy kid with my shirt tail in and my shoes on," Gaines laughed. "Five years later, when Bobby Bryant and I were seniors at Willingham, and Tee and Grover were seniors at Lanier, the *Telegraph* brought the four of us together and had us arranged in the same, identical pose that our 1957 Pony Bowl captains' picture was taken. This time, I had on my varsity letter jacket, so the shirt tail was not a factor.

"When I finished St. Joseph's Elementary School, Willingham had just been built, so I had to choose between Willingham and Mount de Sales High School," Pete said. "Mount de Sales had previously been an all-girls' school, but they admitted boys around 1957-58. They were just starting a sports program, and our seventh grade class would have been the first class with boys to go there. The nuns at St. Joseph's heard that I was thinking about going to Willingham and told me I should go to de Sales, which is where my mom wanted me to go. My dad wanted me to go to Willingham. I ultimately chose Willingham because of the sports program. I was considered to be a bit of a traitor when I chose Willingham, but, when my friend, Don Biggs from St. Joseph's, decided to go to Lanier, that took a little heat off me. We had some great teams at St. Joseph's and some very good athletes. We won the Pony Bowl in football and the championship in basketball, but we lost the city championship in baseball to Ft. Hawkins.

"I had played ball and made friends with a lot of the boys from Willingham, and I was also in the first class to go all the way through from the eighth grade through the twelfth. My years at Willingham were very good ones. I have some great memories from high school like playing football, basketball, and especially baseball. I truly enjoyed playing baseball more than football," Pete said.

"One sports memory in particular was when we played Valdosta High my senior year and lost 12-0, our only loss of the season. I recall that Bobby Bryant ran a slant-route across the middle. They grabbed Bobby by his jersey and slung him to the ground before the ball even got to him, but the officials never threw a flag. Coach Henderson was furious and started throwing things and 'raising cane' in the locker room at halftime. When the half ended and we were returning to the field, I was the first player in line. Valdosta always dressed out over 100 players, and they were filing out onto the field. Coach Henderson asked me 'What are you doing?' and I said 'I'm waiting for Valdosta to get out onto the field.' He screamed, 'You don't wait on them!' and he pushed me right in the middle of the Valdosta players. I thought we going to have a fight right there on the spot. We should have beaten them that night, but we didn't."

Pete Gaines has always had a great sense of humor, and though he was an honor student, quarterback, and the team captain, he was always 'one of the guys,' which meant he was a kidder who also got kidded. "Every year in August, Coach Henderson would take the football team to Jekyll Island for a week of football camp," Pete recalled. "Camp amounted to three-a-day practices in the intense heat and humidity. We were normally up at 6 a.m. to practice while the grass was still wet and before we were really awake. I remember that one morning at camp, which happened to be a Holy Day on the Catholic calendar, Coach Henderson announced, 'Tomorrow morning you'll get to sleep a little later, because Pearman and Coach Garvin have to go to mass since it's a Holy Day.' One of the players asked Pete, 'What did he call you?' I said, 'Pearman.' He asked me, 'Why?' and I said, 'Pearman is my middle name.' He said, 'Oh, I thought maybe Coach Henderson had caught you fishing off the pier when you were supposed to be in your room.'"

Johnny Stallings, a defensive backfield coach at Willingham, was the coach who was responsible for room checks at football camp on Jekyll Island. Stallings recalled, "One night, Pete and his roommate slipped out when they were supposed to be asleep. When I checked their room, of course, it was empty, so I just lay down in Pete's bed and went to sleep. He was pretty surprised when he sneaked back into his room with the lights out and found me sleeping in his bed!"

Stallings said, "Later that week, Pete had to be taken to the hospital in Brunswick because he forgot to take his contact lenses out when he went to sleep, and they stuck to his eyeballs. It was an ordeal getting those lenses out."

* * * * * * * * * *

Gaines' life as a youngster growing up in South Macon mirrored most of his friends' and teammates' lives. Gaines said, "Attending high school at Willingham and growing up in South Macon were very good experiences for me. I always thought my life was pretty normal. Not having a lot of money was no big deal. We really had everything we needed when I was young, and, to this day, I wouldn't take anything for growing up out there. There was a good work ethic among the families in South Macon. It was full of good, hardworking, God-fearing Christian people, and you felt safe out there. It was our own little world, and we didn't know anything different. Who I am today goes back to my family, to where I was raised, and to the people I grew up with."

As a high school leader, Pete's credibility and leadership in Macon went beyond the Willingham community when he was elected President of the Inter-City Student Council. It was an organization made up of all of the public schools in Bibb County and was designed to encourage friendship and sportsmanship. Pete and his friend, Mark Bowen, were both members of Phi Omega Beta fraternity which primarily consisted of Lanier and Stratford boys. Pete remembered, "About two Willingham guys per year were offered membership in POB. We were 'token' South Macon boys, but when Mark, Jimmy Hallman, and I were rushed by POB, the Lanier and Stratford guys began to realize there wasn't a whole lot of difference in us and them.

"I had some outstanding teachers, coaches, and positive influences while growing up in South Macon. Coach Billy Henderson was a great coach and motivator. Neil Bowen, Mark's dad, was my first coach in organized sports, and I played for him in Little League baseball in South Macon. Brother Jimmy Waters, the pastor at Mabel White Baptist Church, was a big influence on me and the other renegades that I hung around with. Diane Waters, Brother Jimmy's daughter, and my sister, Cathy, were good friends, so we all ran in some of the same circles. The nuns at St. Joseph's School had a strong influence on me growing up, too. In those days, I was the kind of guy who pretty much went to school, practiced sports, came home, played out in the yard, and did my homework.

"In school, I had very few problems because the teachers and coaches really took an interest in us," Pete said. "At Willingham, the coaching staff that Coach Henderson put together was tremendous, especially for a young school like ours. In fact, they were so good that we beat Lanier, which had a great sports history and tradition, all three times that we played them during my career. Johnny Stallings, Billy Beale, Dave Hill, Bobby Brown, Henry Middlebrooks, and Mike Garvin were not only great coaches, but were good people who made Willingham successful."

He continued, "In addition to some great coaches, Willingham was blessed with some of the finest teachers anywhere. Mrs. Mary P. Smith was a great teacher because she cared so much about her students. She was just a super person who demanded that we work hard and insisted that we do our best in the classroom. Mr. Leonard Pridgeon taught chemistry and physics. He was a no-nonsense guy who had a great grasp of the subject matter, and when you completed his course, you were ready for college. No one ever cut up in his class. Mary Lamback and our principal, Fred Johnson, expected us to 'toe the line' and do what was expected of us. Willingham had a great faculty and staff.

"I had such good friends during my high school years and have maintained many of those friendships through the years," Pete recalled. "For example, Buck Carroll, who was my center on the football team in 1962 when we had 'The Drive' to beat Lanier, is now a patient of mine. Mark Bowen and I were best friends since Little League days, and we remain close friends today. In fact, when Mark joined the Catholic Church, I became his godfather. He and I were battery mates since Little League days – Mark catching and me pitching, and then in high school - me passing and Mark receiving. Mark had great hands and made some spectacular catches. He made me look like a decent quarterback."

Pete's classmate, Tommy Shaw, was a great friend, and he was the godfather of Erin Gaines, Pete's third daughter. Pete stated, "Tommy died several years ago on the night of our 35th high school reunion. He was the most unselfish fellow that I've ever been around."

Tommy's wife, Belinda Shaw, said about Pete Gaines, their long-time friend, "When Tommy and I began dating, he told me of his friendship with Pete Gaines and how much he admired Pete. In fact, Tommy had already decided, at 19 years of age, that if he ever had a son, he would be named for Pete. Our oldest son is named Turner Jackson (Jack) Shaw, and Pete is his godfather."

Belinda continued, "Growing up, Pete probably took a lot of kidding about being Catholic, but Tommy greatly respected Pete for his strong religious convictions. As teenagers, the guys always ended up at the Gaines' house on Friday for lunch where tuna fish was always served. My daughter has now become Catholic, and I can see even more clearly that theirs is a powerful faith, and why it was so important to Pete for his three girls to be part of that faith.

"Tommy also loved to tease Pete about the evening when some friends were invited to spend the night at the Gaines' house when Pete's parents were out of town. To protect his sister's good name, Pete made the boys spend the night in a hot car outside rather than letting them stay inside the house. Somehow, it never dawned on the boys to just go home."

Belinda recalled, "I have always known Pete to be compassionate and caring. I suppose that's why, in the late 1980's, when my husband had a skin cancer removed, I found myself sitting in Pete's office in tears and looking for some consolation and assurance that this would not be life-threatening for Tommy. Pete's kindness and gentleness have always been his most obvious strengths. I believe he got those traits from his parents. I am so thankful for the loyal and supportive friend that he was to Tommy, and he remains a friend for me today."

* * * * * * * * *

Pete Gaines' high school football career was spectacular. In his first varsity game as a sophomore against Warner Robins, Pete completed all three passes that he attempted, and two went for touchdowns. *The Atlanta Journal's* prep sports reporter, Paul Atkinson, included the following snippet in his column: Quotable Quote: Willingham's football coach, Billy Henderson, on his 15-year-old quarterback, Pete Gaines:

'He's as good a passer at this stage as Francis Tarkenton (Georgia quarterback) was at Athens High.'

Henderson should know – he coached 'em both.'

Pete's senior class (1963) had the best record at that point in Willingham's brief history, going 6-1-3, and he was the team's captain. Pete broke seven school records in the 1962 football season. Those records were:

- 664 yards passing
- most yards total offense – 960
- most passes completed and attempted – 41 of 96
- most passes in a single game – 24 vs. Valdosta
- the longest kickoff return – 93 yards vs. LaGrange
- interceptions in a season with three

Pete was courted by several schools including the University of Georgia and the South Carolina Gamecocks. Gaines recalled, "South Carolina was recruiting me, and when I took my official visit there, Dan Reeves from Americus, GA, who was the quarterback at South Carolina in those days, gave me a tour of the campus and the facilities. Reeves told me, 'Pete, you gotta come play at South Carolina.'

"Mark Bowen, who played end at Willingham, and I had decided that we wanted to go to the same college together, and, since Georgia offered both of us scholarships, we chose UGA. Johnny Griffith was the head coach when we signed with Georgia, but he was fired after my freshman season. Coach Griffith had assured Mark and me that we could play baseball in the spring if we came to Georgia," Pete recalled.

Georgia brought in a young, aggressive, head football coach from Auburn named Vince Dooley who came to Athens at the end of Gaines' freshman year. Pete and Mark went to Coach Dooley shortly after he arrived on campus and told him about the arrangement they had made with Coach Griffith about being able to play baseball in the spring. Coach Dooley quickly informed the two former Rams that if they intended to play football at Georgia, there would be no baseball for them since spring football practice would determine who would be playing in the fall. Case closed.

"When I went to Georgia in 1963," Pete said, "the NCAA had a rule that freshmen weren't allowed to play varsity football. Georgia already had a good number of quarterbacks, so I got to play some defensive back and a little quarterback on the freshman team, but I separated my shoulder during spring practice of Coach Dooley's first year. I missed my entire sophomore year when I fell off an ice truck in the summer and hurt my shoulder again. I wondered if

I would ever be able to play again, but I came back the next year, and all they had me doing was climbing the big hill on campus on all fours. They had me hanging from the goal posts and doing pushups to try to strengthen my shoulder. Pat Hodgson played end for us and was also injured. Pat and I would go to Atlanta for therapy together. I came back my junior year and quarterbacked the scout team. We ran the upcoming opponent's offense in practice each week, and I took a huge beating from our first-team defense. I dressed out for varsity games and relayed the offensive plays from the coaches in the press box to Coach Dooley. My senior year, I was the holder for extra points and field goals.

"When my fourth year in school was completed, I still had one year of athletic eligibility left, but there was no need for me to come back and expect to play," Pete said. "They really weren't going to miss me, and I had already been accepted into dental school at Emory. All in all, I had a very non-descript football career in college, but the friends I made and the camaraderie that I had with those guys at Georgia were some real highlights of my life."

One of the closest friends that Gaines had at the University of Georgia was Tommy Lawhorne who was one year younger than Pete. Lawhorne was from Sylvester, a small, South Georgia town in Worth County. Pete said about his friend, "Tommy played on an awful football team in high school, and he went to Georgia as a kicker, but he ended up playing linebacker, alongside Happy Dicks, who is now a neurosurgeon. Tommy is a vascular surgeon in Columbus, GA. Lawhorne was just ridiculously smart, and we had some really bright guys on that team. In fact, Tommy only one made one 'A' in his entire academic career. The rest of his grades were all 'A-pluses.'"

Gaines recalled about Lawhorne, "In Atlanta, Tommy interviewed for a Rhodes Scholarship which, in those days, only went to people from the Ivy League schools. However, Tommy went to medical school at Johns Hopkins, lived in Baltimore for 10 years, and then went to Oxford, England, to study anyway."

Lawhorne recalled, "I first met Pete when I went to Athens as a freshman in the fall of 1964. We both were on football scholarship at the University of Georgia and consequently lived in the same dorm, Lipscomb Hall. Yet, it was during my sophomore year when our friendship blossomed. Pete was, and is, a very good athlete. He had been a star in several sports at Willingham High in Macon. Indeed, he was quite versatile in his skills and could play any position or any sport, yet he didn't have the size and speed to play quarterback at the college level at that time. During the fall of 1965, Pete was relegated to being the 'scout team' quarterback and was burdened with running the opposing team's plays each week against the No. 1 varsity defense. Of course, Pete was 'protected' by a 'B-team' line. To say the least, that was not a glamorous position. Pete would take a beating regularly, but he never complained, and he performed his duty with dignity and grace. It was then that I began to develop an abiding respect for Pete Gaines.

"Pete roomed next door to me for two years and probably maintained the filthiest dorm room that any human being has ever occupied," Lawhorne said as he began to warm up with memories of his long-time friend. "Let me hasten to add that Pete would faithfully change the sheets on his bed every quarter, whether they needed changing or not. Pete Gaines is not a morning person and he seldom, if ever, attended class before 10 a.m. Nevertheless, Pete was so bright that he graduated from Georgia with honors and went on to become a first-class dentist following graduation from Emory Dental School."

Dr. Tommy Lawhorne has a deep respect for Pete Gaines as a husband, father, athlete, and particularly as a friend. However, their friendship has never prevented Lawhorne from needling his friend at every possible juncture. Lawhorne laughed, "Pete just stood around in practice all day. No sweat. No dirt. It was like, 'Hey, Pete, come hold for the kicking game at the end of practice.'"

"I was a good student in college, but Tommy was incredible," Pete said. "He and I were in a physical chemistry class together, and after class, we had to sprint to get taped and get on the field in time for practice. This class was by far the hardest course that I had ever taken. The test the professor gave was unbelievable, but Lawhorne and I both made 100 on the test. Tommy made 87, and I made 13. With the curve, he made an A+ and I made a C+. People were making 2's and 3's on that exam. I was proud of my 13, but Tommy went back to the teacher to try to get extra credit to get an A without the curve."

Pete said, "We are still very good friends today, and I'm his daughter's godfather. His son and daughter are very bright students, and, after high school, they both went to Princeton. I remember telling Lawhorne, 'Don't let your daughter, Vaise, go up there to Princeton in New Jersey. She's going to meet some Yankee, they'll get married, and you won't ever see her again. Sure enough, Vaise met a guy at Princeton, got engaged, and was about to be married down at Sea Island. Kathi and I had offered to host an engagement party for Vaise, prior to the wedding. One evening, while watching television, I saw Maria Bartiroma of CNBC interviewing Lou Gershner, the CEO of IBM. The name, Gershner, sounded familiar, so I looked at the wedding invitation and discovered that Vaise Lawhorne was marrying Lou Gershner's son. Obviously, the sting of marrying a Yankee was somewhat softened for Tommy by having his daughter marrying into one of the wealthiest families in America."

Lawhorne continued, "Pete is the quintessential person of great faith, and over the years, the most important, under-girding feature of Pete Gaines' life has been his vibrant Catholic faith. He has gone from altar boy to lay reader to faithful worshipper over his lifetime. Pete's faith is strong, and he's loyal and committed to God and the Church. He goes by what the Good Book says and always attends Mass. Pete also goes to Mass every year on the anniversary of his mother's death. Though he is Catholic, and I'm not, I still admire his commitment and his dedication."

Dr. Tommy Lawhorne said, "The years have passed, and though we only see each other about twice a year, Pete and I have talked on the phone about

Pete Gaines, UGA Bulldogs 1967.

five times a week for the past 10 years. We were football teammates in SAE fraternity together—though jocks really weren't 'frat boys' in those days—and Pete was in my wedding. Pete was a solid athlete and student in college, and now he's a great father and husband. He is far from perfect, but he is a wonderful human being. He knows that God loves him, and God knows I love him, but don't tell him."

Georgia's legendary coach, Vince Dooley, remembered Pete Gaines as a steadying influence on his first Georgia team. "Pete was already here when we arrived at Georgia as a new coaching staff, and while he was not as physically gifted as some of the other athletes at the time, we recognized some marvelous, intangible qualities in him. Consequently, we knew that whatever Pete pursued, he would do it well."

Dooley continued, "Pete was the kind of person that everybody liked and respected. He was very mature so he didn't have to learn 'the hard way' as so many young people do at that time in their lives. Pete was the steady member of our team, and he was helpful in preventing some of our more 'spirited players' from straying too far.

"I am very proud of Dr. Pete Gaines," Dooley concluded, "and I can easily see why he would be successful in the medical profession. He was always dependable and was someone that you could trust. Being a quarterback, Pete had excellent hands, and he ended up performing a valuable service for our team by being the holder for extra points and field goals. I know the importance of that because I was a holder myself."

Though Pete Gaines' football career as a Bulldog ended up less-than-stellar, his four years at Georgia were worthwhile, fun, and memorable. During his senior year, he served as president of the G Club (Letterman's Club). "My claim to fame at Georgia happened in 1967," Pete recalled. "We were playing Miami in the Orange Bowl on a Friday night. It was the fourth game of the year, and we were up 6-0. Our kicker, Bob Etter had been perfect on his only two field goal attempts that night, and I was his holder. . We were lining up for a 'chip-shot' field goal to hopefully go up 9-0. The snap went behind me (Tommy Lawhorne interjected, 'The snap hit Pete in a bad spot - right in his hands.'), and Etter began chasing it down. I was left uncovered by their defense because they were homing in on Etter, our kicker-turned-ball carrier. I was over there just begging for the ball because I was wide open. I tried to block Ted Hendricks, who went on to become an All-Pro defensive end with the Oakland Raiders, but he just stepped over me like a piece of firewood. Hendricks threw Etter for about a 20-yard loss. If we'd made that field goal, we would have been up 9-0 at the half. Instead, Miami came back in the second half and scored, kicked the extra point, and beat us, 7-6.

"I was taking a shower after the game," Gaines said, "and this guy with the *Miami Herald* walked through our dressing room. I heard him ask, 'Where's James? Where's Pete James?' Here it was, my only chance for a post-game college football interview, and the reporter was calling me the wrong name and wanted to ask me about the bad snap on the extra point. We went on to beat SMU in the Cotton Bowl that year and ended up the season just one point away from being undefeated my senior year."

Gaines' list of former Bulldog teammates reads like a virtual *Who's Who* of college and professional athletes. "I made some great friendships with the guys that I played ball with, and I'm still close to many of my teammates. Kirby Moore of Dothan, AL, was the first quarterback to play for Coach Dooley. He and I signed football scholarships the same year. Kirby became famous for the 'flea-flicker' pass play to end, Pat Hodgson, who lateraled to halfback, Bob Taylor, who took it the distance. We went for two and made it to beat Alabama and Coach Paul 'Bear' Bryant, 18-17. I still see a lot of my former teammates and stay in touch with guys like Mark Bowen and Tommy Lawhorne, as well as my roommate Stan Crawford, a running back from LaGrange, who now lives in Dalton, GA.

"On that Cotton Bowl team, we had Jake Scott, who left school prior to his senior year to play in the Canadian Football League. He later had a great pro career with the undefeated Miami Dolphins of 1972 (Jake was MVP of Super Bowl VII) and the Washington Redskins. Jake Scott was just different. 'Carefree' would be an understatement. He drove a Corvette back in those days. Coach Dooley told us one day at practice, 'Jake has had a family emergency regarding his mom, and he won't be at practice today.' We all wondered where Jake Scott really was. He was the best athlete I have ever seen and was unlike anybody I had ever been around. Jake could have been All-America as a wide receiver, running back, or defensive back. I recently read in *Sports Illustrated* that he was the only player that didn't return for any of the team reunions of that undefeated 1972 Miami Dolphins championship team. But that's just Jake."

Pete continued about that Cotton Bowl squad, "Billy Payne came to Georgia as a quarterback but ended up playing defensive end. Billy was the Chief Executive Officer for the 1996 Summer Olympic Games in Atlanta. Bill Stanfield from Cairo, GA, played defensive end, made All-America, and also played on the undefeated, Super Bowl champion Miami Dolphins [team]. Ronnie Jenkins was our fullback from Glenville, GA, and he was a 'horse.'"

* * * * * * * * * *

Upon Pete's completion of his undergraduate degree at Georgia in 1967, he entered Emory University's Dental School and graduated in 1971. He then joined the United States Army and went to Fort Bragg, where he became a captain and spent two years serving his country.

Pete returned to Macon to practice dentistry with an Emory classmate, Dr. Robbie Edenfield, also a Macon native, who played quarterback at Lanier High under the legendary coach Selby Buck. Kathi Nicholson was a dental assistant in those days for Dr. Edenfield. Pete had 'set her up' with an old teammate from Georgia, and they had one date. Pete's teammate was coming back to Macon to see Kathi again but called from Jacksonville to tell her that he wasn't going to be able to make it for their date. Always the gentleman, Pete told Kathi, "Then I'll just take you out."

They started dating shortly after that, and Pete soon told her, "We either need to get married, or I'm going to have to fire you, because we can't work together and just date." They were married on December 15, 1973, and Kathi still works with her husband one day a week.

Pete and Kathi Gaines have three daughters who all graduated from Macon's First Presbyterian Day School. Amy (28) lives in Atlanta; Jennifer (26) is married to Patrick Deal of Albany, GA, and Erin (24) is married to Henley Hayes of Dalton, GA. Henley went to Georgia Tech on a scholarship to play basketball for Coach Bobby Cremins. Pete recalled, "In Henley's first semester at Tech, their starting point guard was hurt during the preseason workouts and Henley got to play a lot. Then the starting guard returned, and Henley was relegated to the bench. Coach Cremins only played about five or six guys in those days, so Henley left after one season and went to a junior college to play baseball. He later went to Georgia to play college baseball, and now he's the biggest Bulldog fan I know."

Pete Gaines is a man with many friends who esteem him highly from both a personal and professional perspective. Dr. William (Bill) Argo, Jr., DMD, first met Pete in 1984 as a dental colleague. "I am a periodontist, so we treated patients together," Argo said. "We became social friends over the next few years, and now we feel like we are a part of each other's family. We also play golf together about once a week. Pete is, first and foremost, a man of integrity. He is also very devoted to his savior, Jesus Christ, and has instilled that faith in his daughters. Pete treats everyone as if they were his own family. I know Pete to be honest, caring, family-oriented, positive about life, and his word is as 'good as gold.' I have never heard anyone say a bad word about Pete Gaines."

Never one to be confused with Bob Villa of *Sears Home Care* commercials, Dr. Pete Gaines more closely resembles Tim Allen's character on the *Home Improvement* sitcom. "Around Pete's house," Argo laughed, "it is well-known that if he is doing yard work or is repairing something, you had better be prepared for trouble. For example, Pete wired a light at the end of his driveway, and it worked fine as long as you didn't need the lights in your house to work. And never a threat to Paul Bunyan as a forester, Pete once cut down a pine tree, only to have it fall on his house. He once cut down a cedar tree, and a branch literally stuck in his head and had to be removed at the emergency room. Pete once fell off the roof and had an azalea branch stuck in his back side. What a sight that was!"

Argo continued, "Pete is known for telling and retelling the worst corny jokes you've ever heard. He also has a reputation among his friends and family for being a bottomless pit at mealtime. It is not uncommon for Pete to clean his own plate and then clean up the leftovers from his wife's plate, or from anyone else who may be at the table. This habit occurs as regularly at a very nice restaurant as it does at home. As a matter of fact, Pete actually did this more than once (like at every meal!) on our recent stay in California. It's funny, too, because when Pete's friends' children are at dinner with him, they will make him stick his arms out before they eat their meal to make sure he can't reach their plates and get their food.

"But with all kidding aside," Argo said, "Pete Gaines is married to a wonderful wife, and they have raised three exemplary daughters. He is an excellent dentist who treats his patients with exceptional care. In my opinion, Pete Gaines is successful in life because he is so honest, hard-working, caring, and true to his ideals."

Probably no one outside Pete Gaines' family knows him as well or respects him as much Mark Bowen, owner of The Bowen Insurance Agency in Atlanta. "Pete and I have been best friends since we were six-years old. Pete is my godfather since I joined the Catholic Church as an adult. We played on the same sports teams from Little League through college football at the University of Georgia. Part of our decision about going to Georgia was because we wanted to play college football together, and UGA was one of the schools that offered us both scholarships. After college, we were in each others' weddings and have maintained our friendship throughout the years. Jennifer, Pete's second daughter, had her first job right out of college working for me."

Bowen said, "I can say without reservation that Pete is one of the most honorable people I have ever had the good fortune to encounter. In addition to all of Pete's athletic accomplishments, he was also an honor student as well. He is a dedicated husband, father, loyal friend, and an overall good person. I have always admired Pete's spirituality and his unwavering commitment to Jesus Christ. He is a living example of a Christ-centered person."

Bowen took a good-natured jab at his long-time friend and recalled, "After Pete's senior football season at Willingham, he was named Player of the Year for the city of Macon and was also named to the AAA All-State team. It remains a point of contention with Pete, that although we both made the All-State team, I was the one selected to play in the North-South All Star game.

"At the University of Georgia, Pete had the misfortune of separating his right shoulder during his sophomore year. Since Pete was right-handed and played quarterback, this was a career-threatening injury since he was not able to throw the football with the necessary strength required to play in the Southeastern Conference. Always the team player, Pete became the holder for placements, which required both skill and dexterity, and Pete was Mr.

Dependable at this task."

Bowen continued, "My favorite story about Pete and his college football career happened in the UGA-Kentucky game during his senior year. It was late in the game, and we were driving the ball deep into Kentucky territory. Faced with a fourth down and four yards to go for a first down, Coach Dooley called for the field goal team. He told Pete that we were going to run a fake field goal, and Pete was going to throw a pass. Since he had been injured his entire varsity career and only played during extra points and field goals, Pete was going to have the opportunity to throw his first pass as a major college quarterback. He was pumped, and his dreams were finally going to come true. We lined up for the play, and with visions of glory flashing through Pete's head, Kentucky jumped off sides. The five-yard penalty gave us a first down, and Pete's opportunity to throw a pass went down the tubes."

Bowen again kidded his old friend. "After college, Pete graduated from Emory Dental School and then served in the U.S. Army Medical Corp at Fort Bragg. That was another source of contention, since I served in the Military Police and was sent to Viet Nam. Pete has excelled in all areas of his life as a student, athlete, father, husband, dentist, friend, and person. Do I admire him? You bet!"

Judge J. Taylor Phillips is the retired Senior Judge for the State Court of Georgia and recalled Pete's playing days at Willingham. "I was the president of the school's booster club, and Pete was one of the finest quarterbacks that Willingham ever produced. He was a leader of young men and was accorded great respect from his teammates and the student body, in general."

Every summer, Coach Billy Henderson took his team to Jekyll Island for football camp. Judge Phillips wisecracked, "Some students resented the fact that I helped raise the money so the team could go to the beach and run around in the water. Of course, that's not what they did at all, but whatever they did must have been good training, because it strengthened their legs and made a good football team out of them."

The Judge concluded, "In my mind, no one in life makes friends faster than Pete Gaines, and we have been friends for many years. Pete's approach to life has always been one of great humor, respect, responsibility, and he has done those things well. When life's chapter is written, Pete Gaines will have his rightful place in the annals of sportsmanship, devotion, and duty."

* * * * * * * * * *

In recent years, Pete Gaines' life has revolved around church, professional associations, and being involved in his daughters' sporting lives. He is a past-parish council member, lector, and reader at St. Joseph's Catholic Church. He was elected president of the Central District of the Bibb County Dental Association, is on the executive committee of the Georgia Dental Association, and served as president of the Freedom Park Softball League where his three daughters played.

Recreationally, Pete plays golf at the Idle Hour Club in Macon. He and his cousin, Tommy Reid, learned to play golf left-handed at Bowden Golf Course in Macon when they were teenagers. Now, both men hit it right-handed. Pete also finds time to go fishing.

Gaines concluded, "I would like to be remembered as a good husband and father. Kathi has been the greatest blessing in my life. She is a special lady, is my best friend, and has been the glue that has held our family together. God has blessed us with three daughters who have been a great source of joy and pride for us. As they start their own families, I pray that their spouses and children will be just as loving and supportive as mine have been. And maybe one day, if someone asks, 'Are you Pete Gaines' daughter, grandson, etc.?' they'll say, 'Yes,' with a little tinge of pride."

Left to right: Amy, Jennifer, and Erin Gaines

LBCB
(Lower Bibb County Boy)

Oney Harwick Hudson
Class of 1964

Providing for honest things, not only in the sight of the Lord, but also in the sight of men.
                    –II Corinthians 8:21

For the good that I would, I do not do; but the evil which I would not, that I do.
                    –Romans 7:19

John Ginn, a cousin and life-long friend of Oney Hudson, told the story that thrust Oney into South Macon folklore. "Oney's parents wouldn't allow him to have a car when he turned sixteen, so he saved the money he made working on the family farm. When he was an 18-year-old senior at Willingham, his daddy cashed in a universal life insurance policy that he bought when Oney was very young. With that money, coupled with his savings, Oney bought a maroon, 1964 Pontiac GTO with red interior and a Hurst 4-in-the-floor. He paid about $3,000 for it, and to say it would fly would be absolutely correct. It was common knowledge that Oney's GTO was the first of its kind in Macon, GA.

"One Saturday afternoon back in 1963," Ginn, now a contract agent with the Georgia Power Company in Atlanta, recalled, "Oney and our friend, Carl Puckett, picked me up the day he got the car, and, of course, the first thing we did was take off to Fincher's Barbeque, the drive-in restaurant where people in South Macon 'hung out.' Later, while driving south on Houston Avenue near the old 41 Drive-In, a hot 409 Chevy tried to pass us. And when he did, Oney floored it. I mean, floored it! That was the fastest surge of raw, automotive power that I have ever felt. You truly could not pick a $20 bill off the dashboard under that acceleration. In fact, that's the only car I have ever been in that could 'chirp' the tires in all 4 gears. It was awesome!"

Though Oney Hudson owned the fastest car that most guys in South Macon had ever seen in 1964, he had previously been known for driving a John Deere tractor and farming the rich fields of South Bibb County. Oney was part of a long line of farmers and was named in honor of his great uncle, Oney, who left his 600-acre farm to William Hudson (Oney's dad), Trula Dawn (Oney's sister), and Oney when the old farmer died. As a wealthy farmer and land-owner in those days, the elder Oney Hudson left all of his substantial cash to a variety of his favorite charities and, though the gift of a 600 acre farm was greatly appreciated as a generous gift to William Hudson and his family, it put quite a financial strain on them because of the inheritance taxes they had to pay.

But according to Oney, "God blessed my family and allowed us to make those ends meet at the time. We grew watermelons, sweet potatoes, cantaloupes, and corn, as well as raising cows and hogs, to hold onto our land. Growing up on a farm in South Bibb County, I learned the value of discipline and work, because farming was a tough life. I was taught by my father to work hard and not complain. He farmed the land and made a living while my mother, Gertrude Hudson, kept the books, paid the family's bills, and ran the household."

William Hudson was the primary individual who shaped his son's life at an early age. Oney said, "My dad is the most giving person I have ever seen. He would give anything to anyone, and that influenced me greatly. My parents raised me on a diversified farm, and farming was not an easy way of life. Our family struggled early in my childhood days, but we all had jobs to do, we worked hard, and had enough to get by."

He continued, "My dad taught me to be positive and see the bright side of life. He didn't just talk positively, either. He was a man of faith, and he really believed that good things were going to happen for us. If it was dry and the crops desperately needed rain, he could find a single cloud in the sky and would then plow the field, believing that rain was on the way. He would also plow the field when the weather was dry and say, 'When you plow, the moisture comes to the top, and that'll help the crops.' He could always find something good and positive about any situation.

"My dad was a sharecropper in his younger days," Oney said. "He went 50/50 with my Uncle Oney on the farm. My dad provided the labor and machinery, while my uncle provided the land, fertilizer, and chemicals. Both men worked the 600 acres of land in South Bibb County. My dad began to give me more responsibility as he began to get a little older, and I became old enough to assume more responsibility. I was the one doing the hard, manual labor, and he drove the tractor. For anyone who has farmed, they know that the tractor was the preferred machinery on any farm."

William (90) and Gertrude (88) Hudson are still living in South Bibb on property that was developed by their son. In fact, the Hudson family lives in the same general neighborhood where Oney grew up. The communities in that area of Bibb County were called Rutland, Walden, Skipperton, and Coalneck and were filled with hard-working, blue-collar families who wanted better lives for their children than what they had experienced. John H. Heard School serviced that section of Bibb County and was an excellent school.

"My sister and I attended Heard School, and we had some outstanding teachers that truly shaped our lives. I remember Mrs. Sara Willis, who taught me in the first grade. I got off to a good start in school because she disciplined us, and got us ready for the second grade, where Mrs. Hazel Boyer took over. Mrs. Boyer was just out of college and really demanded a lot from a bunch of second graders. We all had great respect for her. But one teacher at Heard that I really loved was Mrs. Alva Cobb. She taught us in the seventh grade, and though she was a little older, she was a wonderful teacher.

"I also had some great teachers at Willingham. Mrs. Mary P. ('Rock') Smith was my tenth-grade American history teacher. She loved teaching and was a great historian in her own right. She made you want to learn about history and was involved in the lives of her students. Not only did she know our names, but she knew about our families as well. Mrs. Smith took a personal interest in us. That fact is evidenced today, because she continues to attend Willingham High School reunions each summer."

Oney recalled several teachers of note. "Mike Garvin was a great math teacher. As a senior, I had him for Algebra-Trig and always liked the way he worked so hard to make math interesting. I remember Henry Middlebrooks, Billy Henderson, Bobby Brown, and Martin Allman. They all became coaches when the school day ended, but I liked being in their classrooms. I think Coach Allman was from West Virginia, and he had this 'mountaineer' dialect. We would imitate the way he would say, 'I guarantee you.' Coach would get mad at our class and rail, 'I 'garr - un – tee ya, if you don't get quiet, I'm takin' you all to the 'aw-fiss'! We had his accent down pat, especially when his back was turned. We had great teachers who were mostly young and enthusiastic and who really wanted us to learn. They all demanded discipline in class, or they'd whip your butt. They could do that back in those days."

It is interesting to note that most of Oney's favorite teachers were coaches. He explained, "I played football at Heard School, but I never played sports at Willingham because I had to work on the farm. My parents and I hardly ever missed a home football or basketball game that was played at night, though. We didn't have the money to go to the out-of-town games, so I often went with Doris and Ben Lindsey, the parents of my good friend, Duke Lindsey. The Lindseys seemed to have more financial resources than most everyone else in our part of the county. They also took Duke and me to the races in Daytona Beach, FL."

"I absolutely loved Willingham High School! The people, the sports, sock hops and dances after football games, the Junior-Senior proms, Johnny Jenkins and the Pine Toppers. All of it. High school was a great time in my life. I also was in a high school fraternity during my senior year. Phi Omega Beta offered an invitation to join, and I did. There were hardly any Willingham boys in P.O.B. in those days, but I actually made some contacts with guys that have been helpful to me in business."

* * * * * * * * *

After high school, Oney attended Abraham Baldwin Agricultural College (ABAC) in Tifton. He said, "Since Tifton was not exactly a 'bustling town' in those days, we founded a social fraternity on the campus of the junior college and named it Phi Sigma Delta. We brought in bands and had concerts which were usually held in an old tobacco warehouse off campus. It was great! But everybody from around there in conservative Tifton didn't warm to the idea of us bringing in the 'controversial' Doug Clark and his band, 'The Hot Nuts.' We even received some threats, but we had fun anyway."

Oney graduated from ABAC in 1966 and then went to the University of Georgia in Athens, where he graduated with a Bachelor of Science in Agriculture in 1968. John Ginn recalled some of the good days in Athens. "Carl Puckett, Oney, and I roomed together at Georgia for our junior and senior years. We lived in a house built in the 1920's that had one big gas heater in the main room and just a small space heater in one of the three bedrooms. We also had a fourth roommate that tended to get a little tipsy on occasion. Actually, it was more like 'falling down drunk every night.' One night he came in late, left the back door open, and 'free-range' chickens from the yard next door came in and roosted all over the house. It goes without saying that these chickens were not potty trained. We spent the next morning shooing them outside and cleaning up after them. That was a bad day in Athens."

Ginn, Puckett, and Hudson all grew up in South Bibb County, which was a close-knit community within itself. Dr. Rick Lanford, Vice President of Development for the Methodist Children's Home in Macon, is an ordained United Methodist minister who grew up in South Bibb and has known Oney's family for many years. Lanford said, "The fact is that almost everybody in South Bibb knew each other. My father, Dr. Charles Lanford, was the family physician for countless families in that area, and our family also lived in South Bibb County. Oney was a bit older than me and one day he told me, 'Rick, you will always be a LBCB.' And I asked, 'A what?' Oney replied, 'A LBCB. A Lower-Bibb County boy. And no matter how successful you get, or where you go, or what you do, you'll always be a LBCB. So be proud of it.' And I never have forgotten those words, and I've never forgotten where I was raised."

While Oney grew up in Sub-South Bibb County, Anne Brewer Hudson, a Willingham cheerleader and a 1963 McEvoy graduate, grew up in the Bruce School area off Houston Avenue. She and Oney didn't date each other when they were in high school, though she knew about him. Anne said, "When I was at McEvoy, one of my best friends lived right down the road from Oney, and when I would drive past his house, I always thought he was a cute guy with a great personality. Several years later, Oney was dating a classmate at ABAC named Ola. I remember telling him that 'Oney and Ola would never look right on their wedding invitations.' We began dating while Oney was at UGA in 1967."

According to Oney, "One of the crowning moments of my life was the day I married Anne Brewer, March 17, 1968, during my senior year at the University of Georgia. Anne is my dearest and best friend, and we have two fine sons. Lance (32) lives in Greenwood, SC, and is a nurse anesthetist. Matthew (35) helps me with our farm operation, which includes 150 acres of small grain, 90 acres of pecans, 70 acres of corn, and he has given us our two wonderful grandsons, Lance William Hudson, II, and William Dean Hudson. Those little guys love to ride their motorized, miniature John Deere tractors that we gave them. Anne and I have had a wonderful friendship and marriage for the past 37 years."

To Anne Hudson, the feeling is mutual about her husband. She said, "Oney has a lot of patience, which is pretty evident in the fact that we've been married for 37 years. Everyone's life is filled with bumps in the road, but we have been able to keep the lines of communication open and work through those hard times. Our sons still feel comfortable in seeking advice from their daddy, and they truly enjoy his company.

"Oney's faith in God has sustained him his entire life. He is such a kind, loving, and giving person, who helps his family as well as those outside his immediate family. Oney is a dedicated husband, father, and friend. He has never wavered from his responsibilities to his parents, who are nearly 90 years old, and to my 88-year-old mother."

* * * * * * * * * *

Hudson has also never wavered from his commitment to his friends. Oney lost one of his closest friends, Tommy Shaw, back in 1998. Melinda Shaw, Tommy's widow, spoke about the love and admiration that she has for Oney. "We grew up in the Rutland community of south Bibb County, went to Heard School, and I have known him as far back as I can remember. After Tommy and I married, I got to know Oney and Anne very well. It was obvious that he and Tommy had enjoyed a close friendship as teenagers, and now that they were both back in Macon, it would begin to grow into a closeness that few friends can know. They both said that they were each like the brother they never had. They were presidents of their senior classes at Willingham, Tommy in 1963 and Oney in 1964. Our relationship with Oney and Anne was always about having fun. When we were all together, it seemed like we could just turn back the clock and be young forever.

"Tommy and I were married for 33 years," Melinda recalled, "and he died on the evening of his class's 35th high school reunion. Except for my children and me, Oney and Anne Hudson are the ones that I still see who feel a great sense of loss following Tommy's death. In fact, they stayed with me and my family around the clock when we were first faced with Tommy's loss. They really helped give our family strength. That's the kind of friends they were to us."

The Hudsons have remained close friends with Melinda Shaw, who now lives in Birmingham and has three children - Christie Melchiors who lives in Richmond, VA; Jack Shaw of Birmingham, AL, who works for Revere Control Systems and is a married father of three; and Lee Shaw, who is married and lives in Alaska.

"Back in the 1970's," Melinda recalled, "I first heard Oney express an interest in local political issues. I think that he has had a positive impact on the community leaders in Macon and Bibb County, as well as statewide. I am also

Proud Grandparents: Oney and Anne Hudson holding Will and Dean Hudson

proud of his service to the Georgia Farm Bureau and his appointment by Governor Sonny Perdue. Oney's ability to deal with people is one of his greatest assets. In the business world being trustworthy, straightforward, and diplomatic have added up to much success for Oney and Anne.

"But perhaps his most important personal quality is Oney's deep faith in God," Melinda continued. "Oney has definitely been a guiding force for me, personally, in my walk of faith, and I will always remember him for his tender-hearted and compassionate support. A special moment happened in May, 2003, when my daughter, Christie, was married in a South Carolina wedding ceremony. It was Oney that she asked to walk her down the aisle since her daddy had died in 1998. She told Oney that he was the closest thing she had to a dad. I know that this was a proud moment for Oney to be able to stand in for his long-time friend, but it was also a day that was full of difficult emotions. A few years earlier, Oney and Anne had traveled to Montana to be with me and my family for the wedding of my youngest son, which demonstrates what a faithful friend he has been throughout the years. Oney was a loyal and true friend to Tommy and me, and I will continue to cherish his and Anne's friendship and encouragement forever."

Russell Lipford, a partner in the accounting and consulting firm of Clifton, Lipford, Hardison, & Parker, LLC, in Macon, and David Green, part-owner of SSK Realty with Lipford, hold Oney Hudson in very high esteem. Green said, "I have been so impressed that Oney has been such a wonderful son and son-in-law for these many years. He is now taking care of his loved ones as they increase in years. He's a great husband to Anne and father to his two sons.

"As a businessman, I have been involved with Oney for about eight years, and these have been exciting times. Oney is one of the most honest, forth-right, straight-forward individuals you will ever meet. His integrity is impeccable, and it has been a great experience watching him and working with him in our many developments. Oney can build roads, houses, and commercial buildings as economically as anyone I know. It's like he can smell out a deal, and he has good judgment about how to make things work for the betterment of all involved.

"He is a true entrepreneur," Green said. "From farming to building to selling to developing, he is absolutely one of the best, and I'm proud to be his business partner. Oney has made major contributions to the greater-Macon community as a board member of Georgia Farm Bureau and is now on the

Governor's staff for environmental work in Georgia, which is a very big deal. I am really proud to call Oney Hudson my friend."

Russell Lipford, a partner with Oney in several major commercial business ventures, echoed similar sentiments about his friend. "Oney's first exposure to the development business involved the creation of Hudson Estates off Jones Road. There was a considerable risk involved, since Oney's vision was to make this subdivision comparable to those in North Macon, but he stuck to his vision and became involved in the construction business to insure that the lots would be filled with upper-end homes which would upgrade the Sub-South community. Oney's development of Melton Place, a senior adult retirement community where his parents, his mother-in-law, and he and Anne reside, reflects this same 'first-class' attitude in his building and development."

It is easily apparent that Oney and Anne Hudson are in the development business for the long haul, as opposed to many developers who are interested in making the 'quick buck.' Anne said, "In developing land and building a community, Oney has always strived to produce quality growth, which is something that we can look back on and feel good about the end results."

Anne Hudson believed that much of the business success that she and Oney have experienced in recent years is due to his uncanny ability to relate to all types of people. "Oney has always been able to be completely at ease with total strangers, just as easily as he is with long-time friends. His ability to relate has served him well since his high school days as senior class president at Willingham. I've seen him mediate and bring peace and agreement between different groups on many occasions. There's no doubt that Oney has leadership ability, and he has gained a lot of respect in the business world. Oney has received many honors in his life, but one of his greatest honors came when Georgia Governor Sonny Perdue appointed him to the Department of Community Affairs board as an at-large member in 2003."

Oney knows that he is a man who has really been blessed in many ways. "Being able to develop property in the south part of the county has been a good thing for me, personally and professionally," he said, "but I also believe it has been good for South Bibb County. It has produced a lot of jobs and other opportunities for many people. In 1989, my dad, sister, and I developed a plan regarding what we wanted to do with our property. In those early days, residential lots would sell for around $14,000. Today, those same lots would go for $25,900. Nobody ever thought that we would sell lots to build $200,000 houses in sub-South, but we did. We have seen amazing growth in our new-found occupation.

"I remember that I cried when we sold our first lot because we were breaking up the family farm. The only problem I've experienced with commercial and residential development is that it gets slow, then hot, and then slow again. We'll sell a one-acre lot and then build a 'piece of road' to it. The development of neighborhoods and shopping centers gets pretty exciting. Currently, I only owe about $5,000,000!"

Oney recalled, "Since 1988, we have developed Hudson Estates, a residential subdivision with 120 lots built on 106 acres. We took a 100-acre pecan orchard and built 100 houses on it. Also, we've built a condominium subdivision in Centerville and a suburban center on Hartley Bridge Road that includes a doctor's office and a health club that has over 1,200 members. We are revitalizing an old Wal-Mart building on Gray Highway where a Big Lots Discount Center is coming. This puts another building back in use, and that helps neighborhoods. I am a partner in 10-12 corporations locally that buy land and develop neighborhoods, office parks, and shopping centers."

Business partner Russell Lipford stated, "Oney is one of our finest citizens. I'm honored to have known and worked with him for all of these years. His background in development, politics, and business was really put to the test with the Copus Connector project. He recognized the value to the Middle Georgia community of having a large industrial site adjoining I-75 only a few miles from Warner Robins Air Force Base, which is the economic engine for all of Middle Georgia. Oney put together a team with David Green and Frank Walthall to buy the acreage between Hartley Bridge Road and Sardis Church Road. He spent years convincing leaders in the local community about the viability of this project, while his actions and motives were often criticized by his neighbors who could not see the long-term benefits of such a project.

"Likewise, I'm sure Oney had his own emotions to deal with since he would be selling his family farm, but he has continued to work on the Sardis Church Road interchange, and it will enhance the industrial park. It will also ensure that the resulting development will be an asset to the South Bibb County community."

Oney Hudson has worked hard to get that interchange on Sardis Church Road. He said, "When it happens, it will become the Tom Hill Sr. Boulevard of South Bibb County and become the southern-most entrance into Bibb County. This will open up South Bibb County, as well as opening up neighboring Twiggs County, since this connector will join into Sgoda Road near I-16. It will be a good thing for the county to have a Class 'A' site such as this."

Though Oney has, for the most part, gone into development as his primary vocation, he said, "In my mind, I am still, and will always be, a farmer at heart. I would love to farm for a living, but I just got tired of waiting in line for a government subsidy to help me make ends meet. I really do enjoy what I'm doing, but it's still quite a risk. Working with our local Planning and Zoning and trying to change the mindset of politicians are not easy things to do. I got turned down for several projects that made perfect sense, and that's so frustrating. The head of P&Z told me in a meeting once that a certain location would be an ideal place for an office park. I countered with, 'But y'all already turned me down when I tried to get an office park on that very location!' Go figure."

* * * * * * * * *

In addition to developing locations all over Bibb County, Oney is actively involved as a deacon at Grace (formerly Sardis) Primitive Baptist Church. According to Oney, "The best thing that I have ever done was joining the church. God, faith, and the church are very important parts of my life. Recently, my pastor asked an intriguing question that affected me deeply. His question was, 'If you went on trial for being a Christian, would they be able to find enough evidence to convict you?' I want them to be able to find plenty of evidence to that effect in my own life."

Oney has been deeply involved in his church, which was founded in 1864. "We consolidated three small bands of Primitive Baptist churches - Shiloh in Lizella, Elizabeth on Houston Ave, and Sardis in South Bibb County. When the churches joined together to form one congregation, we formed Grace Primitive Baptist Church and meet in the old Sardis Primitive Baptist building."

Always the leader and the good citizen, he serves as an officer of the Porter-Ellis Community Center and the Bibb County Farm Bureau, where he was on the board of directors for eight years. Oney serves on the Department of Community Affairs and was appointed by Governor Sonny Perdue to the Agriculture Advisory committee to promote the governor's agenda.

Oney has been honored twice, along with his dad, as the Soil & Water Conservation's Man of the Year for Georgia in 1972 and 1992. Likewise, he was placed on the Agriculture Commission by Senator Saxby Chambliss. Locally, Oney is a member of the Bibb County Homebuilders Association.

His past and current resume reads like a *Who's Who* among community leaders. He has served as a committee member on the Bibb County Unification Project and was a member of the Bibb County Property Taxes and Land Evaluation Study. He has functioned as a committee member on the 2005 Club to study the future of development of Bibb County. Oney has served as a member Alpha Zeta Agriculture fraternity and is the Middle Georgia Area Director for the UGA Agriculture Alumni, as well as having served on boards for Windsor Academy, the BB&T Bank Board, the Advisory Committee for Bibb County Extension Service, and as a member of the Georgia Cattlemen's Association. He has also served as a Farm Service Agency committee member, a Director of the Ocmulgee Soil and Water Conservation District, and as a Director of the Georgia Farm Bureau Federation for eight years before retiring. He is also a director on no less than ten boards that are directly related to his real estate developments.

* * * * * * * * * *

Serving on boards for the past twenty years the way Oney has can cause some people to lose their sense of humor and perspective on what real life is about. Oney has managed to maintain a solid balance between work, family, and fun. He has always been one who loved a good story. Anne Hudson recalled, "As our sons approached age 16, Oney began to tell them stories of his high school and college experiences with his buddies. I wasn't too thrilled to hear him telling our boys about some of their daddy's exploits, so I told him to 'hush and not put any wrong ideas into their heads.' We developed calluses on our knees from praying for our boys' safety as they were growing up."

John Ginn vividly remembered stories from their younger days. "Oney and I were a lot alike in that we were raised by our parents to avoid the serious stuff that could get you into big trouble. His parents, like mine, just wouldn't stand for anything more than a little 'harmless' trouble, but we still caught grief for that.

"I remember one night at Fincher's Barbeque, Oney and I had been 'breaking training rules' – if you know what I mean. When he got home, he got sick, and his momma had to help clean him up. Oney told her 'he had gotten some bad barbeque at Fincher's!' My question was, 'Who in the world ever heard of bad barbeque at Fincher's?' I'm pretty sure Oney's momma knew exactly what was going on, but she let him off the hook that time."

Ginn continued, "In 1968, Oney and I joined the Georgia Army National Guard. Oney ended up serving four years with the Mobilized Infantry and was a Personnel Carrier with an E-4 rank. He and I went off to basic training together in 1968 at Fort Dix, NJ. This was before the 'new army' was invented, so we caught physical and verbal abuse from the drill sergeants. One of our first Physical Training tests included a one-mile run, and little did we know that we were being timed. For some reason, Oney decided to take it easy on the run, and at the finish, he and about twenty other guys, who were coming in last, got cut out of the group, and their names were taken by one of the instructors. That afternoon as we were finishing, Oney and that group were taken off and made to run up and down a massive pile of dirt that was at least four stories tall. When they got back to the barracks after dark, Oney was so nasty that I thought he had been beaten with a bat. His eyes were black, his ears were black, and (I am not making this up) he had black grit stuck to the top of his front teeth and gums from breathing so hard through his mouth. He looked awful!"

"But the next time we had a PT test, Oney finished way up in the front of the pack!" Ginn recalled with a grin.

"While Oney and I were in New Jersey and stationed at Fort Dix, we ate our first Chinese food ever," Ginn said. "All I can remember is that we smeared a bunch of intensely-hot Chinese mustard all over the meal, and then we couldn't eat it. We thought it was regular mustard like you got in Macon.

"We also rode a Greyhound bus into New York City while we were in New Jersey," Ginn said. "But did we go to the world famous museums, Broadway shows, and other 'must see' attractions? Nawww! We just walked around the streets of New York and almost got mugged several times. We did ride the bus down to the end of the island where you could see the Statue of Liberty from about a mile away. We were 'country come to town!'"

The times have radically changed for Oney and Anne Hudson since the early days of their marriage. Though Oney's time is now occupied with lots, plats, building permits, and house plans, rather than John Deere tractors and plowing long, straight rows, he still finds time to hunt and fish with his sons and

The Hudsons: Matt, Lance, Anne and Oney.

with friends. Wynfield Plantation in Albany is a favorite location to shoot quail for the Hudson boys. He and Anne own a condo at the Beach Club (formerly the old DeSoto Hotel) on Tybee Island near Savannah and go there about once a month.

Oney concluded his story by saying, "With the financial means to live anywhere in Middle Georgia that Anne and I desire, and since we own property all over this area, we have chosen to live in South Bibb County. We have plans to someday build a house out in this area once again, but right now, with my parents and Ann's mother living in the Melton Place Community with us, that's a good thing for all of us.

"If someone asked me about having success in my life, I would tell them it's because of 3 F's: my faith, my family, and our farm. For me, growing up in South Bibb County was a lot of fun. My life story parallels a country song that says something like, 'You don't find happiness in money and success.' I've been blessed because of the success we've had in real estate, but agriculture is my first love. I would trade it all if I could make a living farming, but I can't."

Oney no longer owns that maroon, 1964 Pontiac GTO with red interior and a Hurst 4-in-the-floor that he bought for $3,000. For the past five years, he has driven a navy blue, 1964 Corvette convertible that will also fly, and he continues to believe his own words of wisdom that he conveyed to young Rick Lanford, that 'being a LBCB is truly a good thing.'

"I would want said about me when my time here on earth is done what Jesus said to one of His faithful followers,

"Well done, thou good and faithful servant. You have been faithful over a few things. I will make you ruler over many things. Enter into the joy of the Lord."

—Matthew 25:21

Oney's friends would, in all likelihood, tell him, "Well done."

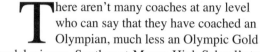

Raised Right

Willie Jay Goolsby, Jr.
Class of 1970

"Never, never, never give up"
—Winston Churchill

There aren't many coaches at any level who can say that they have coached an Olympian, much less an Olympic Gold medal winner. Southwest-Macon High School's track coach, Willie Goolsby, is one of those elite coaches who could (but wouldn't dare) boast about the amazing accomplishments of one of his protégés. Antonio Pettigrew, class of 1987 at Southwest, ran a leg on the USA's Gold Medal-winning 4 x 400 meter relay in the 2000 Olympics in Sydney, Australia. No one was prouder of Pettigrew than his high school track coach in Macon.

Willie Goolsby, in his words, was "raised right." The son of Henrietta and Willie Goolsby, Sr., young Goolsby learned the value of hard work and education at an early age. Willie's dad had a first grade education and his mom finished the fourth grade, but they were honest, hard-working people who taught their three sons – Charles, now 54, Willie, Jr., 52, and Paul, 50 - how to live, succeed, and get along in life.

Goolsby, Sr., worked in Public Works for the City of Macon, while Mrs. Goolsby worked in other people's homes. According to Willie, Jr., "My parents were the greatest, most loving and caring people you could ever meet, and, though they didn't have any formal education, they were both very smart people. Together, my mom and dad built the first two houses that I lived in. They physically did the work. We lived very close to what is now Eisenhower Parkway/U.S. 80, but it was a dirt road in those days, and that area was quite undeveloped. In fact, we had chickens, pigs, and cows in our yard, and, though our house was inside the city limits, it was like we were living in the country.

"My parents were always involved in our lives when we were young. They either took us on school field trips, or they made sure we were able to go to places like Grant's Park in Atlanta, Warm Springs, Stone Mountain, or to the World of Coca Cola," Goolsby recalled. "Those were great times for my brothers and me, because we would sometimes get to ride the Nancy Hanks railway to Atlanta. We didn't have a lot of money, but my folks made sure we never went lacking."

Willie Goolsby, Jr., attended Eugenia Hamilton Elementary School on Pio Nono Avenue and later went to Ballard Hudson Junior High School through the ninth grade. He transferred to Willingham High School as a sophomore when integration became more widespread in Bibb County. "I had always wanted to go to Willingham after watching their football games against Lanier and Valdosta when I was much younger", Goolsby remembered. "I was very familiar with Coach Billy Henderson and the excellent program that he had at Willingham. He was considered by many in the Macon community to be a 'football god' because of his outstanding record against the best teams in the state. Kirk Durham and I were the first two black players on his varsity football team in 1968."

Ben Hinson, president of Mid Georgia Ambulance in Macon and a football teammate and personal friend of Goolsby's back in 1967, wrote the following letter to the editor of *The Macon Telegraph* on March 19, 1994, in honor of his friend:

"In the fall of my sophomore year in high school, I learned many lessons. Playing football for Billy Henderson at Willingham High School taught me a great deal about commitment, hard work, and perseverance.

One of the things I had not had the opportunity to learn, until that point in my life, was how to work well with people that were different from me. In fact, in the ninth grade, I was ejected from a game in Griffin for making racial remarks. The Griffin team had a young black man playing for them. We did not have any blacks on our team at the time, and I had no friends who were black.

I simply didn't understand very much about some of the people who lived around me. I was raised in a family who taught me to love everyone, but the peer pressure of those in school swayed me to be somewhat racist and very proud of it. Then, a most memorable incident occurred. It would change my life.

Our team had returned from football camp at Jekyll Island and was practicing out behind the school when two young black students showed up saying they wanted to go out for the football team. The coaches issued them equipment. Because they had missed the beginning of practice, they were assigned to running laps to get in shape. At the end of practice, they were given the responsibility of running back punts.

Eleven of us were on the punting team and only two of them were returning kicks. I'll never forget that day. As we punted to them, all of us would rush down the field and tackle the one with the ball as the other one would block. They would then jump up and go back to receive the next kick. We would punt the ball again, they would run it back, we would tackle them viciously, and they would get up and run back to receive the next one.

Well, about the seventh or eight repeat of this drill, one of the young men caught the ball and ran it all the way back for a touchdown. Rather than celebrating or making any comment that they had beaten us, the two young men simply trotted back down the field to receive the next punt.

I realized then that there was a level of character and commitment in these two men that I had not seen before. After that practice, I walked off the field determined that I had been wrong about my racial feelings and needed to have a friendship with these two young men who happened to be black.

My life was affected a great deal that day on the football field. I learned a lot about people, a lot about race relations, and a lot about myself and how judgmental and wrong I had been. Those young men taught me a great lesson, one that I have carried into business and use every day in my relations with all people.

The names of the young men were Kirk Durham and Willie Goolsby, the same Willie Goolsby who just led the Southwest Patriot girls' basketball team into the state Class AAAA championship game.

His tremendous character, quiet strength, and resolve to do a good job have changed my life and changed many lives of people around him. We, in Macon, are indeed fortunate to have someone like him among us. Thanks, Willie, for a great job. You mean a lot to a lot of people!"

As much as Ben Hinson's life was changed, because of his observations and encounter with Willie Goolsby, hundreds of young high school students and athletes have prospered under the tutelage of this Willingham High School graduate, class of 1970.

Willie Goolsby lettered in football, basketball, baseball, and track at Willingham (which was renamed Southwest High in 1970-71). He lettered in football three years and was twice named the Macon Touchdown Club's Player of the Week in his senior season. In basketball, Goolsby was named the team's Most Valuable Player and received the Top Athlete Award at Willingham.

"I had a good experience at Willingham, especially in athletics. In those days, you were accepted by the student body more quickly if you were an athlete," Goolsby said. "There was a common bond with all of your teammates, both black and white, in sports. Wayne Jones, Allen McCoury, and Ander Horne were real friends of mine at Willingham.

"I had some very good coaches in high school in Billy Henderson, Billy Beale, Lloyd Bohannon, and Edgar Hatcher. Larry Ramey, my geography teacher, was the first black coach at Willingham. I had great respect for Coach Ramey and Coach Jesse Mays, who died recently. Those men were instrumental in my considering coaching as a profession," Goolsby remembered. "Being a coach in the community where I grew up was significant, because athletics was such an important part of life."

Goolsby was considered a pioneer as both an athlete and a coach. Thomas Krause wrote a feature article about Willie Goolsby in the February 16, 2002, edition of *The Macon Telegraph* in celebration of Black History Month. Portions of Krause's story are quoted below:

When Willie Goolsby tried out for the Willingham football team in

1968, his efforts weren't exactly encouraged. He had the spare time, the talent and the ambition, but he was also black, and attending a school that was 96 percent white. "I just wanted to play football," he said. I didn't really think about it. I knew that there was going to be pressure. I'd heard of Jackie Robinson and those guys, but I just wanted to play."

Goolsby weathered the resistance. He continued to practice hard when other players were out to make him look bad. Eventually, white players and white coaches began to change their minds about him. But many African Americans weren't as quick to change their minds. Coaches from black schools and peers from his neighborhood called him a traitor. Goolsby said, "They didn't like seeing a talented black teen playing for a white team – even though I was the first black student in Bibb County to play for a white varsity team."

Unfortunately, things aren't much different today. Goolsby is the coach at Southwest which is 95 percent black. And no white students play on his team. "They won't come out," he said. "But there's an open invitation. Anyone can come out." And Goolsby suspects white students get peer pressure from their friends about not trying out for a team dominated by players of another race. Goolsby knows those arguments. He heard them himself 22 years ago. He just didn't listen.

"I was looking out for myself," he said. "I wanted to open doors. I've always been an individual. I didn't let people stop me." When Goolsby first decided to go to Willingham, he thought he could learn a thing or two about other people. And he thought he could teach other people a thing or two about African-Americans. His decision to play sports met a lot of resistance but also gave him a certain amount of prestige. Goolsby said, "Athletes are the student leaders. And once I won the respect of my fellow athletes, others on campus began to change their views of me. I don't know what kind of stereotypes they were taught, but they learned that things weren't like they thought."

Henry Ficklin, a teacher at Southwest, said, "Goolsby has shown that people can overcome their differences through athletics. Once people are put on a team together, they learn to respect one another for their abilities and talents. Race becomes irrelevant. He is one who is dedicated to young people, to help make them excel."

After graduating from Willingham, Willie entered Carson-Newman College, a small, Baptist school in Jefferson City, TN. He lettered in track, soccer, and football where he played both wide receiver and defensive back, and he graduated in 1975 with a Bachelor of Science Degree in Education, majoring in Health and Physical Education.

"When I finished college, I moved back to Macon to hopefully find a teaching and coaching position. In junior high school, I learned a lot about coaching and relating to kids from coaches like Robert Slocum, Robert Hudson,

Donald Richardson, and Waders Campbell," he recalled. "It seemed like every kid who was good in sports had dreams of becoming a professional athlete some day, and I was no different. But fortunately, I had enough sense to know that everybody wouldn't make it in the pros, and I knew that an education was really important. I also knew that coaching was a great way to remain a part of the game when I couldn't play any longer."

Player and coach Willie Goolsby with Latavia Coleman (FSU).

Having coached for over 30 years, Willie Goolsby owns some impressive coaching credentials. His coaching career began in 1975 when he coached in middle school. Goolsby coached football, basketball, and track at Southwest High from 1976 to 1987. He then transferred to Southeast-Macon High for four years and became the varsity girls head basketball and track coach from 1987-91 before returning to Southwest when the long-time, highly-successful girls' coach, Albert Sharpe, retired.

"We had some outstanding teams at Southwest in the mid-90's," Albert Sharpe recalled. "I coached for 30 years at Ballard-Hudson and Southwest High Schools in Macon." Sharpe, a recreation specialist at Macon State College, remembered Goolsby fondly. "I met Willie when we tried to get him to play for us at Ballard-Hudson, but, instead, he chose to go to Willingham and play for Coach Henderson. Willie was a very good athlete back in the late 1970's. After he finished college, he came back to Macon and we served on staff together at Southwest. He was my assistant basketball coach on the girls' team before going to Southeast High, where he became their head girls' basketball coach for four years. I decided to retire from active coaching, and I wanted our program to continue playing at a highly-successful level, so I helped get Coach Goolsby back to Southwest."

Sharpe said, "I think Coach Goolsby is a fantastic guy that the players and students all respect. He works extremely well with the kids and has very good work habits. His teams have been exceptional, because he puts so much into their preparation and gets his players to believe in what he is doing. Willie has both a love for the game and a love for kids."

On a lighter note, Sharpe recalled a time when Goolsby, already a track, basketball, and football standout at Willingham, decided to give baseball a try. "Willingham had excellent baseball teams back then, and Willie was determined to play for the Rams. They put him in center field where he promptly missed three or four straight fly balls. After the game, I pulled him aside and told him,

293

'Willie, you really need to stick with football, basketball, and track."

As a coach, Goolsby had some outstanding players and marvelous teams while he coached girls' basketball at Southwest. "We went 24-3, 25-2, 22-3, and 22-5 from 1994 to 1997 and got to the State AAAA finals twice. We put together an amazing 93-13 run from 1987 through 1991."

Goolsby reminisced, "Shana Askew and Latavia Coleman are two of the finest female basketball players to ever come out of Macon. Askew went on to a great career at Auburn, while Coleman became a four-year starter at Florida State."

As a student-athlete, Askew prospered in many ways under Willie Goolsby's tutelage. A 1993 Southwest graduate, Askew said, "I can't say enough good things about Coach Goolsby. As a coach, he was so determined and wanted to win badly, but he also wanted you, as an individual, and us, as a team, to be as good as we could be. He taught me to give everything I had while the game was going on. He didn't want us to say afterward, 'What could have happened?' He is a good man and a great coach who cares deeply about his players beyond athletics. He was interested in what we did with our lives, and he wanted us to be successful.

"Truly, he was my inspiration to go on to college," Askew said, "because I had a child when I was young. I had some special situations that I had to take care of as a mom to be able to play high school sports. Coach Goolsby was a father-figure for me, and he did a lot to help me get to Auburn on scholarship. I played four years of Division I college basketball and graduated in 1997 with a degree in Health and Physical Education."

Shana Askew's life seems to be going well these days, and she attributes much of that success to her high school coach. Today, she is engaged to Marquis Daniels of the NBA Dallas Mavericks, whom she met while both were playing basketball at Auburn.

LaTavia Coleman, Askew's teammate on the 1995-96 play-off teams, played for Goolsby at Southwest from 1992-96 and attended Florida State on a basketball scholarship. Coleman said, "I was 5'10" in the ninth grade and finally decided to give basketball a try. I saw Coach at lunch one day and told him I wanted to play. We were state runners-up against Sequoyah and South Gwinnett my junior and senior years. I really loved playing basketball for Coach Goolsby. He was the first coach that I ever played for, not having been a basketball player in middle school. He made practice fun, but he could also be serious when we needed to focus on a drill so we would do it right. He was extremely focused in regard to conditioning, and we would run drills until we did them perfectly. Coach Goolsby is a great guy, and I am really glad that he was my coach because he helped get my career started in the right way."

Coleman played all over the floor at both Southwest and Florida State – from point guard to post player. She was drafted by the Houston Comets of the WNBA and was immediately traded for two players to the Indiana Fever, where she played in two exhibition games. Coleman played one year in Portugal and is now a probation officer with the City of Atlanta.

Having become the all-time winningest girls' coach in Southwest basketball history, Goolsby takes great pride in all of his former players. He knows what most of them are doing in life and is frequently in touch with them. Pictures of former players and students litter the bulletin board in his office in the old Willingham gym. College posters with several of Goolsby's former players are within easy reach as well. He takes pride in his ability to quickly update a visitor on the whereabouts of former players and coaches.

Wanda Burns, a 1987 Southwest graduate, is another player who flourished as a player for Goolsby. "I think a defining moment in my basketball career happened my junior year in high school. We were playing in the state semi-finals, and four of our five starters fouled out. I was our only starter still on the floor and played the entire game. Coach Goolsby pulled me aside during a time-out and whispered to me, 'Wanda, I want you to prove to everybody right now who you are. I already know who you are. Go out and prove it to the rest of them. You show them what you can do.' We finished the game with four seldom-used substitutes and me, and we played out hearts out. Even though we lost, I'll never forget the faith and trust that he put in me that moment. My career was never the same again."

Burns went on to Florida State where she played for four years and graduated in 1991 with a B.S. in Social Work. She said, "My years playing for Coach Goolsby were special. He was such a motivator and a good friend. He was unlike most coaches in that he looked out for our well-being both on and off the court. If a player couldn't afford to go to camp, he would arrange it so she could attend. If someone needed transportation for a college visit, he took care of it. He was such a caring coach, and I am glad that I played for him."

Today, Wanda Burns is now Wanda Jackson. She is married to Dewayne Jackson and is the proud mother of a seven-year-old daughter and a two-year-old son. She works in Macon for the professional licensing board.

As good as Willie Goolsby's girls' teams were throughout his coaching career, and they were very good, perhaps the most notable athlete that he has ever coached, was Antonio Pettigrew. "Our track team finished 2nd in the state in AAAA during Pettigrew's junior year," Gooslby said. "After graduating from Southwest High, Antonio attended Santa Fe Community College in Lakeland, FL, before transferring to South Dade CC in Hialeah, FL. Finishing at South Dade, he had a great career in track and graduated with a degree in education from St. Augustine's College in Raleigh, NC."

Goolsby recalled, "In 2000 at the age of 32, Antonio finished fourth in the 400-meter qualifying event which allowed him to run on the 4 x 400-meter relay team in the Sydney Olympics. He was on the Gold Medal-winning 4 x 400-meter relay team along with twins, Alvin and Calvin Harrison, and the much-heralded Michael Johnson. Of course, Johnson was the world record holder in the 400-meters. That's some pretty fast company for a kid from Macon, GA.

"Antonio's 400-meter times were just amazing. He ran a 43.1 leg on the

4 x 400-meter relay team at the 1997 World Outdoor Championships. That was the second fastest relay leg in track history. Antonio's personal best times were 20.38 in the 200-meters and 44.21 in the 400. He has really brought some notoriety to Macon and to Southwest throughout his career, and I'm so proud of him," Goolsby concluded.

With Antonio Pettigrew, the feeling is mutual. "Coach Goolsby was my track coach at Southwest from 1985-87, and I ran the 200, 400, 4 x 100, and 4 x 400 relays. He was a great coach and a very good man who knew how to put a team together, and he never gave up on a kid. Coach Goolsby was a great influence on me, and he helped me so much both in my track career and in life. He didn't just prepare me for athletics. He prepared me for life, because he demanded the best I had. Though Coach wasn't much of a talker, he had this 'stare' that said he meant business. But the things he did say made sense and were important to me. He taught me to work hard so I could accomplish something in my life. He deserves good things happening for him because he has been responsible for a lot of good things happening to his athletes. I wish and hope that I will be able to give back to him and the school some day, because they gave me so much."

Today, Antonio Pettigrew is successful as the Director of Sales for Velocity Sales and Performance Center, a training center for athletes in Raleigh.

* * * * * * * * * *

Willie Goolsby has continued to coach girls' basketball at Southwest and is in his 31st season as a high school coach. One man who has observed Goolsby's athletic career since 1969 is Edgar Hatcher, the former head football coach and Athletic Director at Southwest High in Macon. A native Maconite, Hatcher also coached Goolsby in football and basketball at Willingham in 1969-70. Goolsby returned to Macon after graduation from Carson-Newman College and coached football alongside Hatcher at Southwest.

Edgar Hatcher recalled about his long-time friend, "Willie Goolsby is just a winner. He has been a winner as long as I've known him. He came to Willingham during some tough times when there were very few black students, and he stood up and became a leader. Willie was something of a pioneer in those days. He took a stand for what was right and was highly respected by the entire student body. Willingham was a better place because of Willie and his leadership."

Hatcher continued, "He was great athlete. I coached him in varsity basketball in his senior year, and we called him the 'trash man.' Willie was about six feet tall and had to play inside against guys that were 6'8" and 6'9," but when the ball was shot, Willie somehow managed to get it and score. In fact, he seemed to get just about every loose ball, because he was so relentless. Willie practiced hard, played hard, and was disciplined as both a player and a coach. He was always early to practice and always stayed late."

"But I think the best quality that Willie Goolsby possesses is loyalty," Hatcher concluded. "There aren't many folks in today's world that demonstrate loyalty like Willie does. I'll never forget how he looked after Johnny Higdon. Johnny was a good athlete at Willingham who had a tragic fall from a tree and suffered extensive brain damage as a young teenager. Students at Willingham were good to Johnny, but Willie really spent a lot of time with him. He would take Johnny to the store where Higdon always bought bubble gum to give out at school and to our players. If there was any place that Johnny needed to go, Willie took him. Willie's life has been successful because of the great influence that he has had on so many young people and the love he has shown throughout his life."

The Coach and The Gold Medalist. Willie Goolsby (right) and Antonio Pettigrew with Olympic Gold Medal.

Dr. Columbus Watkins agreed with Hatcher in his assessment of Willie Goolsby. Watkins, who retired from the Bibb County school system in 1998, was Goolsby's principal. He said, "I hired Coach Goolsby at Southwest. He was just an excellent coach, man, and human being. I consider him to be a true professional who always gave his best. There is no question that he was a good hire."

Probably no one knows Willie Goolsby better than his daughter, Dr. Tiffany Goolsby, a pharmacist in Washington, DC. Tiffany graduated from Southwest High in 1994 before going to Payne College in Augusta. She graduated from the Howard University School of Pharmacy in Washington, DC, in 2003 and is a registered pharmacist. She has also received an Oncology Pharmacy Fellowship from Howard. About her father, Dr. Goolsby said, "I think my dad has been a success in life because he is doing what he has always wanted to do, and he is at peace. His life has never been about money, and he has had a great influence on so many high school students and athletes. My dad has always been so dedicated to what he has chosen to do with his life, which is to teach and coach basketball. He has always cared deeply about his players, and, when some of them couldn't afford to go to basketball camp in the summer, he made sure that they went, even if he had to pay their way. That's how much he cared about them.

"Running track for my dad was a wonderful experience. I ran the mile and the two-mile for him. Growing up in our home, my dad was very protective of me, his only daughter. In fact, I couldn't date until I was 17. But he let me be a child, and, when it was time, he let me be an adult, which was a very good thing. My emotions were somewhat mixed about going to school where my dad was on the faculty. Once, I went to the principal's office for something very minor, but my dad found out about it, so I was always very careful about what I did."

As single dad for the past three years, Willie is engaged to be married to Evette Mathis. Goolsby's other children are sons, Willie Jay Goolsby, III, and Jayson Goolsby, both of whom live and work in Macon.

Willie believes that kids need to know that they can succeed no matter who they are and regardless of their background. "I tell these kids all the time, 'I don't care where you're from. I don't care if your mom and dad are on crack. You can make it. It may be harder, but you can do it.' I have always used slogans with my players and teams. They are easy to remember and have paid some dividends throughout the years. I tell them 'There's no gain without pain,' because being successful in life and in sports takes hard work and dedication. I encourage my players to 'Work hard. Then, work smart.' And I have always told them to 'Strive to be the very best that they can be.' Then, they won't ever be disappointed, if they've done their best."

He concluded, "I love coaching and being with high school students. If I had my life to live over again, I don't know that I would do anything differently." And because of that, hundreds, maybe thousands, of students' who live in South Macon have been enriched due to the positive influence of Coach Willie Goolsby.

Top of the Class

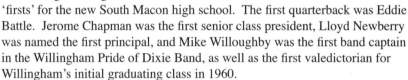

Michael Hill (Mike) Willoughby, M.D.
Class of 1960

"I can do all things through Christ who strengtheneth me."
–Philippians 4:13

In the early days of Willingham, circa 1958, the school opened with grades eight through eleven. There were lots of 'firsts' for the new South Macon high school. The first quarterback was Eddie Battle. Jerome Chapman was the first senior class president, Lloyd Newberry was named the first principal, and Mike Willoughby was the first band captain in the Willingham Pride of Dixie Band, as well as the first valedictorian for Willingham's initial graduating class in 1960.

Regarding the Bibb County tradition in those days of having separate high schools for boys and girls, Willoughby commented, "Linda Adams from McEvoy High and I were both chosen to represent our schools as speakers at the inaugural graduation ceremony. Linda was McEvoy's top senior and I was Willingham's, so we flipped a coin to see who would give the valedictory address, and she won the toss. So I gave the salutatorian's speech at graduation."

In addition to being Willingham's top academic student, Mike was named Senior Superlative, a big deal in those days. However, without his knowledge, the 1960 photo-shoot would take an unusual but excellent turn that would affect the remainder of his life. The *Ram-Scott* (named for the schools' mascots, Willingham Rams and McEvoy Scotties) yearbook staff selected couples for their superlative pictures, and as fate would have it, Mike Willoughby and Lurlene Garrett were chosen to be photographed together. That cold day in February, 1960, was the first time Mike and Lurlene had met. He called her the next week, and they have been together since.

Lurlene recalled, "We dated the rest of our senior year in high school, through four years at Mercer, and then married in June, 1964. Mike went to Medical School at Tulane in New Orleans while I taught French and English there. After Mike finished med school, we moved to Richmond, VA, where he did both his internship and residency in Obstetrics and Gynecology at the Medical College of Virginia.

* * * * * * * * *

Mike Willoughby grew up on Mikado Avenue in the Cynthia H. Weir school district, attended Mikado Baptist Church, pastored by the renowned Dr. E.C.

Sheehan, and began his high school career at Lanier Junior. Mike was part of a multitude of South Macon boys who had to leave Lanier for the new high school on Canterbury Road in 1958. "I liked Lanier and was not very enthusiastic about leaving, because it was such an excellent school with great academics, a good atmosphere, and a rich history and tradition. I had friends at Lanier, many of whom were in the band, so I wasn't looking forward to leaving for a brand new school.

"Certainly there were some cliques at Lanier," Mike said, "and South Macon was seen by many as being 'the other side of the tracks.' I believe that in the eyes of Lanier people and in selected neighborhoods of Macon we were seen as somewhat inferior or maybe second rate, but that was their misguided opinion of South Macon. My own opinion of South Macon was that of a blue-collar community, greatly influenced by two dominant churches, Mikado Baptist and Mabel White Baptist.

"On the other hand," he continued, "as much as I liked Lanier, going to Willingham was also a great experience for me after I transferred there in the 11th grade. Our student body, which was not nearly as large as Lanier's, was very compatible because we had all gone to similar neighborhood elementary schools in South Macon. I think we got closer to each other at Willingham since we were all from the same general area of town. There is no doubt that my life is better, having grown up in South Macon, and that is because of the people that I grew up with, the opportunities I was afforded, and the values and challenges that were presented to me. Additionally, though I wasn't involved in athletics, Willingham gave a lot more guys an opportunity to play high school sports."

Having quality teachers at every educational level helped Mike become an outstanding student. "Mrs. Florence Sanders, my first-grade teacher at Weir, gave me an educational foundation and an enjoyment for school which continued throughout my academic career. Her son, Sonny Sanders, and I went through school together. Discipline was instilled in me by Miss Eva Bates, my third grade teacher. Guyton Carr at Lanier Junior High gave me an appreciation for science and math. He was a man of character, discipline, and integrity.

"But the teacher who was, by far, the most influential in my development in high school was William Bell," Willoughby said. "He was my 11th and 12th grade English teacher and taught me the importance of reading and writing. He was an excellent instructor and helped us with organization." After his teaching career at Willingham ended, William Bell continued to move up the educational ladder in Bibb County, becoming principal at Central (formerly Lanier) High School and later becoming an administrator with the Bibb County Board of Education.

Not only did Mike have outstanding teachers shaping his academic life, but there were others who added to his development as a young man. "My parents, Q.A. and Ethel Willoughby, were the most influential people in my formative years. They gave me guidance, support, and taught me to have character and integrity. My pastor, E.C. Sheehan, taught me important principles in life and about faith in God.

"In my early years," Mike recalled, "I had a close-knit group of friends like Terry Land and Gary Purdy in the Mikado Avenue neighborhood. The three of us lived next door to each other, and we were constantly in each others' homes. I have fond memories of playing neighborhood football, baseball, and just goofing around together with those guys.

"My friends from Willingham days were Billy Winslette, Larry Jackson, Billy Lyles, and Eddie Battle, along with Robert Towe, who graduated from Lanier. Winslette, one of my best friends, and I played in the band together during our elementary school days at Weir, then at Lanier Junior and Senior, and finally at Willingham. Though I played a little baseball in elementary school, my life in those days was pretty much about music and school."

Willoughby said, "Growing up in the 1950's was just a great time for me. We would spend summers at my parents' home in North Georgia on Lake Burton. I was always very interested in music, but not rock and roll. Unlike most of my friends, I listened to progressive jazz and really liked the music of Gerry Mulligan, who played baritone sax, as well as Stan Kenton and Stan Goetz, also a sax player, and the brilliant pianist, Dave Brubeck."

* * * * * * * * * *

Mike Willoughby and Lurlene Garrett were married in June, 1964, after they graduated from Mercer University and waited five years after college to have children. The Willoughbys now have three grown daughters—Laura, Carla, and Camille, and the four Willoughby women can't say enough good things about their husband and father.

Lurlene, now married to Mike for over 40 years, gave some insights into the man she met at the fateful yearbook photo session. "Mike has an uncanny knack for goals and goal-setting. He won't quit at anything until his goal is achieved. His hobbies in recent years have revolved around what our daughters were doing, and whatever they did, Mike was into it 100 percent. Golf is a true love of Mike's, and he really likes hiking and snow skiing, but he hasn't had much time for those activities in recent years because of his involvement in our daughters' lives. Having hiked between villages in England in the past, one of Mike's goals is to hike across England from coast to coast after he retires.

"Mike is just the best son and father in the world," Lurlene said. "As a son, he is remarkable for having taken care of his father during his battle with Alzheimer's. Mike's dad died in 2000, at 86, while his mom, now 93, is living in Sterling, VA. Mike has been a great son to her as well. He simply adores his daughters, and he knows them better than most fathers because he has spent so much time with each of them."

Spending time with his daughters has been Mike's style of parenting for Laura, Carla, and Camille. To say Mike 'has been there for them' doesn't do him justice. Camille, the youngest Willoughby girl, has returned the favor by opening her apartment to her dad for several months since Mike and Lurlene have sold their house in Leesburg and are in the process of relocating. Camille commented, "When I'm too busy with schoolwork, Dad does the dishes. He vacuums when I'm too lazy, and he keeps things working around the apartment. Though he's not a real handyman-type, he tries to do a lot of things around the house, though he just can't figure out the plumbing or electricity. That's when he always calls the professionals.

"Dad oversees my bureaucratic issues like insurance, health issues, doctors' appointments, car maintenance, and other things that I seldom think of. He is a very generous man who has always provided for my sisters and me. I remember when I was growing up, he bought a new flute for me when I was in the seventh grade and a guitar when I was in high school. Throughout the years, he has driven me to ballet lessons, to and from college and boarding school before I had a car, and never grumbled about being my chauffeur."

Camille continued, "When I meet someone who is a patient of Dad's, they always praise him, saying they've been his patient for 30 years and will be so upset when he retires. It is obvious that he is very good to his patients and employees, and when he is on call, I have heard him on the phone speaking in a very gentle and friendly tone with his patients. That always happens, even if it turns out their call was not very important."

She concluded, "My dad gives me good advice when I go to him. He always listens, and though he is a very busy man, I feel very fortunate that I am able to spend this time with him."

Laura Willoughby, Mike and Lurlene's oldest daughter, concurred with her sister. "As a father, Dad is always supportive, rarely loses his temper, and he's so patient. His easy going, down-to-earth manner makes him loved and respected by a wide variety of people. Dad really doesn't like to hear people complain, but when they do, he will say something funny or supportive that will make that person feel better. My dad is a very generous man, both with his time and money. He would give my sisters and me practically anything we wanted, within reason, though he also taught us to value what we work for and not be extravagant. Dad recognized the importance of a good education and saw to it that my sisters and I were able to achieve our career goals by providing a great deal of financial support for our college and graduate school tuition."

Describing her dad when he is away from the office, Laura continued, "He loves anything and everything about food. I think the reason for his love for food is that he grew up in a Southern household. He likes a McDonald's Egg McMuffin or a gourmet meal at a five-star French restaurant. Dad is also a very good cook. He loves to marinate and grill meat, and he even likes to go shopping for food.

"Those of us who know my dad consider him to be a generous and kind father, husband, son, and a devoted physician. He will be best remembered for his sense of humor and his ability to make the best out of any situation. My parents have provided a wonderful home with great opportunities for my sisters and me."

Carla Willoughby, the second of three daughters and the only married Willoughby daughter, presented Mike and Lurlene with their first grandchild, Jonah, in December, 2004. Carla is presently a high school French and Spanish teacher and is considering graduate programs in environmental studies and creative arts. She has observed her dad's best qualities since childhood. "My dad's persistence and devotion to his responsibilities in his various roles throughout the years as a son, student, husband, doctor, father, and friend have endeared him to others. His ability to remain calm, centered, and even-tempered, even in the midst of an emergency, are important qualities that have helped him become such a highly-effective, well-respected physician. Dad is a bright, hard-working man who places the needs of others before his own, which is highly unusual in our current world."

Mike has several passions in life which are presently unfulfilled. For many years, he has dreamed of taking time for himself to walk across England from coast to coast, staying in bed and breakfast inns along the way, and simply enjoying the peace of a day where his only responsibilities are waking up, eating and drinking, and walking toward his destination. Carla said, "Dad deserves to have a day this simple, when his body and mind can feel the joy of being energized through long, meditative walks in nature, and when he also can feel the pure, healthy fatigue that comes at the end of a day filled with physical activity. Dad's life has been filled with too many endless chores, both inside and outside the workplace. The remarkable thing to me is that he has always faithfully completed his responsibilities without a squeak of disdain or resistance. He has unquestioningly accepted and faced each day with all of its responsibilities without complaining."

Mike's second passion is music, which has been tabled in order to fulfill his varied responsibilities as a father, son, doctor, and husband. Carla observed, "It is interesting to watch Dad when he sits down to eat or relax in a chair. He is consistently restless and fidgety, tapping his fingers rhythmically, as if a deep-down part of him knows that if he doesn't express even this tiny amount of his musical nature, he might go crazy. In high school, he played the trumpet, and throughout my life, I have seen him reach out at opportunities to fulfill this musical side of himself again, particularly with the piano. However, he has never really had the time for this creative growth due to his many responsibilities. With his focus, persistence, and meditative nature, it is easy to imagine my dad being successful in a musical career."

Mike's parents survived the Great Depression of the 1930's. Many parents in the 1950's and 60's placed great importance on their children's need to seek financial security and independence. Carla Willoughby surmised, "With different parents and different values in my dad's upbringing, he might have turned his acceptance of routine, responsibility, and hard work into the persistent, life-long musical practice that makes a great musician. I can imagine my dad as a jazz pianist or horn player, but considering the nature of my grandparents and the fact that they were products of the Great Depression,

Dr. Mike Willoughby

the arts would never have been encouraged as an honorable vocation. The medical profession, on the other hand, which promised financial security and an elevated social status, made sense as a direction that would have been encouraged for him.

"My father was born with the gifts of intelligence and perseverance needed to be successful in the medical profession. He is a doctor because he has powerful hands and was born with a healing touch," Carla concluded. "If healing powers were to be measured, not by how accurately a doctor intellectualizes an illness through diagnosis and treatment, but rather by the pure healing energy that emanates from a person, I know that my dad would be among the select few with true healing charisma. I know this because of the strength and gentleness of his touch and the energy that I have felt when holding his hand or receiving a fatherly embrace. Many nights as a child, I suffered from sleeplessness and nightmares, and the only thing that would soothe me would be my father gently rubbing my back so I could fall back asleep. In his hands, he carries all of the love and energy that have helped bring thousands of babies into the world."

Mike has practiced medicine since 1967, and physicians who have worked closely with him have nothing but the highest praise for their physician/friend. As medical partners for the past 26 years, Dr. H. Ronald McLeod has known Mike Willoughby well, as both a physician and friend. "I met Mike in 1968 when we were in post-medical school training at the Medical College of Virginia. He is very smart and combines that with a practical application of medical care for his patients. It is quite obvious that Mike generates respect and confidence in his patients; they know that they are safe in his care. Mike is, likewise, highly respected by his friends and colleagues and has been honored for being the past Chief of Staff of Loudoun Hospital Center, past-President of Loudoun County Medical Society, and past Chief of Department of OB-GYN for Loudoun Hospital Center.

"Mike has been a great friend for many years. He is honest; he loves medicine and is known as a compassionate physician who provides his patients with outstanding care. His dedication to medicine and his patients was demonstrated when he helped develop a plan of improving the care of indigent patients within our community. Mike was also a leader in improving the medical care of women in our community, regardless of their economic conditions," McLeod said.

"Mike Willoughby has been a great husband and father. He loves his family and has done everything he could to provide opportunities for his children to achieve their dreams. He is equally dedicated to providing the finest care possible for all of his patients."

As a medical partner with Dr. Willoughby for the past 10 years, Dr. Anne Brown noted that a common thread in Mike's life is the presence of women. The women in his life are his patients, his very smart wife Lurlene, his three daughters, Dr. Allen, Dr. Wever, and me. He is also a highly-responsible only-son to his elderly mom who lives in this area."

She continued, "Mike is definitely the head of our medical practice, and while he is, in many ways, a typical 'older' physician, he is very progressive. As a younger physician in our practice, I have never been made to feel that my opinions didn't count. I often ask him for advice, due to his many years of experience, and he occasionally asks for mine as well. I feel lucky to have had the good fortune of being his associate for the past ten years."

Though physicians and medical associates have always spoken in glowing terms about Mike, perhaps the one individual who has the best professional insights into the character of the doctor is Belle Ware, his administrative assistant and office manager for 27 years until her retirement four years ago.

Ware said, "Dr. Willoughby was such a great guy to work for. He reminds me of my father who was from Alabama, because both men are such Southern gentlemen. I like the way Mike has lived his life, and I respect the professional manner in which he conducts himself. For the many years that I worked for him, he treated all of his employees with great respect and took very good care of us in regard to financial benefits and retirement plans. The phrase 'you get what you pay for' held true in our office. While other offices down the street constantly had new faces and lots of turnover, the people in our office were happy working for Dr. Willoughby."

In his gynecological practice, Mike Willoughby had a way of making his clientele feel comfortable and relaxed. Belle Ware recalled, "He treated his patients with such compassion and care. He stood when his patients entered the room, he offered them a chair, put them totally at ease, and held the door for them when they left. Regarding the exams, our nurses would do the pre-exam before Dr. Willoughby came in for the actual exam. He always greeted them warmly and was a great listener. Through the years, he had such a dignified way for an undignified exam."

Ware's concluding statements, both professionally and personally, spoke volumes about her confidence in and appreciation for Dr. Mike Willoughby. "People who know Mike are extremely loyal to him. Professionally, my two daughters and two daughters-in-law are his patients, and nine of our eleven grandchildren have been born through his practice. That's how much our family thinks of him."

* * * * * * * * *

Mike and Lurlene Willoughby have lived most of their married life in the once-quaint Northern Virginia community of Leesburg, approximately 30 minutes west of Washington, DC. According to Lurlene, "When we first moved here, we could see for about 30 miles from our house, and there were cows in the pasture next to us. We live in Loudoun County, VA, which has battled Gwinnett County, GA, for the dubious title of the fastest growing county in the country. We have gone from living in a primarily pristine, rural community to a burgeoning, heavily-populated county with awful traffic. We are now in the process of moving from Loudoun County and are building a new home in Williamsburg. Hopefully, it will be completed by the end of 2005."

Mike's resume is impressive and noteworthy after serving his patients as an Obstetrician/Gynecologist for the past 32 years in Northern Virginia. He is a diplomate of the American Board of OB-GYN, is a member of the Medical Society of Virginia, the Loudoun Co. Medical Society, and the Virginia OB-GYN Society.

Moving from being the top student at the brand new A.R. Willingham High School in South Macon, GA, to one of the most highly-respected physicians in his field, Dr. Mike Willoughby's life has been full and rewarding. His life seems to have paralleled Proverbs 22:1, which says, 'A good name is rather to be chosen than great riches; and loving favor than silver or gold.' Without a doubt, Mike Willoughby has a good name and is highly esteemed and greatly respected by those who know him best.

He concluded, "I would like to be remembered as a good father, husband, and physician, and there is no question that the best things that I have ever done were marrying Lurlene, having three wonderful daughters, and becoming a physician."

Not a bad life for the smartest guy in the Class of 1960.

> *"We have nothing to fear, but fear itself."*
> *–Franklin D. Roosevelt*

Michael Willoughby, daughters Laura, Camille, Carla and son-in-law Edgar Arce

Reid to Mann to First

Thomas L. (Tommy) Reid, Jr.
Class of 1961

The bond that links your true family is not one of blood, but of respect and joy in each other's life.
–Richard Bach

Coach Billy Henderson, Willingham High School's football coach and athletic director, had his eye on Tommy Reid. After all, Reid was one of the best athletes in Macon, GA, in the late 1950's and early 60's. As a track athlete, he ran the 440-yard dash in 49.6 seconds. Reid earned a baseball scholarship to the University of Georgia as a shortstop and was a three-year starting guard and team captain of the Willingham Rams' basketball team.

For those reasons, Henderson approached Reid in the hallway at school and invited him to try out for football. Reid's reply was a classic as he told Henderson, "Coach, I don't think I want to play any sport where you have to have an ambulance on the sidelines." Thus, he stuck with the other three sports for the duration of his high school career.

Tommy Reid grew up on Grenada Terrace off Houston Avenue in a neighborhood filled with outstanding athletes. In fact, four guys from Grenada Terrace went on to become college football players - Wilton Marchman (UT-Martin); Bobby Bryant, (University of South Carolina), who was also a baseball player and a defensive back for the Minnesota Vikings; Pete Gaines (UGA); and Tommy Reid (UGA), baseball. In addition, four other athletes within a half-mile of Reid's house played major college football - Mark Bowen and Randy Wheeler (UGA), Doug Boyd (Clemson), and Terry Colson (BYU).

"To my friends and me, South Macon was just like any other part of town in those days," Reid said. "My parents provided everything that my sisters—Ann and Vicki—and I needed. We were healthy and happy. We had three meals a day and parents who loved us. I always had good clothes, because my dad worked at Joseph N. Neel's clothing store for over 40 years. I never thought about all the things that we didn't have. My dad, Thomas L. Reid, Sr., was my biggest fan when I was growing up. He kept newspaper clippings of my entire career. My mother, Marie Beasley Reid, stayed at home and raised the three of us. My dad died in July, 2002, but my mother is still living at age 87."

Pete Gaines, Tommy's cousin, remembered growing up together in South Macon. "We were first cousins who lived on Grenada Terrace and spent our spare time playing whatever sport was in season. Tommy is two years older than me, so I've always sort of tagged along like a little brother. In grammar school at St. Joseph's, I was fortunate enough to play one year alongside Tommy on the baseball and basketball teams. I still remember vividly playing basketball games on those old asphalt courts surrounded by a chain link fence, and our mothers insisted that we wear sock caps because of the cold. There we were – the only two players on the court wearing shorts and sock caps, looking like nerds. But we could dribble and shoot, and that deflected a lot of the cat calls and unsavory comments."

Gaines continued, "For two years at Willingham, Tommy and I were teammates in baseball and basketball (with no sock caps!). In those high school years, I began to appreciate the athletic talent that Tommy possessed. His quickness, speed, and coordination were obvious, but his competitiveness made him the total package. Tommy, as a baseball player at Georgia, and now with his true love, golf, has shown to be, in my opinion, one of the finest all-around athletes that Macon has ever produced. And he is as good a person as he is an athlete. Tommy's faith and integrity have served as an outstanding example to all that know him."

Tommy Reid's formative years were fairly routine, much like Gaines, Bryant, and countless other young athletes. "Growing up in South Macon was great," Reid recalled, "especially in the summers when we played Little League baseball at Ridley Field on Houston Avenue. We also played baseball all day long in the vacant lot behind Doug Boyd's house. I would ride my bike wherever there was a game. I lived close to Bruce School, and we would play basketball and baseball there all the time. We had one bat and one ball. I remember trying to play on the Little League field when the groundskeeper wasn't there, because we could hit home runs over the fence. On other fields, you had to hit it and sprint around the bases for a home run. We wanted to play on a field where you could hit it out of the park, but they didn't want us out there messing up the field and would run us off if they caught us playing there.

"Though baseball was my best sport, I still loved to play them all. I didn't play varsity football at Willingham, but I did play sandlot football for South Macon at Memorial Park on Second Street," Tommy said. "We had a good team with Gene Harrington and Buddy Petty. The Macon Recreation Department would furnish helmets and shoulder pads for the players, and we'd provide our own jerseys. There were no gyms for basketball games in the grammar basketball school leagues. All of the games were played on outdoor courts until your school qualified for the city tournament, and then you could play indoors at Memorial Park. We played our games outdoors in January and February. I remember that you would fall down and skin your knees on those asphalt courts. We didn't have the luxuries that kids have today."

One thing that Tommy Reid did have was plenty of athletic ability. Being Catholic, he played grammar school sports at St. Joseph's Elementary School. At Willingham High, he split time in the spring between track and baseball. In track, Reid long-jumped, ran the 440 and 220-yard dashes, along with the mile relay and the 440-relay and was named the MVP his senior year when

Willingham finished 2nd in the state in Class AAA. Willingham's 440-relay team of Bobby Bryant, Tommy Reid, Jimmy Hallman, and Anthony Wilkes was the fastest sprint relay team in the Macon area in those days. Personally, Reid ran a 49.6 in the 440 and finished second in the state meet his senior year.

As a baseball player at Willingham, Tommy was a three-year letterman and went on to play college baseball at the University of Georgia. In basketball at Willingham, Reid was a three-year letterman, was named Best Offensive Player for three straight years, and was team captain and Most Valuable Player his senior year. "Tommy Reid was one of the five greatest athletes to ever play at Willingham High School, and we had some great ones that came through there from 1958 through 1970," Coach Billy Henderson said. "I never could get him to give football a try, but he was tremendous in baseball, basketball, and track."

"I went to Lanier Junior High in the eighth and ninth grades while Willingham was being built," Reid recalled. "I was really glad when Willingham was started, but I experienced a little disappointment because my cousin, Madden Reid, and my uncle, Richard Reid, both went to Lanier. I had some great coaches at both Lanier and Willingham. I really liked Bobby Brown, Henry Middlebrooks, W.C. Jones, and Johnny Stallings a lot. In baseball, we played some terrific games against Lanier when they had their three big left-handed pitchers - Frank Hall, Charles (Bunny) Richardson, and Charles Haygood. They also had some other great players in Lula Belle Thomas, Robert Towe, Frank Cornelius, Lawrence Dover, and John Breedlove. We had a pretty good pitching staff as well with Jimmy Hammond, Bobby Matthews, Bobby Bryant, and Jimmy Hallman. They were backed up defensively by Buddy Petty, Tack Mote, Olie Goad, and LeRoy Mann. We always played close games against Lanier."

Reid excelled in the classroom at Willingham as well as on the playing field. He graduated from Willingham in 1961 with honors and was selected as a Senior Superlative. When he completed his high school career, he moved easily to the University of Georgia where he had noteworthy academic and athletic careers. Reid lived in the athletic dorm during his career at Georgia. "LeRoy (Mann), Gene (Harrington), and I roomed together at Georgia," Tommy remembered.

Georgia's baseball press guide in 1965 said of Reid, 'Tommy Reid is considered to be one of the best third basemen in UGA baseball history.' Reid said, "I always wanted to play baseball in college, and I thought about playing professionally when I finished at Georgia, but I didn't think I was big enough physically. I was about 5'10" and 170 pounds in college and played shortstop as a freshman and sophomore but moved to third base my last two years."

Reid was the team captain at UGA in 1965 and was the team's leading hitter in 1964, hitting .300 with 24 hits in 20 games, and was second on the team in RBIs. "Two of my greatest memories from playing baseball at Georgia are being involved in one of only two triple plays in school history and playing in a perfect game at Georgia. Don Woeltjen threw a perfect game against Georgia Tech in Atlanta in 1963, and we beat them 5-0. That was quite a thrill. I really enjoyed my career in Athens.

"'Big Jim' Whatley was my baseball coach at UGA from 1961-1965. He wasn't the greatest coach I've ever had, but I always liked him and, for some reason, he liked me as a player. I made All-SEC for him in 1965. Coach Whatley was one of the all-time great athletes at the University of Alabama where he lettered in four sports," Reid recalled.

Tommy Reid has always been aware of people who have been great influences on him, both athletically and personally. "There have been a lot of significant people in my life," he said. "They have shaped me into who I am today. My great-granddaddy, James Early Reid, helped build St. Joseph's Catholic Church. I have always admired my granddaddy, Thomas Jacob Reid, from a spiritual perspective. I received my spiritual foundation at St. Joseph's School and St. Joseph's Catholic Church.

"Coach Billy Henderson was the best baseball coach that I've ever played for," Reid recalled. "He was hard but fair and was always honest with me. He was a coach that could get everything out of you that you were capable of giving. He was the master motivator. I remember that Coach Henderson always had sliding practice in the preseason on those gray mats in the gym. Our teams were always strong in baseball fundamentals, even though he coached us without an assistant coach.

"My uncle, Richard Reid, was also influential in my development as an athlete. He was 10 years older than me so I always looked up to him. He inspired me to be as good as I could be. I used to watch him play at Mercer, and I wanted to be able to play like him. Today, Richard is in the Mercer University Athletic Hall of Fame as an athlete and the Macon Sports Hall of Fame as a coach."

Richard Reid remembered, "When Tommy was in elementary school at St. Joseph's, he suffered badly with asthma. For that reason, I felt that he would be greatly handicapped as an athlete. But as he grew older, he seemed to outgrow this terrible disease and began to excel in several sports. I can recall Coach Tom Porter at Lanier High saying that Tommy had the best stride of any quarter-miler he had ever seen. I also remember playing softball with him on the Buck Moore softball team. He was extremely fast and had great power to all fields. When I think about it, Tommy was probably the best athlete in our family. I always felt that his greatest talent was in baseball and one day he would become a major league player. However, after he received a compound fracture of the ankle, a professional career didn't become a reality. He later became an excellent golfer, though I could never understand how he could bat left-handed in softball and baseball but play golf right-handed. I still marvel at how far he can hit a golf ball. Tommy was an outstanding basketball player at Willingham, and I believe that he would have made a great football player. He gets his athletic ability from both sides of our family. His mother's brother, Ralph Beasley, was a great athlete at Lanier during the late 1940s."

Tommy Reid has been blessed throughout his sports career by playing for a virtual *Who's Who* of high school coaches. "I remember that my high school coaches," Tommy said, "were better than my college coaches. My high school coaches - Bobby Brown, Henry Middlebrooks, and Johnny Stallings – were all such good guys and impressive coaches. They were great influences on young guys like me, and I admired them all. They just seemed different from other men back in those days. They had a great effect on me, and I don't ever remember hearing a single one of my coaches ever cuss at us."

Reid continued, "I even admired Godfrey (Goot) Steiner who coached at Dudley Hughes Vocational School. He was a tough, hard-nosed guy, but he really went to bat for his players, and I liked that. When I broke my ankle one year, he sent me a letter to encourage me. I played American Legion baseball for him. He and Coach Henderson were total opposites as men and in the way they coached. Under their direction, both coaches helped me become a lot more competitive athletically."

Additionally, Reid loved and appreciated many of his high school teachers who likewise made lasting impressions on him. "Mary P. Smith was one of my favorite teachers. She taught history and was such a professional. She didn't tolerate any foolishness in class, and she had great command over all of those boys at Willingham. She was well respected and there was no back-talking Mary P. Smith," Reid said.

"In the classroom, Mike Garvin was a great algebra teacher. He could explain math better than any teacher that I've had. Years after high school, Mike and Carolyn Garvin sponsored us on a Marriage Encounter weekend that was presented by the Catholic Church. Susan and I became close friends with the Garvins."

* * * * * * * * * *

Tommy and Susan Reid have been married since August, 1965. The way they met is a story within itself. Reid, then 14, went to watch his cousin, Pete Gaines play in a state Little League baseball tournament in Cordele, GA. Susan Amsbaugh, along with Kathy Gaines, Pete's sister, Gail Carey, and several other girls from Macon, also went to watch Pete play. Tommy remembered their first meeting, "Susan dropped some money on the ground under the bleachers and then said to me, 'Little boy, will you pick up my dime?' I did, and the rest is, as they say, history."

"Tom and I have been together since forever," Susan Reid said. "The biggest factor in his life, besides his God-given ability and talent in sports, is his tremendous heart and passion for what he does. Tom loves every minute of every game in which he's involved. I was attracted to him, not for his athletic ability, but in spite of it. Little did I know when I first saw him at that Little League game in Cordele that God had sent me to that ballgame specifically to meet Tom Reid—and for him to pick up my dime under the bleachers.

"He hasn't always been fortunate enough to be on a winning team, but

Tom always played like he was. He played by the rules and always played hard. He has officiated for many years because the rules of the game mattered to him. Tom admired a lot of coaches in his career - from Billy Henderson at Willingham to Jim Whatley at Georgia. He was always a great player, but he was a team-player first and foremost."

Susan continued, "Tom is extremely disciplined. He believed that neat, clean uniforms were always a reflection on the game. Sloppy attire disparaged the game. He meticulously polished his baseball spikes, referee's shoes, and golf shoes. He would say, 'If you want to play good, you need to look good.' I guess that mentality has carried over, because Tom even polishes my shoes to this day.

"Tom has always been a caring, supportive husband and father. He has tried to instill a loving relationship with God in our sons, Tripp and Chris. He has modeled character and a great work ethic for them that are carrying over in their lives. Tom is a man of substance, and there is no pretense about him. He loves Macon, his hometown, Willingham High School, and he is still a die-hard University of Georgia Bulldog," Susan Reid concluded.

Today, the Reid's two sons are both married and have presented their parents with four grandchildren. Tripp (37), married to Margie and living in Birmingham, has a son and two daughters. Now living in Atlanta, Chris (32) is married to Aimee, and they have a son.

Tommy Reid began his vocational career in his hometown of Macon after a sterling career in baseball and graduating from the University of Georgia in 1966 with a BBA in Marketing and Accounting. "I went to work for Maxson Electronics, formerly the old Naval Ordinance Plant, right out of college," Reid said. "Allied Chemical Corporation bought that facility and hired me as the plant accountant. The plant made seat belts, and I became the comptroller of plant operations until the plant closed in 1984. I knew that I could either find another job in Macon or move elsewhere. Thus, we moved from Macon to Greenville, AL, which was right outside Montgomery. We ran North American Seat Belt operations and employed over 2,000 workers.

"In 1992, I was promoted within the company and moved to Maryville, TN, where we had two facilities that manufactured air bags," Reid said. "That plant had between 2,400 and 3,000 employees. I took an early retirement with 25 years of service in 1998 and then moved back home to Macon. I took one year off before going to work at Century Small Business Solutions as their general manager. There, I worked with Income Tax services and bookkeeping."

* * * * * * * * * *

With less job and work responsibilities, Tommy Reid now plays a lot of golf, and he plays it very, very well. Reid won the Georgia State Senior Amateur tournament at the West Lake Country Club in Augusta in 2001, defeating Bill Ploeger, the top ranked senior amateur in Georgia and one of the best senior amateurs in America. Reid is currently the twice-reigning senior club champion at River North Country Club (now Healy Point) in Macon and was both club and senior champion at Riverside Country Club (now The Brickyard at Riverside) in Macon. He also was the club champion several times at both Arrowhead CC in Montgomery, AL, and Green Meadow CC in Maryville, TN.

Currently playing golf to a zero handicap, Reid recently won the senior club championship again at Healy Point, his home course, and lost the overall club championship to Hal Johnson, a 30-something young golfer on the fourth hole of sudden death. Reid has had three holes-in-one in his illustrious golf career which, ironically, began in South Macon at Bridgewood Golf Course on Hartley Bridge Road.

When Reid won the Georgia State Senior Amateur in 2001, he vividly recalled, "On the last hole, it was a short par 5. I was tied at 2-under par with one guy (Spencer Sappington) and was one shot up on Bill Ploeger, one of the top senior amateurs in the country. Sappington had just birdied 16 and 17, and, on number 18 we all hit good drives on the short par 5. I remember Sappington asking me, 'You're gonna go for it in two, aren't you?' I didn't answer. So he hit his second shot in the water, and I laid up with a 7-iron, knocked it on the green in three, and two-putted to win the tournament. My nerves were shot!"

After Reid clinched the tournament, Bill Ploeger was quoted in *The Augusta Chronicle,* "Spencer and I shouldn't have let Tom back in the tournament, but we did, and he took advantage of it. But that's how you win golf tournaments."

Reid said, "I remember the nerves most of all. You want your parents and your friends and family to be proud of you, and I wanted to do well for all of them. My knees were nearly shaking I was so nervous! Of course, I always had butterflies when I was playing basketball or was in a big baseball game, so it's the same way in golf. You just have to try to relax enough to handle the pressure."

The Augusta Chronicle was not the only periodical to mention that Reid had won the Georgia Senior Amateur. Shortly after winning in Augusta, he got a phone call from Rick Reilly, a reporter from *Sports Illustrated,* who told Reid that the magazine wanted to run a short feature on him in their weekly *Golf Plus* section if that was OK. Reid obviously obliged. So on page G22 of the November 12, 2001—issue of *SI*—the same issue that featured the Arizona Diamondbacks celebrating their World Series victory over the New York Yankees, you'll find Macon's own Tom Reid in 'Faces In The Crowd.'

The feature read, "Reid, 58, manager of an income tax preparation firm, won the Georgia Senior Amateur by a shot with a 2-under-par 214 at West Lake Country Club in Augusta. Earlier this year, he took the Middle Georgia Senior and the Dixie Amateur, a better-ball event in which he teamed with Jimmy Allen, 53, also of Macon."

Sports Illustrated. 'Faces In The Crowd.' That's pretty impressive for a guy who grew up on Grenada Terrace and now plays golf at such a high competitive level.

In addition to his numerous club championships, Reid has also won other significant golf tournaments. Teaming with Maconite and friend Jimmy Allen in the highly-competitive Dixie Amateur in Macon, Reid and Allen defeated the perennially strong team of Gay McMichael and Jim Stuart in sudden-death in 2001. Reid rolled in an uphill, 12-foot putt on the first hole to claim the title.

"I first knew Tommy Reid through my first cousin, LeRoy Mann, who played baseball with Tommy at Willingham," Jimmy Allen remembered. "I would go to Athens and watch them play ball at Georgia. We became personal friends playing golf at Riverside Country Club. We played our first tournament together in the very first Cherry Blossom Tournament ever held in Macon."

"The thing that has impressed me the most about Tommy is that he is highly competitive. Like a lot of people, he wants to win very badly, but he also wants to play against the best players around to measure how good he can be. That just makes him play even harder. But as competitive as Tommy is, he just really enjoys the game.

"He is solid in every aspect of the game, but I would say his strength is that he is so long off the tee. He is awfully strong to be 61 years old. If there was ever a flaw in his game, it would have been his putting, but even that has gotten better since he went to that 'old man's putter.' Really, I believe his problem was that he couldn't see well enough before he went to the extra-long putter," Allen said.

Reid has never been one to boast or brag about his accomplishments, whether in baseball, golf, or any other sport. But Allen recalled one incident when Reid got close to bragging. Close, for Tommy Reid. "The Georgia State Senior Amateur's final round was played on a Saturday in Augusta, and we had talked on Friday. On Saturday, I was playing golf at Riverside in Macon and my phone rang. It was Tommy and he said, 'What are you doing?' We talked a few minutes and before we hung up, he said, 'Well, I won.' And that was it. No bragging. No details. Just, 'Well, I won.'"

Allen concluded about his friend, "The thing I've always liked about Tommy is that whatever he does, either in sports or in life, he does it right."

Tommy Reid has always been a man who had his priorities in line. God, family, and work took top billing in his life. Reid's older son Tripp has learned many life-lessons from his dad, and most of them have been through their involvement in athletics. "I remember arguing with and resisting my Dad over his advice to me about baseball and golf when I was a teenager. My mom sat me down and told me, 'Your daddy has been playing this game before you were born, and he knows exactly what he is doing, so you really ought to listen to him for your own good.' Since then, I don't argue anymore. I just listen to what he says, and he is proven right most of the time."

Tommy never got mad about any poor plays that his sons made on the ball field, but he couldn't stand it if they didn't hustle. Regardless of anyone's ability or skill, Reid always believed there was no excuse for not hustling. "My dad thought that a bad or disrespectful attitude in any sport was worse than unforgivable," Tripp said. "He would say we 'could go on home' or 'go back to the car and stay there' if we pouted or didn't have a decent attitude," Tripp recalled. "Today, I really respect the way he treated me back in those days.

"Our family was never rich," Tripp Reid said, "but dad always bought Chris and me the best sporting goods, baseball gloves, shoes, and golf equipment available. I always felt rich! For a while when I was growing up, I think all the golf clubs, balls, clothes, and golf shoes I had were won by my dad in golf tournaments. I remember actually having to pay for my first set of golf clubs after I got married. I still have a Ping putter that dad got for me when someone in his playing foursome, who had just bought it in the pro shop, missed a putt, then broke the putter, and threw it into the woods on the first hole. Dad retrieved it, and had it re-shafted. I remember how excited I was when he brought that new putter home to me. I would love to know whose putter I have had for over 20 years.

"Dad always emphasized looking like a ball player. I remember how he taught me to roll up and tuck my leggings and socks into my baseball pants so they wouldn't 'ride down' during a game, and it always worked. He used to clean and polish my baseball cleats and golf shoes if I didn't take proper care of them. I think that is an 'old school' discipline that he may have picked up from my grandfather who always dressed impeccably."

Tripp Reid remembered the first Macon/Middle Georgia Golf Tournament at Bowden Golf Course. "My dad led the tournament after the first day and, on the final day of the tournament, lost on the second hole in a sudden-death playoff to Brian Persons. Most people may not remember that Dad had to make a 50-foot putt on number 18 just to get into the playoff. On the first playoff hole, Dad hit a drive on No. 1 over 300 yards, and this was in the days of the persimmon-wood driver and balata ball. He then hit a sand wedge to within a foot of the cup. All of us thought he had won, but Persons then made an incredibly long putt for birdie to halve the hole and stay alive. Dad was incredibly disappointed after the loss and told my mom that he wanted to win it for his sons. It didn't matter though, because he did not need to prove anything to either of us.

"Dad called me after the final round of the 2001 Georgia Senior Amateur Championship," Tripp said, "and told me that he had won. He had beaten Bill Ploeger, a fine gentleman-golfer who was the No. 2-ranked senior amateur in the country at the time. That was such a highlight! Dad remembered that afterwards there were men who would walk up to him and greet him and call his name as if they were still cheering for him."

Tripp recalled, "My dad taught me so much about how to play golf. He never minded playing golf with someone of lesser ability and never made them feel inferior regardless of how poorly they played. However, slow players even to this day drive him up the wall. He always told me, 'You earn your right to be deliberate on the course.' He believes if you can shoot in the 70's or if you are a decent player, then you can take the time to check the wind, plumb the putts, etc. But if you can't break 100, all of that deliberation just hurts your game

2001 Georgia Senior Amateur Champion, Tom Reid, hoists the trophy.

and slows down the course for everyone else. Today, I probably sound just like him when I see unnecessarily slow players on a golf course. He would also tell me that 'people playing in golf carts are not always faster players,' and he's right."

Reid and his sons spent many summer afternoons at Riverside Golf & Country Club playing golf together, and as much as the elder Reid enjoyed the friendships and competition there, he always thought there were obvious and numerous changes on many of the holes that were either unfair or poor tests of ability. Tom would go stand over in the trees and show his sons where a tee box should be moved. It's interesting to note that Riverside has been purchased by local businessmen and has made many improvements like the ones Reid suggested to his sons.

"My dad always made us practice the hard shots and play from the back tees, so when we played in competition, it didn't seem quite as hard," Tripp recalled. "I remember that the golf professionals at Riverside always wanted him to play with them in tournaments because he was such a good player, and it was fun to play golf with him.

"Dad told me that his only regret in athletics was not following through on trying to play professional baseball. He thought his eyesight was not good enough, but I don't think I have ever seen anyone with such poor eyesight that had such amazing hand-eye coordination."

Handling the mental part of athletics was one of the things that Tommy Reid did so well. One year, Tripp was playing baseball at Vine-Ingle Little League and caught a line drive while playing first base. The runner on first had already taken off for second. There was so much commotion that the younger Reid panicked. Amid the screaming and commotion from both sets of bleachers, Tripp recalled, "I remember the image of my dad running down the third base line away from all of the uproar and 'mouthing' the words to me, 'Just step on the bag.' I think that was the only double play that I ever made, and it was due to my dad's calmness under pressure. He is, by no means, a patient person, but he is amazingly focused and rational during the heat of competition."

Tripp concluded about his dad, "If I can get the USGA to outlaw that long putter that he uses, I might be able to beat him on the golf course some day. Otherwise, it seems that I am going to have to wait until he is in his 80's. Then, if he shoots his age, I will still have to play well to beat him."

In the days before Reid became an accomplished golfer, he was one of the best slow-pitch softball players in the area. Softball in those days relied more on speed, defense, moving runners along, and fundamental skills rather than the power-hitting, home run-derby style of game that is played today. When it came to hitting to all fields, playing defense, and taking the extra base, Tommy Reid was one of the best.

"I played softball on the premier team in Middle Georgia – Buck Moore's Service Station," Reid recalled. "We won tournaments all over the South and had guys like Charles Thurston, LeRoy Mann, Eddie Dudley, Donnie Veal, Clyde Zachary, Richard Reid, W.C. Jones, Winnie Banks, Pug Churchwell, Olie Goad, Kenny Smith, and Lossie Collins. Our coach was Paul Barnes, Buck Moore's son-in-law. Our team won the ASA Regional in the South in 1968 and then drove our cars to the ASA World Slow-Pitch Softball Tournament in Jones Beach, NY. We lost the first game 19-18 and then lost the second game 2-1. After that second loss, we turned right around and drove all the way back to Macon! But we still had a great team."

Reid's son Tripp reminisced about softball and his dad's team. "I remember so many of the guys that he played softball with on Buck Moore's softball team in the 70s. I particularly remember getting the mumps after a long weekend of bat boy duty at a tournament and then giving the mumps to W.C. Jones, the biggest guy on the team. That was not a good time to be a bat boy on my dad's team."

Reid's long-time teammate, roommate, and friend, LeRoy Mann, remembered Tommy Reid fondly. "Tom was an outstanding athlete who excelled in baseball, basketball and track, but possibly his best sport of all was golf. Tom took up golf seriously after his high school days because Willingham did not have a golf team back then. In fact, Macon only had two golf courses that were open to the general public. Bridgewood was located in South Bibb County and was a new course while Bowden Golf Course, located in extreme East Macon, was like driving all the way to another county. Today Tom is a 'scratch' golfer."

Mann continued, "At the University of Georgia, Tom lettered on the freshman baseball team because freshman were not allowed to play varsity sports in 1962. Tom became a three-year letterman on the varsity. While at Georgia, we won fifteen times and lost only once to Georgia Tech, our biggest rival. I remember that in our senior year Tom was elected team captain and earned the Most Valuable Player award."

One special season in Tommy's career at Georgia was his freshman year— 1962. "We won something like 16 games and only lost three or four times. Our freshman coach was an ex-professional baseball player. He was a very competitive guy who absolutely hated losing. He would constantly yell and harass the opposing team's pitcher during the game. I often expected the other pitcher to fire a pitch at the coach in our dugout because of his relentless needling. During a game against Georgia Tech in Atlanta, they rallied to make it a close game. There were some controversial calls that did not go our way, as well as some taunting from the Tech players that set our coach off. He paced in our dugout and told us that if we lost the game that he expected everyone to grab a bat and go after a Yellow Jacket. Fortunately, we won the game and tempers subsided. I am still convinced that he was serious, and a real donnybrook probably would have occurred if Tech had beaten us. Two years later, the coach was dismissed from Georgia because of his involvement in a barroom brawl."

Mann continued, "Tom and I were friends at Willingham, but it was not until we arrived at Georgia that we became close friends. Baseball was the bond that formed that relationship and, by the time we graduated, Tom was my best friend. Aside from his athletic skills, Tom was a genuine person. He was always dependable, trustworthy, honest, a straight arrow, and caring. Tom was always a competitor and was one who always gave it his all. He played hard, but he also played fairly and set a good example for others to follow. Tom was such an encourager, and I've never heard him be critical of a teammate. He is a special man and one that I am proud to call a best friend."

Chris Reid, the younger of Tommy and Susan's two sons, expressed great admiration and respect for his parents. According to Chris, "My parents met in elementary school, they dated most of their high school days, and followed one another to the University of Georgia. They were married in Macon and started their family there. My father worked for the same company for 25 years and moved with the company three times during those years. He supported our family, excelled in athletics, financed college educations for Tripp and me, made sure we had an excellent family vacation every year, and always made time for my mom and him to have dinner together or just take a simple weekend trip together. Dad made sure that the important things in life were handled first."

Chris remembered the difficulty that the family had when they left Macon in 1984 during his seventh grade year. "Allied Signal was relocating and moving their operations out of Macon, which meant that my dad would need to choose another place to move our family. I had always thought that, like my mom and dad, I would grow up in Macon, not necessarily in the same neighborhood, but close to my parents and grandparents. We were lucky to live close to my grandparents because we got to see them on a daily basis, enjoy meals together, and spend time helping them get along. I think my Mom and Dad chose that home so we could be close to them."

"My dad has two sisters who had moved away from Macon years ago, so he was the one that my grandparents relied heavily upon. But sadly, the time came for our family to move to Montgomery, AL, and now it was Auburn vs. Alabama instead of Georgia vs. Georgia Tech. Now it was public school vs. private, Catholic school, and it was new house vs. old house."

"After being gone for 14 years and living in two different cities, my parents moved back to Macon in 1998," Chris recalled. "My dad took the opportunity to work for a past colleague who held him in very high regard, but I believe the main reason they moved back to Macon was to help my grandparents who were getting older. My grandfather passed away in July, 2002, but not before meeting and attending the baptism of my son and his great-grandson, Andrew Thomas Reid. I know my dad was glad to be back in Macon, and, though he misses his father very much, he helps his mother every day."

Chris concluded, "Fathers like mine will always be good fathers, and they usually turn into 'great' grandfathers. I am deeply indebted to my dad for helping me to become a good father, too."

In addition to being a good dad and husband, Tommy Reid was a good brother as well. Tommy's younger sister, Vicki Reid Bronson, had many great memories of growing up in South Macon and being a part of the Reid household. "Having Tommy as a big brother gave me both the best of times and the worst of times," Vicki laughed. "As children, we played outdoor games when Tommy wasn't engaged in organized sports. How lucky we were to have real athletes on our teams! I still remember playing football with Tommy, Mark Bowen and our cousin, Pete Gaines. We even had Bobby Bryant, who became a professional football player. But as good at sports as these boys were, it was common for them to include the girls on their backyard teams. For me, as a teenager, there was probably nothing better than to be the younger sister of a popular athlete, and where else could you find a better place for boyfriends and friends who were boys?"

Vicki continued, "I remember feeling a certain jealousy of Tommy when we were young. But now, as an adult, I can look back and realize that during that time in our history, exceptional male athletes were given a lot of attention. With all of the attention that Tommy received, I never remember thinking that he was impressed with himself. I don't even remember thinking of him as competitive; I just remember him being really good at what he did.

"But even with a measure of jealousy regarding Tommy," Vicki said, "I was always proud to have him as my brother – except once. Tommy and I were students at the University of Georgia at the same time, and it was not uncommon for me to attend the Dawgs' baseball games. I remember one occasion when Georgia was playing South Carolina (I think). The pitcher for USC had a prosthetic leg. And I couldn't believe it when Tommy bunted. I was outraged and thought, 'How could he do that?' That incident helped me to understand Tommy's competitive spirit, but I still want to believe that he was just following orders from the third base coach."

Vicki concluded, "Our older sister Ann and I laugh at our memories from years ago of our 'bratty' brother. We also admit that as grown man, Tommy is as gentle and sweet as they come. One hug from him can melt our hearts and almost bring us to tears. Tommy's athletic prowess may have diminished somewhat with age, though he is an amazing golfer, but he continues to strive to be the best he can be in all that he does – and we both love him for that."

* * * * * * * * * *

Athletics, without question, has been a major part of Tommy Reid's life since his early days growing up on Grenada Terrace. In addition to being one of the best golfers in the Middle Georgia area, he still stays active by officiating high school football games in the fall. He doesn't have the blazing speed or the 'eye at the plate' that he had during his high school or college days, but his competitive fires continue to burn within.

"I can recall the five greatest highlights of my athletic career," Tommy said. "They are:

1.   Winning the Georgia State Senior Amateur Golf tournament in Augusta against Bill Ploeger of Columbus;

2.   Running in the state high school track meet, and our 440-relay team finishing second in the state at Columbus;

3.   Scoring from second base on a bunt. I saw Coach Henderson, who was coaching third base about halfway down the line, waving me home. What a thrill that was!

4.   Being involved in a triple play in high school with LeRoy Mann and Buddy Petty;

5.   Being involved in a perfect game my junior year at UGA behind the pitching of Don Woeltjen. We beat Tech that day."

Life for Tommy and Susan Reid is very good today. They regularly travel to Atlanta and Birmingham to see their two sons and four grandchildren who are all pretty good little athletes in their own right. A thoughtful Tommy Reid reflected on his life, "I want to be remembered as a good Christian, a good son, a good husband, dad, and granddaddy, and as a good competitor and team player."

To all who know Tommy Reid, he is all of those things and much, much more.

Tom and Susan Reid with grandchildren: Josh, Eliza, and Abby. Not pictured is Andrew.

Dartmouth Prof

Prentice L. Knight, III, PhD
Class of 1965

*"And you shall know the truth, and the truth shall
set you free."*
                                        –John 8:32

"The unexamined life is not worth living."
                                        –Socrates

Prentice Knight has been around some real men in his lifetime, men like Joe Swain, Billy Henderson, the coaching staff at Willingham, and his father, Prentice Knight, Jr. All were outstanding role models and were highly influential in Prentice's development, but it was a Methodist preacher named Tom Stroud who really planted the seeds of insight into maximum manhood that blossomed later in Prentice, III's, life.

"Tom Stroud was my minister at Bloomfield Methodist when I was a teenager," Prentice said. "I primarily went to church in those days because some of my friends went, but you couldn't help but listen to Rev. Stroud's sermons. He was always talking with young people, and he spoke a lot about love, empathy, and forgiveness in a practical and believable manner, rather than a sugary or preachy sort of way. He was a smiling, gentle man with a calm demeanor, but he was also strong and confident. Slowly, I came to admire Rev. Stroud and sensed that my cultural image of what a real man should be – strong, tough, silent, athletic, highly competitive, and winner-take-all - didn't fit all real men. Over time, I began to realize that my image of a real man didn't even fit my father who was strong, tough, and athletic on the outside, but also funny, gentle, and tender-hearted on the inside. Tom Stroud planted a seed that blossomed much later into the realization that Jesus is the true model for a real man – principled, resolute, and courageous, but also gentle, empathetic, forgiving, and loving."

Prentice grew up in Sherwood Forest in the Bloomfield community, attended Winship School from grades one through five, and Agnes Barden Elementary School in grades six and seven. His family attended Bloomfield United Methodist Church. Prentice and Linda Harris, a beautiful young McEvoy coed and cheerleader, began to date while they were in high school and married while Prentice was a student at the University of Georgia.

"My parents, Prentice L. and Agnes Gay Knight, were the most influential people in my life," he stated. "They raised five children and stayed married for nearly 50 years until my father's death. They really loved each other, and they showered me with love from the day I was born until the day they died, my dad in 1995 and my mom in 2002. My parents gave me a strong sense of well-being and self-worth, while living full, passionate lives and demonstrating that life, in all of its uncertainty, complexity, richness, and wonder, should be embraced. They set high expectations for me to create a meaningful life but gave me great leeway to decide what that meaningful life would be. My mom and dad worked hard and expected the same from me. They were fun, spontaneous people who brought much joy to their kids and to other people around them. Like everyone, they had their problems and weaknesses, but they were wonderful parents. I wish I had more of their strengths."

Prentice Knight was one of the exceptional young athletes being groomed in the elementary school leagues of the Bibb County school system back in the late 1950's and early 60's. "I played sports from the fifth through the twelfth grades and had many coaches who were positive influences on me. Joe Swain was my grammar school coach at Agnes Barden and was a great teacher/coach who made sports fun. It was through Joe Swain's influence that I first developed a real sense of team, teamwork, and an organized group-purpose. He also stressed individual dedication and achievement within that team framework. At Willingham, Billy Henderson, Mike Garvin, Johnny Stallings, Dave Hill and others expanded on the lessons that Joe Swain initiated. However, the greatest lessons from my Willingham coaches were that a person can give more and achieve more than he realized, and there is a strong correlation between hard work and good results. From Billy Henderson, in particular, I learned the importance of the psychological dimension of achievement—vision, inspiration, and dedication.

"My close friends in high school – Claudie Brown, Wayne Johnson, Mackie Bryant, Dickie Maddox, Chipper Murphy, and several others—had a huge, positive impact on me. They were typical teenagers in that they were silly, fun-loving, and sometimes did stupid things - and we were all just a bunch of 1960's punks! But, they were good people with good values. My close friends were not into drugs, hard drinking, or trouble just for trouble's sake, so I wasn't seriously tempted to be either. These guys were good students who valued academic achievement. In retrospect, I can see that my circle of close friends helped me in an informal, subconscious way to define reasonable limits, set positive expectations, and see the world as filled with opportunities. And, of course, they were fun, supportive, and caring, as all good friends are."

Knight continued, "There was another group of students at Willingham that also had an important influence on me and believed that intellectual curiosity and achievement were important. Some of those classmates are Terry Moore, Tommy Mason, Kenneth Hunt, Gary Lawson, Danny Kennedy, Tommy Hendrick, Donnie Coleman, Orrin Carstarphen, Larry Powell, Jerry Peavy, Jimmy Hightower, Stan Gunter, Frankie Hollingsworth, Dennis Dove, LaDon Walker, Cary Adams, and others. Most of us were together in college prep classes and belonged to the Beta Club. We challenged and supported one another academically. I admired these guys and wanted to be like them in the classroom."

As a long-time high school and college friend, Claudie Brown recalled meeting Prentice Knight. "I first heard of Prentice Knight when I was a seventh grade football player at Bruce School, and we were about to play Agnes Barden, probably our biggest rival. This was pretty unusual in those days, but our principal, Charles Deaton, went to scout a game that Barden was playing and videotaped it for us. He came back and gave us a full scouting report, telling us if we were going to beat Barden, Prentice Knight was the one we were going to have to stop. Understand, this was elementary school football in 1959."

In high school, Prentice Knight was a special football player, earning a varsity letter as a sophomore on a team that included UGA-bound Pete Gaines and Mark Bowen, as well as Bobby Bryant, who went on to the University of South Carolina and the Minnesota Vikings. Prentice's coaches agreed that he, too, would have been a major college prospect if his knees had stayed healthy. The last game of his senior year at Willingham was the last football game Prentice Knight would play.

Prentice and Claudie Brown played all sports against each other in elementary school but became the closest of friends when they entered Willingham High in the eighth grade. "We became teammates in football, basketball, and track in high school," Brown said, "and then went to the University of Georgia and roomed together until Prentice and Linda Harris married. Prentice is one of those people who is intelligent, as well as studious, but has a great sense of humor and knows how to have fun. He was never the life of the party but would tell a joke if two or three friends were around. For the past 45 years, he has been one of the most loyal friends anyone could have.

"Prentice is the ultimate professional," Claudie stated. "He's easy to get to know, he's really accepting of all types of people, and he has been all over the world, but I've never known him to be condescending to anyone. Unlike many of us from South Macon, Prentice was fairly nonreligious when we were young, but as an adult, he has really become a man of great faith with strong Christian values. He leads a Bible study with well over 100 people from his community."

How Prentice chose geography as his college major is a story within itself. Claudie and Prentice were sitting around during a snowy, winter afternoon watching a college basketball game on television, when talk turned to the fact that neither of them had declared a college major. After weeding out several subject areas, they flipped a coin, and Claudie chose math. Prentice decided on geography because he liked the subject. Claudie maintained that Prentice selected geography because he made an 'A' in the introductory course and that it was a 'football course.' Either way, Prentice stayed the course and ultimately made a great life for himself and his family. The fact that he and Linda have been married for over 37 years is a testament of their commitment."

Prentice has been a success in life because of his dedication to whatever task he chose. He has been strongly committed to his family, his church, and the pursuit of his education. Brown joked, "I've always wondered if Prentice was a little lazy, because he stayed in school so long getting advanced degrees. I figured that he kept on going to school because he didn't want to get a real job."

Brown recalled their days in high school when Prentice Knight was a guy whom lots of girls wanted to date. "He asked Linda Harris, also a senior, for a date. She was thrilled to go out with him, but Prentice didn't call or ask her out again for a while. When he finally called back, Linda broke two dates with other guys to go out with him for the second time."

Prentice Knight graduated from the University of Georgia in 1969 with a BS degree and a major in geography and a MA in 1971 from the University of Georgia. He earned his Ph.D. from the University of Illinois in 1977, with specialization in economic development and economic geography.

* * * * * * * * * *

Prentice's community service and civic involvement come primarily through his church, Franklin Presbyterian Church, a small church with about 100 active members. "Our church has several strong programs that help people in need, both locally and around the world," Prentice said. "My family supports and strongly believes in these programs. Our daughter Marla has been a leader in our mission programs and has organized mission trips for our church to Nicaragua, Mexico, and eastern Kentucky.

"One of my favorite activities is teaching our adult Sunday School class. Actually, I function more as a facilitator who has responsibility for selecting biblical and Christian topics, developing a framework for discussing the topics, and then engaging the class in discussion and debate on those subjects. Our class is a thoughtful, tolerant group of Christians who have diverse perspectives on religious questions and enjoy discussing these diverse points of view in an atmosphere of mutual love and respect. This class has helped me mature as a man and a Christian."

Prentice has traveled extensively throughout the world as part of his work. Often, Linda travels with him, and they will tack a vacation on the end of a business trip. Additionally, the Knight family, including their two daughters, Marla Knight-Dutille and Rachel Knight Flowers, along with their sons-in-law, takes a family vacation outside the U.S. every 12-18 months. According to Prentice, "We have recently taken family vacations to Italy, Peru, and Costa Rica. Our 2005 family vacation will be to London and Germany. We have discovered that the earth has such great beauty and enormous diversity, environmentally, economically, culturally, and politically. Experiencing that beauty and diversity is both enriching and humbling. International travel, particularly when you can get away from tourist hotspots and experience local people and their culture, helps develop better understanding and appreciation of not only other places and people, but also of home."

* * * * * * * * * *

Sherwood Forest, Prentice's subdivision, was a section of Bloomfield, a rapidly-expanding, newer neighborhood of South Macon. His grammar school, Agnes Barden, served Bloomfield whose residents were quite similar socioeconomically. "Our neighborhood was mostly middle and lower-middle income families with children and solid family values," Knight said. "To my knowledge, there was essentially no crime, and I always felt safe. Most mothers stayed at home and kept an eye on the neighborhood and the children. My parents let me roam throughout Bloomfield to visit friends and play pick-up sports. When I wasn't in school, I would often be in the neighborhood playing without my parents knowing exactly where I was, although they knew my friends and the places where I could usually be found. The same was true for my friends, and we just considered this the natural state of affairs. My close friends through the seventh grade all lived in Bloomfield, and I have very fond memories of hanging out, playing sports, riding bicycles, or going roller-skating at Durr's Lake with neighborhood friends like Ricky Spires, Larry Boatright, Bobby Floyd, Mike Luzier, Bill Burnett, Doug Benton and others."

Knight felt he grew up in a safe, supportive, friendly neighborhood where he had great boyhood friends. "In retrospect, I see that ours was a very homogenous neighborhood, totally white and mostly Protestant families with parents who had high school educations, worked hard, and believed in the American Dream. There were no black people in Bloomfield or in our schools, and our view of blacks was based mostly on negative stereotypes. From our experience, we assumed that the world that really mattered was made up of white, Anglo-Saxon, Protestant Americans of Southern heritage. This continued to be my general assumption through college until I went off to graduate school at the University of Illinois."

Growing up in Bloomfield, Knight knew that South Macon was considered the 'other side of the tracks' when compared to North Macon, but he never felt any sense of inferiority. "It was my vague perception, right or wrong, that South Macon was more alive, more genuine, and harder working than North Macon. I had very positive feelings about Willingham, which is what defined South Macon for me as a teenager. The fact that Willingham consistently beat Lanier in football, the only sport that really mattered in South Macon in those days, was 'proof positive' for me as a teenager that South Macon was somehow better than the rest of Macon on some elemental level. Of course, a psychologist might well enjoy analyzing my teenage perceptions about this."

Prentice Knight had numbers of teachers and friends who greatly influenced his academic career and personal life. Between Bloomfield and Willingham, his life was greatly enriched and constantly entertained. "Mrs. Abby, my fourth-grade teacher at Winship School, had that rare gift of making each pupil feel special and instilling young students with the feeling that learning is a good thing and can be fun. She was inspiring, supportive, warm, and caring. My early memories of school are positive, and many of those memories are associated with Mrs. Abby.

"Kemp Mabry, who later got his doctorate and taught at Georgia Southern University, was a math teacher at Willingham and was a no-nonsense, get-the-job-done teacher who set high expectations for his students. Mr. Mabry gave honest and direct appraisals of your work but did so in a matter-of-fact manner that did not belittle or anger you. He used praise sparingly, so his praise had a powerful impact. I recall the time that he separated out a few advanced math students in our class to work with self-instructional workbooks, and I distinctly remember the day that he handed a test back to me and said, 'Mr. Knight, you did very well on this test. It's time for you to join the 'big boys.' He immediately sent me off to the lunchroom to join a small group of the math 'big boys' who worked as a small self-directed group using self-instructional workbooks. I worked damned hard on those math workbooks because I was determined not to disappoint Mr. Mabry or suffer the embarrassment of having to leave the 'big boys.' Our small group did not focus entirely on math, however. I distinctly remember us discussing and debating the Vietnam War, which was the first time that I engaged in serious dialogue about the war."

Claudie Brown graduated from Willingham with Prentice and roomed with him at UGA until Knight was married. "Claudie was my best friend in high school. We were quite different in many ways. Claudie was loud—including his attire—was extroverted and full of energy. He loved being the center of attention, while I was quieter and more of an introvert. However, I think our personalities complimented each other, and our common interests in sports drew us to friendship. In retrospect, I now see that the qualities that I admired in Claudie in high school are the same ones that I admire in him today. He speaks the truth as he sees it in a blunt, unvarnished way (though some might say 'too much so'), he is fiercely loyal to his friends, and he loves to act gruff and crusty but is actually tender-hearted. My mother had those same qualities. Claudie works harder than anyone I know at maintaining contact with old friends, and in keeping our old gang informed about one another. Friendships, old and new are at the center of his being. We are still close friends today, and he and his wife Janice visit Linda and me in Kentucky every year.

"Wayne (Buffalo) Johnson and I were close friends throughout our Willingham careers. He was easy going and fun, always laughing, but he was also the hardest-working, most dedicated person I knew. Wayne literally willed himself to be a great football player, and in the process, earned all-state and honorable mention All-America honors and won a football scholarship to Florida State.

Charles Byrd taught senior English literature at Willingham, and Prentice got his first understanding of what a good college course would be like. "Mr. Byrd really wanted his students to learn, and more importantly, he wanted us to learn how to think. He worked hard to excite students about ideas and literature. He challenged us to understand that truth often has many layers and multiple perspectives, but at the end of the day, it was up to the student to demonstrate interest, work hard, and to want more. If you did, then he was ready to help you journey farther by sharing more of his intellectual insight and excitement. If you didn't, well, that was your choice. Just don't get in the way of the rest of the class.

"Mr. Leonard Pridgeon, our chemistry and physics teacher, gave me my first insight into the mind of a scientist. Prior to Mr. Pridgeon's class, I thought of science primarily as subject matter, but from his class I learned that science is also about curiosity, analytical rigor, objectivity, intellectual passion, creativity, and the scientific method.

"Ricky Spires was a good friend in grade school and high school," Prentice recalled. "We lived in the same neighborhood, both attended Agnes Barden School, and we played sports and hung out together on weekends and during the summer. As teenagers, we went to church together and had our first dates together. I was 15 when Ricky got his driver's license, and that access to an automobile provided me with my first real taste of the freedom that a car can provide."

The Class of 1965 at Willingham was an excellent class in many ways. The football team, heavily-laden with '65 class members, led Willingham to an 8-1-1 record, the best in school history, and a second consecutive win over Valdosta, a national high school powerhouse, and a fourth straight win over arch-rival Lanier. Academically, the class was one of the strongest in Willingham's brief history as well. Prentice remembers his friends in the Class of '65 as being a bunch of 'characters.' "You could fill a book with great stories about these guys. People like Carl Summers and Mike Luzier who could continuously think up and do things that I could not even imagine. Richard Whitfield was the best joke-teller I have ever known. I remember him telling hilarious jokes non-stop for two to three hours on football trips. I remember Barney Kinard who had a gift for giving people nicknames that matched their physical characteristics, like Chipper Murphy being the Stump, Macky Bryant being the Quail, and Barney, himself, being the Stork."

Knight continued, "Of course, during my early years of high school, my heroes were upper classmen—Lathrop Holder, Bobby Bryant, Pete Gaines, Tommy Reid, Clint Tucker, Jimmy Hallman, Ralph Pulliam and others. I can now see that I had good role models in those days."

He continued, "It is important to note that Billy Henderson and Fred Johnson played important roles in building the self-esteem and character of the student body at Willingham. Coach Billy Henderson spoke (preached, actually) continuously at pep rallies and school assemblies about school pride and self-esteem. He told us that we could accomplish anything we wanted as individuals and as a school. Being a graduate of Lanier gave Coach Henderson credibility in helping convince our student body that we were as good as anybody, including the people from Lanier and the wealthier areas of Macon. Our principal, Fred Johnson, set high expectations for Willingham's students and teachers. I never heard him say or do anything that would suggest that he thought his student body was inferior to Lanier. My Willingham education was solid, and it prepared me for college. Likewise, Willingham provided excellent athletic programs and coaching for the major sports. I had a ball in high school with lots of good friends and good times, and most of that was in an innocent and positive way.

"South Macon was a good place to grow up, and it had a positive influence on me. I got a good education and had a lot of fun in an environment in which I felt safe. I saw first-hand that life is challenging for most people and that you have to earn your own way in life. On the other hand, I learned that life is full of opportunities, and hard work pays off. I also observed that most people, though not all, are good, and that money, lineage, and power are not measures or determinants of the goodness of people."

Prentice Knight is quick to acknowledge that marrying Linda Harris of McEvoy High and having two daughters, Marla and Rachel, are the best things he has done in his life. "Linda and I have been happily married for 37 years. She has been a wonderful partner, lover, and mother, and we were blessed with two children who were fun to raise and brought us much joy. Marla and Rachel are 12 years apart in age but could not be any closer as sisters. Both girls are now happy, well-adjusted adults who have graduated from college and married fine young men. They make the world a better, more loving place, and I am proud to be associated with that. God has blessed me with wonderful parents, wife, children, friends, and with opportunities galore. Nearly all the good things throughout my life must be credited to God's blessings, along with the kindness and support of others."

* * * * * * * * * *

Currently, Dr. Prentice Knight, PhD, serves as a Chief Learning Officer for CoreNet Global, which is based in Atlanta. CoreNet Global is a professional association of 7,000 members involved with the strategic management of corporate real estate, infrastructure, and the workplace. CoreNet's membership includes most of the world's largest corporations, all of the major real estate service companies, consulting firms, and the largest economic development agencies. CoreNet Global members manage $1.2 trillion in worldwide corporate assets, totaling 700 billion square feet of space.

Prentice's team at CoreNet is responsible for developing and delivering research and education programs throughout the world. One of Prentice's main responsibilities is holding Discovery Forums throughout North America, Europe, and Asia. He deals with industry leaders, examining the most critical and pressing business issues. Each year, over 700 industry leaders are involved in these sessions which attract the most innovative and advanced thinking that is available.

From these Discovery Forums, Prentice has become the opinion leader for the corporate real estate industry by providing insights into the direction, trends, and innovative practices. He also provides the directional framework for the professional development of CoreNet Global. Many have labeled him as the industry's most respected speaker.

Bruce Russell, a Senior Executive at Kodak for years and previously Prentice's boss, quoted executives from two of the largest real estate service companies in the world. They spoke about one of Bloomfield's favorite sons, "Prentice Knight masterfully orchestrates a learning moment for a diverse set of interests in the corporate real estate industry with his Discovery Forum gatherings. Using his teaching-profession background, Prentice manipulates various levels of experience and varied cultures to create a mutually beneficial forum for all to learn. Without the sense of honesty and integrity that Prentice exercises, competing factions would resort to marketplace 'one-upmanship' tactics, rather than participating in the collaborative environment that expands everyone's universe.

Prentice Knight hard at work in Bangkok, Thailand.

"Every once in a while, you are fortunate to run into an individual who combines raw intelligence with the ability to distill disparate sources of information into concepts and ideas that get to the essence of an issue or challenge. Even more rare is to find in that person a level of integrity in dealing with large and small issues alike, that instills confidence and credibility, allowing them to be even more effective in soliciting opinions and developing solutions. Finally, when you add a true compassion for people that transcends roles and titles, you've found the rarest of individuals. Prentice Knight combines all these characteristics into an engaging and highly skilled businessman, and more importantly, a good friend."

Prentice was a professor for 13 years, teaching at Dartmouth College in Hanover, NH, and at the University of Kansas. He taught courses and did research on regional economic development, business location theory and analysis, economic geography, and regional research methods. He has published papers and made professional presentations on these topics. He loved working with students and gradually developed a Socratic method of teaching which he has used in his career since leaving the academic world in 1987. He moved to the world of business and non-profit professional foundations because of his interest in the development and practical application of knowledge to business and economic development issues. Prior to his current position at CoreNet Global, Prentice served as the CEO of the International Development Research Council (IDRC), a large business association with several thousand members throughout the world.

"Prentice Knight is that rare person who combines extremely high intellectual capacity; a comfortable down-home, on-your-level approach to communication; and a refreshing genuineness about everything he does," according to David L. Bibb, Deputy Administrator of the U.S. General Services Administration. "I have watched in amazement and with deep respect as Prentice gets things done that most people just wouldn't expect to be possible. He has been able very quickly to gain information about the constantly evolving practice of corporate real estate and workplace-making from around the world. Prentice can then synthesize that information into easily digestible information that has impacted literally thousands of corporate real estate professionals and, ultimately, the millions of workers who spend so much time in the workplaces that those professionals create."

Bibb continued, "I know that Prentice's thinking and the information flow coming from him, as well as from his colleagues at CoreNet Global Learning, have had a major, positive impact upon the way in which the U.S. General Services Administration goes about its job of providing workplaces for more than a million Federal workers and contractors. We are rapidly moving from our past of being 'order takers' to our present and future of being 'value-added enablers' who help the business of government get done in a way that the American taxpayers deserve and have a right to expect."

Other members of the CoreNet Global Learning Team commented about the impact that Knight has had on their business. "Prentice is one of those few people who can do it all. He is in constant demand by his co-workers because of his talent and experience. Whenever a new initiative comes along, he is involved and often is right in the middle of it. If the leaders in the corporate real estate industry were asked, 'Who is the single most knowledgeable, articulate person in our industry?' many of them would reply, 'Prentice Knight.'

"Prentice is well known for his brilliance, wit, and charm, but what many people do not really appreciate is how much he has shaped the practice of his profession world-wide. As the CEO of the International Development Research Council (IDRC), Prentice set the tone for the corporate real estate industry by developing and delivering programs across North America, South America, Europe, and Asia."

Roy Dohner, past President of the IRDC, said about his friend, Prentice Knight, "Prentice has been and continues to be one of the most prominent and respected thought-leaders, generating both original research and practical education in the field of corporate real estate. He has devoted his professional career to the development of tools and processes, research and education to elevate the quality of corporate real estate management.

"I came to know and appreciate Prentice even more as the elected volunteer President of IDRC. During my tenure, Prentice provided strong staff support while also providing wise counsel and sound advice. I came to better understand not only his professional skills, but also his personal qualities. Prentice is a man of integrity with strong moral values; he always gives his best and can be counted on, not only as a professional colleague, but also as a trusted and valued friend. Prentice Knight is an excellent educator and a true professional."

Bruce Russell has seen the lighter, human side of Prentice Knight. Russell commented, "In addition to the high degree of excellence in which Prentice carries out his responsibilities, he is a wonderful human being with a great sense of humor. The 'absent-minded professor' concept is a time-honored, if not worn, cliché, but it fits Prentice to a 'T.' For example, earlier this year Prentice and two colleagues were traveling in Germany on business, and after a meeting in Frankfurt, they drove south in their rental car.

"One morning, as the group gathered for breakfast in a small hotel situated against the backdrop of the Alps near the Austrian border, Prentice said he had a confession to make. 'I was lying in bed last night about midnight, just thinking, when I realized something very important,' he said with a sheepish grin. 'When we left the hotel in Frankfurt, I forgot to get something out of the safe in my room. It's my passport. It's still there.'"

Russell continued, "This oversight was significant because Prentice and his colleagues planned to drive to Berlin and from there fly to London. The itinerary didn't include going back to Frankfurt, about 240 miles in the opposite direction, yet he wouldn't be able to enter the United Kingdom without the passport. After some good-natured ribbing, Prentice's colleagues agreed to 'swing back' through Frankfurt on the way to Berlin.

"In recent years, Prentice's hair took on a distinguished gray," Russell said. "That, coupled with natural good looks and a beard that he sported in later years, resulted in Prentice's closest friends referring to him good-naturedly as 'Kenny Rogers.' The resemblance was very close. In Asia a few years ago, a Japanese fellow came up to Prentice and was convinced on first sight that Prentice really was the entertainment star and excitedly asked for 'Kenny's' autograph. It took a while for Prentice to persuade the man that, in fact, he was not actually Kenny Rogers."

Another memorable event for Knight's friends was when Prentice was asked to speak at a very prestigious economic development group meeting in Rome, Italy. Prentice and Linda flew from Nashville to Newark, NJ, and then to Rome. At the Rome airport, Italian Customs did not accept the Knights' passports for entry into their country. By mistake, Prentice had picked up their out-of-date passports and left the current ones at home. Unable to persuade either the customs officials or the American Embassy to intervene, Prentice and Linda were put back on a plane returning to the States. The good news is that the airline recognized their own error and immediately upgraded Prentice and

Linda to first class, arranged for a courier to get the correct passports from their home, and get the passports to Newark. When Prentice and Linda arrived in Newark, they were handed their current passports and immediately made the flight back to Rome. In his truest form, Prentice gave his presentation on time.

Russell said, "Needless to say, family and co-workers now carefully check the whereabouts of Prentice's passport before he travels internationally."

Bruce Russell concluded about his friend and colleague, "Prentice has served as the CEO of the International Development Research Council's Research Foundation, a nonprofit foundation that carries out research on strategic corporate real estate management. Corporate Real Estate, 2000, a multimillion-dollar research program of the Foundation, was created under his leadership and has been widely acclaimed throughout the business world."

* * * * * * * * * *

Currently, Prentice and Linda have lived on a farm in Scottsville, KY, for the past seven years. They jointly own and operate the farm with their daughter Marla, and her husband, Phil Dutille, and raise beef cattle. Prentice is involved in his family's genealogy and has researched the four major lines of his family.

Prentice noted, "I enjoy reading on a wide range of topics but particularly enjoy geography, history, and world religions. Linda and I also enjoy walking with our dogs on the farm which has beautiful landscapes and interesting woods and wildlife. We also like family travel, because it is a great way to learn about the world while having fun and creating wonderful family memories."

When quizzed about how he would you like to be remembered, he replied, "I hope people will remember that I was genuinely curious about life and truth; that I really did try to separate the wheat from the chaff, in being a friend, husband, father, son, brother of humankind, and child of God; and a few people are a little better off because I was around for a while. I also try to keep the truth of these three aphorisms in balance.

And you shall know the truth, and the truth shall set you free.
—John 8:32

The unexamined life is not worth living.
—Socrates
Life is too important to be taken seriously.
—Oscar Wilde

Knights in Philadelphia: Linda, Prentice,
Marla Dutille and Racheal Flowers.

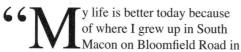
Renaissance Judge

Judge William (Bill) Self
Class of 1967

*"Every job is a self-portrait of the person who did it.
Autograph it with excellence"*
—*Source Unknown*

" "**M**y life is better today because of where I grew up in South Macon on Bloomfield Road in the 1950's and 60's," Judge Bill Self said matter-of-factly. "We lived in a rural setting in those days, and certainly the culture was different. We were free to walk the neighborhoods, and we knew most of our neighbors well enough that their children walked freely into our house, and the Self children did the same at theirs. Our houses were unlocked at night, and we left the keys in the ignition so we didn't misplace them. That way, we always knew where to look for our car keys."

In the 1960's, the home of Judge Tilman E. and Mary Paul Self was a neighborhood gathering place. Bill Self recalled, "Back then, a lot of children came to our house to play ball or chase because our yard was a little larger than the surrounding yards. I attended Agnes Barden in grades one through six and a new school, W.T. Morgan, in the seventh. Things were so radically different in those days, because we could walk to school which was about a mile from home, or catch the bus, ride bikes, or even hitchhike. There's no telling how many times I've hitchhiked to and from Willingham on Williamson Road, and my parents were never concerned about me. I'd stick out my thumb and ride in the first car that stopped. Today, I would never even consider picking up a hitchhiker unless I could see that they were clearly in distress or were in military service."

Bill admits to having a wonderful childhood. The third of four siblings, - Tilman, Jr., Philip, then Bill, and Jill (Til, Phil, Bill, and Jill)—he vividly recalled growing up and rambling through the safe, unhurried neighborhoods of Bloomfield, a relatively young community in those days. "I really enjoyed going to the Little Store that 'Mom' and 'Pop' Childers owned at the corner of Bloomfield and Chambers Roads. Their little country store had two gas pumps out front, and when I walked up there on Saturdays, the Childers would let me pump gas and pay me with a Yoo-Hoo chocolate drink. I liked pumping gas for some reason. The Childers had this chest-type drink box where you had to lean over and slide your drink through a maze to the front of the box where the drinks came out. I always wanted the coldest drink, which was usually in the back corner of the drink box. They were so cold that they had ice in them, and it was worth the extra effort to maneuver the other drinks out of the way to get the one I wanted."

The Childers' son, Garner, owned a barber shop behind The Little Store where Bill would also spend time on Saturdays, sweeping floors, helping around the barber shop, and would also be paid with a soft drink. "RC's and Double Colas were pretty popular with us back then, since those were the biggest drinks you could find, and we had to eat a Moon Pie with the RC Cola. You can tell that I worked pretty cheap back in those days," Bill laughed.

Bill graduated from Willingham in 1967 and made great memories through his involvement in the Willingham Pride of Dixie Marching Band, under the direction of the legendary Jim Littlefield. Quinton Childers, no relation to the previously-mentioned Childers family, transferred to Willingham in 1964, and, like Bill, was also in the band. "Bill played flute, piccolo, and tenor sax," Childers recalled. "We had some good times on band trips, riding the bus to out-of-town ball games, and cruising on the weekends.

"Persistence has always been an important trait of Bill's, one that has pushed him to be a success in life and as a lawyer and judge," Quinton Childers said, "but Bill's tenacity nearly caused his undoing one time. There was an occasion when we were in high school, and Bill didn't know when to quit. He is the only person I have ever known who parked a motorcycle in a pine tree. Literally. This happened back in the days when we were young enough, that if you fell, you bounced. Now, things tend to break. Bill and I were riding the motorcycles on a pipeline when we came to a creek. Since Bill's bike was lighter, he went across the creek first. The water appeared to be just a few inches deep, so Bill jumped the creek and his front tire cleared the water. However, when his rear tire landed, he hit the water which was actually a couple of feet deep. Bill was thrown off the back of the bike, but he managed to hold onto the handlebars. Picture Bill hanging on while chasing behind the dirt bike until it hit a pine tree! The motorcycle lodged its front tire on one side of the tree trunk, and the rear tire ended up on the other side of the tree, about three feet off the ground. Bill finally turned loose of the bike, and when he did, it stayed there, stuck in the pine tree. He never even considered turning the motorcycle loose until he parked it around the pine tree."

* * * * * * * * * *

Judge Tilman E. and Mary Paul Self raised their four children in a house on Bloomfield Road when there were few houses in sight of theirs. The Selfs' neighborhood was considered 'in the country,' because they were actually outside the city limits of Macon. People raised cows and chickens next door to the Selfs', but things changed as Bloomfield grew at a rapid rate, and the Selfs' country-home was gradually surrounded by scores of new houses. Agnes Barden School was soon joined by Jessie Rice, W.T. Morgan, and later Minnie Burghard Elementary Schools in the ever-expanding Bloomfield area.

Soon, the idea of annexation became a real possibility, and with old Lanier High becoming over-crowded, Willingham High serviced the South Macon community. Bill Self recalled, "My brother Tilman who is nine years older than I, went to Lanier because it was the only option in town. My brother Philip and I were excited to go to the new school, but, when you socialized outside South Macon, you became aware that folks sorta treated you like you were from the wrong, or poor, side of the tracks. I don't remember anything being blatant or flagrant, but you knew there were some things different. Macon has always had the influential, socially accepted, powerful people who lived in historic downtown, Shirley Hills, Vineville/Ingleside area, or the Idle Hour Estates sections of town. My father was about the only lawyer in Macon who didn't live in the right part of town, other than Judge J. Taylor Phillips and lawyers Frank McKinney and Virgil Shepherd, who both lived out in the south Bibb County/ Byron areas. The influential, powerful lawyers didn't live in South Macon."

Growing up in South Macon was a very positive experience for Self. He even saw the segregation of boys and girls at Willingham and McEvoy as a positive thing. He recalled, "Certainly, I think there were some problems with, and a fair amount of objections to, the separate education of the sexes in Bibb County. On the other hand, there was something about the experience of not going to class with the opposite sex that helped mold us. Interestingly, there are now some pilot programs in Georgia where boys and girls are being separated for educational purposes. The thinking is that there are fewer distractions without the attraction of the opposite sex in classes together.

"I distinctly remember going to the University of Georgia and attending my first class with a girl sitting next to me. She was wearing a short skirt, and it took a while to get used to being in class with girls. I think there was something formative about that Willingham experience. Today, some may call it cruelty, and there would be some parents who would threaten to sue if boys and girls were segregated, but somehow, there was the knowledge of and enforcement of discipline. It was very clear that we were in school to learn, and that fact was reinforced because the purpose of our being there was for an education."

Bill continued, "All of these things combined to make my growing-up experience a positive one. Understand, too, that my attitude about South Macon comes from never having known what it is like to grow up in a wealthy neighborhood or going to school at Stratford. Though I was never in a high school fraternity, I recall that even the cliques were divided by where you lived or went to school. You could be in whatever fraternity or sorority you wanted, but even then, there was a hierarchy that was run by Lanier or Stratford boys."

Bill Self was asked how he rated his high school experience at Willingham.

"Academically, it was a *nine*. We had good teachers. Education meant something back then, and I came from a family that insisted that I study and make good grades. Parents supported the schools and teachers in those days. Teachers taught. Not much time had to be spent babysitting, and you didn't play around in Leonard Pridgeon's chemistry or physics classes. I would have been more likely to cut up in Coach Mike Garvin's trig class than I would in Mr. Pridgeon's.

"I recall Mike Garvin on more than one occasion standing at the door of his classroom and just popping you one with his paddle when you came in. He said, 'I don't have time to stop in the middle of class today, so that's for whatever it is you thought you were gonna do in my class!' I still see Mike Garvin these days, and he just recently became a grandfather. When I had a grandchild before he did, I thought, 'What's wrong with this picture?'"

Bill recalled that in the mid-to-late '60s there were some challenging days during integration. "We had band camp at Willingham the week before school started and practiced marching at old Cranford Field, located across Williamson Road. We were a week ahead of the rest of the school by having that week's exposure to our first black band member, Wilfred Anderson. After camp was over and school had started, Wilfred came into the lunchroom and sat down next to me. I was not about to get up and leave. Ronnie Carr joined us, and it immediately became obvious that we were being stared at. Things went downhill quickly from there, but somehow we worked through those tense, difficult times. In fact, years later, one boy who had been antagonistic toward me in high school because of his racial attitudes came to me and apologized for the way people had been treated back then. Those were some trying, demanding years that we all managed to get past somehow."

Bill Self believes that the camaraderie that was present in the Willingham band helped to solidify some relationships among band members. He recalled, "Everett Tharpe, a sharp, young black student, was our bass drummer at Willingham. His skin was very dark, and he was extremely witty. Everett also didn't put up with a lot of junk. One day, on the way to a Willingham band event that was out of town, we stopped at a restaurant for lunch. We all piled out of the bus and went into the restaurant, thinking everything was fine. Suddenly, a woman who worked there said bluntly, 'We don't serve niggers in here,' and Everett responded immediately, 'That's all right, I don't eat them, either!' A couple of people had already gotten their food and were eating, but we all stood up together, took ketchup bottles, poured it on the food, and walked out without paying. We weren't having one of our own treated like that."

Bill recalled another occasion when Willingham's band went to St. Augustine for band camp and planned to march in a parade. "The motel owners weren't going to let Everett stay at the motel with the rest of the band. We protested that we were going to leave, so they agreed that our black band members, Everett and Francis Hicks, could stay there and room together.

"Even though there were people in the band that weren't necessarily happy about Willingham being integrated, the attitude in the band was, 'We're the band. All for one, and one for all. It's all right for us to pick on each other and maybe treat each other badly some times, but now you're talking about the band. So, we reacted in unison and came together as one."

Jim Littlefield, the Willingham band director, helped his band deal with the issue of integration in a straight-forward manner. Bill vividly recalled that when Wilfred Anderson chose to be part of the Willingham band in 1964, Littlefield said to his band members, prior to Anderson's arrival, 'We're going to deal with this issue. Wilfred is going to be a member of this band, and he'll be treated like every other member of this band. Period!'"

Self stated, "I believe Wilfred's sense of humor made things a lot easier for all of us. He would make a comment like, 'When the cheerleaders get here, they'll notice me, because I'm the tall, dark, and handsome one in the band.' Littlefield wisecracked, 'Well, you're tall and dark...'"

Bill Self credits Littlefield as the one teacher who had the greatest and longest-lasting influence on his life. "Jim Littlefield's greatest impact on me was that he taught me to love music and to love all kinds of music. Since I was not active in sports, I got my discipline training from my band director. Band was where we learned about a team effort, discipline, supporting each other, and working together for a common cause.

"Littlefield was a strict disciplinarian and wielded a paddle that he had made," Self remembered less-than-fondly. "The handle was a baseball bat handle, and the paddle part was a boat oar. He secured the bat handle to the oar with bolts and drilled holes in the oar part to make it sting. We named it 'Big Bertha,' and he used it frequently."

On a sad note, Jim Littlefield died in 2004, and Bill Self was called upon to eulogize his former band director. "Officiating Jim Littlefield's funeral was an honor but was one of the most difficult things I've ever done," Bill said. "He had the longest-lasting influence on my life and continued to influence me until his death. In fact, I saw Jim at the Bibb County Courthouse shortly before he died. Interestingly, he was at the courthouse filing a new will.

"I said, 'Papa Jim, how ya doing?' and he said in that blunt, straight-forward way of his, 'Trying to get your staff to help me out.' I said, 'Well, you know who their leader is,' and he said, 'That's what I was surmising!' I responded, 'Well, guess who taught me?!'

"He was without words for a moment."

Self continued, "I asked, 'What are you doing here?' and he said, 'Just making a few changes, putting my new will in, and grabbing the old will out.' I said, 'You aren't about to die, are you?' and he instantly shot back, 'We're all gonna die.'

"I said, "Yeah, that's right,' patted him on the back, and then excused myself.' He died the next day after our meeting at the courthouse. It was both a tremendous honor and a tremendous burden that I had regarding his funeral," Bill said.

"Recently, I got a note from Jim's widow who told me that she thinks 'Big Bertha' still exists, and if she can find it, it's mine. In the eleventh grade, I never would have thought 'Big Bertha' could end up being something that I would treasure."

Bill Self credits numbers of people – teachers, pastors, and friends—for having made a difference in his life and development. He said, "Though it's true Jim Littlefield had the longest-lasting influence on me, my parents were by far, without question, the most influential people in the whole of my life. I think that it was Abraham Lincoln who once said, 'All that I am, or ever hope to be, I owe to godly parents.' I could make that same statement. I cannot, nor would I ever desire, to deny, disclaim, or escape the very considerable influence Mom and Pop had upon who and what I am. While they deserve no blame for my faults and failures, they deserve all the credit, as they raised me in obedience to God's great guidance as they understood it, for all that is good within me.

"My Aunt Ann and Uncle Jesse Self were like a second set of parents to me," Bill said. "Their son Jerry was my closest friend while we were growing up. We spent countless nights at each other's homes and roomed together at UGA. Jerry and I remained best friends until his tragic death in an automobile accident in 1977."

Others who have had positive effects on Bill Self's life are Rev. Blackie and Rilla Bellury, who were family friends of the Selfs. "They were wonderful influences on all who came to know them," Bill stated. "Rev. Bellury married Jane and me in December, 1971. O.M. Cates baptized me at Cherokee Heights Baptist Church. My uncle, Rev. Bill Self, pastored that church prior to Rev. Cates."

Considering teachers who greatly influenced his life and career, Self credited a law professor at the University of Georgia named Sam Davis. "Sam taught family and juvenile law and was the one that I found who most genuinely admired the practice of law. Most law professors are so bound up in theory and academia and don't have much practical experience. Many law professors never hung a shingle or practiced law and earned their keep. Sam Davis had an air about him that supported those of us who genuinely wanted to practice law."

At Willingham, Lenoir LaMountt taught English when Bill was in junior high. "She died shortly after we graduated from Willingham, but she was one of the best influences on me as a teacher, simply because she gave me such a great foundation in the basics of English and grammar. She taught me a love and appreciation for the English language."

* * * * * * * * * *

After graduating from the University of Georgia in 1971 and the UGA 's Lumpkin School of Law in 1974, Bill began his legal career as a lawyer and worked with his father before establishing his own practice in Macon from 1980-'89. He was elected Judge of Probate Court of Bibb County in 1989, succeeding his father, Judge Tilman E. Self, Sr., who died in February, 1989.

Without question, Bill is a man of great energy with multiple skill sets, who is deeply involved in civic affairs. He has been active in the legal profession, both as a lawyer and judge, and has written countless articles for legal journals, as well as being published in Christian periodicals. Regarding his community involvement, Bill is a member of Vineville Baptist Church, participates in Habitat for Humanity, and lectures frequently for churches, civic groups, schools, and professional organizations.

Numbers of long-time friends weighed in on the virtues of Bill Self. Quinton Childers, a former tax accountant who has known Bill since childhood, said about his friend, "Bill's greatest strengths are his intelligence and honesty. For Bill, there are no gray areas. There is right, and there is wrong, and he always strives for what is right. Bill has been a leader in this community as long as I can remember. He served as President of the Sertoma Club of Macon, as well as Governor, and State Director for Sertoma International. Bill has assumed leadership roles in local churches as an Interim Music Director and Sunday School teacher."

Childers kidded his friend by asking, "How many lawyers do you know that can truly be called an 'honest lawyer?' Bill is one of them. He is also a very talented actor, having performed in numerous Theatre Macon productions. And of course, Bill has always been an accomplished musician.

"One of the things that I have admired the most about Bill as a judge," Childers added, "is that he has dedicated himself to help those who cannot help themselves. He has such a heart for the elderly and disenfranchised children, as well as those trying to deal with the final business of recently departed loved ones."

Paula Castro-Poveda, a 1967 graduate of McEvoy High and a classmate of Bill's, also attended UGA. She and her husband, Ozzie, lived in the same trailer park where Bill and his cousin Jerry lived. "I recall an occasion when a mobile home was destroyed by fire," Castro-Poveda stated, "trapping and killing the family pet. Bill found the animal and carefully buried it before the owner arrived so she would not have to see the charred remains of her beloved pet. This extraordinary act of kindness toward a total stranger exemplifies the way Bill treats people, no matter their race, religion, or social standing. Bill Self is an honest, forthright, caring, and compassionate man who loves God and country. He loves and respects the law and defends it rather spiritedly at times! Those qualities make him a good judge, a good person, and a true friend."

Castro-Poveda, a South Macon product like Self, has been impressed with Bill's varied interests and talents and sees the judge as something of a Renaissance Man. "Bill designed, created, landscaped, and maintains his beautiful yard. He is a terrific cook, and I am sure that we are not the only family who invites Bill over to eat and then asks him to do the cooking. He is so talented and plays musical instruments, sings, and has even been choir director at several churches. Bill loves the theatre, has dabbled in oil painting, has learned some Spanish, and took a course in 'signing' for the deaf so he can better communicate with people. That tells a lot about the type of person Bill Self is."

She concluded, "On a fishing trip to South America, Bill met a little girl who needed surgery which her family could not afford. When he came home, Bill sent letters to many friends and acquaintances to solicit their help on her behalf. This exemplifies how Bill Self treats people."

Ann Young has been Bill and Jane Self's Sunday School Teacher for several

Jane and Judge Bill Self.

years at Vineville Baptist Church in Macon. "Bill is a person who excels in all areas of life. He is a wonderful Christian man who puts God first, family second, and his fellow man third. Bill radiates love in his life and has fulfillment in life through many avenues. He has a lovely, talented wife, Jane, and they have two children, Mary Catherine and Tonya, who is married to Dustin Allen. The Allens have two children, Tristen and Peyton Allen. Bill has an incredibly busy life but makes time to help others. He is one of Macon's outstanding citizens, who also maintains his community spirit through his acting ability in many substantial roles performed with Theatre Macon."

Praising Bill's parents, Young said, "Judge Tilman and Mary Paul Self raised Bill to have the highest level of personal character and professional success. Judge Self, Sr., and Mrs. Self always expected the best from their children. On many occasions, Mrs. Self has been known to say, 'Expect the best; get the best.' What father would not beam with pride and joy at the decision his son made to follow in his dad's chosen profession and, ultimately, to the elected position of Judge of Probate Court?"

Bill and Jane are active members at Vineville Baptist Church. "Bill was once called on to substitute teach my Sunday School Class," Young recalled. "On the Sunday when he taught the lesson, it was the largest crowd that we have ever had in Sunday School. Bill gave an excellent presentation that morning but said he spent over 16 hours preparing for the lesson. This is another example of always doing his best. His parents taught him well."

Ann Young continued, "No better example of Bill's character can be seen than the story of his trip to Venezuela. While there, he met an eight-year-old girl named Jessa, whose father, Jose, was one of Bill's fishing guides. Jose told Bill and his brothers, Philip and Tilman, Jr., that Jessa was losing her eyesight. She had already lost most of the sight in one eye, and the same thing was happening with the other eye. The doctor in San Fernando did not seem to know exactly what her problem was. Bill and his brothers told Jose that if Jessa's doctors could refer her to Emory in Atlanta, his family would see to it that she and whoever might accompany her would be taken care of. Upon returning home, Bill approached his Sunday School Class and other friends about forming a prayer chain for this child. Hundreds of people in the United States were praying for Jessa. The outcome has been the return of sight in the girl's good eye and the evidence of healing taking place through the prayers of people. Bill could have listened to this father's concern for his child, gone fishing, and said goodbye forever, but his love and compassion compelled him to do what he could for Jessa and her parents."

As a stellar churchman, Bill once served on his church's search committee to find an assistant pastor. Young recounted the story. "A young man with outstanding credentials was found. The interviews and talks were going well, and the young man thought he was about to be called to the position when negotiations took a downward turn. The problem? The future associate pastor was a big-time Florida fan, and Bill Self is a Georgia Bulldog alum. The young man had to do some fast talking and praying to overcome that hurdle, but he got the job, nonetheless."

She concluded, "1 John 2:5, reminds me of Bill Self. It says, "If anyone obeys God's word, His love is truly made complete in him.""

Tilman E. (Tripp) Self, III, is an attorney with the prestigious Macon law firm, Sell & Melton, and a nephew of Judge Bill Self. Tripp said, "I have the unique pleasure of knowing Bill as an uncle, a judge, and a fellow member of the Bar. Perhaps the best compliment I can give is that he is extremely consistent in every role. Bill is detail-oriented, loyal, hard-working, and tough, and displays his passion for his work, as well as his hobbies, in all that he does. Because Bill is so driven, he rarely misses the mark.

"While Bill enjoys the reputation for being polite, courteous, and has never refused to answer a snide legal question, he also has little patience for the unprepared lawyer, the disrespectful litigant, and I feel sorry for anyone who considers his court inferior. Bill has fought hard to raise the stature of the Probate Court, and folks are wise to respect his court. He has always been willing to give me personal or professional advice, and he has always been accurate and on-target."

There is little doubt that Bill Self has kept the Self family name regarded in high esteem in Bibb County. His peers voted him the Outstanding Probate Judge of the Year in 2000, while he has been elected Probate Judge five times since his election in 1989. Tripp said, "I believe Bill will be remembered as a judge who loves his court and relishes its mission to serve others. He is known, too, as a man who is devoted to his wife, daughters, and grandchildren. Bill is faithful to God and serves Him well through his musical talents. He is, likewise, totally devoted to his profession."

Belinda Griffin was already serving as the Probate Judge of Crisp County in Cordele when Bill was elected in Bibb County. Griffin said, "I knew and loved his father, Tilman, who preceded Bill in office, and I have found that Bill and his dad shared many character traits. When I first began to see Bill at our training sessions, he appeared to be fairly quiet and less-outgoing than Tilman. I soon learned that I had gotten the wrong impression, because Bill is most definitely a people-loving person. He is extremely intelligent, very knowledgeable of the law and of life experience."

Judge Griffin continued, "Bill is always willing to share his knowledge with his fellow judges who may have questions, and he has prepared a number of informational publications which he freely shares with the general public. Bill would be an excellent professor if he chose to do something other than serve as a Probate Judge.

"It is also obvious that his mama and daddy 'raised him right,'" she said. "If I had to use one phrase to describe Bill, I would have to say that he is a true Christian, Southern gentleman. He is kind, courteous, and considerate of everyone he encounters. Because of, or perhaps in spite of, all of his saintly qualities, Bill is a fun guy to be around. He usually has a good, clean joke to share, and he can 'cut a rug' with the best of them. He is just a good guy, and I think Bill Self is simply one of the best."

Sarah Harris is an attorney with Harris & James in Macon and has been associated with Bill Self for the past 20 years in the legal field, first as a fellow attorney and then as Judge of the Probate Court. She said, "Bill always makes those who come to his court feel comfortable, particularly those who are dealing with the loss of a loved one. He is an advocate for the Probate Court, the issues of the elderly, and those who are incapacitated.

"Bill has always been one who is willing to work with people," Harris stated. "Bill appreciates compromise that will help everyone work together in a more meaningful way. In 1991, after my first child was born, I decided I wanted to work part-time, so I went to see Bill since 85 percent of my practice was in his court, and I needed to find out if this was a possibility. He listened to my thoughts and ideas of how this might work with court appearances and hearings. Other than my husband, he was the primary supporter and advocate of my decision. Without his help and flexibility, I would not have been able to maintain my elder law practice. I continue to work part-time 13 years later, and I credit the success of my law practice to Bill's encouragement, support, and trust."

Presiding over Probate Court, Judge Bill Self has witnessed the virulent extremes of humankind. Sarah Harris was there to observe one of those moments. "Once, during a very difficult guardianship proceeding, my 89-year old client, suffering from advanced stages of both dementia and syphilis, decided to give Judge Self a sign of exactly how she felt about him. When she finished her testimony, she stood up, turned to face Bill, and lifted her dress over her head. Unbeknownst to me or anyone else, my client had nothing on underneath. Bill, in a very composed manner, thanked her for her testimony and recessed court for a break."

Over the past 20 years, Harris has had the opportunity to observe cases involving contested wills, guardianships over older adults, and other probate matters. "Bill handles each case with studied care and truly strives to make the correct legal ruling each time. In guardianships, you generally have siblings fighting over what they think is best for their mother or father. Bill always tries to strike a balance to keep or restore harmony in the family. He is always looking out for the best interest of the incapacitated individual, and he seeks to help the elderly, disabled or mentally handicapped person maintain their dignity and retain as much independence as possible."

In the legal profession, the character, integrity, and qualities of an individual are easily observed by those who work together. Marla Moore works in the Administrative Office of the Courts and has known Judge Bill Self for years. She stated, "The Administrative Office of the Courts works with all judges, but my particular duty is to work with probate judges and to provide staff support to the Council of Probate Court Judges and the Judges' Training Council. When Judge Tilman Self, Sr., died in 1989, I was pleased to know that his son would succeed him as judge of the Probate Court. Judge Bill Self took everything with good humor, including a requirement that he attend a 40-hour orientation program after he had been in office nearly four years. He soon became the quintessential probate judge, the mentor, the one to go to when you have a question or concern about the law or a case that is before you. Judge Self is always available to answer questions, either by phone or email. He also moved up in the leadership of the Council of Probate Court Judges by serving on committees and eventually becoming President of the Council; he has been honored as the Probate Court Judge of the Year."

In his 15-plus years on the bench, Self has achieved a reputation for his kindness, his sense of humor, patience with his contemporaries, and being an excellent teacher for those in training. Moore said, "He is a champion for those whose circumstances have caused them to be in guardianship situations, either because of age or incapacitation, and will work to bring equitable settlements of family conflicts that arise over the division of property when a person dies. He deals with every one even-handedly and will fight for what is right and fair and just."

According to Moore and others who know Self well, whatever he has to say about any topic is generally worth listening to. "He fights for the right thing," she continued, "not just for the popular thing. For example, he is strongly in favor of the non-partisan election for probate judges. Likewise, he volunteers his time to mentor and train new judges. His desire is to make the probate court a place where anyone can go and get the service they need, whether or not they have an attorney or the money needed to proceed. Judge Self has the ability to listen, think, make the right decisions, and cause the people around him to feel that they are important."

* * * * * * * * *

Judge Bill Self has lived a life which has greatly influenced those around him. From his early days as a student at Willingham who befriended a new, young black band member to a lawyer and judge who seeks to help those who pass through his court, Bill is a man who is actively living out his Christian faith. As a family man, he believes the best things he has done in his life are marrying his wife Jane, being the father of two fine daughters, and maintaining a close, loving relationship with his own family and his in-laws.

"I hope to be remembered in life as one who has succeeded. Ralph Waldo Emerson is credited, by many, as having written the prose entitled,

Success

'To laugh often and much; to win the respect of intelligent people and the affection of children; to earn the appreciation of honest critics and endure the betrayal of false friends; to appreciate beauty (and, I would add, music); to find the best in others; to leave the world a bit better, whether by a healthy child, a garden patch or a redeemed social condition; to know even one life has breathed easier because you lived. This is to have succeeded.'

Bill continued, "I hope that people recognized my Christian faith in the way that I lived and treated my fellow man. I pray that my wife and daughters will recall me as a good husband and father, who loved them dearly. I hope that they can forgive and forget the many, many times that I fell far short of the mark.

"In my professional life, I hope to be remembered as a lawyer and judge who possessed and displayed honesty and integrity. I hope that there will be those who say of me, 'He was a good and faithful friend.' In the whole of my life, I pray that I will have somehow added to the esteem with which the name Self is held in this community, for I want not to blemish that good name which my father created.

"Lastly, I hope that more people will remember me fondly than otherwise."

In all likelihood, that wish will certainly happen.

Bill Self family 1988:
Jane, Tonya, Mary Catherine, and Bill

Do The Right Thing At The Right Time

H. Darrell Young
Class of 1966

And do not be conformed to this world, but be
transformed by the renewing of your mind,
That you may prove what the will of God is, that
which is good and acceptable and perfect.
—Romans 12:2 (NAS)

Darrell Young's first commission check as a young salesman for Minnesota Mining & Manufacturing (The 3M Company) in 1973 was $0.38. That's thirty-eight cents! His second check was a whopping $5.50. With a $230 a month rent payment, along with a wife and young son, he learned that something had to change in a hurry. Darrell 'got it in gear' quickly as he developed an amazingly unorthodox sales method and multiplied his meager initial earnings.

To say his sales methods were unconventional would be a grave understatement. While working for the 3M Company in 1973 and trying to sell storage and retrieval products using microfilm and microfiche to hospitals and textile manufacturers, the truth was that Darrell wasn't even sure what his products were—much less what they did. Sales training in those days at Darrell's one person Greenville office was not a district strong point.

In those early days, Young would walk into the office of a potential customer (usually a patient accounting or accounts payable department) and approach the person whom he presumed was responsible for purchasing. His appeal to them was, "I have a product and I need for you to help me figure out why somebody like you would want what I'm selling. Would you mind reading this brochure about my product and tell me what it does and how you could benefit from it?"

And they would read it!

Then the customer would tell Darrell about his own product and how he or she—the customer—could actually benefit from what Darrell was trying to sell to them. Amazingly, people began to buy 3M products from Darrell. His 'gut-level-honest method of sales,' along with his ability to connect with the customer, became his formula for success as a salesman.

Walter Huff, founder and Chief Executive Officer of HBO & Company (not the Home Box Office HBO), experienced first-hand what an amazing salesman Darrell was. Likewise, he worked closely with Darrell for over 15 years and watched him rise to the position of President of HBO's Mini-Computer Group, as well as becoming President of HBO & Company.

According to Huff, "With HBO, Darrell was consistently placed in situations where an office or a district was struggling for survival. He would go to the stagnant or ineffective office, often-times away from his home and family, and immediately turn a losing situation into a highly-profitable business."

'Team player' is a term Huff attached to Young. "Darrell would relocate wherever HBO felt he could be best used. Not only did he produce the desired results for us at HBO, but he delivered a quality product, and consistently had the highest sales volume."

His performance was so good, in fact, that he was moved into a business area that he knew virtually nothing about! In 1984, Walter Huff elevated Darrell to Vice President of Research and Development – a job that he learned 'on the fly' since his background was in sales. Knowing little about the nuts and bolts of how computer software was created, developed, etc., Darrell knew something that was much more valuable. He knew what the customer wanted, because he had such a close relationship with his customers. They were used to telling him what they needed, and now he was in a position to respond to what the customer requested. His R & D team would now create whatever it was that the customer would buy. Talk about 'customer service.' Darrell Young led the team that ushered in a new era in the computer software age for medical clients. The new product was named STAR, and has become one of, if not the most successful, information systems installed in hospitals around the world in the last 20 years.

* * * * * * * * * *

Darrell Young didn't learn about customer service and sales, though, as an adult in Atlanta. He learned how to sell and treat customers growing up as a kid in Macon. His dad, Harry Young, and his uncle, Zack Young (they were actually brothers-in-law), owned the Georgia Market House, a full-service grocery business operating in downtown Macon, GA. By working with and observing his dad, Darrell quickly identified who the customer was. He began to develop solid work habits at the age of 12 when he worked in his dad's grocery business – sweeping floors, bagging groceries, delivering, and cleaning up at the end of the day. Young continued his work at Georgia Market House even during the Christmas holidays while he was in college.

His work history went from the grocery business to upscale men's clothing when he went to work at the Oxford Shop in downtown Macon. Young states, "Lessons that I learned in retail were to respect every customer and understand who is responsible for your paycheck."

Darrell's parents and grandparents taught him a strong work ethic which was reinforced by living in South Macon, the blue-collar, working-class side of town. His grandfathers never retired. One grandfather was Welsh, the other was Scottish, and they worked and drove themselves awfully hard until they each died at 85.

Darrell's high school academic career mirrored those of many of his friends, being lack-luster at best. As a classic underachiever, Darrell moved through his high school years with little academic fanfare. He did have some success in athletics as a young guy. He played elementary school sports at Cynthia H. Weir Elementary school, but his greatest athletic achievements came because of his baseball ability, making numerous all-star teams in Little League, Pony League, and Colt League in the summers.

Becoming more of the social creature than an academic learner, Darrell gave up high school baseball when he got suspended for one game in his junior year because he stayed out beyond curfew on the night of the Junior-Senior prom. Darrell remembered, "My high school baseball coach actually called my house on a Saturday around 12:30 a.m. just to see if I was at home in bed. And I wasn't home, but neither were most of my teammates since we had all been to the Junior-Senior. So my dad answered the early-morning phone call. He was told by the coach that I didn't need to plan on making the road trip to Albany that morning. That episode pretty much ended my high school baseball career."

By this time though, the high school social scene in Macon seemed more appealing to him than high school baseball, but perhaps his high school claim to fame was being voted president of his high school fraternity (Alpha Omega Sigma, aka, AOS). Local fraternities and sororities enjoyed much popularity in the mid-60's in Macon because the public schools were segregated by sex. Willingham, Lanier, and Mark Smith were boys' schools while Miller, McEvoy, and Lasseter were for girls. Thus, high school fraternities and sororities gave many Macon teens an opportunity to meet students from their rival schools. Lanier and Miller were, by far, the most affluent and socially sophisticated schools in town. Seldom, if ever, had a Willingham boy been selected president of a fraternity that had a preponderance of Lanier boys. However, his nomination speech was so moving and inspirational that Darrell won the fraternity presidency in a land-slide. The speech of note was delivered by Connell (Connie) Stafford, who later became the campaign manager for Georgia Senator Sam Nunn of Perry.

Though Darrell's high school career was uninspiring, he had several teachers and coaches who had an influence on his young life. Coaches Mike Garvin and Billy Beale were two outstanding math teachers. Likewise, Johnny Stallings and Tommy Mixon were two coaches whom Darrell held in high regard. Mixon was a particularly good coach to Darrell in his high school years.

Graduating from Willingham High School in 1966, Darrell attended Middle Georgia College, a two-year school in Cochran located 35 miles south of Macon. He arrived without any idea of what he wanted to do with his future. Darrell achieved a 4.0 socially at Middle Georgia but struggled academically in his first year, primarily because his class work and social life were at serious odds. However, after meeting Brenda Kiker, an attractive young coed from Atlanta, Darrell's academic focus became clearer. His grades improved drastically and immediately. His grade point average suddenly became a priority.

Darrell Young took his first psychology course at MGC and was introduced to a subject that he didn't even know existed. Coupled with the study of business, the field of Industrial Psychology became attractive to him. Higher education suddenly began to make sense. It also revealed how little he actually knew about "how and why" people behaved as they did.

Upon graduating from Middle Georgia, Darrell enrolled at the University of Georgia in Athens and graduated with a B.S. in Psychology in 1970. As a result of marrying Brenda Kiker when he was a junior at UGA, Darrell went to work in the psychology department where he worked in an animal lab and in a human learning lab daily for two hours per lab. His grades continued to spiral upward, and, in his last two quarters at UGA, he made the Dean's List and graduated with a 3.3 grade point average.

According to Young, "I began to read books that dealt with behavioral concepts, relationships, and leadership. I was intrigued with how people dealt with each other and how hard it was for people to build sustainable relationships."

The race toward an education for Darrell Young was officially on.

As a junior at the University of Georgia, he completed his last two years of class work at age 21. Darrell was greatly influenced by the two psychology professors he worked for - Dr. Clyde Noble and Dr. Roger Thomas. Dr. Noble taught Darrell the joy of learning through critical thinking, which resulted in a new understanding of how to read - not as a youngster would read - but how to read critically and to understand what the author was trying to communicate. Dr. Thomas is credited with being the academic encourager that Darrell had never had but had desperately needed. Drs. Noble and Thomas helped Darrell realize that his potential was much greater and he was a more capable student than he had ever believed. Young gradually began to realize that he had a lot more academic ability that had gone untapped. Thus, his academic career began to flourish.

* * * * * * * * *

After graduating from UGA, he joined the U.S. Army reserves and served his five months active duty at Fort Ord, California, near Monterey. It was after returning to Atlanta that he took his first "real selling job" with The Lipton Tea Company and moved to South Carolina. He learned about sales by going into the back rooms of grocery stores – much like the one in Macon where he grew up working for his dad - and talking with the manager and assistant managers of local grocery stores. Because of his background, Darrell knew the grocery business about as well as the grocery store personnel. More importantly, he knew the importance of relationships with store managers, and he knew how to talk to them. They realized that this was a young man much like themselves whose background was like their own.

Promoted by Lipton in less than one year, Darrell moved with Brenda and now young Brent to Raliegh. There, he would handle the regional warehouse accounts for Winn-Dixie, Colonial, and A & P Grocery. As a sidebar, the tea-buyer for Winn-Dixie/Raleigh happened to be a bi-vocational preacher. With Darrell's strong foundation growing up in Mikado Baptist Church in Macon, he treated the buyer/preacher more like a preacher than a grocery store employee. Before he knew it, Darrell was stacking Lipton Tea boxes and Lipton products literally from the floor to the ceiling. Because of the trust factor, there was nothing the buyer/preacher wouldn't buy from Darrell Young.

Seeking a more sophisticated product than tea with an opportunity to make more money, Darrell went to work for Hank Brooks of Minnesota Mining and Manufacturing in Greenville, in 1973. In Darrell's words, "Hank was a tough, tough boss but was one who was fair."

And Darrell's product? Microfilm and microfiche systems that would be used in healthcare and the textile manufacturing world.

Darrell went from Columbia, to Raleigh, to Greenville, to sell a product that no one at 3M had been successful in selling, primarily because it was a one-man show with the closest support being in Atlanta. It was here that Darrell first learned the concept of entrepreneurship. Darrell was given a three-month guaranteed salary, after which he would be paid entirely by commission on what he had sold. It was in Greenville that Darrell learned what 'cold calls' were, and it was in this setting that Darrell's first commission check was for 38 cents.

But he pressed on, learned the trade, and by the end of his first year, his previous salary had doubled. He soon sold several huge accounts in Greenville and Spartanburg. Roger Milliken of the Milliken Mills family became his major account. They were buying what he was selling.

Now, things were beginning to pick up speed professionally for the Young family.

While a member of a medical unit in the Army Reserves, Darrell began meeting with doctors during their down-time. He advised them about how they could store information, keep up with patients more accurately and efficiently, and even bill them more proficiently by using his 3M microfilm/microfiche products. Darrell taught them how to index information on computers, then roll to a number or an image, and go directly to the desired file.

Few had sold microfilm and microfiche like South Macon's Darrell Young. He went to 3M's home office in Minnesota and explained to the 3M people what he was selling and how he was doing it. As a result, a sales training film is produced on *What's Up In Greenville*. Thus, 3M wanted to take Young out of the South and move him to Harrisburg, PA, or to Minneapolis.

But instead of leaving his native South, Darrell again looked for a more sophisticated product with the opportunity to make more money in the process. Ultimately, he went to work with HBO & Company, knowing little about information systems and how they brought value to hospitals

At first, it was apparent that Darrell wasn't going to get the job with HBO. He was told by Mike Rogers, the interviewer, "You're not qualified for this job."

Darrell responded, "I've never been qualified for any job I've ever had when I started."

Upon his insistence that he wanted to work for HBO, he was asked, "How do you know that you can be successful in a line of work you've never done?"

Young replied, "I have never *not* been successful! And, if I'm not successful here, then I'll leave." Darrell Young got the job with HBO.

In preparation for his sales position with HBO, Darrell drove from Greenville to Atlanta and met with Chris Clarke, the president of Northside Hospital in Atlanta. After meeting with Clarke for five hours, Darrell learned an enormous amount about hospital data collection and communications systems, how to market his product, and virtually how to begin the job that he had been hired to do.

Not surprisingly, Northside Hospital became one of HBO's best customers. In 1981 Chris Clarke allowed Darrell Young and his associates from around the country to demonstrate their computer system to 56 hospital administrators in one week during the American Hospital Association conference held in Atlanta. Sales were eventually made to most of the 56 hospitals for hospital-wide computer systems which addressed data collection, registration for admittance, nurse-staffing, and order entry.

Darrell's sales and marketing strategy was similar to the one he had used with 3M. Going to the office of the Hospital Administrator in a Hialeah, FL, hospital, Darrell discussed with him HBO's new computer system for hospitals and said, "I don't know all of the benefits that this system has. Would you mind looking over this brochure and help me?"

The hospital administrator looked over the HBO brochure, and said, "What you have here is...", and then taught Darrell about his own product. Miracle of miracles, the hospital administrator, within three months, bought the system that he just explained to Young.

After being notified of the decision to buy, Darrell was extremely excited about selling a computer system to one of the major hospitals in South Florida. He couldn't wait to call HBO's home office and inform them of his great news. Darrell was greeted with, "They aren't buying our system. We've never sold anyone a computer system that has taken less than a year to explain, sell, and close the deal. And you're telling us you've closed this deal in three months? They won't buy from you."

Darrell was told by his boss that no one was flying all the way from Atlanta to Hialeah, FL, to close this deal without first getting a letter from the administrator of their intent to buy the computer system. Young went to the hospital administrator, explained his dilemma, and the man promptly signed a letter of intent. Young returned to Atlanta with the letter of intent to buy clutched in his hand. The deal was done.

When asked by hospital presidents, administrators, and decision-makers why they should buy a million-plus-dollar computer system from him, Darrell would give them two reasons: "First, HBO & Company is driven by customer satisfaction and customer loyalty, and, as a result, you don't pay until the software you bought has been installed in your hospital; and second, I will take responsibility and be accountable for both your satisfaction and loyalty."

Those reasons were apparently good enough for five hospitals in Miami, Hialeah, and Ormond Beach, FL, to sign up within the next nine months with the new, up-and-coming HBO medical software company. At age 27, Darrell Young had become a key player in one of the youngest, most aggressive software companies in U.S. Healthcare.

* * * * * * * * * *

However, success had its down side as Darrell was called on to begin a two and a half year sales and management stint in San Francisco, selling the merits of HBO products. With his Southern accent in tow, Young found that initially he was not well-received by some of his potential Californian customers.

He remembered thinking, "You know, some of these folks actually believe that all Southerners have chickens running around in their back yards and didn't attend school past the seventh grade."

Times were interesting for the Young family as they began their new journey. They moved into a culture and life-style that were very different from anything they had previously experienced. Thousands, though it seemed like millions, of miles away from home, family, and friends, Darrell was going to be challenged professionally like never before. HBO computer software sales, plus building a regional office, required a level of commitment far beyond anything the Young family had ever experienced. Having never previously failed in business, Darrell Young was getting a serious test in his young professional life. Life wasn't really good for the young salesman from South Macon.

Church and friends had always been cornerstones in Darrell Young's life as he grew up on Glendale Avenue in Macon. His social life as a teenager revolved around activities with friends at Mikado Baptist Church on Houston Avenue. "Friends like Ricky and Sheila Payne, Harris and Brenda Stokes, Jimmy and Ronnie Lambert, Diane Driggars, Randy Jackson, and Ricky Dorman gave me a sense of security and well-being when I was a teenager," Young recalled.

Darrell's spiritual life, somewhat dormant since the days of mandatory church attendance as a child and young teenager, began to come alive again. Attending Calvary Church (Conservative Baptist in doctrine and theology but not listing 'Baptist' on the marquee, so as not to scare the locals!) in Los Gatos, CA, from 1977-80, he experienced something of a spiritual awakening.

Young remembered, "Calvary Church was not a place you went expecting traditional worship. It could be best described as a church whose focus was on relationships and love rather than on rules, regulations, and ceremony. Its methods of communication were exciting with lots of drama, big screen televisions, and a music director named Ace, who led a new style of music from a nine-foot grand piano with a swing-away, 'Stevie Wonder-type' microphone. I experienced biblical application teaching there, and every Sunday we had unpredictable worship experiences."

Young's reaction was, "Man! This was church like I had never experienced." The cool, young, 32-year-old pastor of Calvary Church in Los Gatos explained very clearly that God was in control of things on this earth and in Darrell's life as well. The Lord taught Darrell that he wasn't the one in control.

God had the attention of the tough, young, aggressive, successful sales manager from Macon.

The next thing he knew, Darrell Young was the new teacher of a seventh-grade boys' Sunday school class which had periodic visitors from a local detention home. For the first time, California suddenly didn't seem so bad after all. In fact, it would become the most significant learning and growth experience of Darrell's 29-plus years, both relationally and spiritually. As a matter of fact, things had also begun to pick up in sales, and HBO went from three hospitals to 33 hospitals in Darrell's two and a half years in the California office. They went from two employees to 60 employees in that same time span.

However, the lure of raising his family back home in Georgia was great enough that Darrell took a demotion with HBO to return to his home state. He went from a regional sales manager with HBO to a salesman. He went from a big, plush office to a cubicle. Times were not that good professionally for Darrell Young.

As in the past, he was again called upon by the Chief Executive Officer, and he soon righted another HBO-ship in the form of some Tennessee hospitals which were considering leaving HBO as a client. Within three months of his return to Atlanta, Young was promoted to southeastern regional manager, which was two steps above his current job and one step above the job in California.

Young remembers, "Things were very good in the Southeast for the next two years. However, as the company continued to grow and, as a result of going public, it was felt that the company needed more 'professional management.'

Once again Darrell was demoted due to experience and maturity. This time it lasted for eight months. In 1983, Darrell was promoted to Vice President for Research and Development. The irony here is that he knew virtually nothing about R&D, but the HBO customers trusted him.

He explained to his R&D staff, "I don't know all that you know, but I do know about customers, and I do know about sales and operations. Our customers will tell us what they need, and we will meet those needs." In 1986 Darrell was promoted to President of HBO's Product Group and then served as CEO and President of HBO of Georgia.

In 1992, Darrell resigned from the company because of philosophical and strategic differences concerning future directions. In 1994, he founded HIE, a healthcare technology company which developed software tools that integrated disparate software computer systems. In 1997, Darrell took the company public, and the company was sold in 2001.

Darrell Young has developed several tenets that have brought him success in business at various levels. Those tenets say:

1. You must maintain your ability to improve continually and create new value for both internal and external customers;

2. You must create new wealth for the corporation through revenue growth, profit, and leadership;

3. You must never attempt to lead and grow a business by only managing expenses; and

4. You must never look to outsiders to create future value for your customers or your company.

* * * * * * * * * *

Today, Darrell has begun a new business called Transformance Concepts, which bridges the communication gap between insurance companies and hospitals. In addition, he has co-authored a leadership workbook with Dr. Joseph P. Hester entitled *Leadership Under Construction,* which was published by Scarecrow Publishers. The workbook, released in March, 2004, outlines practical ways for leaders to achieve their purpose, establish incentives, maximum strategies, and develop a personal business plan. The concepts of ethical and servant leadership which are addressed in the workbook link thought to purpose, purpose to performance, and performance to relationships.

Also, in the past several years, Darrell has participated in laying the foundation for the University of Georgia's Terry College Leadership Institute and has assisted in the development of a youth leadership program at the UGA Fanning Leadership Institute. With a strong emphasis on leadership at the college level, Young's passion for leadership development, however, has not been lost on high school students. He is a co-founder of the Leadership Academy for Cobb County (GA) High Schools.

According to Young, "I have spent large blocks of time teaching young Cobb County athletes about leadership and service. In recent years, we took two athletes (one male, one female) from each public high school in Cobb County and taught them over a 10-week period about values, service to others, and leadership. It was an incredibly rewarding experience."

One young businessman who benefited greatly from Young's influence was Jeb Stewart (now age 34) of the SciHealth Holdings software company. They met through a mutual friend who had been a member of Darrell's Sunday School class at Eastside Baptist Church in Marietta. Darrell is the coach; Stewart is the student.

Stewart confesses, "Darrell Young played a huge role in my life personally, spiritually, and professionally. He mentored me in business and was a wise counselor regarding my investments. The one thing that impressed me the most about Darrell Young was his ability to relate to people of all ages without being threatened. He is as comfortable mentoring a high school senior as he is sitting around a board room table with millionaires or PhDs."

Jeb Stewart learned a tremendous amount about business and life from Darrell, and he learned as much from observing Darrell's life as he did listening to what he said. Young once asked young Stewart the question, "If you were sitting with potential investors and they asked you what you thought it took to be successful in business, what would you tell them?"

Stewart gave what he thought was an insightful and correct answer when he replied, "Work hard and make good decisions."

Young replied, "That's incorrect! To be successful in business, the timing must be right, and you must have the right business model. You have to do the right thing at the right time." And for that reason, Darrell Young spends an inordinate amount of time with clients, as well as with young businessmen, to make sure the business model for their operation is one that can bring them success.

Jeb Stewart and Walter Huff, two men who know Darrell well, give him their highest marks in character, ethics, and loyalty. Young, a very bright guy who could assess a situation and create 'do-able' solutions, was also the consummate team player. From relocating his family to working in an area of business where he had no background, even to taking a lesser position, if that's what the company needed at that time, Darrell did all of those things.

Jim Stratman lives in Dallas, TX, and knew Darrell through 3M, HBO, and HIE (Health Information Enterprise). Jim stayed with 3M long after Darrell moved on and then reconnected with his old friend nearly ten years later when he came across Darrell's name in *Fortune Magazine*. There was a feature on Darrell titled 'Rebuilding Your Sales Organization.'

Stratman says about his long-time friend, "Darrell Young is a strong leader. He is a man who has fiber in his makeup. He has built trust with others because he is not a manipulator. One thing I've always admired about Darrell is that he puts people in 'win-win' situations. It's no secret that Darrell is opinionated, but his opinions are usually correct and well-thought-out."

He continued, "I have seen Darrell embrace what was right for him and his family, especially while he was in California. For him to move back to Georgia for a lesser position and less money was amazing! But Darrell had a trust factor about what God had for him and his future. It was a very bold and insightful move for a young man, but he had strength of character going for him. I have the utmost respect for Darrell Young."

From a business perspective, Darrell's most important job, however, was not being a CEO. It wasn't even being a VP of Research and Development. Young's finest moment in business was the opportunity to lead in the creation of a product line which would ultimately impact hundreds of thousands of lives around the world in a meaningful way.

* * * * * * * * * *

Business and profession have always been vital and life-giving to Young,

Darrell Young family from left: Amanda and Billy Pero, Darrell and Brenda Young, Brent and Ellen Young with Jessie and Jada. Jake was not yet born.

but family takes precedence in his life these days. Darrell and Brenda Young have been married for 35 years, have raised a son Brent, and daughter Amanda, and are now grandparents to Brent and Ellen's three young ones Jessie, Jada, and Jake. Darrell and Brenda are active members of North Point Community Church in Alpharetta, and he continues to teach seventh-grade boys in Sunday School, as he did while living in California.

Darrell is now able to pull away from work and the pressures that which accompany the business world and play golf at his home course, The Atlanta Country Club. Though previously an outstanding tennis player, his primary sport these days is golf. His son Brent became a highly-decorated golfer in the Atlanta area, winning a number of junior tournaments before going off to college to play competitively at Furman and then Georgia State University in

Atlanta. Brent has earned a Masters of Business Administration degree in Real Estate and currently works for Hewlett-Packard.

Darrell and Brenda's daughter Amanda earned both an undergraduate and Master's degree in education and is now an inspiring teacher in a suburban Atlanta elementary school. In 2004, Amanda married Billy Pero, who, along with his dad, are restaurant owners in Buckhead.

With retirement not entering his mind, Darrell, at age 56, vigorously pursues his professional passions. Thus, he continues to work, write, read, teach, and coach. Darrell's desire is to be remembered as a man who has continued to grow in every area of his life - professionally, intellectually, personally, and spiritually. Although his academic life started slowly through his high school and junior college years, one of his present goals is to learn something new each day. Likewise, after his spiritual re-commitment to Christ and to the faith of his youth, another of Darrell's passions has been personal spiritual growth on a daily basis.

Darrell's life has been lived well. He is a man who was not afraid to try and fail, though his victories and successes far outnumbered his defeats. Darrell has become a man who, though extraordinarily successful in business at many levels, is willing to serve others in many and various capacities. The age-old concept of servant leadership, which was modeled 2,000 years ago by Jesus, has taken a firm hold on his life.

The life of Darrell Young has been one that has gone from mediocrity as a youngster to a life of excellence as an adult. His has been a life marked by values, ethics, and improvement. His life is one that has been, and will continue to be, transformed in every way, just as his life verse indicates.

Mann to Reid to First

Edward LeRoy (Roy) Mann, Jr.
Class of 1961

*"Do not boast about tomorrow, for you do not know
what a day may bring forth."*
–Proverbs 27:1

R oy Mann played by the book. In banking and baseball, in the military and in class, and in life in general, he did things the way they were supposed to be done, and that philosophy has served him well in life. Roy has always been somewhat of a 'straight arrow' that made people who knew him proud to be associated with him. He did the right things for the right reasons, and his life has been successful as a result.

Always the baseball player, Roy Mann's game was solid with no frills. As a second baseman, he turned the 4-6-3 double play (second to short to first) with Tommy Reid as well as anyone whoever played the game in Macon. He and Reid, his shortstop in high school and college, knew each other's every move. They knew where and how to deliver the ball so the double play could be turned with precision. And they turned hundreds of double plays in the seven years when they formed the keystone combination at Willingham High from 1959-61 and then at the University of Georgia.

Roy played by the book when he served in the military immediately after he left Athens. "Nobody wanted to go into the Army in those days," Mann said, "so the Air Force had their pick of who they wanted to enlist. Upon graduating from the University of Georgia in 1966, I joined the US Air Force, entered Officer's Training School (OTS) at Lackland Air Force Base in San Antonio, TX, graduated in October, 1966, and was commissioned as a 2nd Lieutenant and assigned to Hill Air Force Base in Ogden, UT. Hill was one of the country's largest Air Force installations with an employment base of approximately 24,000 civilian and military personnel."

Mann said, "During my military career, I spent two years at Hill AFB and two years at Headquarters Command at Wright Patterson AFB in Dayton, OH. Upon completion of my military service, I was honorably discharged in October, 1970. At that time, I had attained the rank of Captain."

As in other areas of Mann's life, he had success militarily and was named the Outstanding Procurement Officer at Hill AFB in 1967. His responsibility at Hill AFB was procurement of spare parts for F-101 and F-4 aircraft and awarding multi-million dollar contracts for the repair and overhaul of these battle-damaged airplanes being returned from Viet Nam. At Wright Patterson

AFB, he was in a staff position responsible for developing procurement policies and procedures for the operation air bases in the Air Force Logistics Command. Roy received two Commendation Medals for excellent work during his four-year stint in the Air Force.

Mann recalled, "I was selected for Officer's Training School (OTS) in 1966. There were approximately 1,200 students in OTS with the student population sub-divided into flights. The members of each flight became very close-knit because this was the group that you literally lived with twenty-four hours a day for twelve weeks. We shared the same barracks, attended class together, ate every meal as a group, drilled and endured daily physical training exercises. There were 14 in my flight – a very impressive group of high-caliber, highly educated individuals. Of those in my flight, 11 had master's degrees and one had a doctorate."

He continued, "Our Flight Training Officer was Captain Lyon, a man with a fearsome reputation. He was known to be a 'hard-core, no-nonsense' military man and one who always 'washed out' one or more of his students. It was said that, in his two years as an instructor, no flight of his had ever graduated 100 percent of its students. The penalty for 'washing out' was to enter the service as an Airman, the equivalent rank of Private in the Army.

"The academic load and the accompanying stress they put on you was unbelievable. We spent eight hours a day in class and were told that in the twelve weeks we were in OTS we covered about 60 percent of the curriculum taught at the Air Force Academy over four years. Testing was administered frequently, and, if one failed any test, he immediately 'washed out.' Everyone stayed stressed until the grades were received. From 5:30 a.m. to 7:30 p.m., Monday through Saturday, life was a high-speed race as we hustled from one scheduled activity – i.e. classes, inspections, drill, and physical training. Meals were a welcomed respite, although we were only allowed seven minutes to gulp it down.

"The last hurdle to graduation was a five-mile run through an horrific obstacle course under a hot, mid-day Texas sun. I was in shape, but I have never felt fatigue like I experienced that day after crossing the finish line. Most of us were too exhausted to climb into the back of the trucks to return to the barracks and had to be physically lifted in. But it was all worth it. Graduation was a great event as we paraded in review with jets streaking overhead and the Air Force band playing a litany of patriotic music. Pinning on the gold 2nd Lieutenant bars was especially meaningful, given the price we had paid to receive that honor. Looking back, it was one of the most difficult experiences of my life but one that I take immense pride for having successfully completed. As others have often said, 'I wouldn't take anything for having gone through it, but I wouldn't want to do it again,'" Roy stated.

"Our flight was the first under Captain Lyon to graduate all of its students. It was a proud accomplishment because we had set a goal on 'day one' to graduate the entire group. Teamwork was the key. Whenever a classmate struggled, others in the flight assisted. Together we made it!"

An only child, Mann grew up on Houston Avenue in South Macon, attended Cynthia H. Weir Elementary School, and was known as 'LeRoy' Mann in those days. "My parents were honest, God-fearing, hard-working people," Roy recalled. "My dad, LeRoy, Sr., suffered from tuberculosis and lung problems which greatly hampered his health, but he still managed to build and manage five duplex apartments to earn some money for our family. My mom ran Martha Mann's Florist Shop downtown at the Georgia Market House where she worked six days a week.

"My parents were strong Christians and were very active at Houston Heights Baptist Church where my mom played the organ," Mann said. "My dad was a deacon and a Sunday School teacher for 12-year-old boys. He called every kid on his class roll every single week to invite them to church and, according to our pastor, Rev. Stephen Krysalka, every boy that my dad ever taught in Sunday School accepted Christ and became a Christian. What a great legacy my dad left when he died in 1982."

Mann apparently observed the faith and strength of his parents as he was growing up, because he has had situations in life that stretched his own faith. James Turner has known Roy Mann for most of their banking careers but became good friends when they were co-workers at the C&S Bank in Augusta. Turner, now retired and living in Covington, GA, remembered a serious situation which happened with Mann. "Roy had a mole on his back that had been examined by his general practitioner who thought it was no problem," Turner said. "Subsequently, Roy had one of his banking customers, Dr. Joseph Still, also look at the mole. He immediately diagnosed it as a malignant melanoma. As you can imagine, we were all taken aback by this development, and I'm sure that this was a severe five-year trial in Roy and Bonnie's lives. He had surgery and went through a long immunotherapy program at Duke University Hospital. Fortunately, the cancer has never returned. Roy demonstrated amazing durability and great faith during this experience."

"My parents taught me right from wrong, but it was my mom who was the disciplinarian in our home," Mann remembered. "I could negotiate my misdeeds with Dad, but Mom would grab a long, wooden-handled clothes brush and wear me out if I misbehaved. I recall that our neighborhood consisted of honest, hard-working families. There was no crime to speak of in those days. There was a strong work ethic among the families in our area. We had good role models in the adults that we knew, and they taught us how life was supposed to be lived. Our neighborhood provided positive values for children, and being a good citizen was both demonstrated and expected of young people. I didn't know a single family that was a broken home in those days. The husbands worked and most of the wives and mothers took care of the homes. That was the typical American family in the 1960's.

"Willingham was a great school," Mann said. "To me, as a new school, it was a showplace, and the students were proud of their school. I went to Lanier

Junior High in the eighth and ninth grades before Willingham opened. We had some excellent teachers like Mike Garvin who taught math and Mr. Pridgeon and Mr. Bunch in science. I was very prepared to go on to college. My Willingham High School days were some of the best days of my life."

For Mann, simply growing up in South Macon was a memorable time. "I remember eating at Fincher's Barbeque, 'dragging' Cherry Street, high school football games, and sock hops after the games. We would go to movies like the 41 Drive-In, the Rialto, Bibb, Capital, and Grand theaters on our dates. And Lakeside Park was a popular place to go dancing on the weekends."

Roy Mann and Bonnie Baxley, a McEvoy student, began dating while both were in high school and continued to date when he went to the University of Georgia in Athens to play baseball. Roy graduated from UGA in 1965 with a BBA and completed his MBA at Georgia in 1966. They got married in 1966 before Mann went off to OCS. "Our honeymoon consisted of us going to Atlanta on Saturday and me being inducted into the Air Force on Monday. We then drove from Atlanta to San Antonio, TX," Mann recalled. "Bonnie drove out with me and then caught a bus back to Macon by herself."

After leaving the Air Force in 1970, Mann worked for the Citizens and Southern Bank (C & S, which became NationsBank and later the Bank of America) in Augusta from 1970 through 1994. The Manns moved back to Macon in 1994, where Roy served as a Senior Vice President until his retirement. He was head of Commercial Lending for the Central Georgia Region which stretched within a 75-mile radius of Macon. Roy Mann retired in 2000 after 30 years of service.

To become more qualified as a banker and to continue to move upward in the banking industry, he graduated from the Stonier Graduate School of Banking at Rutgers University in New Jersey in 1982. Mann recalled, "This was a grueling three-year program. Graduating from the Stonier Graduate School was one of the proudest moments of my banking career because of the hard work that was involved while I was making a living and raising a family. After my retirement from the Bank of America, I went back to work as a Senior Vice President from 2000-2002 for Colonial Bank. In November, 2002, I retired for good."

Roy Mann has been a highly respected banker and businessman throughout the years. John McSween of Colonial Bank in Macon has known Mann since their early years growing up in the old C & S National Bank. According to McSween, "Roy spent most of his banking career in Augusta, while I spent my career split between Atlanta and Rome, GA. I first remember hearing Roy's voice on our old Community Bank credit committee conference calls. He was steady and professional and always seemed calm and knew the right answers. Roy was always a strong advocate for his clients."

He continued, "In 1994, through some realignment, I was asked to move to Macon as city president and regional manager of the North Georgia Community Bank. I asked Roy to return home and join me as the No. 2 guy and credit officer for the group. Later when we both were 'retired' from Bank of America, I got the job of local President and CEO of Colonial Bank in Macon. After taking a look at the portfolio, I knew I needed a top quality credit man that had 'been around the barn' a few times like me, so I cajoled, begged, and basically asked Roy to join me in Macon. He honored me by saying, 'Yes,' but he also made it clear that when he reached 60 (he's a few years older than me), he was going to retire for good. And he did at the end of 2002. We try to have lunch together once a month to see how low his golf handicap has gotten. His 'retirement grin' has made all of us who are still in banking envious.

"I would identify Roy Mann as honest, trustworthy, loyal, and an excellent banker. He is just solid in every way," McSween said. "I consider him to be very forthright and full of integrity. Unlike many 'higher-ups,' Roy learned to be a good follower, which made him a better leader to those under his authority, in my view. He communicated the bank's mission and then would set about accomplishing it regardless of the bureaucracy. He was always steady. We were a good team. I was 'Mr. Outside', and he was 'Mr. Inside.' Roy's staff respected him completely.

"Roy will be remembered as a quiet, competent leader who always shifted the credit to others. He showed a lot of self confidence, and that raised the level of success of our entire team. He never promoted himself, which is somewhat unusual in our profession. And I have been so impressed with the way Roy has diligently looked after his mother who has basically been an invalid for the past ten years," McSween continued. Today, Mann's mother Martha (90) is living in Bolingreen Nursing Home in Bolingbroke, GA, near Macon.

McSween recalled some lighter moments while working with Mann. "Once in awhile, Roy would get going on old C&S Bank or UGA baseball stories, and few people could tell a story like Roy. I remember one story that he told about this 'squirrel in the house/Christmas tree episode.' We were all on the floor laughing."

Roy recounted the story that McSween referenced, "This squirrel got into our house here in Macon. I chased that thing all over the house for thirty minutes but never could capture it. Bonnie was asked to help, but every time it ran in her direction, she would drop her broom, scream, and run off into another room. Finally, after the interior of our house had nearly been destroyed, I resorted to the only alternative left. I decided to shoot the squirrel. Bonnie had a fit when she saw me with the gun, thinking I was about to blow a hole through the living room wall. Actually, it was only a pellet gun, but she didn't know the difference. The squirrel had become exhausted and had taken refuge in our Christmas tree which, by now, was leaning at a 45-degree angle with most of the Christmas ornaments scattered about the floor. While the squirrel was making those 'clucking' noises that they often make, I 'popped it' right between the eyes and with one shot the squirrel was 'history.'"

"Bonnie actually wrote a poem to the rhythm of *Twas The Night Before Christmas* about this misadventure which many of our friends have enjoyed.

This situation is funny now, but at the time, I was so exasperated that I didn't know who to shoot – the squirrel or Bonnie," Mann laughed.

"I'll always remember Roy Mann as a friend and as someone that I counted on, trusted, and valued his opinions. His wife Bonnie is great, and they are a wonderful couple," McSween concluded.

Jimmy Turner, now a retired banker who worked with Roy Mann in Augusta, remembered his banker friend as competent, well trained, steady, and good with people at all levels. "Roy was always very dependable and has a good strength of character. When he made mistakes, he fixed them and moved on with the plan. Roy has always been a good family man and was dedicated to his entire family – his wife, children, parents, and granddaughter.

"Roy relates to people well at all levels internally in the bank and also with customers at all levels of authority. He had a good ability to focus on the business at hand. I think he was more of a consensus manager at the time that we worked together, but he was a good leader and was willing to take responsibility for the actions of those who worked for him. Not many leaders are willing to do that, and he has managed a very long, good career with a large banking institution, which is no small task. And wherever he has been, he has always a part of the solution and not the problem."

Turner continued his assessment of Mann with a tongue-in-cheek comment, "The very best thing that Roy has done was to have the good judgment to marry Bonnie. He was a very good athlete at UGA, as well as at the local softball fields around Augusta. However, he is still waiting on his Masters invitation, which will likely be a very long time.

"In short, Roy Mann is true blue. The Lord has blessed us both," said Turner. "I think that anything Roy has done has been done because the Lord gave him the strength and the talent to do it. The Lord was also merciful to him and spared him to be a positive influence on other people whom he would touch in one way or another. He has done that and continues to do so even today."

Wherever he worked, Mann seemed to always have the respect and admiration of his co-workers. Dan Forrester of Security Bank in Macon is a native Maconite like Mann. He knew Roy when both worked for C & S and then Nations Bank in Augusta. Regarding Mann, Forrester said, "He was my 'worst nightmare' in banking, because it was a no-win situation trying to follow him. Roy was that good at what he did. I have followed him on more than one occasion as a branch manager, and I always had to work hard to keep the pace that Roy set.

"I have known Roy Mann for my entire banking career, having worked with him in Augusta and again in Macon. We were both management trainees at C & S Bank in Augusta, GA. Roy is a great person, and I have always considered him a good friend. He has great character and is someone you can always count on to do what's right.

"I also remember that he was a good baseball player when he played second base at UGA," Forrester continued. "He is a good family man, a very good manager of people, and always ran his areas of responsibilities well. People think highly of Roy Mann in the community because he has such strong moral character. He is a leader by example, is soft-spoken, intelligent, and is a good instructor. He is a loyal employee and is a strong, solid Christian man."

Remembering a light side about his friend, Forrester recalled, "Roy told me about the time he returned home from the Air Force only to find that his mother had trashed his life-long collection of baseball cards. He had a card of just about every player who had been in the big leagues. Roy was in total disbelief! All of those cards from all of those years...gone!"

Another contemporary of Mann's is Dave McBride, a native of Albany, who is now retired from Bank of America in Macon and living in Ponte Vedra Beach, FL. "Roy Mann and I worked in credit risk management in different cities for C & S Bank (now Bank of America) for years. We met in 1980 when Roy was senior credit officer in Augusta and I was a credit review officer in Atlanta. Beginning about 1983, our respective careers became functionally closer as we both served different geographic regions of Georgia as senior credit officers. From 1983 through 1995, Roy and I became close friends, sharing the camaraderie of similar work routines and growing in mutual respect. It was in 1995 that Roy returned home to Macon as senior commercial lender. I had been transferred to Macon in 1992 as regional senior credit officer, so in 1995, Roy and I, now both in Macon, began a closer working relationship that continued until our respective retirements from Bank of America. We have maintained a close personal relationship that continues to this day."

McBride said, "Roy is one of the most trustworthy people I have ever known, and I think that's probably his greatest strength and asset. As I think back over the years, the interactions we've had, the meetings we've attended together, the customers we've solicited, and even the one-on-one lunches we've shared - all those who have come to know Roy realize that he would never mislead them or betray a personal or professional trust. Roy's interactions with others are always above-board and honest. Professionally, he levels with others about banking issues. Sometimes, these conversations are pleasant, and sometimes they are not. But even during the latter, I've seen Roy state facts clearly and without being unfairly judgmental, leaving bank customers or subordinates with a feeling that they've received a complete and fair hearing. Personally, he comes across as low-key and reserved, but, as his personal relationships deepen, others get to see his dry wit. He relates to other people on their level. I've been with Roy to negotiate loan proposals with corporate officers and watched him handle intricate details with total professionalism. Likewise, I've been with Roy as we kidded around with the elderly couple who operated our neighborhood dry cleaners.

"'Follow me' would describe Roy's leadership style," McBride said. "Low key. Professional. Thorough. Subordinates learned from Roy by watching him work. He came to work on time, didn't goof off, didn't procrastinate, and was 'available' to anyone who needed him. He demonstrated to his peers and subordinates a strong work ethic. What he did, who he was, and what he stood for were all good for the bank, for his community, and for those who interacted with him."

"I would call Roy Mann a 'complete person.' He is a good husband and father to his wife and sons. He's a good son to his mother. To his banking family, customers, and co-workers he is a quiet professional. And to his friends, he is a nice guy and the kind of person you can count on at any time to help. To all who know Roy, he is a good person to know and to be around."

McBride continued, "In 1995, Roy had just moved back home to Macon after 25-plus years in Augusta. It was about the time of Macon's International Cherry Blossom Festival. I recall it was a beautiful spring day and several bank officers decided to walk to Central City Park for lunch outdoors. Vendors were set up everywhere, so lunch choices were many. The four of us decided on a barbeque vendor from North Carolina. As we approached, there was a sign explaining the choices for barbeque sauce: Mild, Hot, Extra Hot, and 'Thermo-nuclear.' Three of us ordered sandwich lunches with hot sauce. Roy, surprisingly, insisted on the 'Thermo-nuclear' sauce even after the vendor warned him twice that it was 'very hot.' Roy's mind was made up. He said he 'really liked hot sauce.' So as we began to eat, the three of us discovered the hot sauce was really, really HOT! But Roy said nothing. The rest of us were about to die!

"Finally, after eating about half of his barbeque sandwich, Roy said something to the effect that 'his sandwich was so hot he couldn't taste anything!' Knowing that Roy's sandwich had to be much hotter than ours, we started to laugh. He began to sweat profusely and could not finish his sandwich. We all dashed over for some ice cream, but Roy said his mouth was too numb to eat, and for years, we laughed at Roy every time barbeque was mentioned. He later told us his mouth was numb the rest of that day. In subsequent years, we always asked Roy if he wanted to revisit the barbeque vendor from North Carolina."

Dave McBride noticed the deep and caring nature which his friend has demonstrated throughout the years. "I have always been impressed with Roy's handling of his mother's illness. I know deep down that her slow deterioration has been wrenching for him and Bonnie. But Roy's steadfast devotion to her needs, even to the point of moving back to Macon to better attend to her, says a lot about him. And in 1999, one of Roy's administrative assistants at the bank suffered with cancer. She passed away at age 43. I was, and remain, thoroughly impressed with Roy's kindness toward her and her family during that time. He went over and above the corporate protocol for handling this type crisis in the workplace."

McBride concluded, "Roy Mann is a friend that I would call on if I really needed a favor or help with anything. He is such a good and honest person that I would reciprocate without hesitation. He has such a winsome way about him with this dry wit and is one of the funniest guys around. He used to be a good baseball player, and he continues to be a very good golfer. I miss not being around Roy these days!"

Roy Mann credits his success personally and in business to numbers of people who have played major roles in his life. "Certainly, my Dad and Mom had the greatest influences on me, because both were such strong believers in Christ. My high school baseball coach, Billy Henderson, was a tremendous motivator. He made you perform way above your ability level and insisted that everyone on his team 'give 110 percent.'"

"My uncle 'Duff' McGill was an engineer in Savannah, GA, with Union Camp. He was always so positive. With him, the sun was always shining! He had such a great attitude and gave me a lot of positive reinforcement. He was very funny and had a great personality. He was married to my mom's sister and was someone you just wanted to be around.

"I had some great teachers in my career, too," Mann recalled. "Mrs. Reese was my 5th grade teacher at Weir School. She was great with kids, was always so personable, and could get you to do whatever she wanted. She was a very patient teacher."

Mann remembered several personal 'firsts' and other meaningful moments while growing up in South Macon. My first job was at Kroger in the Cherokee Plaza Shopping Center. My first car was a 1955 Chevy Bel Air. I loved that car! I remember playing baseball at Willingham, and we were playing against Dudley Hughes Vocational School. They were coached by Godfrey (Goot) Steiner, who was one tough character. One day we were playing Dudley Hughes and during the game, some of the Willingham players on the bench began to mock Steiner who was coaching third base by chanting 'Goot, Goot, Goot.' This wasn't too smart since Willingham's dugout was on the third base line and only a few feet away from Steiner. Their mocking was so loud that I could hear it from my position at second base. Steiner had heard enough, and he stormed toward the dugout threatening anyone who called his name again. I don't know what he said, but when I got to the dugout, all the players on the bench looked like zombies, or like they had just seen a ghost. Needless to say, there were no more taunts from the bench during the game."

Mann recalled about his Willingham High School baseball days, "We played Jordon High of Columbus at Luther Williams Field in Macon. We really played a sorry game and lost 13-12. I remember that somebody laughed or cut up on the bus going back to Willingham after the game. Coach Henderson stood up and said, 'We'll practice when we get back to the school. Nobody leaves.' He had us sprint from home to third and then slide hard into third. The ground around third base was like pavement. We were raw from sliding on that awful, hard ground, and each of us must have run from home to third about 25 times. Thankfully, Larry Jackson's mother came to pick him up at dark and demanded that Coach Henderson let us go. Whenever I think of that instance, I always want to thank Mrs. Jackson for coming to our rescue. Otherwise, Coach Henderson would have kept us there all night. You can bet nobody ever cut up on the bus again after a loss.

"We had some great games against our cross-town rival Lanier. Both teams had tons of talented players," Mann remembered. "We had guys like Eddie Battle, Larry Fowler, Bobby Mathews, Jimmy Hammond, Jimmy Hallman, Buddy Petty, Tack Mote, Joel Dickens, Olie Goad, Bobby Bryant, Richard Powers, and Tommy Reid. Those guys could really play the game. But so could Lanier, and unlike most high schools, the Poets had three top-quality left-handed pitchers in Frank Hall, Charles (Bunny) Richardson, and Charles Haygood. We were tied for the region with Lanier and had to play them in a best-of-three game playoff. We barely lost both games to them and must have played 20 innings of baseball. High school baseball in Georgia didn't get much better than the caliber of ball that was played in Macon.

"I roomed with Tommy Reid for four years at Georgia and played high school ball with him three years at Willingham," Mann said. "He was one of the best athletes I have ever been around. He could play baseball, basketball, track, and he's now a top-flight senior golfer."

Mann was a pretty fair athlete himself, playing high school baseball and basketball at Willingham and then going to Georgia to play college baseball. According to the 1965 UGA baseball guide, Mann led the Bulldogs in runs scored as senior and batted .300 as a freshman. A three-year varsity letterman, Mann was primarily a 2nd baseman throughout his career but played some shortstop as well when teammate Tommy Reid was moved to third. While at Georgia, he played for the Bulldogs' long-time coach, Big Jim Whatley.

"I have many great memories from my years in baseball," Mann said. "At UGA, our varsity baseball team only lost one game to Georgia Tech in my four years. I was playing when Don Woeltjen went down in Georgia baseball history by throwing a perfect game against Tech in Atlanta in 1963. "We beat them 5-0, and he struck out 11.

"During the summer season while at UGA," Mann recalled, "I played semi-pro baseball for the Johnson Chicks of Macon. It was a team that was made up of former college and ex-pro baseball players. We had guys like Bartow Irby who was involved in a trade for Roger Maris when he was in the minor leagues. We played against the Atlanta Federal Prison, and the game was actually inside the Penitentiary. The inmates were pulling for us! There were guards stationed in the machine gun towers. It was quite an experience! Our team seldom lost. We went to the National Semi-Pro Baseball Tournament in Wichita, KS. Enos Slaughter, who played for the St. Louis Cardinals, played in this tournament after he retired from major league baseball. Some of our players included Tommy Mixon, who played professional baseball and basketball; Donnie Veal, who played at Mercer, and whose brother, Inman (Coot) Veal, played for the Detroit Tigers; Gary Stillwell, who played in the St. Louis Cardinals organization; Bartow Irby, who played in the New York Yankees organization and was in a trade involving Roger Maris; Dopey Dean, Tack Mote, and others. It was a great group of players, and we enjoyed traveling around the state beating up on other teams. That was some amazing baseball in those days.

"I have had some great friends throughout my years while growing up in South Macon, and we have some incredible memories of those days," Mann remembered. "Buddy Petty was one of my closest childhood friends. We grew up a few houses across the street from each other, and one day I was at Buddy's house when Theron Sapp was there visiting with one of his friends. At that time, Theron Sapp was the 'football stud' of Macon, having established himself as one of the best running backs in the state. He went on to star at the University of Georgia and scored the touchdown that broke a long losing streak against Georgia

Roy and Bonnie Mann.

Tech. He is also one of only four football players at Georgia to have his jersey retired. The papers claimed that his touchdown 'broke the drought,' so he was quite the Macon hero and eventually played for the Pittsburgh Steelers and the Philadelphia Eagles in the NFL.

"At the time, I was probably 11-12 years old, and Buddy and I idolized Theron Sapp. But as kids are prone to do, Buddy and I began to pick at Sapp until he finally had had enough and threatened to take our pants off if we didn't leave him alone. To kids our age, the threat of having your pants removed was a scary proposition and also one of great embarrassment. However, as kids will do, we continued on until Sapp jumped up and acted like he was 'going to get us,' so out the door we flew! Back in those days, I was as skinny as a rail but was also as agile as a monkey. Buddy's house had a huge Chinaberry tree next to it, and I shot up that tree, and within seconds, was on the roof of his house. I don't know where Buddy ran, but I stayed up there about an hour before getting up the nerve to come down. I never saw Theron Sapp come out of the house, but I know he scared the living daylights out of me. You can bet we didn't bother Mr. Sapp again."

Roy Mann, at age 61, continues to live a full life since retiring in Macon in 2002. His life has had meaning, and the relationships he has formed over the years through banking, baseball, and the church remain strong and significant to him and Bonnie. Roy is extremely proud of his two sons, Mike (35), and Alan (33), as well as his only grandchild - Alyse, Alan's 14-year-old daughter. All live in Augusta.

Roy has always been a good, solid citizen wherever he has lived. Currently, he is an active member of both the Macon Exchange Club and Tattnall Square Baptist Church. He was especially connected in the civic community while living in Augusta. He was involved in the Renaissance Housing Partnership, Westlake Country Club, the Optimist Club, Board President of the Boys Club, and was Chairman of fund raising for the American Heart Association in Augusta. But perhaps one of his favorite accomplishments is being a member of the 'G Club,' the letterman's club at the University of Georgia. Today, he spends his gradually-increasing leisure time playing golf, watching sports, reading, and working crossword puzzles.

Friends like Jimmy Turner, who has known Roy Mann for a long time, speak glowingly of his character and his commitment to do the right things. According to Turner, "Roy was and is a good family man. He has been a good friend of mine over the years even though our paths haven't crossed as much recently. I suspect, like the rest of us, that there are things that he would do over in life but not that many things when you come right down to it. I know his marriage to Bonnie has been a good one. I know Roy and Bonnie Mann as totally trustworthy people."

Indeed, the love of Mann's life has been his high school sweetheart. "We have been married thirty-seven wonderful years" Mann said. "She has been faithful and a helpmate, especially during those times when life got a little bumpy. I will never forget when we were newlyweds and moved to Ogden, UT. It was a beautiful location at the foothills of the Wasatch Mountain range, but for the first year, Bonnie had a severe case of the homesick blues. She had never lived far from home, and everyday, when she would look out our front window toward the mountains, she would say they blocked her way home. But after one year, she adjusted and began to enjoy the beauty of Utah. However, home was never far from her heart."

Roy continued, "The summer following our move to Utah, we took vacation and came back to Macon to visit our family and friends. When the train crossed the Georgia line, I thought we were going to have to stop so Bonnie could get out and kiss the ground! She did enjoy our stay in Utah and subsequently adjusted well to the other places we have resided during our marriage. Bonnie has been a wonderful wife, mother, and a gift from God to me. She has always loved children and started a very successful Mother's Day Out program at Warren Baptist Church in Augusta which continues in operation to this day.

"Since we moved to Macon," he said, "Bonnie went to work as an administrative assistant at Tattnall Square Baptist Church. She has been my helpmate and support throughout the years, and I love her with all my heart. As I once told the Rev. Stephen Krysalka, the minister who married us, that when he ties the knot, he really ties it tight! I thank God for Bonnie, one of the greatest blessings in life that God has given me."

As Mann spoke about the future, he said, "I hope that others will remember me as a man who was principled in all areas of life. I want them to think of me as a person of integrity who had high character. I hope that my life has demonstrated humility, because whatever I have achieved has been through the grace of God. Christ and faith have always been important in my life. The *23rd Psalm* tells me that 'the Lord is my Shepherd.' That verse has been a source of strength and assurance for me, especially when times have been difficult."

Man of character. Straight arrow. High-level baseball player and quality banker. Teammate and friend. Roy Mann has been a success in life at every level.

The Mann family: Roy, Alan, Bonnie, and Mike Mann

Willingham's Last Graduate

Dr. Kim Walden Johnston
Class of 1970-ish

*"What lies behind us and what lies before us are
tiny matters compared to what lies within us."*
–Ralph Waldo Emerson

Kim Johnston is a true son of South
Macon/Bibb County and Willingham High School. Kim grew up
on a farm and drove a tractor as a second grader. He joined Liberty
United Methodist Church, attended John H. Heard School, and was scheduled to
graduate from Willingham High in 1971. However, when the federal courts, in
1969, struck from existence the names of Lanier, Mark Smith, Ballard-Hudson,
Peter G. Appling, Dudley Hughes Vocational, and Willingham High Schools
in favor of compass-oriented names for the public high schools (Southwest,
Northeast, and Central), Kim's graduation from Willingham suddenly looked
like an impossible situation. Rather than attending Southwest High in his
senior year, Kim enrolled early at Middle Georgia College in Cochran in lieu of
actually completing his high school requirements. Kim said, "After I finished
my freshman year in college, Mr. Fred Johnson, the principal at Willingham,
asked if I wanted Willingham or Southwest on my high school diploma. That
was an easy choice for me. I wanted a Willingham diploma, which probably
made me the last boy to officially graduate from A.R. Willingham School for
Boys."

After attending Middle Georgia for two years, Johnston graduated from
Valdosta State and then got a master's degree at Georgia Southern University,
where he served as a teaching assistant for two years. Kim taught biology for
a year at Southern and studied genetics before being accepted at the Medical
College of Georgia in Augusta. He has been a practicing neurosurgeon in
Macon with Georgia Neurosurgical Institute since 1987.

Kim and his two brothers, Carey and Mark, six and ten years younger
respectively than Kim, were raised on a farm on Walden Road. Their dad
farmed 350 acres of their own land in addition to 200 rented acres. "My parents
put me on the road that they thought I should go in life," Kim said, "and they
were always there to encourage me. My dad worked hard on the farm, and so
did my brothers and I, but we enjoyed that kind of life. I got to drive a truck in
the fields when I was so young that I could barely reach the pedals. I gained a
lot of confidence and have such great memories from growing up on a farm."

He continued, "We grew sweet potatoes, and my dad had to drive to Atlanta
to sell them at the Farmers' Market. Those were the days before I-75, and he'd

have to leave at 2 a.m. I would go out and pack the sweet potatoes in boxes. My daddy said, 'You can go with me to Atlanta if you're awake at 2 in the morning,' and I remember sitting in the bed trying to keep my eyes open so I could ride to Atlanta with him.

"Some of my memories of life on the farm would be eating cans of sardines with Saltine crackers at lunch. Daddy knew that if we left the fields and went home for lunch, by the time we got there, ate, and returned to the fields, it would take too much time away from working; so we took sardines and ate them in the truck. We hunted dove, quail, and fished a little, but one of my fondest memories was lying outside on the grass at night and just gazing up at the stars. The sky was clear, the moon was bright, and the stars were everywhere. The simple things in my life, when I was growing up, are the things that have meant the most to me."

In the Johnston household, life was fairly uncomplicated. "Unlike the lives of our own children today," Kim recalled, "we had no summer camps, no advanced reading classes, no videos, and no SAT prep classes. Our lives back then weren't highly organized like children's lives are now. We had to create our own fun, and in the summer, we would ride bicycles from our house to Vinson's Valley to go swimming. Our lives were unhurried, and we had a great time growing up. Another good thing about living on the farm was that I didn't have to worry about getting a summer job."

Kim played a little baseball in the summer at South Macon Park, located at Willingham High School. He loved the game, but his dad's opinion about sports in the summer was, "Why are you playing baseball when you could be working?" Kim said, "One problem I had regarding sports was that we lived so far from town that it was quite a chore to get to and from Willingham where our games were played. I played basketball at Willingham in junior high, but after practice, I would have to walk to Westgate to catch the bus, then ride downtown and catch another bus at the Trailways station, and ride almost to Warner Robins before getting home. It was about 8 p.m. when I finally got home. That made it pretty difficult when you had to eat supper and then do homework; so sports in high school didn't work out well for me."

If sports weren't Kim Johnston's forte in school, then academics were. "I had some outstanding teachers at Heard School, and it's no exaggeration that every one of my teachers was excellent," he stated matter-of-factly. "My education at Heard School was unbelievable, starting with Miss Sara Willis, who must have taught half of the world. Miss Joyce Ray, who is still living and is in her upper-90's, taught us history. Her seventh-grade history class was harder than any college history course that I have taken. For example, with Civil War battles, she wanted the generals' names, the number of casualties, who won, where the battle was fought, and the dates. In just one test question, she must have had 20 fill-in-the-blanks. We learned history in her class, and she actually taught me to enjoy history. Thinking back, I love Civil War history, and Miss Ray is the reason. I took American History courses at Willingham and in college, and thought, 'Hey, I've been in Miss Ray's class. I already know this stuff.' Hazel Stanton was another of my outstanding teachers at Heard School. You couldn't have found better teachers to prepare you academically than mine."

At Willingham, Coach Eddie Battle was highly influential during Kim's high school years. Harold Watson taught math and was a favorite of Johnston's, but two science teachers seemed to have the greatest academic influence on Kim's future. "E.J. Hancock instilled in me a will to learn. He had this phrase that we all laughed at: 'Bless Pat, y'all haven't studied!' As eighth graders, he had us build a transistor radio for a science project, which was a pretty neat thing to do back in the 1960's. Though he had taught science for a long time, he was extremely enthusiastic about teaching and about life.

"Of course, Leonard Pridgeon taught Chemistry and Physics, and I was so well-prepared from his courses that I didn't have to crack a book in my first two chemistry courses in college. Everybody respected him tremendously, and nobody ever cut up in his class. But I remember one day, somebody didn't realize where Mr. Pridgeon's room was and foolishly pushed a set of lockers in front of his classroom door and left them there. Suddenly, they must have realized whose room it was and immediately got those lockers moved. That shows how respected he was because he certainly wasn't a physical threat."

Charles Deaton, former principal at Willingham Junior High, was another name that Kim recalled from high school days. "I got to know Charles Deaton more personally when his younger son Richard was a patient of mine. Richard and I were married on the same day, our sons were about the same age, and they were teammates in baseball, so we used to go to Atlanta together for their games. Richard called me one day and said, 'I was working under my car, and when I got up, I didn't know where I was. I was just lost."

I said, "Richard, that doesn't sound good; so he came down to the hospital, and we did an MRI scan. Sadly, he had a malignant brain tumor. Through Richard's illness, I got to know Mr. Deaton and his lovely wife, and I gained a tremendous amount of respect for that family. I also learned that Mr. Deaton had been a medic at Iwo Jima years ago; so we had that medical connection in common."

High school and South Macon for Kim Johnston were great places. "Educationally, you could get whatever you wanted at Willingham. You could just slip through and barely graduate, or you could be highly challenged and get a top-quality education. I give Willingham high marks. I got an excellent education as a result of some outstanding teachers. Today's schools aren't the real world because they don't reflect balanced segments of the society. To me, Willingham was the real world."

He continued, "I thought South Macon was heaven. Where we lived was really in the country. In fact, a portion of Highway 247 was a dirt road way back then. I grew up on Walden Road and remember when they barricaded and closed the old Cornfield Road just past Vinson's Valley. People used to go out there on Friday and Saturday nights and drag race. They would uncap the headers off their cars, and you could hear the rumbling all the way to our house.

"We had our own culture back then, and there was no better place to live. Our neighborhood was like some of the rural places that today's affluent people think are so wonderful. Our farmland wrapped around what is now the Macon Municipal Airport. In fact, the airport was built on land that my granddaddy, Robert Johnston, owned."

Long-time Macon residents may remember one of the most infamous events in Middle Georgia's history. The Byron Pop Festival took place in the summer of 1970 and was a smaller, southern version of New York's Woodstock. Johnston recalled, "My dad rented a farm that abutted Vinson's Valley, a family-type environment with a lake and small rides. I remember that when the Byron Pop Festival began, an estimated crowd of over 250,000 people pretty much took over portions of Houston, Peach, and Bibb County, which included Vinson's Valley, even though the owners had hired some people with shot guns to try to keep the people out and protect their property. The owners had some serious concerns about drugs and wondered what would happen, legally, if someone got hurt or drowned. What a crowd that was!

"I remember that during the festival we were plowing on tractors, and people would just come walking out of the woods naked," Kim recalled. "It was unbelievable! People from Macon and the surrounding communities would ride down there just to look at what was happening. One day, my dad had to drive a big truck loaded with soy beans or grain toward Byron. People were just jumping on our truck to get a ride to the Pop Festival. Most of them were wearing nothing or next to nothing. The expression on my dad's face was priceless."

* * * * * * * * * *

When Kim and Jane Johnston first moved back to Macon in 1987, he joined Georgia Neurosurgical Institute and practiced with Drs. Hugh Smisson, Sr., and Joe Sam Robinson, Jr. "Shortly after I returned, however, Dr. Smisson retired and Dr. Perry Cone died. All of a sudden, it was just Joe Sam and me. We covered the emergency room at The Medical Center of Central Georgia every other night for several years. It was as bad for me as residency, but you do what you have to do when there were just two of us. I would operate one day, and when I finally got finished, I would hurry home and sleep because I would be on call the next day."

Despite working ridiculous hours throughout his medical career, Kim and Jane Johnston, his wife of 30 years, raised two fine sons who both graduated from Macon's Stratford Academy. Kim said, "I tried to make as many of my sons' games and activities when they were growing up as possible. Jane did a great job for both of us keeping stability in our home. Though Kyle and Blake are now in college, we still have a great relationship."

Few people know someone like other family members. Johnston's sons,

Blake and Kyle, both have the utmost respect for their dad. Blake, Kim's younger son, is completing his freshman year at the University of Colorado in Boulder and stated, "He has always been a loving father, and even though he was tremendously busy when Kyle and I were young, he was still there for us. Dad has gone from the farm to the city, but he continues to escape back to the country when he can get away. He is successful professionally because he works so hard, and, relationally, he is unbelievably the nicest, most genuine person you will ever meet.

"For fun, Dad goes outdoors. He still loves to fish, hunt deer and doves, and we recently planted about 200 trees at our log cabin in Macon County. We also try to get away and go to our place at the beach near Pensacola. I'm just so proud to have him as my dad."

Kyle Johnston is a rising senior and a varsity baseball player at Mercer University. "The top two priorities in my dad's life are God and family. Any success he has had in life is a direct result of his faith in God and the fact that he is a praying man. I have a godly dad who loves being a doctor. Years ago, there were times when his work kept him away from home more than he wanted, but his career has now taken second place to the importance of his family. There were also times when he would frequently get home late, but his goal is to try and get home between 6 and 6:30 p.m. so we can have dinner together."

Kyle continued, "Anybody who knows my dad knows that he is an extremely hard-working physician and has always been one to set and achieve goals in his life. Going to Blake's and my games or other activities has always been a priority for dad. He seldom, if ever, missed one of my games and even tries to catch my Mercer baseball games. He did everything possible to go to Gainesville, FL, last year for our game against the University of Florida. He is so supportive of everything Blake and I do.

"One thing that I love about my dad is that he is one who would never brag about anything that he has ever done. However, when he went off to college, he paid his own way through graduate and medical school by working and with scholarships and with loans that he took out. He truly had nothing in those days, but he has now become very successful in life, though he has never been affected by his financial success."

Co-workers, friends, and other medical people in the Macon area can't say enough good things about Dr. Kim Johnston. In 1982, Dr. Dan Strawn of Radiology Associates in Macon and the son of Macon dentist, Dr. Loy Strawn, first met Kim. Strawn was a junior med student at the Medical College of Georgia in Augusta, while Johnston was a mid-level resident in neurosurgery. "Kim was absolutely a pleasure to work for and learn from," Strawn said. "Always a gentleman, he was so good to medical students, and that was not always the norm in med school. Some young doctors were somewhat difficult to work for, and many of them rode us pretty hard, but not Kim. He was a joy to be around."

Strawn recalled, "In 1989, our family moved back to Macon from Memphis.

I ran into Kim at The Medical Center of Central Georgia and was surprised when he recognized me seven years later. He is the same guy now that he was back in those earlier days in Augusta. The most impressive thing, in my mind, about Kim Johnston is that he doesn't have the typical ego that normally accompanies a neurosurgeon. He's humble, uses good medical judgment, and has a wonderful bedside manner. I know that there is no arrogance in Kim, because I see him practically every day since he uses our imaging system and CAT scans. He sees the sickest of the sick as he deals with spinal cord injuries, head traumas, and other serious neurological problems. I just can't say enough good things about Dr. Kim Johnston."

Dr Joe Sam Robinson, Jr. has been Kim's friend and professional associate at Georgia Neurosurgical Institute since 1987, and acknowledged, "He is a very kind, Christian gentleman who has always done his utmost for all of his patients. Kim's uniform affect is one of kindness, and he rarely, if ever, raises his voice in anger. For him, nothing is too good for his patients. He is successful as a physician and in life because of his overwhelming interest in other people.

"Besides his concern for his patients, Kim has always done everything he can for his two sons, Kyle and Blake. He has backed them to the hilt and followed all of their activities closely while attempting to give them appropriate fatherly counsel."

Dr. Robinson concluded, "One thing we laugh at around our office is when a doctor calls for him, and if Kim is really busy, or if you ask him to do something and he really doesn't have time, he will rant and rave. He will insist that he is not going to do it, but in about three minutes, he will come back and say, 'OK, go ahead and do it.' He is such a softy!"

When Kim first went to work with Georgia Neurosurgical, Laurie Faircloth was assigned to the 'new guy' to help him learn what to do and where to go. She recalled, "I didn't know for sure if his name was Johnson or Johnston, so when I asked him, he said, 'it's just plain old K-I-M, Kim.' That is the kind of man he is, not pretentious, or flashy. He's just himself. Dr. Johnston came back to Macon with his lovely wife, Jane, and their two sons, Kyle and Blake. I never knew how many folks one man could know, and they all seemed to come from the area where he grew up and went to school. He has always been proud of growing up on Walden Road. His reply, when asked by patients where he is from, is, 'I grew up in South Bibb County in the country on farm land.'

"His love for his family is first and foremost, and I don't think he has ever missed a single ball game that Kyle has ever played. He is so proud of his sons, which is very evident when he speaks of them. They are the type of sons that men dream about having. Blake and Kyle are hard-working, Christian, athletic, and handsome young men. It is also easy to see the influence of Kim's parents on their oldest son. His father, Sanders Johnston, was one of the kindest men I have ever met, and he seemed to have passed that same kindness on to Dr. Johnston. His mother Jeanette is a true Southern lady, and her genteelness is also evidenced in Kim."

One of Kim's greatest strengths as a physician has always been his bedside manner. "All of his patients and their families just love him," Faircloth said. "He is often seen issuing a hug to a patient, along with advice. Families love him because he is thorough and concise. He does not have to be urged to do things. He is the easiest doctor in the practice of five to work for because he does everything before he has to be asked. His only 'down-side' is the fact that he is so popular. He always has a long list of patients waiting to see him, and it's truly amazing, but I have never heard an unkind word uttered about him. If Kim ever gets distressed, he is apologizing before you even realize he was mad."

Faircloth concluded, "Many people in different fields seem to measure success in their ability to make money, but not Kim. I think the thing that makes him successful is that he is so genuine, gentle, and kind. I believe he would rather die a pauper and know that he had done things right and honorably than to have had all the riches in the world. I truly believe that he is one of the richest men I know regarding things that truly matter in life."

A medical associate of Johnston's, Dr. Carlos Feltes, is a native of Paraguay in South America. Dr. Feltes, married with two daughters, plans to return to his native Paraguay to practice with his father when he completes his work in Macon. He serves as a Neurosurgical Fellow and works very closely with Kim Johnston in the Operating Room. Feltes spoke of his connection with Kim, "Dr. Johnston, the physician, has achieved a masterful control of the field of neurosurgery, due to his long years of experience and solid training at the Medical College of Georgia in Augusta. His skills are blended well with his unmatched bedside manners. He addresses each patient's problems as if they were his own family member and dedicates the necessary amount of time to each. The patient feels very satisfied after their consultation."

Dr. Feltes continued, "After only the initial visit with a patient, he can create the appropriate bond that is necessary in the patient/doctor relationship. In neurosurgery, not all doctors are able to achieve what Dr. Johnston can, in part, due to the stress and high profile diseases that must be treated. Dr. Johnston's patients love and trust him unequivocally. To prove my point, discussing patient care and problems with him are true reflections of what his thoughts are and of what he has talked to the patients about. He is natural and honest with the patient at all times, and that is a special virtue. Dr. Johnston's dedication to work meets the highest standards in his field. He always comes to work early, is never late, and never leaves any matters unfinished.

"Dr. Kim Johnston, the surgeon, has unlimited patience, steady-as-steel hands, courage and knowledge in this field. Those qualities make him a complete surgeon. He also shares his skills with his colleagues when they are in need, and he has the honesty to ask somebody for an opinion when one is needed."

Feltes concluded, "Dr. Kim Johnston is an amazing teacher. I can personally testify that he has done everything in his power to transmit his knowledge as a neurosurgeon to his pupils. He simply is an honest and

Dr. Kim Johnston, Neurosurgeon.

dedicated person who will take someone under his wing when it is necessary, like a father would help and mentor a son. For me, Dr. Johnston has taught skills that I will take to my grave. His talent, skills, and ethics will be a model for me for the remainder of my medical career."

Since beginning his practice in Macon in 1987, Kim has made many friends in varied avenues of his life. One long-time friend is Charlie Cantrell, owner and President of 5-Star Automotive Group in Macon. "Kim Johnston is, without a doubt, one of the finest Christian men I have ever met," Cantrell stated. "We have known each other since 1994 when my daughter, Christy, started dating Kim's son, Kyle. We have become close friends since that time. Kim is such a role model in so many areas of his life. He always goes above and beyond the call of duty to help people, which, in my opinion, is why he is such a great physician. Kim is humble to the point that you wouldn't know he's a doctor if you just met him."

Cantrell continued, "Kim is just unique. He's a special person and is unlike anybody I have ever met. One thing that I really admire about him is the way he treats people, and helping somebody else comes so naturally to him. Maybe some of that came from his upbringing on a farm in South Bibb County. As much as Kim would have liked to, I know that he didn't get to play sports in high school, primarily because he was milking cows and working 80-100 hours a week. That same work ethic has continued on into his adult life."

* * * * * * * * * *

The practice of medicine for Kim Johnston draws comparisons to a double-edged sword. One edge is the joy and sense of accomplishment that comes from being highly-skilled, doing one's job well, and fulfilling one's life's calling. The other side of the medical profession is the ungodly amount of time and energy which are required when you're a neurosurgeon with the huge time commitment that frequently takes you away from your home and family.

Kim said, "Basically, Jane and our sons had to do a lot of things without me for such a long time. In my field of medical training, there were no time limits invoked. As an intern and resident at the Medical College of Georgia in Augusta from 1981-87, the first five years consisted of working approximately 140 hours a week. My sixth year as chief resident of neurosurgery, I was on call 24 hours a day, seven days a week, 365 days a year except for two weeks vacation. I remember operating for three straight days and nights, and when I finally left the hospital, I couldn't even remember where my car was parked. The training in those days was absolutely brutal, and it was so unhealthy for a family's life and for us, personally, as doctors."

"But, Doc, weren't you doing what you thought you ought to be doing with your life and saving other people's lives at the same time?"

"I understand that only the good Lord saves lives, but, yes, I was working to help people," Kim said. "Today, most folks don't understand that what we, as physicians, are able to do is only through the grace of God. I have often wondered why I have been fortunate enough that God has given me the opportunities and the abilities to do what I do in life."

He continued, "There are certainly rewards for what I do. My family has never missed a meal, we live in a nice home, and my two sons are attending the college of their choice, but still, it's awfully difficult on the entire family. I remember when we first moved to Macon, and our burglar alarm went off. I was involved in surgery, operating on a gunshot wound to the patient's head. My family was at the house, and I'm doing surgery on the gunshot patient, and we just hoped the sheriff would get there in time. Thankfully, it turned out that a window was broken. That is sort of a capsule of what frequently happens when you're overworked and you're not at home a lot to take care of the things that a 'normal' husband and father does. But I have no regrets about going into the field of neurosurgery. None at all."

Though he still works long days with irregular hours, Kim Johnston continues to be in great demand as a neurosurgeon. A recent guest of Kim's waited while he took six phone calls in a one-hour interview. Apologetically, but in true Kim Johnston-style, he seemed somewhat frustrated, not because this was a nuisance to him, but because he didn't want his guest to be inconvenienced. Thankfully, Kim is able to take some much-deserved time off these days, due in part to a somewhat larger medical staff at Georgia Neurosurgical. "In my spare time, I like to hunt and fish. We bought a farm down in Macon County and built a log cabin there. It looks like you can't get the 'country boy' out of me. I try to go down there as often as I can to enjoy the farm land and outdoors."

Apart from work, Kim has been on Stratford Academy's Board of Directors and in the school's booster club. Additionally, he has served on numerous boards and committees in the medical field. More importantly, though, Kim has served on the original board of directors for the Fellowship of Christian Athletes (FCA) in Macon. "One of the most meaningful things that I have done in my life would be my involvement with FCA, because it has such a life-changing, enduring impact on students' lives. FCA has brought me so much satisfaction, and a major reason for that fulfillment and joy is directly related to Scott Adams, the local FCA leader. Charlie Cantrell, Dr. Joe Johnson, Dr. Chuck Hawkins, and I helped fund the position to bring Scott on staff and to establish FCA in several Macon schools. That was the best money I have ever spent."

Scott Adams, the Executive Director of FCA in Macon, spoke about his friend, Kim Johnston, in equally glowing terms. "Kim is a very faithful man. Middle Georgia FCA depends on a handful of core people for our major financial stability, and Kim is one of those people. He caught the vision of what FCA could do in this community, for the schools in our area, and he wanted to be a part of getting it started and keeping it going.

"Sometimes doctors get separated from reality by the nature of their work and the status they have obtained because of their profession, but Kim has never done that. He remains a truly humble person with great people skills. I'm sure that is why his practice has been so successful."

Adams continued, "I think Kim will be remembered as a great father. He has raised two fine sons, Blake and Kyle. His older son, Kyle, was named Middle Georgia FCA Athlete of the Year in his senior year of high school. That's an award given as much for character and faith in God as it is for athletic achievement. You don't end up with a son like Kyle Johnston without having a great role model in the home. I don't think there's any greater compliment in life than to have your child honored for his character."

There is no question that Kim Johnston has established a successful medical practice which is well respected throughout Middle Georgia. Adams said, "I have never heard anyone speak an unkind word about Kim, which is unusual for a doctor in his area of expertise. I think Kim is such a genuinely caring person that he has gained the respect of patients and other doctors as well. Everyone who knows Kim knows that he is very open and approachable, and just like with his patients, he is always interested in what's going on in the ministry of FCA, and how he might be of help.

"I think Kim is successful in life because he had a vision for how he wanted to live his life and has been faithful to the plan. He has allowed God to direct his steps in life and has been blessed because of it. Like all of us, Kim has dealt with some hard issues in life, but he remains the same person through all of the trials and tribulation. He is truly a person to be admired for his spirit and caring for others."

* * * * * * * * * *

"I hope that I will be remembered as a loving dad to Kyle and Blake," Kim said. "As far as being remembered as an outstanding doctor, I would rather be thought of as a caring doctor. That is something really important to me these days because we have depersonalized medicine so thoroughly. For some reason, we don't treat every patient like they could be my brother or my family member. Every patient that comes into our office is someone's daughter or son, mother or father, and we've lost some of that mentality. As a physician, you obviously want to be much more than adequate, but we've lost the caring attitude that ought to be present in medicine today."

Kim concluded, "The other thing about a legacy is that I have tried my best to help people. There's no greater joy that I can get than a simple 'thank you' or a Christmas card from a patient. With the terrible traumas that we see all the time, it is easy to get emotionally worn down. Recently, we had one patient that had a severe head injury, and we operated on him for six hours. When I saw his mother after the surgery, she didn't say a word. She just walked up and hugged me. That was worth..." and his sentence faded out, unfinished.

"It has nothing to do with the money we make," he added. "It has everything to do with the lives that we touch. Sure, I haven't gone lacking, financially for anything, but at this stage in life, those friends and relationships are the things that matter the most.

"The opportunity to help someone at critical times in their lives is a blessing to me," Kim stated. "The friends and relationships that are made are what matters the most. I feel very blessed in life."

The truth is that Macon and Middle Georgia should feel equally blessed that there are still doctors like Kim Johnston, Willingham's last graduate.

The Johnston Guys: Kyle, Dr. Kim, and Blake

Faculty and Staff

Without question, Willingham High had one of the finest faculties and staff anywhere from 1958 through 1970. In *31206*, 25, high-achieving, successful-in-life graduates of Willingham paid homage to those men and women who were responsible for the education of thousands of young men. Willingham's staff worked for relatively low pay from 8 a.m. until way past 3 p.m. when the students left, Monday through Friday, and frequently on weekends and after school. Willingham's faculty and staff were people who took up tickets at games, chaperoned sock hops and dances in the Willingham gym (which, oddly enough, had bleachers on only one side). They worked closely with parents to see that their sons were doing what was expected, both in the classroom and on the practice fields, and generally involved themselves in the lives of students at a young school that was rapidly seeking and suddenly finding a new identity in the heart of South Macon.

Lloyd Newberry, Willingham's first principal when the South Macon school opened in 1958, was tragically injured in (and ultimately died from) an automobile accident at the conclusion of the school's first year. Newberry was replaced as principal by Fred Johnson in 1959-60. The following pages contain brief biographies and updates of several long-time teachers, coaches, staff, and administrators who served with merit at Willingham during its brief 12-year history.

Fred Johnson

Meeting and talking with Fred Johnson for the first time in over 40 years can be unnerving at best. Seldom is a school principal sought out for dialogue and interviews, but, five minutes into the conversation with Willingham's former principal, any anxiety was melted away. Fred Johnson looks the same as he did when he walked, or perhaps strolled in his own inimitable way, the hallways of Willingham in the 1960's. Still mentally sharp, physically fit, and uncharacteristically funny for a man who is nearing 90, Mr. Johnson is more impressive in the 2000's than he was in the 1960's for the simple fact that he doesn't seem to have aged. He has walked the carpeted levels of the Colonial Mall of Macon for years, and, in his words, "inherited some good genes'"—both being primary factors in Johnson's ability to remain bright and fit.

When A.R. Willingham High School for Boys opened on Canterbury Road in 1958, Fred Johnson was the principal at Alexander IV Elementary School on Ridge Avenue. He previously taught at Lanier Junior High, and Mike Garvin, who would later coach at Willingham, coached Johnson's grammar school teams in the mid-1950's.

"I grew up in North Georgia at the foot of Ripshin Mountain and Double-Head Gap," Johnson laughed. "There's a mountain range up there called Brawley Mountain, and I was born at the foot of that mountain. It is below where the Appalachian Trail starts in North Georgia and is near Sharp Top Mountain. I lived there until I was four years old and then moved to Blue Ridge, GA, the county seat of Fannin County. I went to school at Blue Ridge Elementary and was one of the first students to attend the new school that opened in Fannin County. Also, I was one of the last seniors that finished in the eleventh grade which was our senior year."

After Johnson graduated from high school and during the Depression, there was little work to be found and no money to be made, so he began doing odd jobs for a few years to help his family. "Then I got a chance to go over to Berry College in Rome in the fall of 1936," he recalled. "I drove a truck at Berry as my full-time job during the fall semester, started taking classes in the spring, and stayed there and worked every summer. I hardly ever got home but was able to get home to go to my father's funeral. I had to hitch a ride to Atlanta and then find a ride home to Blue Ridge. Travel in those days was nothing like it is today. I got my first car when I was 32 years old. When I went in the Navy at 26, I didn't need a car."

Johnson continued, "By going to school in the summers at Berry, I finished my academics in four years. I guess I had an idea that I might want to go into education because the courses were pretty easy for me. I majored in English and took enough teaching courses to get a teacher's certification. After I finished at Berry, I went to visit my sister in Dublin, OH, which was about the time they passed the draft law that said everybody must go into the military for one year. Being a very smart man, I said, 'I will go ahead and get my one year military obligation done, and when I get out, there will be jobs available.' I volunteered and went into a V-6 program in the Navy where they train people to be officers. I was assigned to the *USS Prairie State,* which was an old ship-hulk tied up in New York Harbor. I spent the winters of 1940 and 1941 in training in New York and was commissioned as an ensign in February, 1941.

"In the Navy back in 1941, I thought I pulled a pretty smart deal when I volunteered for communications duty," Johnson recalled. "It sounded good to me because I could go to a warm climate in an area that everybody wanted to visit. I got stationed in Hawaii. I volunteered for that duty, and that's how I ended up in Pearl Harbor. What started out well didn't end up very well."

So, Mr. Johnson, were you there when Pearl Harbor was bombed?

"Oh yeah!" he said, "I was on the *USS Maryland* but was pretty fortunate, because I had been on the *USS West Virginia* until a week before the Japanese bombed Pearl Harbor. I worked with the staff commander who was in charge of the Pacific battle fleet. He moved his staff over to the *Maryland* about a week before Pearl Harbor was bombed. If I had stayed on the *West Virginia,* I would have been right where a 2,000-pound bomb was dropped, because that's where my battle station would have been. In fact, a couple of days before Pearl Harbor was bombed, the USS Oklahoma arrived, and, because we were short of birthing space for ships, our ship was tied up elsewhere. The Oklahoma took five torpedoes along the side that would have hit our ship if we had been there."

While conducting this interview in the presence of Doris Hunnicutt Johnson, his wife of 58 years, Fred Johnson commented, "I believe that the Good Lord was looking out for this old boy from Blue Ridge. I think I must have been the luckiest man that ever lived. I used to tell Doris that 'the Lord saved me just for you.'"

His wife smiled and replied, "Then why did I end up getting all the bad luck?"

Fred Johnson was in the Navy for five and a half years, and when he left the military at age 32, he worked for the Boy Scouts of South Carolina and went through their training program for about a year. Johnson recalled, "I didn't like the guy I was working for, and I wasn't making but $100 a month, driving my own car and paying my own travel expenses. That's when I went to a teachers' employment agency in Atlanta. I already had a teaching certificate, but it was about to run out. They told me, 'We have two jobs available—one in Ft. Lauderdale and the other in Macon, GA. Dr. Mark Smith was the school superintendent in Bibb County at that time, and the young lady at the employment agency talked me into coming to Macon, so I started teaching at Lanier Junior High for Boys in 1946. Lanier was a great school in those days."

When did you know you wanted to be a principal?

"When I found out that they made more money than I made as a teacher," he laughed. "When they offered me the principal's job at Willingham, I was excited about that. I was going to make about $600 a month—not $600 a month more, just $600 a month—in comparison to about $400 a month that I was making as a grammar school principal. When I started teaching, I was making about $200 a month. Teachers still don't make a lot of money, but it seemed like we made more in buying power back in those days. In education, you'll never get rich, but you have a chance to be successful, and you can do a lot of good. After all, you'll never see a Brinks Truck in a funeral procession."

When asked about his early years at Willingham, Mr. Johnson replied, "The people out there were good folks, and they worked with you. I recall a funny story when Chipper Murphy's mother came by the school early in the year and told me, 'If Chipper gives you any trouble, you just slap the boy next to him, and Chipper will quiet down.' We had parents who were interested in their children's education, and they cooperated well with the school and the athletic program, which was a big plus for any school. That concept is quite different nowadays. Obviously, there were some who didn't care much for me as the principal, but that was OK. School principals aren't supposed to be popular."

He continued, "We had many good teachers that worked at Willingham. Mary P. Smith, Leonard Pridgeon, Charles Byrd, and William Bell were some of the finest teachers anywhere. Bell and Bird both became principals later on. When Charles Bird came to us, he had never had an education course, but I gave him a job based on his promise that he would get certified as a teacher. Nelson Mathews was one of the best shop teachers I have ever seen, and he wasn't college-educated. Of course, Billy Henderson did an outstanding job with our athletes and sports teams."

Johnson attended most of Willingham's games and sock hops during his tenure as principal. "I enjoyed my years at Willingham, especially in those early days. When I first went there, I felt like I was an educator. Toward the end, I felt more like a policeman, and I wasn't cut out to be a policeman. That wasn't my calling in life. If it had been, I would have joined the FBI."

Fred Johnson experienced the early years of excitement and growth of the new high school, and in 1964-65, experienced the beginning of integration in Bibb County. He recalled, "Wilfred Anderson was our first and only black student that year. He had a good sense of humor, which was very helpful in the adjustment for both Wilfred and Willingham. For example, on Senior Day, our seniors could bring their parents to lunch at school. Wilfred came by the office and asked Mrs. Lamback, the school's receptionist, 'Will you call me when my mother arrives? I think you'll recognize her when she gets here.'

"On Wilfred's first day at Willingham when his father came with him to enroll, I didn't know what to expect. I made a point to be here early before school started and stayed late after school ended. His daddy brought him to the office that morning, and I pretty much escorted him around all day. When Wilfred was in the lunch room, so was I, though he didn't always know that I was nearby. One day he told me, 'Mr. Johnson, I'm going out on the playground after lunch.' I didn't think it was a good idea, but I finally said, 'OK.' I alerted the teachers, and they helped monitor where Wilfred was and what the other students were doing. We decided early on that we weren't going to tolerate any bad behavior for any reason."

On Wilfred's first day at Willingham, a teacher sent Fred Johnson a note that some former students were camped outside the first hallway waiting for school to end. Johnson recalled, "While they were waiting, I walked over to them, and I didn't tell them a lie, but I said, 'You see all those cars over there? There are 10-12 Secret Service agents in those cars. You fellows are not supposed to be here. You need to leave right now and don't come back, and they all left.' I wasn't bluffing; there were people out there in the parking lot, but it may not have been 10-12 Secret Service agents. Those boys left the school, and thankfully, we didn't have any trouble."

Demonstrating how seamless integration actually was at Willingham, Johnson remembered, "After Wilfred had been there a while, he told me he was going to play intramural football after school. I thought, 'Uh, oh.' I told one of his teammates that Wilfred wanted to play, and the boy said, 'That's right.' I asked him, 'What are you going to do if a player on the other team jumps on Wilfred? What are you going to do, then?' He never hesitated and said, 'Then he'll have to whip all of us.' I knew then that we were making some progress, and I went on home that afternoon. It was just a matter of us getting used to each other."

Fred Johnson remembered that there were very few serious incidents in those days at Willingham. "Every public school in practically every town has had fights from time to time, and Willingham was no exception. The fact that integration happened somehow led the local media to expect that problems were happening when they weren't. A reporter came to the school after getting a 'tip' that a riot was about to happen. She was trying to find a story which never happened, and she showed up at school the second time. She said, 'I want to speak to him (meaning Wilfred), and if he doesn't come out and speak to me, then I'll make up a story.' At the time, I was pretty busy and didn't have time to talk with her. Her editor called and said, 'We heard that Willingham was having a free-for-all, and my reporter was sent there to do a story.' I told him, 'I'll tell you everything that I know, but I don't want your people out here threatening me.' He asked if he should run the story, and I told him, 'I can't tell you what to do. You just do your job, and I'll do mine.' He ended up not running the story."

After 13 years at Willingham and Southwest High School, Fred Johnson became principal at Union Elementary School in Macon for a couple of years before retiring in 1975. He spends time gardening, doing some house repairs, and fishing. "I used to fish in the Gulf of Mexico every year when Dr. Julius Gholson, the Bibb County school superintendent, would take the principals fishing."

Johnson acknowledges that he is in very good health these days. He is in such good health that he went to the last all-year Willingham reunion at the City Auditorium in 2003. "I have one sister who is 94. My secret to long life is that I just keep on breathing. I remember that Judge (William) Bootle, on his 100th birthday, said, 'You just have to live a long time to be 100!' And he's so right. I try to get some exercise every day, I go to the mall every morning and walk, and I still drive."

"Mr. Johnson, are you enjoying your life these days?"

"Oh yeah. I have a view of the Ocmulgee River from the main level of my son's house in River North. We have walkie-talkies to be able to speak with them upstairs. I lived in the same place on Shadowlawn Drive off Ayers Road near Country Club Estates for 50 years. We were in the poor section of that neighborhood, however! My wife and I have two sons. Harold, who is not married and lives in New Mexico. He is a compliance officer for an energy department. Our son Joe Johnson is an insulation contractor, and we live in the basement-level of his house. We have two grandchildren."

When asked if he ever regretted leaving the classroom to become a principal, he answered, 'No, you just leave one set of problems for another set.

Being a principal was easier for me since it was more about organization and administration. The biggest headache that a principal has is the parents, but, for the most part, we had great parents at Willingham."

Fred Johnson, the self-described 'country boy from the foothills of the Appalachian Mountains,' has seen a lot more in his nearly 90 years than he ever dreamed about while growing up. He got to see the South Pacific and the Fiji Islands, and he narrowly avoided catastrophe when Pearl Harbor was bombed. He had the privilege of leading a new public high school located in the working-class side of town in only its second year of existence and made some memories that have lasted a lifetime.

* * * * * * * * * *

Billy Henderson

In 1958, when Billy Henderson was named as the first head football coach at Willingham, South Macon's brand new high school, he was an unknown entity to the young men he would be coaching. To their parents' generation, however, he was one of the greatest and most highly-acclaimed athletes in the history of sports in Macon. Henderson's athletic biography was well-chronicled with success from high school, college, and the professional ranks.

When he graduated from Lanier High in 1946, Billy Henderson had earned 14 letters in football, basketball, baseball, and track and he was named the top athlete in Georgia in both football and baseball as a junior and senior. Additionally, he was All-America in both sports for two years, but perhaps the highlight of Henderson's high school career was being selected to play in the East-West All-America baseball game at the Polo Grounds in New York.

When Henderson left Lanier for the University of Georgia in 1946, freshmen were eligible for varsity competition, and he played four years for the Bulldogs in football and baseball, earning eight varsity letters. He also played on two SEC Championship football teams, coached by the legendary Wally Butts and played in the Gator, Sugar and Orange Bowls.

"I played on the Sugar Bowl team of 1946 against North Carolina," Henderson recalled. "Fosky West had 'rung my bell' when I was 17, but we were planning to wait four years before getting married. Then it became three years and then two years. I remember that I was in my hotel room after the Sugar Bowl game, and all of the other players were putting on their coats and ties and heading to Bourbon Street. I was on the telephone calling Fosky. We got married on January 23, 1947, and have been married 58 years."

After a highly successful college career and a two-year stint playing minor league baseball in the Chicago Cubs organization, Billy Henderson was named athletic director and head football coach at Willingham at the ripe young age of 29. When the school opened its doors in September, 1958, he was returning to the city where his life had been molded by such coaching legends as Tom

Porter, H.P. Bell, Lem Clark, and Stooge Davis. Henderson always credited the Boys Club and the YMCA in Macon as being important contributors to his life during his formative years.

Henderson explained how he got the Willingham job at such a young age. "I came to Willingham after having coached in Jefferson (GA), at Athens High and later at Furman University and the University of South Carolina. I remember that I was on a recruiting trip in Orlando for South Carolina in December, and it was snowing for the first time in years down there. Somehow I learned that there was a brand new school being built in Macon, my home town. I called and asked about the job on my return trip back to Columbia, so I drove over to Macon for the interview and was hired by Dr. Mark Smith, the Bibb County School superintendent, in February, 1958. The building hadn't even been completed at that time.

"I went back to Columbia to tell my head football coach, Warren Giese, that I had been chosen for the new position at Willingham. He was a man who had a tremendous influence on me. Coach Giese was a physical fitness fanatic, and he insisted that his coaching staff be in excellent shape. Every day at lunch, he took me with him to the YMCA to play handball. I'll never forget that he taught me how to play the game. One day, I finally caught up with him and whipped him in handball. He made us play 10 or 15 games that day, and I beat him every time. We were both exhausted so I told him, 'Warren, I'll see you next week. I have to get ready to leave to go on a recruiting trip in the morning,' and he said, 'Oh, no. I'm reassigning that recruiting trip to somebody else. You're staying here, and we're gonna play handball again tomorrow.' That's how competitive the man was."

Coach Henderson continued, "I told Warren that we were going to move back home to Macon and help start a new high school. He asked if I'd signed a contract, and I told him I had not. Then he said, 'Don't do anything just yet.' The next thing I knew, he had put a briefcase on his desk and said, 'I can't give you a raise because of the system that we have but consider this to be a raise.' It was a considerable amount of cash that I would be able to use to buy a home for my family. My mouth dropped open, but I told him, 'I can't take that.' He asked me again, 'Have you signed anything?' I told him, 'No, but I gave them my word that I'm coming.' As I look back, I'm so glad I made that decision, because we have had some of our happiest moments and greatest days at Willingham."

* * * * * * * * *

Friday night high school football games for Coach Billy Henderson were preceded by his Friday afternoon ritual. After school and the obligatory pep rallies on game days, he would go to the YMCA downtown to get a massage, sit in the steam room, and then go home to eat oyster stew at 4 p.m. sharp. Fosky Henderson prepared his pre-game dinner every week, while the coach just relaxed and got mentally prepared.

Billy Henderson coached for 45 years with the majority of those seasons at Willingham (12 years), and later at Clarke-Central (23 years) in Athens until his retirement in 1996. Having coached literally thousands of young athletes in his career, Henderson learned early on about the struggles of providing for a young, growing family on a coach's salary. He was consistently looking for ways to supplement the family's income by managing a bowling alley, helping in a fast-food restaurant, or running a summer recreation program at local schools so Fosky could stay at home with their children. But financially, times were always tough on a coaching and teaching salary in the Henderson household.

"We had four young children—Brad, Fran, Carol, and Johnny. Chris had not arrived yet. I remember going to the bank to borrow some money, since it was time for Santa Claus to come, and I learned a lesson the hard way. The young banking assistant told me, 'Billy, you don't have any collateral for this loan.' I told him point blank, 'I gave you my word. If I live, you're going to get your money back, and if I die, you're still going to get paid.' But he rejected my application for the loan. That episode made me think a little. I taught this lesson to my students and my children, that if it's possible, don't ever go to an assistant; always go to the person who makes the decisions and is in charge."

Though coaching and education have never been high-paying professions, Henderson never considered doing anything else for a living. With an amazing recall of statistics, game situations, players, and even the years certain games were played, Coach Henderson recalled many players from Willingham days. In his opinion, Bobby Bryant and Darrell Parker rank as perhaps the greatest athletes who ever attended Willingham, along with Brad Henderson, Tommy Reid, Eddie Battle, Randy Wheeler, and countless others. However, conversations with the coach soon revealed that he remembered substitutes and average athletes with the same ease and pride that he remembered all-state performers. For years, the coach would have pictures under the glass on his desk of former Rams who had died.

Going back to the early days of Willingham, Henderson said, "Eddie Battle is one of those fringe benefits in my life. Being a teacher and a coach, you love all of your students and players, but many of them maintain contact with you, even into adulthood. Eddie Battle is one of those people, and I talk with him on a regular basis. He was our first quarterback and was a co-captain at Willingham in 1958. Eddie was an outstanding athlete who played football, basketball, and baseball and was the first Willingham athlete to play in the Georgia High School All-Star baseball game in Atlanta at the old Ponce de Leon Park, the home of the Atlanta Crackers. He was a pioneer and a great leader who helped put

Willingham on the map."

Henderson recalled, "Cecil Bentley, who played Little League with my son Brad, once wrote an article remembering Brad's last high school football game before his untimely death on Labor Day, 1964. The title of it was *'Remembering Brad,'* and he recalled that Brad threw for 170-something yards against Warner Robins in his last game, which was the opening game of the season. That was back during the days when the forward pass was 'only a rumor' at Willingham."

He continued in detail, "The very next game after Brad's death was against Dougherty High of Albany, and John Duke, a former UGA teammate of mine, was their coach. We won something like 26-6, and after the game, the score was the farthest thing from my mind. I remember us shaking hands after the game, and he was all upset with me because he thought we had run up the score. But that's life. And unless you're in someone else's shoes, you really don't understand."

The coach recalled a story about one of Willingham's greatest athletes. "Bobby Bryant was an all-time great person and an all-time great athlete. I'll never forget this story that happened when I was in my early 30's. In 1962, I was so unyielding; it was my way or the highway. I've told young coaches this story on many occasions, and the lesson is—don't ever give a youngster an ultimatum. There are times when you just need to keep your mouth shut. Bobby and I had a disagreement about an issue, and my word to him was 'do it my way or get off the field.' So Bobby started walking to the dressing room. As he was leaving the field, I was hollering at him, 'Hey! Just remember who the baseball coach is!' *I* was the baseball coach, and I knew that Bobby loved baseball, so I was thinking he would turn around and come back, but he didn't. And sure enough, I didn't let him come out for baseball that spring.

"Bobby was an exceptionally talented track athlete in the 440, sprints, relays, and the high jump. One afternoon at track practice, he was running laps around the football and baseball fields while I'm hitting ground balls to the baseball team. Finally, I sucked up my pride and said, 'Come on, Bobby. You need to be playing baseball.' And he was back."

Henderson acknowledged that his methods of dealing with young athletes have changed over the years. "I'll never forget the era when long hair was becoming an issue during my days at Willingham. Understand, I associated long hair and facial hair with flag burners and non-patriots, so I had three local barbers with three chairs lined up at the gym door when the football team reported for fall practice. I was the judge, jury, and executioner. Wayne Jones, who was just one of the finest kids you have ever seen, showed up with hair about halfway down his forehead. He had tears in his eyes when he told me, 'Coach, I'll get my hair cut, but it won't make me a better football player.' I learned something from Wayne that day. In fact, when I took over the Clarke-Central job in 1973, I showed up in the parking lot with my crew cut. The first young men that I saw all had long hair and facial hair. They eyed me suspiciously until I told them, 'You don't mess with my hair, and I won't mess with yours.'"

* * * * * * * * * *

With his long and storied coaching career which has produced three State Championships in football, three in baseball, and one in swimming, Coach Henderson recalled some of his proudest coaching moments, several of which came during his early years at Willingham. "I was 30 years old in those days, and I had already coached at Furman, South Carolina, and had played four years at Georgia, so I had been around the very best in athletics. In our first year at Willingham, we were gonna whip everybody, because I knew everything, but we got our brains beat out.

"That first Rams team in 1958 went 0-7-3. It got to the point where we used to celebrate when we made a first down. In fact, it got so bad late in the season that I got frustrated and really embarrassed myself against Moultrie one night in Porter Stadium. They rode Bobby Mathews out of bounds and deserved a 15-yard penalty for a late hit, but the official didn't call a penalty. I got so irritated that I got up in the official's face and I screamed, 'Call it! Call it!' But he wouldn't call a penalty on them, and as he went to get the ball from Bobby, I spotted the yellow flag in his pocket. I grabbed his flag and threw it down - boom! Then I got in his face again and said, 'Now call it!' And he did. He walked off 15 yards against Moultrie. He should have thrown me out of the stadium. Our players were laughing so hard that I had to tell them, 'That's the last time you'll ever see me make a tail out of myself.' That wasn't necessarily a proud moment in my life, but it is certainly one I'll never forget."

On another occasion in that inaugural season, Henderson recalled, "We were playing LaGrange and this time Bobby Mathews was knocked out cold and had to be taken to the hospital. We didn't have seniors on that team and were getting shut out that night. We got the ball on our own 20-yard line late in the game and drove it the length of the field and finally scored. That was one of my proudest moments as a coach. After the game, one of the officials came up to me and said, 'Billy, if your kids hadn't put the ball in the end zone, I was gonna put it in the end zone for them.' He said he had never seen a bunch of kids with that kind of heart and determination who just wouldn't give up."

Willingham's 0-7-3 record in 1958 turned into a 6-4 season in 1959, and the football foundation had been laid for the future. Things got better so quickly at Willingham that the Rams defeated arch-rival Lanier in Willingham's third season of existence. The Rams dominated their cross-town rivals by beating the Poets six consecutive years and became the only school in Georgia football history to beat Coach Wright Bazemore's Valdosta Wildcats three consecutive years (1963-64-65). After coaching for two years (1970-72) at Mount de Sales Academy in Macon with Mike Garvin (the Cavaliers' head football coach and athletic director), Coach Henderson's success followed him to Clarke-Central High School in Athens, where he won three state football crowns and appeared in the state finals three consecutive years. Perhaps his greatest point of pride as a coach, however, was producing 167 athletes who won college football scholarships.

"Other proud moments that I recall would be the first win in school history at Willingham in 1959 against Dudley Hughes, and who could forget the first time we beat Lanier, 13-7, in 1960? Nobody but our players and coaches gave us a prayer to beat Lanier. In that game, Jimmy Hammond blocked a punt, and Lathrop Holder caught it and scored. Clint Tucker scored the winning touchdown for us. What a great game that was!"

One of the hardest things that the coach ever experienced in his coaching career was watching Valdosta High beat Athens High in the state playoffs in 1965. "We had already beaten Valdosta that same year. Jordan of Columbus upset us, 35-13, the week after we beat Valdosta, giving Valdosta the region championship. In those days, only one team from each region went to the playoffs. Someone from Valdosta had a sign that read, 'Thank you, Jordan!'"

Henderson continued, "I'll never forget Mike Garvin, one of our bright young coaches, as he became an instigator the week of the Willingham-Lanier game. He was the brains behind our students sneaking over to Lanier and attaching a helium-filled weather balloon with the words, 'Smear Lanier,' and then greasing the flag pole so no one could get the balloon down. Garvin and Johnny Stallings would make sure our mascot, Sam the Ram, would be hidden so Lanier couldn't kidnap him the week of the big game."

Henderson reminisced, "We had such a terrific booster club at Willingham in those early days. With booster club meetings on Monday nights, parents had to get to the school cafeteria early to get a seat to watch the film of the previous Friday night's game. Our parents raised money any way they could to help earn money for our athletic program. We had great parents who supported whatever we did.

"Our Friday pep rallies and Thursday night bonfires were something to behold. I'll never forget the night we were playing Lanier at Porter Stadium, and they locked us in our dressing room. Everybody was wondering where we were. Willingham-Lanier games always had great bands, and they competed with each other just like our football teams did. Jim Littlefield of Willingham was the master of creativity, and Lanier's Bob Barnette was close behind. One year, Lanier had James Bond as Agent 007 enter the stadium on a pulley-and-wire contraption that was unbelievable. Both schools were constantly trying to outdo each other, which made that week so much fun."

Henderson confessed that one of the most painful things that he has ever done was showing the Willingham-Warner Robins film after his son Brad and Brad's friend, Diane Driggars, were killed. Billy Henderson had always been a man who constantly talked to his teams about overcoming adversity and how quitting was never an option. Thus, he had the limousines and family car take him and the coaching staff to the school for football practice after Brad's and Diane's funeral. Billy Henderson was a man who practiced what he preached and he didn't ask his players and coaches to do things he wasn't willing to do.

Henderson continued with a brief summary of his motivation in life. "My dad died when I was eight years old and left my mother with four children. She taught me that folks live on, even when things look bleak and hopeless. Her principles of discipline and hard work lived on through me. My mother

demanded the best of me and instilled the principles of doing the right thing and treating people the way they should be treated. That has never changed. I am sick of people, schools, and educators whose principles change with the times. Our methods may change, but
our principles don't.

"Something that was always been important to me was trying to balance family time and coaching. Our family always ate at least one meal around the table together. We had devotionals daily at 6:30 a.m., and each of our children would pray while we held hands. Our son Johnny would get this big frown on his face, so I would tell him to go back to his room and don't come back until he got a smile. My family went on baseball trips with the team. Fosky was the model mother and coach's wife. I remember when we beat Valdosta in 1963; she was trick-or-treating with our young children."

Henderson's coaching philosophy came straight out of his Lanier High School background. With coaches Bell, Davis, Porter, and Clark as his mentors, the Coach tried his best to make Willingham as much like Lanier as possible, and it all started with discipline and respect. "Lanier's motto was 'We Lead,' and I coupled that with 'It Can Be Done.' Everyone who knows me well knows that *The Impossible Dream* was the song that I sang every morning in the shower to start the day.

"If I had any strong points as a coach and an educator, it would be that I cared about people. I learned the importance of motivation from my teachers and coaches at Lanier. In those early days, all of the coaches coached a sport each season, and they encouraged kids to play all sports, unlike today where athletes are encouraged to play one sport year-round."

Billy Henderson has always been an observer of people who are successful and who do things the right way. He learned that lesson up-close and personal in the East-West all-star baseball game at the Polo Grounds in New York. "We took a train to New York for the all-star game. Babe Ruth was my coach while Ty Cobb coached the other team. I was catching in front of 25,000 spectators; the count on the batter was 3-2, they had runners on first and second, and the game was tied. The runner on second took off for third and I didn't hear the umpire call ball four; so I fired it to third, but the ball went all the way to the left-field wall. Our left-fielder ran it down and threw the ball against the screen behind home plate. The batter who walked came all the way around to score.

"After we got the third out and we had our turn at bat, I started back out to warm-up our pitcher for the next inning. Babe Ruth shouted toward me and cursed, 'Give me another %# $*@%# catcher!' I remember seeing my tears falling in the dust at my feet as I took off my catching equipment. He said nothing to our left-fielder. That episode taught me a lesson about how we, as coaches, can motivate or destroy a player with what we say
and how we say it. We never shouted at players for physical errors. Mental mistakes and not hustling are different from physical errors and
we dealt with that strongly. We could live with physical errors. I know that

lesson well, because one game, I fumbled four times against Columbus High. Coach Davis made me carry a football to class, when I rode the bus, and I had to sleep with it. That reminded me of what I needed to do with the ball."

Henderson also learned another important lesson about coaching and life from the New York baseball experience. He said, "Babe Ruth was considered the model character for America back then. He was seen as a gregarious, fun-loving man who was beloved by the press. On the other hand, Ty Cobb, from Royston, GA, had the reputation for being surly and combative. In New York, I went to a banquet for the players and coaches and sat across from a well-dressed, well-mannered gentleman in a suit. I later found out that he was Ty Cobb, and he was nothing like the man the press had described. I learned that things aren't always like they seem with people. The Wayne Jones-hair incident and the guys at Clarke-Central with long hair and facial hair are great examples of this. I learned that it's what is in the heart of a person that really matters."

Billy Henderson had a different philosophy than many high school coaches, because he never cut a player. In fact, he stated publicly that if a player came out for football in the eighth grade, worked hard, and paid the price, he would start on the varsity before he graduated. Henderson re-enforced this attitude when he arrived at Clarke-Central in 1973. With only 18 players showing up for spring practice in his first year at Clarke-Central, Coach Henderson quickly began to win over the student/athletes in Athens with his enthusiasm and fervor. He told his players, "We are going to the top of the mountain, and all of you can go if you play by the rules, but no individual will keep us from getting there."

Coach Henderson has won enough awards and recognitions to fill multiple trophy cases and scrapbooks. He was the National Baseball Coach of the Year in 1972 after winning two state titles at Mount de Sales and one at Willingham. He won three state football crowns at Clarke-Central (1977, 1979, 1985), and was in the state football finals three consecutive years (1984, 1985, 1986). After beating Lanier and LaGrange six straight years at Willingham, his Clarke-Central team defeated cross-town rival Cedar Shoals 13-consecutive years. Clarke-Central's football stadium was formerly known as Death Valley but was renamed 'Billy Henderson Stadium' in 1996.

Today, the Coach is now officially retired and lives in Athens with his wife, Fosky. He maintains his life-long commitment to fitness by going to the YMCA in Athens to workout and swim each day. And yes, he still wears that trademark crew cut which is now more 'salt than pepper.' The walls in his house, as well as those in the carport, are covered with pictures of his former players, team photos, and family members. Coach and Mrs. Henderson are now the proud grandparents of five grandsons and four granddaughters.

It is truly a humbling experience for a former student to sit in the Coach's modest but comfortable den and watch and listen to him reminisce about teams and players who are as familiar to him in 2005 as they were in 1958. Billy Henderson is one of the most remarkable men that Macon, and specifically South Macon, has ever known. Though his greatest athletic achievements may have taken place in Athens - at the University of Georgia and later at Clarke-

Central – undoubtedly his greatest work and finest accomplishment came when he built a program from scratch and gave pride and hope to a blue-collar, working-class South Macon community. Willingham's Rams believe that may have been his best work ever. And though he left Macon in 1973, Billy Henderson's roots will forever be planted in Macon, GA.

Coach, Macon misses you greatly, the Willingham family thanks you profusely, and we all appreciate your leadership in the development of something great and long-lasting – Willingham High School.

* * * * * * * * * *

Mike Garvin

Mike Garvin, who never lettered in a varsity sport at Lanier High School, became one of the finest football coaches in the state of Georgia. Though he began his high school coaching career at Willingham in 1959-60, his record as a head coach at Mount de Sales Academy in Macon earned his admission into the Macon Sports Hall of Fame in 2003. While attending Mercer University, Garvin actually got his first taste of coaching at Alexander IV Elementary School in Macon. His 1957 Alexander IV squad, featuring running back Grover Bradley, won the coveted Pony Bowl championship on Thanksgiving Day. Garvin's team beat a Charles H. Bruce School team which featured Bobby Bryant (who played collegiately at South Carolina and later for the Minnesota Vikings) and Mark Bowen, who would earn a football scholarship to the University of Georgia.

Garvin's Alexander IV principal was Fred Johnson, who would become the principal at Willingham in 1959-60. With a desire to coach at Lanier, his alma mater, Garvin interviewed there but was not offered a job. He ultimately accepted a coaching and teaching position at Willingham.

"I absolutely loved teaching math and coaching at Willingham," he said enthusiastically. "Those were eight of the most exciting years of my life. We had an amazing young, energetic staff of coaches, and Willingham had some outstanding classroom teachers. Our coaching staff got along so well, and though we didn't always agree on every issue, we always came out of a meeting in one accord. Coach Henderson did a great job of hiring the staff and keeping everybody moving in the same direction. Johnny Stallings, Dave Hill, Henry Middlebrooks, Jesse Duckworth, Billy Beale, and Mack Edwards were several guys who coached at Willingham for a while, and all were exceptional high school coaches."

Garvin coached during fall, winter, and spring, and during his Willingham career, he coached basketball, football, wrestling, and track. Football and wrestling were the sports, however, where he had the greatest successes. "As far as I know, Willingham was the only school in Georgia history to beat Valdosta three years in a row in football. Another highlight was when we were second in the state in wrestling to Briarcliff from Atlanta for two straight years. Willingham was strong in just about every sport back in the early days. Certainly football was the most high profile sport, but wrestling was strong, and track and baseball were both really good."

"Academically, Willingham was a fine school with teachers like Leonard Pridgeon, Mary P. Smith, Charles Byrd, and many others. Ed Cain may have been the brightest kid that I ever taught at Willingham, but there were a lot of great students back then," Garvin recalled.

In an all-boys' school, pranks and practical jokes ran amok. However, a lot of mischief originated with the young coaching staff assembled by Billy Henderson. "Johnny Stallings was such a character," Garvin recalled. "He started our wrestling program, and it was one of the best in the state under his leadership. Later, he was admitted into the National Wrestling Hall of Fame, the Georgia Athletic Coaches Association Hall of Fame, and the Macon Sports Hall of Fame. I remember one time when Coach Henderson got upset with some of the assistant coaches over the use of his office phone. He decided that he wouldn't let us use his phone any more, so Stallings just changed the lock on Henderson's door, and he couldn't get into his own office. I've seen Stallings take the cap off a Coca-Cola bottle with his teeth. He was really something, but he was also a great coach.

"Working at an all-boys' school, we seldom had girls in the gym, so the girls' rest rooms were practically unused during the day. A few of the coaches used the ladies' room as their own 'executive washroom.' I remember one day when Coach Dave Hill was in the girls' rest room, and some cheerleaders from McEvoy walked in. They didn't know he was in there, but Dave heard them walking in. He didn't know whether to run out and be seen or just stay in there. He just pulled his feet up on the toilet lid and waited quietly until they left. I don't think Dave used their rest room much after that."

Garvin remembered, "One year Martin Allman and I were coaching eighth-grade football together. We drove over to LaGrange, played poorly, and lost. It was just one of those bad games that you have once in a while, and the trip back to Macon from LaGrange was a long one, especially after a loss. Some of the boys were having a little too much fun on the way home, and Coach Allman had just about heard enough. He jumped up, started walking to the back of the bus, and said in his West Virginia-way, 'If I'd known I was fighting World War II for a bunch of boys like y'all, I'd have lost the war!' Everybody got pretty quiet the rest of the way home.

"Lanier was the school in Macon that had all of the history and tradition, but when Willingham was created, we saw ourselves starting a new tradition," Garvin said. "We accomplished a lot with some poor facilities in a very short time. The gym was about the best thing we had, even though it only had bleachers on one side. Willingham had no football practice facilities, no dressing rooms for athletics, no track, and no baseball field. For a while, we practiced in a cow pasture across Williamson Road. The coaches tried to raise money to help improve facilities by going to businesses in the South Macon community. Later 'McWill Night' was created by Coach Henderson to help raise funds for the school and to showcase the P.E. program. About the only things I didn't enjoy back then were raising money and having to drive the 'Yellow Hound' (school bus) to games. I had no bus-driving experience and no confidence in my driving ability."

In addition to teaching and coaching in Willingham's early years, coaches were expected to scout their upcoming opponents. "Scouting in those days was not easy," Garvin recalled. "I-75 wasn't completed so we had a long, difficult drive to Valdosta on Friday nights. I saw them play so much I started to join their booster club. I drove my old Corvair – not Corvette! – to Valdosta, Moultrie, LaGrange, Columbus, and Albany a lot of times."

Garvin was an important part of the staff that brought immediate notoriety to Willingham and South Macon. "My best moments at Willingham would have been when we had several state individual wrestling champions and our team finished second in the state twice to an established Atlanta powerhouse. My favorite football memory would have to be when we beat Lanier for the first time in 1960. Nobody thought we had a chance, but we beat them, 13-7. We went on to beat Lanier six years in a row. Because we were the blue collar school in town, we would sometimes mention that we were playing the 'rich kids across town,' which was pretty good motivation for our players.

"We always got great support from the South Macon community. They really believed in us as a coaching staff. We had people involved in the program who didn't even have kids in the school, and on Monday nights during football season, we filled up the cafeteria when we showed the game films from the previous Friday night's game."

Though most of Garvin's experiences at Willingham were good ones, one of the worst experiences which he and the rest of the staff had was losing to Jordan of Columbus the week after beating Valdosta in 1965. The drive home after the Jordan game was one of those 'forgettable moments' in Willingham history, but for Garvin, the good times greatly overwhelmed the not-so-good moments. Garvin stated, "All in all, those were great years, and they were outstanding preparation for me to ultimately become the head football coach at Mount de Sales. I learned that you can do whatever you set your mind to do. For example, I had never coached varsity girls' basketball, but I learned to coach it, and we had some success at Mount de Sales."

Boys at Willingham who knew Mike Garvin frequently teased him about being single. Garvin's standard reply was, 'You can't trust women. The only thing you can trust is a math book.' However, that philosophy changed when Garvin started a conversation with Carolyn Robertson at the College

Hill Pharmacy in Macon. Carolyn, who taught at Joseph N. Neel School, was tutoring a high school student in math and needed a math book. Mike brought it to her, and the rest was history. They were married in 1965 and now have three grown sons – Michael (37) lives in New York City, while Rob (35) and Matt (34) both live in Macon. All three sons are married, and the Garvins now have two grandchildren.

Mike Garvin left Willingham in 1967 to become the head football coach and athletic director at Mount de Sales Academy where he won three state titles in football. Today he teaches two classes of Beginning Algebra at Macon State College while Carolyn works in the Tift College School of Education at Mercer University in field placement and teacher certification.

Stating his philosophy of life, Garvin said, "I have a God-given talent to help kids understand math. I believe that I have the ability to be able to get something out of somebody, and I believe that work always precedes success, except in the dictionary."

* * * * * * * * * *

Mary B. Lamback

Mary Lamback called herself a 'flunky' who worked in the office at Willingham, but those who knew her knew better. She served as secretary, receptionist, and administrative assistant to both Lloyd Newberry and Fred Johnson, the two men who served as principal at Willingham from 1958 until 1969, when she retired.

"I loved every day that I worked at Willingham," Mrs. Lamback said. "The boys were funny and cute and nice, but, of course, I didn't have to teach them either. Working at Willingham, there were so many interesting things that happened in those days. I guess I've heard just about every excuse in the book about why boys were late or absent from school."

Lamback recalled, "A particularly bizarre story happened one day after school. Boys would stand around out front of the school to wait on their bus after the school day ended. One boy took another boy's cap off and tossed it on top of the breezeway. The boy who owned the cap climbed up the railing to get it but couldn't reach the cap. He found a mop handle which was long enough to retrieve the cap, but the boy lost his footing and fell on the long stick. Ouch!

"This boy came walking very gingerly into the office with a pained look on his face. When he fell on the mop handle, it broke and was sticking out of the boy's rear-end. I can only imagine how painful that must have been. Mr. Johnson came out of his office, saw the boy's predicament, and took him into his office. Several of us went along as chaperones and watched while Mr. Johnson carefully removed the implanted stick. After making sure the boy was all right, Mr. Johnson instructed him to get his mother to take him to the doctor as soon as he got home. I've been in education a long time, but I have never heard of a situation like that ever happening."

Mary Brown, a native Maconite, met her future husband, Sam Lamback from Augusta, while playing tennis at the Baconsfield Park tennis courts on Nottingham Drive. "We both had dates with other people when we went to play mixed doubles. Sam and I were on opposite sides of the court, so I got to watch him across the net," she mused. "I must have looked like the 'wrath of the Almighty,' because I was sweaty, sunburned, and exhausted. Miraculously, though, we were married two years later. Sam had been living at the YMCA in downtown Macon and worked at Woolworth's department store. We had to walk wherever we went because he had no car. On weekends, though, we were able to borrow my dad's car and would go to Lakeside Park to swim or dance."

Soon Sam Lamback would get his own Woolworth's store, and the newlyweds would move to Jasper, AL, where they lived for several years. Later, the Lambacks moved back to Macon, and Sam began a career in banking at Home Federal Savings and Loan, where he became an executive officer. They had three children—the Rev. Sam Lamback, Jr., daughters Palmer Jones and Louise Watson, and seven grandchildren. All three Lamback children now live in Macon. Sam Lamback, Sr., died in 1997 after being married to 'Mary B,' as she was affectionately known, for 60 years.

"Those early days at Willingham were wonderful days," Mary B. Lamback said. "We went to Porter Stadium and the City Auditorium for football and basketball games. We had such a good faculty and staff, and everybody got along so well."

Oney Hudson, president of Willingham's class of 1964, has fond memories of Mary B. Lamback. "She was Mr. Johnson's secretary. She was deeply-loved and so well-respected that the class of 1962 dedicated the yearbook to her. That showed what people thought about her. She was like a second mom to many Willingham students."

Mrs. Lamback's daughter Louise recalled many fond memories and excellent stories of her mother's years at Willingham. "One of my mother's friends called to see if she would be interested in the job at Willingham, and since all three of her children would soon be in college, she decided to start working to help with our college expenses. Mama worked at Willingham from the time it opened in 1958, which was the year my sister (her oldest child) entered college, until I (her youngest) left graduate school in 1969."

Louise continued, "Mama thoroughly enjoyed her years at Willingham and would entertain us with stories of funny things that the boys and the faculty said and did. She enjoyed being around the boys, and she had great love and respect for Mr. Newberry and Mr. Johnson, the two principals that she worked with. Mama was a person of tremendous energy and determination. She told me that there was a 'no running in the halls' rule at Willingham, but she couldn't seem to slow down to a walk. As she would run down the hall to deliver messages to the teachers, the boys loved to stop her and remind her of the rule. She tried to run only while classes were in session so no one would see her running.

"Mama developed some close friendships with several people who worked at Willingham. She still stays in touch with her librarian friend, Martha Hutcherson, who is now 95-years old and lives in Winder, GA, with her daughter Page House. Dixie Cutter, a science teacher who rode to work with Mama every day, was also a close personal friend."

* * * * * * * * * *

As a mother, Mary B. Lamback was adamantly opposed to her children having a television in the home when they were growing up. Louise recalled, "Mama had visions of having to pry us away from the TV to get us to do our homework, read, play games, or go outside to play. She was always full of creative ideas of things for us to do. She and Daddy taught us to play tennis, and all of us spent lots of time on the red-clay courts at Baconsfield Park, which is where my parents met. With Mama's encouragement, we built our own marionette stage, made the backdrops, props and marionettes, wrote the scripts, and put on marionette shows for our friends in the neighborhood. She was always full of energy and great ideas."

Mary B.'s three children felt greatly deprived, because they didn't have a TV and maintained hope that their mother would one day change her mind. Louise Watson recalled, "One year Daddy gave her a TV for her birthday, and Palmer, Sammy, and I were so excited. I'll never forget that the entire family watched *I Love Lucy* the first night. The three of us dared to believe that we would actually become a 'normal' family once we had a television. That illusion vanished the next day when Mama exchanged the TV for a refrigerator. I can't begin to tell you how sick we were about that!

"While Mama was the secretary at Willingham, she saved Write-Right coupons from the school's paper shop, and, sure enough, one of the first things she did when I left for college was to send in her coupons and get a TV," Louise confessed.

It was no secret that periodically students would call in bomb threats to the Willingham office. Louise re-told a story that her mother had shared with her children. "Frequently, the student who had called in the bomb threat would be standing on a nearby hill so he could properly enjoy watching the students and faculty file out of the building. Sometimes Mama and Mr. Johnson could figure out who had made the call by looking through the list of boys who were absent that day. It was quite a disruption in the school day, and it annoyed Mama that these boys where able to pull off this unseemly prank. One day, when a boy called the school to say that a bomb was in the school, Mama simply told him he had the wrong number, and he quickly hung up. We decided that life was much simpler in those days."

Louise Watson recalled the story about the year school pictures were to be taken at Willingham. "When the photographer arrived at the school, he came into the office and asked Mama if he could take a picture of her at her desk. Not wanting to be photographed, she quickly turned her head away, but he snapped her picture anyway. When the pictures arrived a few months later, there was a full set of pictures of the back of my mother's head – from 8" by 10s" to wallet-sizes. We all thought it was so funny, and my brother carried this picture in his wallet for a long time."

Her family told the story about the time Mary B. and a few of her friends from church decided to take a class at Dudley Hughes Vocational School and learn how to hook rugs. All of these women were very artistic and would meet once a week to dye the wool, cut it into thin strips, and work on their attractive, hand-hooked rugs. Louise recalled, "This was about the same time when some of their children started attending college; thus, the word 'hooker' took on a new meaning. However, these sweet little ladies had no idea what the word, 'hooker,' meant, as evidenced by the fact they had always called themselves 'The Hookers.'

Louise continued, "We would get letters at school from Mama telling us what 'The Hookers' were doing. We had a wonderful time reading her letters to our friends in the dorm. When their children finally clued their mothers in to the word's new meaning, 'The Hookers' loved it and started calling themselves 'The Happy Hookers' after the title of a current book by a member of the world's oldest profession. This group of talented ladies met in each other's homes for over 50 years."

Mary B. has always loved tennis, played from childhood into her late 70's, and still watches tennis on television. Louise told the story about the time Sam, Jr., Palmer, and she decided to organize a surprise tennis tournament in their mother's honor for her 70th birthday. "Unfortunately, Mama couldn't play in the tournament, because a few days prior to her birthday, she broke her wrist when she fell out of the magnolia tree she was cutting down in her yard. Thus, the Mary B. Lamback Tournament never materialized. On the other hand, we still had the birthday party/tournament, but, since Mama couldn't play, it became more of a birthday party at the tennis courts."

Mrs. Lamback (88) now lives with her daughter Palmer in Macon's Shirley Hills neighborhood. Mary B. played tennis until she had a stroke several years ago and now uses a walker to aid in her balance and give her mobility. Always gracious and kind, Mrs. Lamback continues to be the essence of a true Southern lady.

* * * * * * * * * *

Mary P. Smith

Oh, the stories that Mary P. Smith tells! Most are funny; all are true; some can barely be remembered, but they all happened and can be verified by her daughter, Pam Wacter, who was entertained nightly by her mother's tales of Willingham. Mrs. Smith said, "I came home every night and told stories at the dinner table to Smitty (her nickname for her husband, W.E. Smith) and Pam, and they would be in stitches. These weren't bad stories or mean stories; they were just funny stories that naturally occurred in an all-boys public high school in the 1960's."

Known to her students as 'Rock,' Mrs. Smith laughed that deep, muffled laugh that was famously hers and explained how the nickname happened. "Johnny Wires is the student that first called me 'Rock.' I had scheduled a test for his class, and they were just whining and begging me to postpone it. I said, 'No, I'm not going to do that. You're going to take this test because I scheduled it with plenty of time for you to study.'

"Johnny said, 'Aw, y'all don't talk to her. She's not going to change her mind. She has a heart as hard as a rock.' I walked into my classroom one morning and there was a rock on my desk, so they all started calling me 'Rock.' I would go to basketball games, and when I entered the gym and the boys would spot me, they would shout in unison and extend the word for several seconds - 'Rrrrrrroooooooocccckkkk!' I loved it!"

Mary P. Smith was born in Bolivar, Missouri, the home of Southwest Baptist University and grew up in small towns throughout Missouri. She said, "My parents were both students at the college when I was born. My dad was a singer and was studying for the ministry. He led the singing in Ingleside Baptist Church in Shreveport after the preacher got upset and resigned about something that happened in the church. They accepted the preacher's resignation and called my dad to be their pastor. We moved to Shreveport when I was about eleven years old."

When the question was asked how a teenage girl from Missouri - by way of Louisiana - ended up in Macon and at Mercer, Smith answered, "That's another story. Those who know me know that I'm a different kind of person. When I was a teenager, I didn't know a single person in Georgia; I had no connections whatsoever. I finished high school in 1934, and my dad wanted me to go to Louisiana College, a Baptist school. I had heard of Mercer and knew it was a Baptist college, so I thought, 'I'll go to Georgia,' and so I did. My parents didn't even bring me over here. I got on a bus, and when I arrived at the bus station in Macon, I called the registrar at Mercer and said, 'I'm here, now. What do I do next?' The registrar told me to call a cab and go out to 421 Adams Street, because that's where the girls were staying. While I was at Mercer, I majored in English and minored in history. History ended up being my first academic love."

Smith stated, "I actually began my teaching career in Newton County's Porterdale Community after graduating from Mercer University in 1938. I taught all of the subjects when I was a sixth-grade teacher in Porterdale, a Bibb Manufacturing village near Covington. Mr. Pittman of the Bibb Company that was based in Macon tried to hire teachers from the different churches, because everybody who taught school also taught Sunday School and Baptist Training Union. He went over to Mercer and told them he needed a Baptist teacher in Porterdale. Though Mr. Pittman was officially employed by Bibb Manufacturing, he was in charge of the schools in all of the Bibb Manufacturing villages. Mercer passed my name along to him, and I got the job because I was a Baptist and a teacher. Later, I returned to Mercer and got a master's degree."

Mary P. Smith returned to Macon in 1957. "My husband was working on the railroad in Macon, so I came down to see Dr. Mark Smith, the Bibb County school superintendent. He said he would give me a job immediately because he was putting a staff together at McEvoy, Macon's new girls' school. Dr. Smith offered, and I accepted. Thus, I went to work in Macon and taught English at McEvoy High, Willingham's sister-school, which was in its first year of operation. When Willingham opened in 1958-1959, I moved down the hill to the all-boys school."

Some would ask Mrs. Smith, "Why would you want to leave a brandnew, all-girls school for an all-boys school?"

Her reply was simple, "Because I had to teach English at McEvoy, and I really wanted to teach social studies. I accused Mr. William Brake, McEvoy's principal, of having too many social studies teachers; so when Mr. Lloyd Newberry, Willingham's founding principal and a classmate of mine at Mercer, offered a social studies teaching position at Willingham, I accepted his offer and was excited about going to Willingham. I had a lot of wonderful experiences there, and I taught in Macon from 1957 until I retired from Southwest High in 1976. Some of my contemporaries at Willingham in those days were Martha Hutcheson, Mary Lamback, and Fred Johnson. I have no misgivings or second thoughts about teaching all boys. Those years were great for me.

"When the girls from Covington, GA, heard that I was teaching at Willingham in Macon," Smith laughed, "they weren't surprised. In fact, they said they were glad I was finally teaching at an all-boys' school because they always knew that I liked teaching boys better than girls.

"By the time I retired from full-time teaching, it had become much more difficult because that was a period of great unrest in the schools. I had more and more students who were not prepared, and many of my students simply couldn't do the work. I recall one student who was just pitiful; I mean he didn't know anything, and there was no point in failing him, because he still wouldn't know anything. One time, I gave his class a true-false test, and he put 'true' by every single answer, thinking he might get half of them right. I actually changed some of his answers to 'false' just to help him pass the test."

"Mrs. Smith, are you telling us that the woman they called 'Rock' changed answers for a student?"

"I sure did," she confessed. "He may have stayed there until he was 70 years old, and he still wouldn't have passed my class."

It was common knowledge at Willingham that Mary P. Smith didn't have discipline problems in her classroom. "Even after I retired," she said, "I would substitute in Macon's schools, mostly at Central. I would introduce myself as a retired history teacher who previously taught at Willingham. Those students must have thought, 'Wow! If she could handle herself over there, then she can do anything.'"

One of her memories about teaching at Willingham was how much pride the students, parents, and faculty had in the school. "For some reason, I didn't quite sense that same feeling of pride when I taught at McEvoy. Willingham had a good faculty led by Mike Garvin, Leonard Pridgeon, and Dave Hill, but Willingham's real strength was in the students. The boys sensed that they were in a special place, and so did I."

Smith recalled the time she taught summer school at Lanier. "I primarily taught Lanier boys, and we got into some real arguments about school-related things. Of course, my neighborhood had a lot of Lanier boys, and they gave me fits because I taught at Willingham."

Mrs. Smith could only recall one bad experience while teaching in South Macon. She said, "Actually, it happened when I was supply-teaching at Southwest. I was teaching a history class for a fellow who was in the National Guard and had been called into service. He had already made out the final exam for the class. There was one student who never paid any attention to a single thing that I said. One day a girl stayed after class and told me the teacher had already given them the test. They already had the answers to the objective test that the teacher wanted me to give. I told the girl, 'Thanks.' That evening, my daughter Pam and I rearranged the test questions. We still used the same questions; we just changed the order of the questions. You should have seen the looks on their faces. That class didn't like me even a little bit!"

* * * * * * * * * *

After teaching for a total of 36 years and substituting another six years, Mary P. Smith stated, "I have no regrets. I retired and was able to take my grandsons to kindergarten and pick them up after school."

Sadly, she fell on a cold day and broke her hip on November 23, 2003. "I lay on the ground just outside my house for about three hours and was unable to move. Finally, some neighbors saw me lying on the carport floor and rescued me. I spent several weeks at HealthSouth in Macon, recuperating from that broken hip."

The interesting part of that otherwise sad story involved the van driver who transported Mrs. Smith from The Medical Center in Macon to HealthSouth. She said, "When the van left the hospital, the driver said, 'Mrs. Smith, did you and your daughter once teach at Willingham or Southwest? I said, 'Yes. Did I teach you?' He said, 'You did. My name is Willie Morris,' and I said, 'Oh, Willie, I remember you. You had a rock band in high school, and you played football, too.'"

Willie said, "You know what I remember about you, Mrs. Smith?"

I thought, 'Oh, me!' "No, what do you remember?"

Willie said, "You didn't take no crap off nobody."

"I remember Willie Morris for one thing in particular. We were studying the Civil War, and I tried so hard and was so careful about what I said and how I said it. I never wanted to offend any of my students. Interestingly, I had many of my black students tell me that 'I was all right,' she laughed. "But when I was teaching, I would use the term 'Negroes.'

"One day, Willie spoke up in class and said, 'Mrs. Smith, I wish you wouldn't say that.' And I asked, 'Say what?'"

He said, "Negro."

"I told Willie that I always tried to call people whatever they wanted to be called. I used to say 'colored' and then found out you didn't want 'colored.' Just tell me what you want to be called, and I'll use that term. Willie said, 'Black. Refer to me as black.' I said, 'OK, then that's what I'll use.' And so I did."

Weeks later, when Mrs. Smith was in therapy at HealthSouth, Willie would walk over to her wheelchair and kiss her on the cheek. She laughed and said, "The girls that worked at HealthSouth looked on in disbelief; I was very fond of my former student, Willie Morris."

Smith's husband worked as a telegraph operator for the railroad. "He was also a native Georgian and a Methodist, but I converted him to be a Baptist," she stated proudly. "I was teaching at Willingham when he had a heart attack and died at age 61. We had one child, Pam (Wacter), who now has retired from public education after having served as a teacher at Southwest and Southeast and principal at Central High School (formerly Lanier) in Macon."

Today, Mrs. Smith lives alone, works cross-word puzzles, and reads every word of *The Macon Telegraph*. She spends her time rooting for the Atlanta Braves and more recently has become a big fan of the Georgia Bulldogs. "I like the Georgia coach a lot," she confessed. "Mark Richt is a fine young man. Having grown up in Louisiana, LSU was always my favorite team, but now I've become a Bulldog fan. I've been a member of Vineville Baptist Church for a long, long time, but with my back problems, sitting on a church pew is not very comfortable."

Mary P. 'Rock' Smith was accused of having a hard-heart by some marginally-motivated high school boys in 1962 due to her unwillingness to reschedule a history test. The truth is, however, that her heart has always been large and full of love and compassion for her students. No teacher ever cared more for 'her boys' than the transplanted Missouri girl who came to Macon without knowing a soul and to Mercer, because she was a Baptist.

Not only did Mary P. Smith become one of the all-time great history teachers at Willingham, but she was also one of the most beloved.

Willingham Men Who Died in Vietnam

Twenty-five men from South Macon and Willingham High School have been honored in *31206* for their successful lives. There were many men from Willingham and South Macon who fought for their country and for the freedom of others in the Vietnam War. Six of these men, our friends and classmates, were killed in action in Vietnam. Thus, they did not have the same privilege and opportunity to live out their lives as we and they all would have wanted. Their lives were, nonetheless, successful in a very real and meaningful way to all of us who knew them. They deeply touched our lives.

These six men are heroes, and in this small way, we honor them accordingly.

This short, but hopefully meaningful, chapter is in honor and memory of the six men from Willingham who fought and died in Vietnam. Their service to our country has not gone unnoticed or unappreciated by the rest of us—their former classmates, teammates, brothers, and friends. May their eternal souls rest in peace.

The following information on each soldier was gleaned from the website, *http://thewall-usa.com/*. It lists their age, rank, birth date, pertinent information, and notes from friends or family which were sent on their behalf. Our friends are listed alphabetically.

Willis Lee Furney
(Willingham Class of 1964)

SGT - E5 - Army - Regular
173rd Airborne Brigade
20 year old Single, Caucasian, Male
Born on Aug 13, 1946
From MACON, GEORGIA
Length of service 2 years.
His tour of duty began on Jun 25, 1966
Casualty was on Mar 09, 1967
in TAY NINH, SOUTH VIETNAM
HOSTILE, GROUND CASUALTY
GUN, SMALL ARMS FIRE
Body was recovered
Religion
BAPTIST

John Daly
John was there when Furney died.
I haven't forgotten you, old friend, John Daly
April 12, 2002

Allen Carson Hardison
(Willingham Class of 1962)

SP5 - E5 - Army - Selective Service
1st AVN BDE
25 year old Single, Caucasian, Male
Born on Oct 23, 1942
From MACON, GEORGIA
Length of service 1 year.
His tour of duty began on Sep 29, 1967
Casualty was on Feb 02, 1968
in PHONG DINH, SOUTH VIETNAM
HOSTILE, HELICOPTER – CREW
AIR LOSS, CRASH ON LAND
Body was recovered
Religion
METHODIST

Sandra Hardison
Sister-In-Law
3914 Hartley Bridge Road
Macon, GA 31216 USA

Carson, We Miss You.
We miss this really great hero as much today as we have for
so many years.
Tuesday, September 21, 2004

Stanley Patrick
Friend in Vietnam
8719 N. Spearsville Rd.
Morgantown, INDIANA46160 U.S.A.

A gentle giant that I will always remember. I miss you Kit.
Saturday, June 03, 2000

Tricia Roberts Hall
Childhood friends
Spartanburg/Greenville, SC USA

To you, Carson, and all the memories - through football, dances, dates, Adel, your
young adult life and then, finally, your leaving for the
military. You were always an absolutely super guy. Through these years since, if

I've thought of you once, I've thought of you a million times and missed you, especially knowing you were gone. If it had to be, thank you for making life safe for me and mine.
Tricia remembers.
Friday, February 04, 2000

Terry Kent Jackson
(Willingham Class of 1965)

LCPL - E3 - Marine Corps – Regular
21 year old Married, Caucasian, Male
Born on Mar 27, 1947
from HAWKINSVILLE, GEORGIA
Length of service 1 year.
His tour of duty began on Aug 16, 1968
Casualty was on Feb 13, 1969
in QUANG TRI, SOUTH VIETNAM
HOSTILE, GROUND CASUALTY
ARTILLERY, ROCKET, or MORTAR
Body was recovered

Ken Beck
Plt. 1085 PI Boot Camp brother
Salisbury, NC 28

I was at the dedication ceremony in Macon, GA, for the eternal flame for Terry.
Although we were not together in Vietnam, I have still lost a brother. God bless him, and his family.
Ken Beck Corporal of Marines, Semper Fi, brother
Saturday, November 13, 2004

Charles I. Wagner
Capt., USMC(Ret)

"We few, we happy few, we band of brothers, for he today that sheds his blood with me shall always be my brother." (Shakespeare). Although I didn't know you, you are my brother and I mourn for you. Semper Fi, Marine!
Thursday, March 27, 2003

Bricey Elrod Lamb
(Willingham Class of 1964)

2LT - O1 - Army – Reserve
21 year old Single, Caucasian, Male
Born on Aug 25, 1946
From MACON, GEORGIA
Length of service 1 year.
His tour of duty began on Jun 01, 1967
Casualty was on Sep 11, 1967
in PLEIKU, SOUTH VIETNAM
Hostile, died of wounds
GROUND CASUALTY
MISADVENTURE
Body was recovered
Religion
BAPTIST

Bennie Frank Holmes
Friend, fellow church member
Marietta, GA USA

God's Piano Player
Bricey was a gentle young man with a love for God and his family
that led him to join the service to protect their future.
His sacrifice was not in vain. He died so that I might live.
Thank you, God, for Bricey's life and sacrifice.
Thursday, November 11, 2004

Franklin Dwight Ruis
(Willingham Class of 1966)

PFC – E2 – Marine Corps – Regular
18 year old Single, Caucasian, Male
Born on Oct 05, 1948
From: MACON, GEORGIA
Casualty was on Mar 19, 1967
in QUANG NAM, SOUTH VIETNAM
NON-HOSTILE, GROUND CASUALTY
ACCIDENTAL HOMICIDE
Body was recovered
Religion
PROTESTANT
C T

Eternal Rest grant unto them O Lord, and let perpetual light shine upon them. May they rest in peace. Amen.
Thursday, March 18, 2004

John Paul Sharpless
(Willingham Class of 1969)

Marine Corps - PFC - E2
Age – 21
Date of Birth: Nov 22, 1948
From: MACON, GEORGIA
PFC - E2 - Marine Corps - Regular
21 year old Single, Caucasian, Male
Born on Nov 22, 1948
From MACON, GEORGIA
His tour of duty began on Feb 04, 1970
Casualty was on Jun 28, 1970
in QUANG NAM, SOUTH VIETNAM
HOSTILE, GROUND CASUALTY
MULTIPLE FRAGMENTATION WOUNDS
Body was recovered
Religion
PROTESTANT

Jimmy Carroll
I was in boot camp with John. I will remember him and all of my other friends and heroes who gave so much.
Friday, September 20, 2002